In Your Own Voice

In Your Own Voice

A Writer's Reader

Andrew Merton
University of New Hampshire

HarperCollins*CollegePublishers*

Acquisitions Editor: Patricia Rossi
Project Editor: Brigitte Pelner
Design Supervisor: Mary Archondes
Cover Design: Kay Petronio
Electronic Production Manager: Valerie A. Sawyer
Desktop Administrator: Sarah Johnson
Manufacturing Manager: Helene Landers
Electronic Page Makeup: RR Donnelley Barbados
Printer and Binder: RR Donnelley & Sons Company
Cover Printer: RR Donnelley & Sons Company

In Your Own Voice: A Writer's Reader

Library of Congress Cataloging-in-Publication Data

In your own voice : a writer's reader / (compiled by) Andrew Merton.
      p. cm
   Includes index.
   ISBN 0-06-501763-3 (Student Edition)
   0-06-502485-0 (Instructor Edition)
   1. College readers. 2. English language — Rhetoric .   I . Merton.
Andrew H., 1944-   .
PE1417.152   1995
808' .0427 — dc20

94 95 96 97 9 8 7 6 5 4 3 2 1

For Gail, Gabe, and Rachel

Contents

Preface

Students in composition courses do not think of themselves as writers, but as students. This is natural. But unfortunately, as long as they persist in clinging to the identity of students, they will not reach their full potential as writers. This is because students and writers have profoundly different views of both their audiences and their relationships to those audiences.

Students automatically write for an audience of one. That *one* is the instructor. And students write with two unarticulated assumptions about this singular audience: (1) *The instructor* has *to read what I write,* and (2) *The instructor knows more than I do about whatever it is I'm writing about.*

These assumptions do not lead to good writing. If a piece of writing *must* be read, then it need not be engaging or compelling. And if the audience knows more about the subject matter than the student does, then the student might naturally believe it is permissible to use generalities, vague references, inexact wording. The student thinks: *The instructor will know what I mean.* The result is bland, unoriginal, and boring.

Writers operate differently. Writers assume that they are writing for a general audience, a large audience, hundreds, thousands, millions. This audience does not have to read what the writers write. And this audience knows less about the material at hand than the writer does.

These assumptions lead to good writing. If no one *has* to read a piece of writing, then it is up to the writer to compel the reader to continue reading. And if the writer, not the audience, is the expert, then the writer must be precise, exact, specific, and clear.

Unfortunately, it is not enough for an instructor simply to tell a student to write compellingly. Nor is it enough to show the student well-written pieces—to point out their themes, their organizational schemes, their use of different kinds of data—and to say, "Try doing it this way." It is not that the student won't try. The student, who is accustomed to being rewarded for following instructions well, will, indeed, try. Too often, though, the result is a pale imitation of the original—a schematic drawing of an eagle, rather than an eagle.

And that is because the transformation from student to writer is as much a visceral process as an intellectual one. It must come from the inside.

But how to make students feel like *writers*?

By having them approach their material the way a writer does: not safely, passively, in the manner of a supplicant, but aggressively, authoritatively, with a distinct point of view and a voice with which to express it.

All students have voices. Few have learned to express those voices in writing. In fact, it is likely that the majority have been trained explicitly *not* to use, let alone refine, their natural writing voices. And as long as that conditioning remains unchallenged, these students will never become strong writers.

The purpose of assembling this collection is to show students that good writing begins on the inside, with the writer's voice. Each piece has been chosen primarily for its voice. Students should be encouraged to immerse themselves in the sounds, the rhythms, the sensibilities of each one, and then to explore how the voice contributes to the overall intellectual and emotional impact of the piece.

Beyond that, the introduction to the book and the To Think About and To Do sections following each piece are designed to help students discover and refine their own voices, a process that begins with the absorption and imitation of the voices of others, then continues as the students try variations of their own.

Every accomplished writer begins by emulating the work of accomplished writers who came before. This is the first step on the journey from student to writer. Unfortunately, students often perceive an unbridgeable gulf between themselves and the writers who are set before them as models. For this reason, most of the pieces in this book are short and easily accessible, while their subjects are timely and provocative. I have tested them in my own classroom, and found that they work both as models for writing and triggers for lively discussions.

The table of contents is arranged alphabetically, by author. There is a supplemental table of contents, in the back of the book, arranged thematically in six parts: Writers on Writing; Becoming Who We Are; Life and Death; Moral Questions, and Answers; Subcultures; and Social Commentary. Students should be encouraged to sample the book in a random manner, for the process of discovering one's voice is more intuitive than logical.

During my twenty years as a teacher of writing I have found that I function most effectively by creating conditions that maximize my students' chances of achieving apparently serendipitous breakthroughs. *In Your Own Voice* was designed with this process in mind.

Thanks to Dot Kasik, John Lofty, Don Murray, Dan Reagan, Sue Wheeler, and my editor at HarperCollins, Patricia Rossi, for their careful readings and constructive criticism of this book at various stages from the original proposal to the finished product. Thanks to Cheryl Penner and Chris Ransom for keeping me organized. And, for their expertise, enthusiasm, and moral support, thanks to all the teaching assistants, instructors, and lecturers I had the privilege of working with during my term as director of the composition program at UNH.

Andrew Merton

Introduction

Let me introduce myself:

Merton the writer and teacher of writing arrives at the Massachusetts Maritime Academy gymnasium in Buzzard's Bay at 7:45 P.M. Thursday, September 19, arrives out of the North and the dark in his yellow Fiat sedan to run with the world champion Boston Celtics who are the fastest-breaking team on the planet. For the last half-hour on Route 6, unspeakable things have been happening in the pit of Merton's stomach but he wants this trip. He gets out of his car and walks past an Audi, a couple of Mercedeses, and a white Lincoln Continental with California plates, into the bare modern lobby of the gym. For Christ's sake, let us get *on* with this.

Here I am again:

I am going to tell you a secret about men. But first let me remind you of something you already know, although, if you are a woman, part of you keeps denying it—the part that takes over late at night as you are drifting off to sleep, alone, and whispers things like, *How come I never have any luck with men? How come the only guys I ever meet are insensitive louts or oversensitive wimps both rolled into one?* The implication being that everybody else is meeting men who are wonderful.

Here is the good news: There's nothing wrong with *you*.

And one more time:

In Montreal, 19 years ago, I was with a woman in a Hungarian cafe when a group of German men at a nearby table began singing: *"Deutschland, Deutschland, über alles/Über alles auf der Welt."*

At first it was merely loud; soon it was raucous, militant, bullying. The men were middle-aged, red-faced, paunchy and drunk; from everything about them it was clear that they were reliving the glories of the Third Reich. The few other patrons in the place were silent. I motioned to the resident gypsy fiddler and whispered a request. He smiled and nodded. The moment the Germans paused for breath, the fiddler launched into a spirited version of "Havah Negillah." I raised my glass to the Germans, who did not respond.

These are the leads of three pieces of mine, written between 1974 and 1988. Each is written in a different voice; each voice reflects a different aspect of me. In the first, I am a man on a mission, serious, intense, and, as the reader might infer, overmatched. In the second, I am a confidant, a friend, reassuring my companion over a drink or a cup of coffee. In the third, I am a man of some sophistication and moral courage, with maybe a bit too much self-righteousness thrown in. Three different readers, each reading a different one of these pieces, might be expected to imagine three different Andrew Mertons. And yet, I hope, a single reader, reading all three, would have no trouble imagining that all emerged from the same person, the same writer.

I have other voices which I use in my writing. I like to think that they are infinite; in practice, there are probably half a dozen that I have come to rely upon regularly. But this has not always been the case. In fact, until I was about twenty years old I had no voice at all.

Well, that's not true. What I mean is, I had no *writing* voice. Certainly I had many speaking voices. There was the voice I used with my buddies in my college dorm. This was a bantering voice, a know-it-all voice, designed to cover up the fact that I knew very little. There was the voice I used with my widowed mother, 300 miles away, on the telephone—the voice of the dutiful, mature son (a voice that did not always feel natural). There was the voice I used with my girlfriend. There were the voices I used with my instructors—a different voice with each, depending on (1) how well or poorly I was doing in a given course, and (2) how well the instructor was taking it. And so on. In fact, my voice varied with each person I spoke with.

But I had no writing voice of my own. When I wrote, I sounded like this:

> A main trading commodity was frankincense, a commodity then in great demand for ritual and other purposes in the lands of high civilization—in Egypt and Mesopotamia north of Arabia, and later across the Mediterranean in Greece and the Roman Empire. Most of the frankincense was grown or collected in south Arabia itself, particularly in the Mahra region and in Dhofar. This trade also carried the commodities brought by sea from India and East Africa to the ports of Cana (Hisn al-Ghurab) and Aden.

I did not, in fact, write this. It comes from the article on Arabia in the *Encyclopaedia Britannica.* It is written in basic textbook/encyclopedia style. It is no worse than most such material; in terms of clarity, it is better than some. Yet the only readers who would pick up such an article voluntarily are those with an unquenchable thirst for the information contained within its pages. To my knowledge, no one has ever said of the *Britannica:* "What a page-turner! I simply couldn't put it down."

My high school classmates and I read fiction—the short stories of Flannery O'Connor, *Arrowsmith* by Sinclair Lewis, and the avant garde sensation from the young J. D. Salinger, *The Catcher in the Rye.* We studied these as literature. And yet, none of our teachers thought to use these books as models for our own writing. When we were given writing assignments, the stylistic model we were implicitly compelled to follow was: *Britannica.*

HOW NOT TO WRITE

I say "implicitly compelled to follow" because, in those days, writing, as a distinct discipline, was not taught. My teachers made no distinction between writing and grammar, and we students were given to understand that once we had mastered grammar, we would have no trouble writing. We would remain trouble-free if we followed eight simple rules:

1. Never write in the first person.
2. Never express an opinion of your own.
3. Never comment directly on the opinions of others; rather, to show diverging views, quote two published sources, separated by the phrase "on the other hand."
4. Use the passive voice whenever possible in order to guard against allowing your own opinion to slip into the material.
5. Use long words rather than short ones. This will show readers that you have a good vocabulary. (For the same reason, avoid using the same word twice in a paper, even if you have to stretch for a synonym.)
6. Write long, complex sentences rather than short, simple ones. This will show readers that you have a fine grasp of grammar.
7. In summary, always write in the dry and lifeless style of a failed, septuagenarian academic (and never mind that most *successful* academics write lively, provocative stuff).
8. If the writing seems, in any way, fun, you are doing it wrong. Start over. The more it seems like drudgework, the better it is.

I tried to follow orders. Compared to the stuff I churned out in high school, the *Britannica* article on Arabia is compelling. I passed my courses. I knew I was not a *writer;* clearly there was no resemblance between my stuff and the work of Salinger, Lewis, or O'Connor. Still, I had faith that if I followed my teachers' injunctions, somehow I still had time to become a writer. It did not occur to me that most readers—myself included—do not judge a piece of writing by the size of the author's vocabulary, or the author's ability to write twenty-six complex sentences in a row.

When I got to college it was the same thing. My instructor in freshman English, a doctoral candidate, had no apparent interest in pieces of writing which sane, intelligent people might reasonably choose to read. The more arcane, impenetrable, and obscure our prose, the more pleased he was. (I have no sympathy for teachers who assign this stuff, and then complain about the awful writing they get from their students. They deserve it.)

In short, writing, as it was taught to me, meant rehashing what others had already written, and doing it poorly.

Then one day I discovered that I had a writing voice. It happened accidentally. I had finished reading a piece by the humorist Art Buchwald, and I began pondering certain campus issues. And I found myself thinking about those issues *in Buchwald's voice*. It was a wry, wisecracking, tongue-in-cheek voice, the voice of a city guy, an insider. I went to my typewriter (a Remington manual) and wrote a humor piece, imitating Art Buchwald.

It was not deathless prose. On the other hand, I thought, it was readable. With great trepidation I submitted it to the editor of the student newspaper, who—bless her heart—read it, laughed, and ran it in the next edition. The rest may not be history, but it sure has been fun. I imitated Buchwald for a while, then threw in some Max Schulman (whom connoisseurs of vintage reruns might recognize as the creator of Dobie Gillis), then Kurt Vonnegut, Hemingway, Joan Didion, Nora Ephron, and on, and on. Today it is nearly automatic. Every time I come across a new writer whom I like—be he or she a novelist, a poet, an essayist, a journalist—a little bit of that voice sticks with me.

By this time, the various voices emerging onto the page when I write are syntheses of hundreds of voices I have read—syntheses not exactly like any others. They are mine.

I learned by accident what all good writers learn, one way or another: Writers learn to write by imitating other writers.

This should not be surprising. Painters are influenced by other painters. Composers learn from composers. Sculptors, choreographers, photographers, and filmmakers, as well as architects and chefs, do not master their work in a vacuum. All are influenced by what and who have come before. The secret is to find writers you like, then think about *why* you like them, and then try to do what they do.

Here is what they do, these successful writers:

They use their voices to form relationships with their readers. As you read each piece in this anthology, think about the persona the author projects. You might even try imagining a picture of the writer from the sound of the voice; is he heavy, thin, tall, short? Is she wearing an elegant suit, or bluejeans and a sweater? Is he a city person or a country person? What is her economic status? And so on. Then think about the relationship of that persona to you, the reader: Is it friendly, distant, forbidding? Are you equals, friends, adversaries? Is the writer casting himself in the role of a teacher, a cynic, a mystic, a fool? The writer's voice establishes, maintains, and sometimes alters the relationship throughout the piece.

Because a relationship exists—because good writers establish bonds with their readers from the outset—we, the readers, are willing, even eager, to read about subjects in which we have no previous interest. Anyone can write a piece about, say, the Los Angeles Dodgers that baseball fans will read, but it takes a skilled writer to write a piece about the Dodgers that readers with no previous interest in baseball will have trouble putting down.

In addition, good writers convey attitudes about the material they are dealing with. In all of these pieces you can tell—often without the writers having to explain it—how they feel about the people, the places, the situations they are writing about. It is the writer's voice that conveys these feelings.

WHAT IS VOICE?

What, exactly, do I mean by "voice"?

I divide the components of voice into two categories: the tangible and the intangible. The tangible components—the things that we can see, hear, measure—are rhythm, pace, inflection, sound. The intangible components are the writer's attitude toward his or her subject, the writer's attitude toward the readers, and the writer's underlying sensibility.

Examine, for example, two contrasting voices:

(1)Fred Salvucci knew the time was right. Even an MIT graduate in civil and transportation engineering could be subject to fits of passion. The mood took hold of him after he left a North End church where he had gone to Sunday mass.

The weather was warm, the air fresh, the day pleasant. As the North End kids rolled up the last remnants of winter and pelted one another with snowballs, Fred Salvucci inhaled deeply and thought to himself with all the poetry of a technician, "Jesus Christ, what the hell am I waiting for? We've been going together long enough." So he went to a phone booth and called Mary Ann D'Agostino in Concord.

She took the train to Boston and he picked her up at North Station, and they just drove around downtown. There wasn't much traffic, it being Sunday, so they could just talk to each other without being interrupted by some *gibbone* honking his horn. Finally, Salvucci stopped at what only a member of Local 32 of the Bricklayers, Masons, and Plasterers Union, at what only a transportation major at MIT would consider a romantic spot. Under the Central Artery, right near the High Street ramp. Very lovely in the spring. You can sit and watch the wet winter grunge slop down over the superstructure.

Fred Salvucci looked deep into the eyes of Mary Ann D'Agostino as the afternoon sun glinted off the sediment stuck to the windshield, and, rising verbally to a level of passion he had never before attained, he said, or perhaps muttered, "What the heck. Let's get married."

Somewhere in Ward 3, a mandolin strummed.

(2)It is an altogether curious structure, this one-story one-million-four dream house of Ronald and Nancy Reagan's. Were the house on the market (which it will probably not be, since, at the time it was costing a million-four, local real estate agents seemed to agree on $300,000 as the top price ever paid for a house in Sacramento County), the words used to describe it would be "open" and "contemporary," although technically it is neither. "Flow" is a word that crops up quite a bit when one is walking through the place, and so is "resemble." The walls "resemble" local adobe, but they are not; they are the same concrete blocks, plastered and painted a rather stale yellowed cream, used in so many supermarkets and housing projects and Coca-Cola bottling plants. The door frames and the exposed beams "resemble" native redwood, but they are not; they are construction-grade lumber of indeterminate quality, stained brown. If anyone ever moves in, the concrete floors will be carpeted, wall to wall. If anyone ever moves in, the thirty-five exterior wood and glass doors, possibly the single distinctive feature of the house, will be, according to plan, "draped." The bathrooms are small and standard. The family bedrooms open directly onto the nonexistent swimming pool, with all its potential for noise and distraction. To one side of the fireplace in the formal living room there is what is known in the trade as a "wet bar," a cabinet for bottles and glasses with a sink and a long vinyl-topped counter. (This vinyl "resembles" slate.) In the entire house there are only enough bookshelves for a set of the World Book and some Books of the Month, plus maybe three Royal Doulton figurines and a back file of Connoisseur, but there is $90,000 worth of other teak cabinetry, including the "refreshment center" in the "recreation room." There is that most ubiquitous of all "luxury features," a bidet in the master bathroom. There is one of those kitchens which seem designed exclusively for defrosting by microwave and compacting trash. It is a house built for a family of snackers.

All we see here are the words on the page. Yet these voices are so strong, so distinctive that it is possible to conjure up a mental profile of each narrator. Is the person a man or a woman? Tall, medium, short? Thin, medium, stocky? What is he or she wearing? Is the narrator a city person or a country person? What is his or her economic status? Ethnic background? Stop here and compose your own narrator for each voice before continuing.

There are several possible answers to each of these questions, yet it is likely that most readers of voice 1 will come up with a male city dweller, probably 30 to 50 years of age, informally dressed, probably of Italian background; *no* reader will imagine a wealthy WASP CEO in a Brooks Brothers suit or Laura Ashley ensemble. (It is important to separate the *writer* from the *narrator*. It does not matter whether or not the writer actually fits the description implied by the voice; the same writer is capable of writing in other narrative voices implying other backgrounds.)

Now, three more questions about voice 1:

What is the narrator's attitude toward his subject, Fred Salvucci?

What is the nature of the relationship the writer sets up with us, the readers? (To begin exploring this question you might also ask yourself: How does this piece of writing make me feel? Comfortable? Uncomfortable? Relaxed? On guard? Respected? Ridiculed? Confided in? Condescended to?)

What is the underlying sensibility of this voice?

While some readers may interpret this passage as a put-down, most are likely to sense that the narrator speaks about Fred Salvucci the way an affectionate uncle speaks of his favorite nephew. He uses sarcasm, but it is light, friendly sarcasm:

"Finally, Salvucci stopped at what only a member of Local 32 of the Bricklayers, Masons, and Plasterers Union, at what only a transportation major at MIT would consider a romantic spot . . . "

He *likes* Salvucci.

The narrator likes us readers as well, I think, and he is treating us as equals, contemporaries, friends. I picture him talking to me (us) on a street corner, perhaps, or over coffee in a local diner, telling me about his young friend, Fred.

And the sensibility underlying all this is tolerant, generous, kind, practical, knowing.

So although we have never seen this narrator, and never actually heard his voice, there is much we have inferred about him. Certainly the contents of the passage have helped, but it is the voice that gives the narrator away.

It is a relaxed voice. The pace is slow to moderate, the rhythm relaxed, like a blues guitar. The sound is predominantly thick, low, with b's, d's, u's, and o's predominating. (Even the t's sound like d's.) Read it aloud, the way you imagine the narrator would read it. (It might help to imagine how a character actor might recite these lines. I think, for example, of Peter Falk in the role of Lieutenant Columbo.) "Fred Salvucci looked deep into the eyes of Mary Ann D'Agostino as the afternoon sun glinted off the sediment stuck to the windshield, and, rising verbally to a level of passion he had never before attained, he said, or perhaps muttered, "What the heck. Let's get married."

Now think about voice 2, and about the narrator you have imagined. Does he or she travel in the same circles as the narrator of voice 1?

While it would be possible to imagine voice 2 as either male or female, I suspect that most readers will settle on a female voice. I think also that most would decide that she is slim, elegantly dressed in an understated way, and fairly well-to-do. She may live in the city or the country, but wherever she lives, it is in the best neighborhood. She is well educated and certain in her tastes. And she is comfortable with money. In fact, hers is the voice of old money, expressing its contempt for the new.

Her attitude toward her subjects, the Reagans and their house, ranges from disdain to contempt. Her attitude toward her readers is not as generous as is the attitude of voice 1; one gets the feeling that to disagree with her would be to commit an egregious gaffe. The underlying sensibility is that of a person with rigorous standards and little patience with anyone or anything that does not meet them.

The rhythm of this piece is tighter, less relaxed than the rhythm of piece 1. The rhythm here is that of a schoolteacher tapping on a desk: measured, insistent. The pace is a little quicker. The sounds are crisp, well-defined, the p's and c's spat out delicately, the s's hissed. The t's do *not* sound like d's. Repetition and quotation marks are used to devastating effect. Read the following passage aloud, the way you imagine the narrator would: "'Flow' is a word that crops up quite a bit when one is walking through the place, and so is 'resemble.' The walls 'resemble' local adobe, but they are not; they are the same concrete blocks, plastered and painted a rather stale yellowed cream, used in so many supermarkets and housing projects and Coca-Cola bottling plants. The door frames and the exposed beams 'resemble' native redwood, but they are not; they are construction-grade lumber of indeterminate quality, stained brown."

For the record, the writer behind voice 1 is Alan Lupo. The piece, "The Mysterious Fred Salvucci Strikes Again," appeared in *Boston Magazine* in March 1974. The writer behind voice 2 is Joan Didion. The piece is "Many Mansions." It appears in her collection, *The White Album.* Also, for the record and for another, more important reason: each of the two passages represents only one of the several voices of each author. Didion's prose, while always exacting, is not always so biting, and, sometimes, is tinged with a profound melancholia; Lupo, always informal, often shows a more reflective and analytical side (for example, see his "A House and Its Memories," Chapter 30 of this book). This is important because *all* writers have several voices at their disposal. (In theory, at least, we have just as many writing voices as we have speaking voices.)

It is evident from "The Mysterious Fred Salvucci Strikes Again" and "Many Mansions" that the writer with a strong voice becomes a character in his or her own work. Whether or not the word "I" appears, the writer is there, an active presence, a narrator supplying the emotional and intellectual context for the material at hand.

DISCOVERING YOUR VOICE

How to begin to discover your own writer's voice? Flip through this book. Find a piece you like. Read a few paragraphs aloud, doing your best to re-create the voice on the page. Think about that voice. What is the rhythm? The sound? The attitude conveyed by the rhythm and the sound? The relationship the writer has established with you, the reader, with that voice? Then close the book. See if you can keep the rhythm, the sound, the attitude going in your head. (The process is like spending time with people who speak English with an accent different from yours—Southerners, New Englanders, Britishers, Jamaicans, Brooklynites; after a while, you find yourself speaking the way they do.) Now think about something you want to write about. And start writing, maintaining that rhythm, that sound, that sensibility.

In the beginning the process will seem awkward. There are two reasons for this. First, you will be acutely aware that you are not, in fact, Dave Barry or Annie Dillard; this is his voice or her voice you are using, not your own. It may be a rough fit, awkward, like a new pair of shoes. (If it is *too* rough a fit, it may be the wrong voice—but try it for at least ten minutes before looking for something else.)

Second, you may have the feeling that you are stealing something— that this is not, in fact, original writing that you are doing, but something you are taking from someone else. It's not true. Imitation is not plagiarism. You may be borrowing someone else's technique, but you are applying it to your own material, adapting it to your own sensibilities.

Stick with it. And, after a few paragraphs, you will discover that a subtle, wonderful thing is taking place. You will notice that you are no longer writing in Dave Barry's voice, or Dillard's; you are writing in your own voice. But it is a much more natural, relaxed voice than the other one, the voice of the encyclopedia which nobody reads by choice. *This* voice is a pleasure to write in, which means it will be a pleasure to read. It is the voice of someone who has something to say, and who knows how to say it.

THE IMPORTANCE OF VOICE TO A GOOD FIRST DRAFT

The pieces appearing in this anthology are not first drafts. The writers have added, cut, reorganized, and polished them until they are as close to perfect as possible. Yet the fact remains: without a strong first draft, the odds against a strong finished piece rise astronomically.

There is a story about Michelangelo, the great artist of the Renaissance. It is said that an awe-struck admirer once asked him: "How is it possible for any human to create a work of art as beautiful as your statue of David?" And Michelangelo replied: "It is easy. I begin with a block of marble, and cut away everything that does not look like David."

This is a fair analogy to the process of writing—except that unlike the sculptor, the writer must create the block of marble. And that is the first draft. As with the marble, it is the texture, the tone, the strength, and the integrity of the raw material that determine whether or not it has the potential to be transformed into a finished work of high quality.

A first draft that is a dry, passive, and sterile vessel full of generalities and secondhand information leads nowhere—even if it is perfectly organized and grammatically correct. But a first draft infused with the voice of a writer with something to say—with the proper chipping, molding, and shaping, such a draft may turn out to be a David.

YOUR VOICE IS A VERSATILE TOOL

The voice of an accomplished writer is just as versatile as the voice of an orator or an opera singer. It is a trained voice, honed and refined through years of practice and experimentation. It is constantly acquiring more subtle nuances, achieving greater resonance as the writer matures. And the accomplished writer learns to play with his or her voice in surprising ways. Watch, for example, as Paul H. Harasim adopts the persona of an inept reporter in order to express what he thinks of the doings of the Central Intelligence Agency in Cincinnati. Note the way Jennifer Allen imposes the awareness of an adult on the voice of a young girl to capture and explain the girl's fascination with sex. And see how Annie Dillard hypnotizes you with the sound of her voice; writing about writing, she takes on the persona of a mystic. You must listen; you must write!

The pieces of writing on display in this book argue, persuade, instruct, ponder, entertain. They are as varied as the people who wrote them. But they have these things in common: they all have strong voices. They are never dull. And they are fun to read, which is compelling evidence that they were fun to write. Read them. Think about the voice in each of them. Try to imagine the narrators—what they look like, how they dress, where they're from, how they talk and act and think. Read passages out loud, the way you think the narrators would. Borrow from them when you write. And soon a new voice will emerge. It is all yours. Use it—because you have something to say.

1

The Corps

Henry Allen

The Vietnam War had gone badly for the United States. The morale among the military establishment was poor. But in one small corner of the country, a dot of an island off the coast of South Carolina, little had changed since the glory days of World War II. On Parris Island the United States Marine Corps still turned boys into men, men into Marines.

It was decidedly out of synch with the mood of the rest of the country.

In February of 1972, Henry Allen, a reporter for the Washington Post, *paid a visit to Parris Island. The result was "The Corps." It is a remarkable piece of writing, more than simply an accurate factual account of life on the island. By re-creating the sound, the rhythm, the ethos of the place, Allen has allowed his readers to share the experience vicariously. The result is frightening and exhilarating.*

1   PARRIS ISLAND, S.C.—He is seething, he is rabid, he is wound up tight as a golf ball, with more adrenalin surging through his hypothalamus than a cornered slum rat, he is everything these Marine recruits with their heads shaved to dirty nubs have ever feared or even hoped a drill instructor might be.

2   He is Staff Sgt. Douglas Berry and he is rushing down the squad bay of Receiving Barracks to leap onto a table and brace at parade rest in which none of the recruits, daring glances from the position of attention, can see any more of him under the rake of his campaign hat than his lipless mouth chopping at them like a disaster teletype: WHEN I GIVE YOU THE WORD YOU WILL WALK YOU WILL NOT RUN DOWN

THESE STEPS WHERE YOU WILL RUN YOU WILL NOT WALK TO THE YELLOW FOOTMARKS. . . .

3   Outside, Berry's two junior drill instructors, in raincoats over dress greens, sweat in a muggy February drizzle which shrinks the view down to this wooden World War II barracks, to the galvanized Butler hut across the company street, the overground steam pipes, a couple of palmetto trees, the raindrops beading on spitshined black shoes.

4   Sgt. Hudson mans the steps, Sgt. Burley the footmarks. They pace with a mannered strut, like men wearing white tie and tails, their hands folded behind their backs, their jaw muscles flexing. One senses there's none of the wisecracking "See Here, Private Hargrove," or "Sgt. Bilko" Army routine here, no hotshot recruits outsmarting dumb sarge for passes to town.

5   In fact, during his 63 days of training at Parris Island, unless a member of his immediate family dies, a recruit will get no liberty at all. He will also get no talking, no phone calls, no books or magazines, no television, radio or record players, no candy or gum, one movie, one newspaper a week, and three cigarettes a day. Unless he fouls up, gets sent to the brig or to motivation platoon, and loses the cigarettes.

6   WHEN I GIVE YOU THE WORD TO MOVE OUT YOU WILL MOVE OUT DO YOU UNDERSTAND ME?

7   Hudson meets the first one at the steps like a rotary mower ripping into a toad, so psyched he's actually dancing on tiptoe, with his face a choleric three-quarters of an inch from the private FASTER PRIVATE FASTER JUST TAKE YOUR DUMB TIME SWEETHEART MOVE! MOVE! as this hog, as recruits are colloquially known, piles out of the barracks in a stumble of new boots, poncho, laundry bag and the worst trouble his young ass has ever been in, no doubt about it when Burley meets him just like Hudson, in an astonishment of rage that roars him all the way down to the right front set of yellow footprints YOU LOCK YOUR BODY AT ATTENTION YOU LOCK YOUR BODY. . . .

8   Or maybe Burley writhes up around this private to hiss in his ear— and Burley is very good at this—*you hate me, don't you, you hate me, private, you'd better hate me because I hate you,* or any of the other litanies drill instructors have been barking and hissing at their charges ever since the first of more than one million Parris Island graduates arrived on this flea-ridden sand barren in 1911.

9   Until there are 60 of them out there in the drizzle with the drill instructors shouting themselves hoarse, 60 volunteers who had heard from countless older brothers and street corner buddies and roommates that it would be exactly like this but they volunteered anyhow, to be Marines.

10   Right now, with lips trembling, eyes shuttling YOU BETTER STOP THAT EYEBALLING, PRIVATE!! fat and forlorn, they look like 60 sex

perverts trapped by a lynch mob. They are scared. They are scared as fraternity pledges during a cleverly staged hell week, shaking like boys about to abandon their virginity.

11   It's a primal dread that drill instructors invoke and exploit in eight weeks (soon to revert to the pre-Vietnam 11 weeks) of folk theater, a spectacle staged on the scale of the Passion Play at Oberammergau, an initiation that may be the only true rite of passage to manhood that America hasn't yet scoured away as an anthropological anachronism.

12   Fifteen minutes after that first recruit panicked out of receiving barracks, Berry, Burley and Hudson have stampeded all of them into their new squad bay. While 1st Lt. Roger McElrath lectures them on the vast variety of crimes and punishments on display in the Uniform Code of Military Justice, the D.I.s are hidden in a room called the drill instructor's house, changing their uniforms. Squared-away drill instructors change uniforms up to six times a day. It is no more possible for a drill instructor to appear sweatstained, soiled or wrinkled than a Vatican priest.

13   "Goddam, goddam, goddam," Hudson is saying, over and over. Fresh sweat blisters his brow. All of them are flushed and breathing hard, swearing and fumbling for cigarettes like a roller derby team at half time.

14   "They look good," Berry says. He's baby-faced, actually, earnest with a flair of cynicism, like a professional athlete. "We got 15 brothers (blacks). They'll pick up drill right away. The others can get the rhythm off them. Not too many fatbodies, not too many belligerents. This'll be a good platoon."

15   The problem for D.I.s picking up platoons isn't exhaustion, though, or even getting psyched to that glitter of madness, but "getting too psyched up, so psyched you might grab a kid to straighten him out and BAM, that's it, it's your stripes," says Gunnery Sgt. Ronald Burns, a drill field veteran who now meets the late night buses hauling recruits in from the Charleston and Savannah airports.

16   Brutality to the Marines is like usury to Jews—a nightmare that threatens their very existence. It is also the leading figment of the Marine mystique and the stock brag of any Parris Island graduate. It is a legend like that of the "Old Corps," which always seems to have ended about three years ago. In the Old Corps, Marines tell each other, there was none of this Standard Operating Procedure (SOP) for recruit training, none of these maltreatment questionnaires and "swoop teams" of inspectors to hamstring the drill instructors.

17   Nothing to keep a D.I. from working over recruits during nightly "thump call," from slamming the whole platoon into "Chinese thinking position," an excruciating calisthenic in which you prop yourself solely on elbows and toes, and not to be confused with other outlawed old

favorites such as six-point kneeling, steam engines, dry shaving, blanket parties, smoking under a blanket, the game of Flood and Air Raid, ethnic taunts, profanity, and allowing a recruit to eat all two pounds of the divinity fudge his girlfriend mailed him, eat it in three minutes flat, lover boy, every goddam crumb.

18   All outlawed now and outlawed too back in 1956, when rumors of Truman's plans to merge the Corps into the Army still haunted Marines, and Staff Sgt. Matthew McKeon made every front page in America by leading an unauthorized night march into Ribbon Creek, out behind the rifle range, and six recruits drowned in a mass panic.

19   Since then, enforcement of the SOP has been screwed down tighter every year at both Parris Island and San Diego, a more recent recruit training base that trains enlistees from the western half of the country.

20   The SOP orders drill instructors to instill "instant obedience to orders." It also forbids them on pain of court-martial from touching a recruit, except to adjust a military position.

21   It prescribes 63 days of training which will include: 89 hours on firing the M-14 rifle, 60 hours of drill, 57 hours of physical training (PT), 23 hours of inspections and testing, 12 hours on clothing and equipment, 10 hours on history of the Marine Corps, and 114 hours of "commander's time," to include one hour each night of "free time" for writing and reading letters and doing anything else that does not involve talking, smoking, eating or leaving the squad bay. There are also endless hours of rifle cleaning, shoe shining, and singing of the Marine Corps hymn:

> *From the halls of Montezuma*
> *To the shores of Tripoli . . .*

22   "Parris Island is a game. If you can play by the rules, you do very well," says Lt. Scott Shaffer, a Navy psychologist (the Marines get medical and religious services from the Navy) who interviews a daily parade of bedwetters, attempted suicides, weepers, catatonics and others suspected mentally unfit for the Marine Corps.

23   "It's very behaviorally oriented, like a big Skinner box. You do well, you get rewarded. You do badly and you're punished. Positive and negative reinforcement. Personally, I'd like to see more positive reinforcement (reward)."

24   This doesn't explain, though, why anybody joins in the first place, especially in an age of beer machines in Navy barracks, and Army boot camps that promise you don't have to lose your dignity to get your training.

25   "They join because they want their girl to be proud of them, or their parents, or the gang on the block. Or they want to be proud of themselves. They want to be somebody, want to be able to go home a big, bad-

ass Marine," says Gunnery Sgt. Mike "Big Mac" McCormick, who is all of that at 6-feet-4$^{1}/_{2}$ and 212 pounds, with five years on Parris Island drilling recruits and training drill instructors. "That's the best lever you've got on that recruit—pride. Next comes fear."

26 But neither pride, fear nor game theory can explain to anyone who has been through Parris Island why he endured those long, dusty, staggering exhaustions of runs, or the standing at attention in chow lines, thumbs locked to trouser seams while sand fleas put on a flying circus in his ears.

27 Or the incessant, insane, "Catch-22" paradoxes—a recruit pumping out jumping jacks, sweating his T-shirt translucent while his D.I. yells "DO YOU WANT TO DO MORE?" and the private, of course, answers "NO SIR," until he realizes the correct answer is "YES, SIR," and the drill instructor tells him to stop doing any more, of course.

28 Given the fact that there are choices, such as the Air Force, which at least offers job-skill training, it would seem the only reason any human being puts up with Marine boot camp is that he wants to—a horrendous thought, if you're an enlightened believer in the basic rationality and pleasure drives of modern, educated man.

29 Think about it: drill instructors might as well be Pueblo shamans scaring candidates for tribal membership and manhood with nothing but masks and chants. (That wry ferocity drill instructors cultivate, the squinted eyes and the mouth about as generous as a snapping turtle's, and the jutjawed arrogance of their back-of-the-throat voices.)

30 And recruits, swaddled in their new uniforms and shorn of hair, are no more civilized, perhaps, than Australian aborigine boys who are circumcised and wrapped in blankets to be purified and symbolically reborn.

31 In *Man and His Symbols*, Joseph Henderson, a disciple of Carl Jung, states that the archetypal initiation that has pervaded all primitive cultures involves submission (enlistment), symbolic death by ordeal (degradation and physical demands far beyond what the recruit believes possible), and symbolic rebirth as a member of the collective consciousness (the Marine Corps).

32 It all fits, even the fact that the lessons taught at Parris Island involve stress or ceremony but few combat skills, except "instant obedience." The Marines leave the grenade throwing and small unit tactics and camouflage to Camp Lejeune, in North Carolina, where, for the first time, recruits are greeted as "Marine." Rifle firing is strictly on a formal bull's-eye target range, in the official National Rifle Association positions.

33 In fact, drill instructors may gain their extraordinary power from invoking all the archetypal terrors of initiation while never actually

threatening the life of the recruit—a threat that would break the bond of trust between recruit and D.I., a bond so strong after only a few weeks that some drill instructors have been able to thump hell out of recruits with no fear they'll turn him in.

34   Like a score of fellow recruits, Pvt. John Hedrick, 19, of Lynchburg, Va., answers only "Yessir my drill instructors treat me well, Nossir, there's no maltreatment, Yessir, I'd enlist again if I had it to do over."

35   Of course, there is bound to be some falling away from the faith, apostasies that drill instructors watch for with those quick glares, stalking up and down a row of recruits in a mess hall, say, making sure the hogs or ladies or maggots are popping those heels and squaring those corners.

36   The drill instructors watch because once a recruit sees the whole ritual is just a magic show, he loses both his fear of the D.I., and his motivation. And motivation is what Parris Island is all about. It not only makes you a Marine, not only makes you like it, but also makes you believe in it.

37   ("The worst thumping I ever got was when the D.I. called the retreat from the Chosin reservoir an 'advance to the rear,' and I snickered," says Mike Jerace, who went through Parris Island in 1963.)

38   So secret doubters who stop shouting those yessirs at peak bellow, who stop trembling and panting like a dog in a thunderstorm to crank out one more pull-up, are apt to spend one to 10 days at motivation platoon: Last year, 3,384 of 28,153 Parris Island initiates did time at motivation platoon, and 557 were later discharged from the Marines "for reasons of defective attitude," said Capt. John Woggon, who directs Special Training Branch. (Which, besides motivating recruits who aren't putting out 100 percent, also takes a pound a day off "fatbodies," reconditions hospital discharges, and punishes legal offenders in its Correctional Custody Platoon.)

39   Motivation platoon is a ferocious speed-up of the carrot-and-stick routine, starting with eight to 20 maddening, grueling miles of speed march broken only by patriotic lectures and movies about epic Marine heroisms at Tarawa, Iwo Jima, Khe Sanh . . . Then fighting with padded "pugil sticks" between recruits who may never have been in a fight in their lives. And finally, lining up sweating and gritty, muscles shrill with fatigue, for The Ditch.

40   What happens to most recruits in eight weeks happens to most of motivation platoon in 30 minutes in The Ditch. The Ditch is Parris Island's last-chance purgatory, 480 meters of sand, mud, barbed wire and corrugated storm pipe all half-flooded with tidewater that these recruits will crawl through on their knees and bellies with metal rifle frames YOU WILL JUMP INTO THIS FIRST WATER OBSTACLE YOU WILL

COMPLETELY IMMERSE YOURSELF YOU WILL THEN CRAWL ON YOUR KNEES DOWN THAT DITCH YELLING MARINE CORPS WITH EVERY BREATH YOU BREATHE. . . .

41   Baptism in a waist-deep mud puddle and the crawl begins. Shaved heads stream mud and water, mouths yaw wide as anatomy displays gasping MARINE CORPS, MARINE CORPS as they grind their way down that ditch like nothing so much as Mexican *penitentes* struggling on their knees for miles to win salvation at the Shrine of Our Lady, the ultimate prostration, the last plea . . .

42   Under the frantic frustration of the barbed wire, through the drain-pipes that deliver them into a mock-up of an Indochinese village where they form up shivering and chanting MARINE CORPS while Staff Sgt. Sam Michaux pounds time with his boot. Then Michaux delivers the last speech before the penitents are sent back filthy and exhausted to their platoons.

43   "This is the world, sweeties, and your drill instructor wants to help you BUT BY GOD YOU BETTER HELP YOURSELVES because when the going gets rough, you can't say anymore I'M GONNA TAKE MY LITTLE RED WAGON AND GO HOME. The next time you think you can slack off you'd best remember that a HARD HEAD MAKES A SOFT ASS and yours is GONNA GET KICKED."

44   Meanwhile, Platoon 220, like another platoon yesterday, and another tomorrow, is just beginning its long initiation back in its barracks, or "barn," as the drill instructors call it, with its paint-flaked bunks lined up like stanchions, its bathroom of cement floors and naked squads of gleaming seatless toilets.

45   Cardboard placards advertise the Eleven General Orders like religious mottoes in the bare-bulb glare of this drizzly afternoon indoors. Decades of sweat and pivoting boots have worn the floors to a shine. Platoon 220's home is shabby but immaculate, like the tin-roof shack of a "good nigger," like Parris Island itself, in fact, a grim, mundane 3,300 habitable acres on which neatness and thrift are the only aesthetics, instant obedience the only ethic.

46   In the next eight weeks, Berry, Burley and Hudson will whipsaw these 60 recruits with reward and punishment. As former Marine commandant Gen. David M. Shoup once said, they will "receive, degrade, sanitize, immunize, clothe, equip, train, pain, scold, mold, sand and polish."

47   They will condition this stampede of adolescence until it understands a great paradox called military fear, a first law of survival that states the only thing you have to fear is not being scared enough to put up with the insult and hassle that are any military existence, with the chronic disaster of war.

48   Platoon 220 will discover the ease and convenience of this tautology just as they will discover that this fear, bleakness and degradation can yield a beauty they'll never be able to explain to anyone who hasn't gone through it and made it.

49   Eight weeks later, for instance, in the lambency of a Southern twilight in spring, Platoon 220 may fall out on the grinder for close order drill, which they'll be very good at by then, and they'll feel the cool flutter of their new tropical uniforms against their legs, and their rifles will flip from shoulder arms to port arms with one, crisp crash, and they'll lean back in a limber strut to the singsong of the D.I.'s cadence—a voice burnished by years of too much fatigue, coffee and cigarettes—the whole platoon floating across the quiet parade field like a ship at sea.

TO THINK ABOUT

1. What persona does Allen's narrator take on? What is the implied role of the reader?
2. What is Allen's attitude toward his subject matter? Is it simple or complex? What was your attitude toward the Marines before you read the piece? What is it now?
3. What is the effect of the last paragraph of the piece?
4. On page 16 Allen cites Joseph Henderson's description of archetypal initiation: submission, symbolic death by ordeal, and symbolic rebirth as a member of the collective consciousness. Can you think of any nonmilitary organizations using initiation rites of this sort? Are there any on your campus? What are the advantages of such procedures? What are the drawbacks?

TO DO

1. Read the first two paragraphs of "The Corps" aloud, in the voice Henry Allen intended. For best results, read it to a room full of people.
2. Make a list of clubs, organizations, and institutions you are curious about. Pick the one that intrigues you the most. Do some library research on that organization. Then arrange to spend a day or two observing members of the organization doing whatever it is they do. When you are done, write a piece about your observations.

TIP

As a writer in the field you must perform a tricky balancing act. It is important to allow yourself to develop feelings about your subject matter; it is equally important to remain detached enough to retain an outsider's perspective on what you are observing. This takes practice. Begin with situations you know you can handle.

2

Sex

Jennifer Allen

We are eighteen, or twenty-eight, or fifty. We know certain things about ourselves and about the world, how we work and how it works. We know more than we did last year. We know a lot more than we did ten years ago. And we are embarrassed when we think about all the things we didn't know back then. Who was that person who was us?

We are right to think about those days. We are wrong to be embarrassed. What we should be doing with that material is writing about it.

When Jennifer Allen was nine she did not know much about sex. But she had lots of curiosity and lots of clues. When she grew up, she wrote about those days, with a child's enthusiasm and an adult's wisdom. Her voice contains elements of both.

1   I am eight or nine years old, and my brother's friend Phil is sleeping over. Phil is as tall as a tree, with huge feet and hands and a prematurely deep voice that make him seem, at thirteen, almost like a grown man. Like my brother, Phil loves rock music. He wants to buy a motorcycle. He dresses like a slob. He is my dream man.

2   Phil rarely speaks to me, but he and my brother and I have pillow fights whenever he sleeps over. On this night, we are in the basement pummeling each other with our bed pillows. My brother gets distracted by something, so Phil and I go at it, one on one, holding onto our pillows and thwacking away. Phil smiles when he starts tickling and pummeling me and I, up too late, giggling too loud, flattered beyond belief, am in a state of bliss close to frenzy. Suddenly, with a force that stops me dead, I have a thought: This activity could get me pregnant. I am so stunned that I blurt it out loud: "I might get a baby from this!"

3   I knew the accepted wisdom as to where babies came from. I had had some sex education in school; my mother had read me a library book that covered the basics. In the book, sex was a show of affection, harmless as a bear hug, but remote. First you had to fall in love, get married, decide to have children. In sex education, it was more antiseptic but just as distant. Intercourse. Ovulate. Penetrate. Ejaculate. Fertilize. Vocabulary-test kinds of words. Formidable, maybe, but dry, not scary. Intercourse was part of being an adult, like having a job.

4   But that wasn't the whole story. Any child growing up in the early sixties couldn't help getting wind of the first rumblings of the sexual revolution. Popular culture was saturated with it; the signs, the words, were all around us, in ads and movies and magazines, on the tongues of older siblings. Sex. Sexy. Sex appeal. Sex drive. Orgy. French kiss. Fruit. Fairy. Topless beach. Bikini. Blue movie. *Sex and the Single Girl.* Go-go girl. Sexpot. Sex kitten. Ski bunny. Stewardess. Slut. *Peyton Place.* Fourth base. Bachelor pad. Promiscuous. Playboy. Swinger. Animal. Rapist. Sex maniac. Sex fiend. Sex pervert. Kids co-opted words from the adult vernacular—you screamed "sex maniac!" for example, at any boy who chased you during recess. Husbands never said to wives, proudly, "Well, you're looking like a sexpot today." They seemed satisfied with Intercourse. To this day, a small part of me thinks that dirty movies are tinted blue, that stripteasing involves sticking your tongue out as you take your clothes off and that a bachelor's apartment is furnished in wall-to-wall pillows that turn it into one big pad, the better to French-kiss sexpots.

5   You didn't have to be a genius to see that sex was much bigger than a soundless, discreet activity like Intercourse. Intercourse was self-contained, it never left the bedroom; sex was insidious, it snuck in everywhere. If sex was invisible but pervasive, like air, wasn't it possible to catch it, or take part in it, without knowing it? Maybe Phil and I were having some form of sex, invisible to the naked eye, that just looked like a pillow fight. Maybe sex was like rubbing two sticks together. Phil and I were the sticks; somehow, unseen sparks might pass between us, like germs, and I would have a baby growing inside me. Conjured out of thin air.

6   It was no use asking any adult about sex. Enlightened as they were on the subject of sex education, they seemed in favor of Intercourse, opposed to sex. They never talked about sex appeal, never said French kiss or sex kitten or slut. They seemed satisfied with Intercourse. Any manifestation of sex, or the body, or private parts, made them nervous. My mother had a reminder that she used to deliver to my sister and me: *Protect your modesty.* "Protect your modesty," she would say when we

sat with our skirts hitched up, knees wide apart, and we would know to straighten up, draw our legs together.

7 Though they never mentioned it, you got the message: Adults didn't like sex. But the phenomenon stared us in the face, far more real than Intercourse. Protecting your Modesty seemed profoundly beside the point.

8 So I put my radar out for sex, was fascinated by what I could not understand. At eight, ten, twelve years old, we had it at our fingertips. Playboy bunnies did much more than have Intercourse. They had sex— with their ears on, perhaps at *orgies*. Go-go girls were almost certainly promiscuous—maybe that was why they were kept in cages to dance for customers. Jack Paar was probably a *swinger*.

9 But the most compelling references to sex were in rock-and-roll. All you needed was an older brother who filled the house with a more sinister brand of rock. *Light my fire, light my fire, light my fire.* Jim Morrison offered the chant, over and over. I would close my eyes and try to think of what "light my fire" could mean; all I could see was a bonfire. But it meant more than that, of course: The way Morrison sang it, shouted it, made me think of a coyote howling at the moon. Animal. *Sex maniac.* What was it about sex that made him want it so badly? The words "light my fire" were a code, and I couldn't crack it. The Animals sang a song that chilled me: "There is a house in New Orleans, they call it the Rising Sun. It's been the ruin of many a poor boy, and God, I know I'm one." Eric Burdon, the Animals' lead singer, looked haunted, and had a waxy complexion. Ruined. Sex went on at that house, sex so dangerous, so monstrous, that by the time you stumbled out, as the sun rose, you had been ruined.

10 Sex could do worse than ruin you. It could kill you. Marilyn Monroe had killed herself—after realizing, as I understood it, what she really was. A sex kitten. A sexpot. A slut. It had made her want to die. (Monroe's death so upset my mother that she broke her silence on the subject of sex: Monroe had died because "men" had forced her to pose naked for years; now she wouldn't have to do it anymore.)

11 There were plenty of real-life sex crimes, too—you could read them in papers and magazines. I followed a series on the Boston Strangler with ghoulish fascination. Why did all the Strangler's victims let him in, when they knew there was a killer on the loose? The magazine said he had hypnotic eyes. Aha, I thought, this was the magazine's code for *sex appeal.* That was it: he got through the door on sex appeal and by then it was too late. A person could have sex appeal, then, but be a *sex fiend* underneath. Could you learn to tell the difference?

12   I grew up a little, I got to be fourteen, fifteen, sixteen. I developed serious crushes on a couple of eighteen-year-olds and learned what going weak in the knees meant. I began to see what the fuss was about; sex lost some of its morbid, fantastical edge. But it stayed dangerous. I skimmed for the Good Parts in the few suggestive books I found and knew this did not speak well for my character. I found a copy of Terry Southern and Mason Hoffenberg's *Candy*, which was one long Good Part, and felt sickened and in need of a bath after speeding my way through it. *Candy* confirmed what I'd thought all along: that sex was a toppling from grace into a messy world. But more important, had I put the book down? Had I made any move to Protect my Modesty? No! I hadn't been able to tear myself away. I was as filthy-minded as Candy, or worse. I had fallen, irretrievably; I could never turn back.

13   I took a look at *Candy* the other day. It is a period piece, spottily funny, way too long. It would be a chore to read through. But I resisted looking at Terry Southern's dust-jacket photograph. I didn't want to remember what he looked like, this man whom I had gone to fourth base with. He hadn't even touched me, but it had happened. Sure and invisible as air.

14   I don't think sex, or most sex, is grubby, or deadly or dire. I think, though, that the notion of sex I grew up with had one resounding element of truth. Sex *is* everywhere, informing everything we do. You can have sex without realizing it at all, seduce and not know it, be attacked and never touched. It is insidious, mutable, in ways that still astonish me; a tyrant sometimes, a traitor at others.

15   And another thing. While I think sex has a great many qualities—sublime, infuriating, farcical, electric, exhausting, crazy-making—it is never, to its credit, even remotely as banal as a bear hug. Even a child knows that.

TO THINK ABOUT

1. Certain elements of the narrator's voice are childlike; others clearly come from an adult. See if you can identify these various elements.
2. In the third paragraph Allen presents a list of sex-related terms adults used in the presence of children. In the fourth paragraph she presents another list, this one of sexy terms not on the adults' approved list. What is the difference between the two sets of terms? Why do you think adults preferred the first set, while children preferred the second?

3. Which terms on the second list are still current? Why do you think certain terms are now obsolete?
4. Allen cites the connection between sex and rock-and-roll. Is it still there? Contrast the rock of the 1960s with the rock of the 90s. What does each imply about its own era?

TO DO

1. Allen writes: "Sex *is* everywhere, informing everything we do." Put your radar out for sex—not Intercourse, but the stuff in the air. Write an essay about what you know and about what you find.
2. Make a list of misconceptions you had as a child—things you thought you understood, but didn't. Write a piece about one or more of them.
3. Make a list of songs that have meant something to you. Pick one. Write an essay about that song in the context of your life.

TIP

Allen writes that sex ". . . is never, to its credit, even remotely as banal as a bear hug." But written material about sex sometimes is. Usually that happens when the writer is nervous about the subject, and distances himself or herself from it with abstractions. Natalie Goldberg has the best advice:

> Always begin with yourself and let that carry you. . . . If you are nervous, look around the room. Begin with something small and concrete—your teacup in its saucer, the thin slice of an apple, an Oreo cookie crumb on your red lips. Sometimes you have to begin far away from the answer and then down-spiral back to it. Writing is an act of discovery. You want to discover your relationship with a topic, not the dictionary definition.

3

Infidelity

Barbara Lazear Ascher

Often we tend to divide nonfiction writing into "personal nar-
ratives," on the one hand, and "research papers" on the other. The
distinction is both false and harmful, for it implies that anything
"personal" is able to stand on its own, without research, and that
anything involving "research" is impersonal, flat, and dull.

In fact, most good nonfiction writing may be placed on a con-
tinuum between the purely personal narrative and the pure research
paper. In Chapter 21 the distinguished scientist Stephen J. Gould
makes science not only accessible, but also enjoyable, by infusing
his scientific judgment with his own personality. And here, Barbara
Lazear Ascher leavens an intensely personal approach to an in-
tensely personal subject—adultery—with numerous references to
history and literature.

Often we set out to defend a given supposition, only to find
our supposition changing as we read and write. But sometimes our
original idea gains strength as we proceed. I suspect this is what
happened when Ascher set out to defend marital fidelity. Her voice
is passionate and authoritative.

1   Well, I can tell you what I'd do if I discovered that my husband was
having a love affair. I'd go get a gun. None of the pertinent information
would filter through the buzzing sound that fills the brain when the
heart is hurt. I would forget the facts: that I adore him, that there's a family to consider, that he makes a better living than I, that criminal lawyers
are expensive. The possibility of widowhood, poverty or prison would
not deter. Infidelity is reason enough for strict gun control.

2   It's hearts like mine that have put laws on the books and the question in the minds of judges and juries: "Is infidelity sufficient provoca-
tion to reduce a charge of murder to manslaughter?" Yes, according to
eighteenth-century case law, if the killer commits the act "in the first
transport of passion." Yes, according to the 1977 English case of *Mossa* v.
the Queen, if the defendant has been told by his wife, "I've had inter-

course with every man on the street" and then throws a telephone at him. Yes, said the law of New Mexico in 1963, it is a *complete* defense if the accused witnessed the adulterous act. How the defendant would prove this was left to our imaginations (which is probably why the law was repealed in 1973).

3   I realize that there are people who appear to act rationally in the face of infidelity. Most of them exist in nineteenth- and early-twentieth-century fiction. Consider Maggie, for instance, in Henry James's *The Golden Bowl.* Upon learning that her husband, the Prince, was romantically involved with her best friend, who was also her stepmother, she devised a plan that was a work of art. Arms negotiations could not match the complexity of bringing Maggie's husband back to her. It worked, but it seemed to take forever. Few of our hearts are strong enough to cling to flotsam that long—to wait for the whim of current to carry us back to shore.

. . .

4   Consider Leonora, the wife of Edward Ashburnham in Ford Madox Ford's *The Good Soldier,* who facilitated her husband's known infidelities by keeping the object of his affections close at hand. "I suppose," muses Ford's narrator, "that Leonora was pimping for Edward."

5   Models of restraint. But the lady from Oklahoma wins my admiration. The year was 1927, Manhattan was a long train ride from Tulsa and there were three little children playing about her knees when her sister-in-law approached with grave news. Her husband, the father of these children, was keeping company in New York with a certain actress. Our young mother sent the children off with their aunt and took the next train east.

6   She went to his hotel, and finding him in the dining room in the company of the lovely miss, stood before the entire crowd of diners and announced: "Samuel, you are either coming home with me immediately or you are never coming home again. You are either raising our children with me or I will do it alone, in which case, you will never see them again." My friend, the now-sixty-five-year-old daughter of this woman, smiles. She is proud of her mother. "He came home," she says.

7   Of the people who sit it out with honor, who wait for their spouses to "get over" extramarital infatuation, who martyr themselves for the cause of marriage, family or economics, I would want to know, was it worth it?

8   I have an eighty-year-old friend who tells me, "The hardest time in my life was when my husband had a love affair, and it lasted many years." I ask her, "Why didn't you leave?" revealing myself to be a member of the "me" generation, ill-equipped to handle frustration or psychic pain for more than a week, let alone years. "Oh, I thought of being passionate, of

walking out the door," she replies, "but I had to think of the welfare of the family as a whole."

9   As I look at her family as a whole—the grandchildren, the companionship of husband and wife over the dinner table—I am almost persuaded. But then I don't know the price she paid: conceiving, bearing and raising his children, knowing all the while that his heart and passions were elsewhere. If these weren't intensely private matters, I would ask her, How long did it take for warmth to return to your body? To your heart?

10   In spite of the latest *Playboy* survey, which would have it that infidelity is a matter of fact of life—48 percent of men and 83 percent of women questioned said they were or had been engaged in extramarital affairs—infidelity is no fair. Somebody is left out. Somebody else is having all the fun. And even that isn't quite true, because guilt hovers about the door of even the most carefree transgression. If you're very lucky it won't knock louder than your heart or knees when you are in that illicit embrace.

11   It is that embrace that is visualized by anyone who has ever been betrayed: one's beloved in the arms and bed of another. Imagine it and tell me that your heart doesn't go belly up like a dead fish.

12   Some of us struggled to understand the hippies' generosity of spirit. If they were willing to share spouses and lovers, we asked, why weren't we? After all, we had so much in common: make love not war—we agreed there; eat grains not flesh—that's cool. We thought that our desire for fidelity must be small and selfish, some tight little knot in our hearts, a nasty wart on our souls.

13   Now, I wonder, how much did the flower children really know about love? In infidelity someone is the outsider. Being an outsider hurts. Memories of birthday parties we weren't invited to, teams we weren't chosen for, being a child in a world run by and for grown-ups. Betrayal dredges up all these old feelings, raw and fresh as if age had neglected to install a protective layer of insulation between childhood and adulthood.

14   So I question the honorable selflessness of James's Maggie, who desires not only the return of her husband but that he be protected from guilt and loss of honor. I question the hippies' magnanimous gestures. I question those who say of their "unsuspecting" spouses, "He (or she) will never find out." "It had nothing to do with you." That's like a pickpocket leaving behind a note saying, "Nothing personal." It may not be personal, but all the same you've been robbed. You've been had.

15   In *The Good Soldier* and *The Golden Bowl* hearts and circumstance failed to mesh. The Prince married Maggie because he couldn't afford to marry his true but penniless love. Obligations of their parents bound

Leonora and Edward. In the enlightened 1980's it is hoped that we marry for love.

16   A friend of mine, divorced for ten sexually active years before re-marriage, tells me: "I never knew that fidelity would feel so good. There is something lush about each encounter when you both know that each of you is the only one."

17   I would describe it as a feeling of being alone in the world without loneliness. Of being complete but uncrowded. Of total peace and security. Like finding yourself under a tropical sun in February, or listening to Stern and Rose play Brahms' Double Concerto, or having your new-born, still connected by a cord, stare straight into your eyes. Nothing to give up without a gun.

TO THINK ABOUT

1. What effect do Ascher's first two sentences have on you? Her first full paragraph? Try to form a mental portrait of the narrator from this one paragraph alone.
2. Do you think Ascher is serious about the gun? Why or why not?
3. Both Ascher and Harry Stein ("The Big A," Chapter 44) oppose adultery, but their voices and sensibilities differ. Try to imagine a conversation between them on the subject of adultery. Now imagine joining the conversation. Compare your voice to each of theirs.
4. What is the effect of Ascher's final paragraph? How does she achieve that effect?

TO DO

1. Make a list of the literary and historical references in Ascher's essay. (If the piece were footnoted, how many footnotes would it require?)
2. Free-write for 30 minutes on a broad subject which is of interest to you. The death penalty, gun control, legalized drugs, euthanasia—whatever you're feeling strongly about. Then go to the library and spend a full day researching your topic. Then rewrite the essay. Compare your first and second drafts.

TIP

Experienced writers work research material into personal narratives so naturally that it *looks* as though no research was necessary—that the writers had this stuff in their heads all along. It's an illusion.

Do not look on research with dread. Go to the library. Read. And soon your writing will bristle with an authority that your readers will assume came naturally.

4

Un Nintended Benefits
Commencement

Dave Barry

Dave Barry is a very funny man. He is wild, manic, over-the-edge funny, an everyman dealing with this crazy world the only way he knows how—by writing manic (but hardly ever depressive) columns about it. In "Un Nintended Benefits" Barry defends his son Robby's addiction to Nintendo video games. It is a typical Barry piece, filled with the kind of wild logic that enables a drowning man to take solace in the fact that he needed a bath anyway.

Every once in a while, another side of Dave Barry creeps out from behind his wildly grinning computer keyboard. This is the Dave Barry who, like every other parent who ever lived, cannot protect his child from the world, no matter how much he wants to. When this happens, his voice changes, as it does in "Commencement." "Commencement" is a more complex piece than "Un Nintended Benefits." Note the two voices here: the confident, encouraging voice of Barry the father, and the anxious inner voice of Barry the Narrator.

Un Nintended Benefits

1   Ok, I bought my child a Nintendo video-game system. I realize I should not admit this. I realize the Child Psychology Police may arrest me for getting my child a mindless addictive antisocial electronic device instead of a constructive old-fashioned educational toy such as an Erector Set. Well let me tell you something: All my childhood friends had Erector Sets, and although I am not proud of this, I happen to know

for a fact that, in addition to the recommended educational projects such as the Truck, the Crane, and the Carousel, it was possible to build the Bug Pulper, the Worm Extender, and the Gears of Pain.

2   And speaking of pain, you have no idea how hard my son made my life before I caved in and bought Nintendo. The technique he used was Power Wistfulness. Remember the old comic strip "Dondi," starring the little syndicated orphan boy who always looked heartbreakingly sad and orphanous and never got adopted, possibly because he had eye sockets the size of manhole covers? Well, my son looked like that. He'd start first thing in the morning, standing around with Dondi-like eyes, emitting armor-piercing wistfulness rays and sighing over the fact that he was the only child outside of the Third World who didn't have Nintendo. Pretty soon I'd be weeping all over my toast, thinking how *tragic* it was—my own son, an orphan—until finally I just had to go to the Toys "Я" Approximately a Third of the Gross National Product store, because after all we're talking about a child's happiness here, and you can't put a price tag on . . . What? It cost HOW MUCH? What does it DO for that kind of money? Penetrate Soviet airspace?

3   No, really, it's worth every penny. I know you've probably read a lot of articles by Leading Child Psychologists (defined as "people whose children probably wet the bed through graduate school") telling you why Nintendo is a bad thing, so let me discuss some of the benefits:

4   **Benefit No. 1—Nintendo enables the child to develop a sense of self-worth by mastering a complex, demanding task that makes his father look like a total goober.**

5   The typical Nintendo game involves controlling a little man who runs around the screen trying to stay alive while numerous powerful and inexplicably hostile forces try to kill him; in other words, it's exactly like real life. When I play, the little man becomes highly suicidal. If he can't locate a hostile force to get killed by, he will deliberately swallow the contents of a little electronic Valium bottle. So all my games end instantly, whereas my son can keep the little man alive through several presidential administrations. He is always trying to cheer me up by saying "Good try, Dad!" in the same sincerely patronizing voice that I once used to praise him for not getting peas in his hair. What is worse, he gives me Helpful Nintendo Hints that are far too complex for the adult mind to comprehend. Here's a verbatim example: "OK, there's Ganon and miniature Ganon and there's these things like jelly beans and the miniature Ganon is more powerfuller, because when you touch him the flying eagles come down and the octopus shoots red rocks and the swamp takes longer."

6   And the hell of it is, I know he's *right*.

7   **Benefit No. 2—Nintendo strengthens the community.**

8   One evening I got an emergency telephone call from our next-door neighbor, Linda, who said, her voice breathless with urgency: "Is Robby there? Because we just got Gunsmoke [a Nintendo game] and we can't get past the horse." Of course I notified Robby immediately. "It's the Liebmans," I said. "They just got Gunsmoke, and they can't get past the horse." He was out the door in seconds, striding across the yard, a Man on a Mission. Of course he got them past the horse. He can get his man all the way to the bazooka. *My* man dies during the opening credits.

9   **Benefit No. 3—When a child is playing Nintendo, the child can't watch regular television.**

10   Recently on the local news, one relentlessly personable anchorperson was telling us about the murder at a Pizza Hut, and when she was done, the other relentlessly personable anchorperson got a frowny look on his face, shook his head sadly, and said—I am not making this quotation up—"A senseless tragedy, and one that I am sure was unforeseen by the victims involved."

11   I don't want my child exposed to this.

12   **Benefit No. 4—A child who is playing Nintendo is a child who is probably not burping as loud as he can.**

13   I mention this only so I can relate the following true exchange I witnessed recently between a mother and her eight-year-old son:

SON: Burp. Burp. Burp. Burp. Bu. . .
MOTHER: Stop burping!
SON: But, Mom, it's my *hobby.*

14   So, Mr. and Ms. Child Psychologist, don't try to tell me that Nintendo is so terrible. OK? Don't tell me it makes children detached and aggressive and antisocial. In fact don't tell me anything. Not while the octopus is shooting these rocks.

Commencement

1   We're taking our son, Robby, to his first day of kindergarten. He is being Very Brave. So are we.

2   We're saying: "This is great!" And: "You're going to have a *wonderful time!*"

3   Robby's thinking: this is it. The fun part of life is over now.

4   We're thinking: "Please, please, PLEASE let him not hate this and let the other kids be nice to him and let his teachers see, among all those

little bobbing heads and skinny arms and Band-Aided legs, what a wonderful little boy this is.

5   I know this is just as rough for everybody else. I know *all* the kids are special. I know the teachers are very, very nice and that, over the years, they've had hundreds of kids like Robby.

6   But not *Robby*.

7   I think: If only they could put him to bed just one time, hear him talk to his stuffed dolphin, hear the dolphin answer back in a squeaky version of Robby's little voice. If only they could have seen him burst into tears in the part of the Saturday TV movie when it looked like Godzilla had been killed by the Japanese army. He slept with his Godzilla doll that night, comforting it.

8   We're getting near the school, and Robby is trying so hard to be brave that I am about ready to turn around and drive back home and sit down on the living room floor and play with him and hug him forever and the hell with developing Motor Skills and Language Skills and Math Skills and Socialization and growing up in general.

9   "This is going to be *great*," I say. I give him his lunch money. I wish I could give him my muscles, to keep in the pocket of his little blue shorts in case a big kid tries to bully him. I wish I could give him my mind, so he'd understand why he has to go to school. I wish *I* understood it.

10   "I remember when I started kindergarten!" I say, sounding to myself like Mr. Rogers. "It was scary at first, but I made a lot of friends!"

11   What I'm really remembering is the way kids got teased in kindergarten. Because they were fat. Because they were short. For no reason at all. We teased them and teased them and teased them, and it must have been hell for them. I still remember the kids we teased. I'm sure they still remember.

12   Please forgive me, Craig and Susan. Please God, don't let the kids tease Robby.

13   We're at his classroom. We're supposed to leave right away. They told us that in Parents' Orientation. They said hanging around only makes it worse. It couldn't be any worse. Robby is fighting panic, asking questions, stalling to keep us there, tears running quietly down his cheeks.

14   "How many hours will it be?" he asks.

15   Thousand, I think. Thousands and thousands, in classrooms, away from us, until you've learned to accept it, and you don't cry when we leave you, and your dolphin never talks anymore.

TO THINK ABOUT

1. Compare "Commencement" to "Un Nintended Benefits." How are the narrative voices different? How are they alike? *— clean or precise*
2. What is the theme of "Un Nintended Benefits"? Is it explicit or implicit? *— understood though only implied*
3. In "Commencement" Barry devotes a paragraph to Robby's stuffed dolphin and Godzilla. Why is this information important? What is its effect on you, the reader?
4. Why does Barry bring the dolphin back at the end? What is the effect of the last paragraph?
5. Read "Fresh Crayolas: A Busy First Day at Kindergarten" by Michael Winerip (Chapter 55). How do Winerip's narrative voice and perspective differ from Barry's in "Commencement"?

TO DO

1. Think of an activity you enjoyed as a child or you enjoy now that your parents, teachers, and other adults might disapprove of. Write a defense of that activity using "Un Nintended Benefits" as a model.
2. Barry divides kindergartners into two categories: the teasers and the teased. (He was a teaser.) Think about your own kindergarten experience (or, if you like, a later grade). How were the various social groupings defined? Which group did you belong to? Write a piece about it.
3. Make a list of actions you took that you now regret. Pick one. Write about it. The episode you picked should be far enough in the past to give you a balanced perspective from which to write.

TIP

Listen for the times when your inner voice and your outer voice are saying two different things. For most of us this happens several times a day; the self we present to the world differs, at least a little, from our inner self. When it happens, make a note of it. These discrepancies often make for good writing.

5

Stalin
Andrei Codrescu

*Andrei Codrescu is a poet and a commentator on National
Public Radio's news program* All Things Considered. *Codrescu grew
up in Romania when that country was under the thumb of Soviet
dictator Joseph Stalin. His prose is poetic: brief, concise, on the bor-
der between the real and the surreal. His Eastern European sensibility acknowledges magic as a matter-of-fact, everyday phenomenon;
it is there, in the closet, nestling inside the umbrella. What is com-
monplace—a mustache, in this case—is transformed into a universal symbol for something that is missing. (For similar magic see
Chapter 43, "Reading Philosophy at Night," by Charles Simic.)*

*Here, in five paragraphs, Codrescu recaptures the world of an
eight-year-old boy in the process of losing a hero. The piece was
written as a radio commentary; the sentences are economical and
unhurried. Here is the voice of a mature man, expressing sorrow for
a lost ideal.*

1   Nobody dies like Stalin did. He didn't just die, he took the world
with him. My world, at any rate. I was eight years old when it happened.
At school all the kids had been crying and I'd been crying the most. For
us, Stalin was that saintly, fatherly figure that smiled from above, surrounded by adoring children. For me, personally, he was father, pure and
simple, because I didn't have one of my own. On my little nightstand
table I had his portrait and I slept securely under the shadow of his moustache.

2   Devastated, disbelieving, I came home from school through the
back alleys, hiding my tears from everyone. When I got home I saw my
stepfather and another man sitting soberly at the kitchen table.
Unnoticed, I slipped into the room and hid, too upset to talk.

3   "I'm glad the sonofabitch is dead," the man said, and my stepfather
concurred.

4   My world was there and then shattered and lost forever. Later, I watched the people cry and tear their hair publicly on the streets, but I somehow knew that it was all a show. They were just using the occasion to grieve, weep, and cry for other sorrows. Stalin was just an excuse to mourn for the world. And I suspected fraud about the whole race of fathers, leaders, and men larger than life.

5   There are no fathers, I later decided, only moustaches which scatter in the wind, hair by hair, which vanish, disappear, betray, and leave you alone at night.

TO THINK ABOUT

1. To most of the world Joseph Stalin was a cruel tyrant, responsible for the deaths of millions of his own subjects. How is it possible that, until his death, he was a hero to a Romanian boy?
2. This is a before-and-after piece. The first paragraph shows the narrator's world as it was. What is the organization of the remainder of the essay? (Note that the turning point is *not* the death of Stalin.)
3. Codrescu is a poet. Can you find elements of poetry in his prose?

TO DO

1. Make a list of turning points in your life. Pick one of them. Write about it.
2. Make a list of your heroes, current and past. Do you remember why you became disillusioned with the old ones? Did they change, or did you?
3. In this piece Stalin's mustache takes on mythical significance. Think of the physical characteristics of important people in your life. Which are (or were) the most significant? Why? Write about the ones that intrigue you the most. (You should include in your considerations items of clothing and accessories such as glasses and key chains.)

TIP

A piece about a turning point must be balanced. Beginning writers often make the mistake of putting too much emphasis on *before*. Each element—before, during, after—must be represented.

6

Silent Dancing

Judith Ortiz Cofer

Who are we? We remember so little from childhood. What we remember, we are afraid to trust. And there is so much we never knew. So we search for clues.

There are always clues. There are photographs (Grandfather in his Army uniform, Grandmother in a sequined gown), mementos, documents, old letters. There are, as well, witnesses to the past: parents, grandparents, assorted relatives, their friends. We work from these. We try to piece it together.

Here a woman who moved from Puerto Rico to Paterson, New Jersey, at the age of three, explores her heritage with the aid of a home movie. The film is silent and only five minutes long. It speaks volumes. The narrator speaks quietly, but toward the end her voice becomes tinged with bitterness.

1 *We have a home movie of this party. Several times my mother and I have watched it together, and I have asked questions about the silent revelers coming in and out of focus. It is grainy and of short duration, but it's a great visual aid to my memory of life at that time. And it is in color—the only complete scene in color I can recall from those years.*

2 We lived in Puerto Rico until my brother was born in 1954. Soon after, because of economic pressures on our growing family, my father joined the United States Navy. He was assigned to duty on a ship in Brooklyn Yard—a place of cement and steel that was to be his home base in the States until his retirement more than twenty years later. He left the Island first, alone, going to New York City and tracking down his uncle who lived with his family across the Hudson River in Paterson, New Jersey. There my father found a tiny apartment in a huge tenement that had once housed Jewish families but was just being taken over and transformed by Puerto Ricans, overflowing from New York City. In 1955 he sent for us. My mother was only twenty years old, I was not quite three,

and my brother was a toddler when we arrived at El Building, as the place had been christened by its newest residents.

3   My memories of life in Paterson during those first few years are all in shades of gray. Maybe I was too young to absorb vivid colors and details, or to discriminate between the slate blue of the winter sky and the darker hues of the snow-bearing clouds, but that single color washes over the whole period. The building we lived in was gray, as were the streets, filled with slush the first few months of my life there. The coat my father had bought for me was similar in color and too big; it sat heavily on my thin frame.

4   I do remember the way the heater pipes banged and rattled, startling all of us out of sleep until we got so used to the sound that we automatically shut it out or raised our voices above the racket. The hiss from the valve punctuated my sleep (which has always been fitful) like a nonhuman presence in the room—a dragon sleeping at the entrance of my childhood. But the pipes were also a connection to all the other lives being lived around us. Having come from a house designed for a single family back in Puerto Rico—my mother's extended-family home—it was curious to know that strangers lived under our floor and above our heads, and that the heater pipe went through everyone's apartment. (My first spanking in Paterson came as a result of playing tunes on the pipes in my room to see if there would be an answer.) My mother was as new to this concept of beehive life as I was, but she had been given strict orders by my father to keep the doors locked, the noise down, ourselves to ourselves.

5   It seems that Father had learned some painful lessons about prejudice while searching for an apartment in Paterson. Not until years later did I hear how much resistance he had encountered with landlords who were panicking at the influx of Latinos into a neighborhood that had been Jewish for a couple of generations. It made no difference that it was the American phenomenon of ethnic turnover which was changing the urban core of Paterson, and that the human flood could not be held back with an accusing finger.

6   "You Cuban?" one man had asked my father, pointing at his name tag on the navy uniform—even though my father had the fair skin and light brown hair of his northern Spanish background, and the name Ortiz is as common in Puerto Rico as Johnson is in the United States.

7   "No," my father had answered, looking past the finger into his adversary's angry eyes. "I'm Puerto Rican."

8   "Same shit." And the door closed.

9   My father could have passed as European, but we couldn't. My brother and I both have our mother's black hair and olive skin, and so we lived in El Building and visited our great-uncle and his fair children on

the next block. It was their private joke that they were the German branch of the family. Not many years later that area too would be mainly Puerto Rican. It was as if the heart of the city map were being gradually colored brown—*café con leche* brown. Our color.

10   *The movie opens with a sweep of the living room. It is "typical" immigrant Puerto Rican decor for the time: the sofa and chairs are square and hard-looking, upholstered in bright colors (blue and yellow in this instance) and covered with the transparent plastic that furniture salesmen then were so adept at convincing women to buy. The linoleum on the floor is light blue; where it had been subjected to spike heels, as it was in most places, there were dime-size indentations all over it that cannot be seen in this movie. The room is full of people dressed up: dark suits for the men, red dresses for the women. When I have asked my mother why most of the women are in red that night, she has shrugged and said, "I don't remember. Just a coincidence." She doesn't have my obsession for assigning symbolism to everything.*

11   *The three women in red sitting on the couch are my mother, my eighteen-year-old cousin, and her brother's girlfriend. The* novia *is just up from the Island, which is apparent in her body language. She sits up formally, her dress pulled over her knees. She is a pretty girl, but her posture makes her look insecure, lost in her full-skirted dress, which she has carefully tucked around her to make room for my gorgeous cousin, her future sister-in-law. My cousin has grown up in Paterson and is in her last year of high school. She doesn't have a trace of what Puerto Ricans call* la mancha *(literally, the stain: the mark of the new immigrant—something about the posture, the voice, or the humble demeanor that makes it obvious to everyone the person has just arrived on the mainland). My cousin is wearing a tight, sequined, cocktail dress. Her brown hair has been lightened with peroxide around the bangs, and she is holding a cigarette expertly between her fingers, bringing it up to her mouth in a sensuous arc of her arm as she talks animatedly. My mother, who has come up to sit between the two women, both only a few years younger than herself, is somewhere between the poles they represent in our culture.*

12   It became my father's obsession to get out of the barrio, and thus we were never permitted to form bonds with the place or with the people who lived there. Yet El Building was a comfort to my mother, who never got over yearning for *la isla.* She felt surrounded by her language: the walls were thin, and voices speaking and arguing in Spanish could be heard all day. *Salsas* blasted out of radios, turned on early in the morning and left on for company. Women seemed to cook rice and beans perpetually—the strong aroma of boiling red kidney beans permeated the hallways.

13   Though Father preferred that we do our grocery shopping at the supermarket when he came home on weekend leaves, my mother insisted that she could cook only with products whose labels she could read. Consequently, during the week I accompanied her and my little brother to La Bodega—a hole-in-the-wall grocery store across the street from El Building. There we squeezed down three narrow aisles jammed with various products. Goya and Libby's—those were the trademarks that were trusted by her *mamá,* so my mother bought many cans of Goya beans, soups, and condiments, as well as little cans of Libby's fruit juices for us. And she also bought Colgate toothpaste and Palmolive soap. (The final *e* is pronounced in both these products in Spanish, so for many years I believed that they were manufactured on the Island. I remember my surprise at first hearing a commercial on television in which "Colgate" rhymed with "ate.") We always lingered at La Bodega, for it was there that Mother breathed best, taking in the familiar aromas of the foods she knew from Mamá's kitchen. It was also there that she got to speak to the other women of El Building without violating outright Father's dictates against fraternizing with our neighbors.

14   Yet Father did his best to make our "assimilation" painless. I can still see him carrying a real Christmas tree up several flights of stairs to our apartment, leaving a trail of aromatic pine. He carried it formally, as if it were a flag in a parade. We were the only ones in El Building that I knew of who got presents on both Christmas and *día de Reyes,* the day when the Three Kings brought gifts to Christ and to Hispanic children.

15   Our supreme luxury in El Building was having our own television set. It must have been a result of Father's guilt feelings over the isolation he had imposed on us, but we were among the first in the barrio to have one. My brother quickly became an avid watcher of Captain Kangaroo and Jungle Jim, while I loved all the series showing families. By the time I started first grade, I could have drawn a map of Middle America as exemplified by the lives of characters in *Father Knows Best, The Donna Reed Show, Leave It to Beaver, My Three Sons,* and (my favorite) *Bachelor Father,* where John Forsythe treated his adopted teenage daughter like a princess because he was rich and had a Chinese houseboy to do everything for him. In truth, compared to our neighbors in El Building, *we* were rich. My father's navy check provided us with financial security and a standard of living that the factory workers envied. The only thing his money could not buy us was a place to live away from the barrio—his greatest wish, Mother's greatest fear.

16   *In the home movie the men are shown next, sitting around a card table set up in one corner of the living room, playing dominoes. The clack of the ivory pieces was a familiar sound. I heard it in many houses on the Island and in many apartments in Paterson. In* Leave It to Beaver,

the Cleavers played bridge in every other episode; in my childhood, the men started every social occasion with a hotly debated round of dominoes. The women would sit around and watch, but they never participated in the games.

17   *Here and there you can see a small child. Children were always brought to parties and, whenever they got sleepy, were put to bed in the host's bedroom. Babysitting was a concept unrecognized by the Puerto Rican women I knew: a responsible mother did not leave her children with any stranger. And in a culture where children are not considered intrusive, there was no need to leave the children at home. We went where our mother went.*

18   Of my preschool years I have only impressions: the sharp bite of the wind in December as we walked with our parents toward the brightly lit stores downtown; how I felt like a stuffed doll in my heavy coat, boots, and mittens; how good it was to walk into the five-and-dime and sit at the counter drinking hot chocolate. On Saturdays our whole family would walk downtown to shop at the big department stores on Broadway. Mother bought all our clothes at Penney's and Sears, and she liked to buy her dresses at the women's specialty shops like Lerner's and Diana's. At some point we'd go into Woolworth's and sit at the soda fountain to eat.

19   We never ran into other Latinos at these stores or when eating out, and it became clear to me only years later that the women from El Building shopped mainly in other places—stores owned by other Puerto Ricans or by Jewish merchants who had philosophically accepted our presence in the city and decided to make us their good customers, if not real neighbors and friends. These establishments were located not downtown but in the blocks around our street, and they were referred to generically as La Tienda, El Bazar, La Bodega, La Botánica. Everyone knew what was meant. These were the stores where your face did not turn a clerk to stone, where your money was as green as anyone else's.

20   One New Year's Eve we were dressed up like child models in the Sears catalogue: my brother in a miniature man's suit and bow tie, and I in black patent-leather shoes and a frilly dress with several layers of crinoline underneath. My mother wore a bright red dress that night, I remember, and spike heels; her long black hair hung to her waist. Father, who usually wore his navy uniform during his short visits home, had put on a dark civilian suit for the occasion: we had been invited to his uncle's house for a big celebration. Everyone was excited because my mother's brother Hernan—a bachelor who could indulge himself with luxuries—had bought a home movie camera, which he would be trying out that night.

21   Even the home movie cannot fill in the sensory details such a gathering left imprinted in a child's brain. The thick sweetness of women's perfumes mixing with the ever-present smells of food cooking in the kitchen: meat and plantain *pasteles,* as well as the ubiquitous rice dish made special with pigeon peas—*gandules*—and seasoned with precious *sofrito* sent up from the Island by somebody's mother or smuggled in by a recent traveler. *Sofrito* was one of the items that women hoarded, since it was hardly ever in stock at La Bodega. It was the flavor of Puerto Rico.

22   The men drank Palo Viejo rum, and some of the younger ones got weepy. The first time I saw a grown man cry was at a New Year's Eve party: he had been reminded of his mother by the smells in the kitchen. But what I remember most were the boiled *pasteles,* plantain or yucca rectangles stuffed with corned beef or other meats, olives, and many other savory ingredients, all wrapped in banana leaves. Everybody had to fish one out with a fork. There was always a "trick" *pastel*—one without stuffing—and whoever got that one was the "New Year's Fool."

23   There was also the music. Long-playing albums were treated like precious china in these homes. Mexican recordings were popular, but the songs that brought tears to my mother's eyes were sung by the melancholy Daniel Santos, whose life as a drug addict was the stuff of legend. Felipe Rodríguez was a particular favorite of couples, since he sang about faithless women and brokenhearted men. There is a snatch of one lyric that has stuck in my mind like a needle on a worn groove: *De piedra ha de ser mi cama, de piedra la cabezera . . . la mujer que a mi me quiera . . . ha de quererme de veras. Ay, Ay, Ay, corazón, porque no amas . . .* I must have heard it a thousand times since the idea of a bed made of stone, and its connection to love, first troubled me with its disturbing images.

24   The five-minute home movie ends with people dancing in a circle— the creative filmmaker must have set it up, so that all of them could file past him. It is both comical and sad to watch silent dancing. Since there is no justification for the absurd movements that music provides for some of us, people appear frantic, their faces embarrassingly intense. It's as if you were watching sex. Yet for years, I've had dreams in the form of this home movie. In a recurring scene, familiar faces push themselves forward into my mind's eye, plastering their features into distorted close-ups. And I'm asking them: "Who is *she?* Who is the old woman I don't recognize? Is she an aunt? Somebody's wife? Tell me who she is."

"See the beauty mark on her cheek as big as a hill on the lunar landscape of her face—well, that runs in the family. The women on your father's side of the family wrinkle early; it's the price they pay for that fair skin. The young girl with the green stain on her wedding dress is *la novia*—just up from the Island. See, she lowers her eyes when she approaches the camera, as she's supposed to. Decent girls never look at you directly in the face. *Humilde*, humble, a girl should express humility in all her actions. She will make a good wife for your cousin. He should consider himself lucky to have met her only weeks after she arrived here. If he marries her quickly, she will make him a good Puerto Rican–style wife; but if he waits too long, she will be corrupted by the city, just like your cousin there."

"She means me. I do what I want. This is not some primitive island I live on. Do they expect me to wear a black mantilla on my head and go to mass every day? Not me. I'm an American woman, and I will do as I please. I can type faster than anyone in my senior class at Central High, and I'm going to be a secretary to a lawyer when I graduate. I can pass for an American girl anywhere—I've tried it. At least for Italian, anyway—I never speak Spanish in public. I hate these parties, but I wanted the dress. I look better than any of these *humildes* here. *My* life is going to be different. I have an American boyfriend. He is older and has a car. My parents don't know it, but I sneak out of the house late at night sometimes to be with him. If I marry him, even my name will be American. I hate rice and beans— that's what makes these women fat."

"Your *prima* is pregnant by that man she's been sneaking around with. Would I lie to you? I'm your *tía política*, your great-uncle's common-law wife—the one he abandoned on the Island to go marry your cousin's mother. *I* was not invited to this party, of course, but I came anyway. I came to tell you that story about your cousin that you've always wanted to hear. Do you remember the comment your mother made to a neighbor that has always haunted you? The only thing you heard was your cousin's name, and then you saw your mother pick up your doll from the couch and say: 'It was as big as this doll when they flushed it down the toilet.' This image has bothered you for years, hasn't it? You had nightmares about babies being flushed down the toilet, and you wondered why anyone would do such a horrible thing. You didn't dare ask your mother about it. She would only tell you that you had not heard her right, and yell at you for listening to adult conversations. But later, when you were old enough to know about abortions, you suspected.
"I am here to tell you that you were right. Your cousin was growing an *americanito* in her belly when this movie was made. Soon after, she put something long and pointy into her pretty self, thinking maybe she could get rid of the problem before breakfast and still make it to her first class at the high school. Well, *niña*, her screams could be heard downtown. Your aunt, her *mamá*, who had been a midwife on the Island, managed to pull the little thing out. Yes, they probably flushed it down the toilet. What else could they do

with it—give it a Christian burial in a little white casket with blue bows and ribbons? Nobody wanted that baby—least of all the father, a teacher at her school with a house in West Paterson that he was filling with real children, and a wife who was a natural blonde.

"Girl, the scandal sent your uncle back to the bottle. And guess where your cousin ended up? Irony of ironies. She was sent to a village in Puerto Rico to live with a relative on her mother's side: a place so far away from civilization that you have to ride a mule to reach it. A real change in scenery. She found a man there—women like that cannot live without male company—but believe me, the men in Puerto Rico know how to put a saddle on a woman like her. *La gringa*, they call her. Ha, ha, ha. *La gringa* is what she always wanted to be . . . "

The old woman's mouth becomes a cavernous black hole I fall into. And as I fall, I can feel the reverberations of her laughter. I hear the echoes of her last mocking words: *la gringa, la gringa!* And the conga line keeps moving silently past me. There is no music in my dream for the dancers.

25   When Odysseus visits Hades to see the spirit of his mother, he makes an offering of sacrificial blood, but since all the souls crave an audience with the living, he has to listen to many of them before he can ask questions. I, too, have to hear the dead and the forgotten speak in my dream. Those who are still part of my life remain silent, going around and around in their dance. The others keep pressing their faces forward to say things about the past.

26   My father's uncle is last in line. He is dying of alcoholism, shrunken and shriveled like a monkey, his face a mass of wrinkles and broken arteries. As he comes closer I realize that in his features I can see my whole family. If you were to stretch that rubbery flesh, you could find my father's face, and deep within *that* face—my own. I don't want to look into those eyes ringed in purple. In a few years he will retreat into silence, and take a long, long time to die. *Move back, Tío, I tell him. I don't want to hear what you have to say. Give the dancers room to move. Soon it will be midnight. Who is the New Year's Fool this time!*

TO THINK ABOUT

1. Cofer opens with the film and frequently returns to it. What is her purpose? How does the film affect the focus of the essay?
2. Cofer gives us a sense of the *barrio* culture through small, telling details. What are some of these? What do they tell us about the lives of Puerto Rican immigrants in the United States?
3. There is some factual information in the essay, as well as a great deal that is imagined or dreamed by the narrator. What is the effect of this mixing of the real and the imagined?

4. The piece ends with the narrator addressing her uncle: *I don't want to hear what you have to say. Give the dancers room to move. Soon it will be midnight. Who is the New Year's Fool this time?* How does this ending affect the way you, the reader, come away from the piece?
5. In 1954 the narrator's father encountered prejudice and discrimination when he attempted to rent an apartment. What, if anything, has changed in the last four decades? Have you ever experienced discrimination based on race, sex, or other factors?

TO DO

1. Make a list of items you consider clues to your past. (You can add to it next time you are home with your parents, but your memory should give you a start.) Study the list. Concentrate on the items that trigger memories, stories, impressions, emotions. Then, using one or more of the items, try to reconstruct a bit of your past.
2. Next time you are home with your parents, explore the house. Add to your list. And ask questions about family history. You may come away with a rich load of material for future writing.

TIP

There are two kinds of history. The first is archival: names, ages, dates, places, conditions. The second is anecdotal: incidents that occurred at parties, weddings, funerals, or in between that bring the archival material to life and illustrate the sensibilities, values, and dreams of the subjects. In a piece of writing the two types complement each other. They are equally important. Seek them both.

7

A Newspaper We Can Do Without

Richard Cohen

Back in the 1980s we used to read a newspaper called USA Today. *We read it to find out what the latest trend was, because* USA Today *was a catalog of trends.* USA Today *could spot a trend in a flat tire or a fortune cookie, and we would learn about them through headlines such as "We Eat More Fortune Cookies" and "We Change Fewer Tires." We read it only intermittently, however, because its chummy habit of referring to itself and its readers, collectively, as "we" drove us crazy.*

As it turns out, we were not the only ones who were bothered by this habit. Gary Trudeau, the cartoonist who draws Doonesbury, *lampooned* USA Today *in a series of strips entitled "We Eat More Beets." And syndicated columnist Richard Cohen delivered the following critique, which proves that imitation is not always flattery.*

*Oh, yes—*USA Today *is still on the newsstands, but "we" bit the dust several years ago.*

1   WASHINGTON—We are sick of USA Today. We are tired of it using the words "we" and "our" to create a false sense of community, to enlist us in movements and trends that we know nothing about and have no desire to join. We want no more of this sort of thing. And we are tired of arguing back at a newspaper that declared, as it did just the other day, "We're Tangled Up Again In Knitting." The hell we are.

2   The trouble with USA Today is that it does not report, it embraces. It incessantly wants to identify with me, but it manages to do just the opposite. I diet for weeks on end, eat nothing for days, drink only water and gargle Perrier and USA Today says, "We Like Steak, Gooey Desserts." We do not. We avoid them like the plague.

3   Sometimes USA Today tells me that I'm healthy, sometimes that I'm on the verge of death and sometimes that I've made a wonderful

recovery: "More Of Us Now Recover From Stroke." I didn't know I had one.

4   I learn that "We're Spiking More Dishes With Spirits" which explains, among other things, why we're having so many strokes, not to mention this urge to knit that I just know you have been noticing. Sober people would not knit nor, for that matter, would they sleep in the buff, which is what USA Today says that one out of eight of us does. "We're Ready To Stand Up And Cheer," says the paper. OK, but before we do, we'd better put some clothes on.

5   The idea behind all this chumminess is to make all of America into one big, intimate community. But instead I feel excluded. I feel like someone reading the foreign press. Who is this "we" they're always talking about? How come I never hear of these things? Why have I been left out again? Reading USA Today recreates the high school experience for me. Once again, I get to feel excluded—the feeling that everyone, the whole damn school, is at a party I know nothing about.

6   There's something wrong with that newspaper. On days when someone I admire dies, the paper says, "We're Curbing Disease, Living Longer." When I'm sick as a dog, the paper says, "We Feel Healthy Even With Aches And Pains." No we don't. We feel awful and we want everyone to know it. Oooh. Aaah. Don't believe a thing you read in that paper. We're sick as a dog.

7   If USA Today were really my paper, which is what it pretends to be, it would headline, "We Hurt, But We Came to Work Anyway." It would say, "We're Dieting And Not Losing Weight, Which Is The Story of Our Lives." It would say, "We're Worrying About Money And Not Getting Rich," and, "We Fear Death But Think We Can Avoid It," and, "We Read Sex Surveys To See If We're Normal." My paper would say, "We're Wonderful And Unappreciated And We Wish Everyone Else The Worst."

8   My paper would say, "We Fear Putting Our Hand Down Garbage Disposal Even Though It's Off," or, after a weekend of yard work, "Our Yards Look Better." Once a month my paper would say, "We Get Haircuts" and, more often, "We Cut Nails." Every once in a while, my paper would headline, "We Buy Suit On Sale And Salesman Says It Is Us," and those of us who are the parents of teenagers would see a headline that says, "Our Children Are Nuts And We Wonder Why We Had Them In The First Place."

9   I get none of this from USA Today—no sense of belonging, no way I can identify with the rest of the country. Its financial section tells me all of you are "Zeroing In On STRIPS That Could Hurt Brokers." I don't even know what STRIPS are. It could be worse. I could be a broker.

10   The paper tells me all of you are in exercise class, buying a phone that dials itself, being intrigued by India, getting more choice in IRAs,

watching "Dynasty," having more sex than some but less than others—running, dancing, eating booze, drinking steak and doing it all together. We are exhausted.

11   Cancel our subscription.

TO THINK ABOUT

1. How would you describe the persona of Cohen's narrator in this piece? How does it compare to the persona of the voice he is criticizing?
2. Nearly all magazines and newspapers strive to present a distinctive voice. The voice of the *New York Times* is easy to distinguish from the voices of *Cosmopolitan, Ebony, Rolling Stone.* Which magazines and newspapers do you read regularly? What sorts of voices do they have?
3. Cohen says *USA Today* creates "a false sense of community." He writes: "The idea behind all this chumminess is to make all of America into one big, intimate community. But instead I feel excluded." What is the difference between a false sense of community and a true one? Consider efforts by politicians, advertisers, and neighborhood groups to create a sense of community, nationally or locally. Which ones work, and which do not?

TO DO

1. Spend an afternoon in the periodical room of your college library. Flip through dozens of magazines and newspapers to get a sense of their voices. Make a list of the voices you like and the ones you don't like. In both cases, list specific reasons.
2. Write an essay critiquing one of these publications, imitating the voice of that publication.

TIP

When you imitate a voice in order to criticize it, the voice you use will be slightly different from the original. Perhaps you will exaggerate the dominant characteristic of the voice slightly, or add a touch of stridency or ill humor. (In the piece you have just read, Richard Cohen faithfully imitated the rhetorical style and cadence of *USA Today*, but allowed some grumpiness to creep in.)

8

Rolling into the '80s

Sara Davidson

This is a story about a place and a time. The place is Venice, California, near Los Angeles, and the time is the late 1970s. A story about a place and a time is usually about the people who live there, then. In this case one of those people, the central character, is the writer herself. In "Rolling into the '80s," journalist and novelist Sara Davidson transformed herself into a symbol of the matrix of time and place in which she lived. She was not easy on herself. Her voice is both analytical and wistful.

1   "Who is the rich man?" asks the Talmud. The question has never seemed more relevant. The answer of the sages is: "He who is satisfied with what he has."

2   I live in a house by the ocean with an outdoor Jacuzzi. I owned, until an embarrassing little accident, a pair of roller skates. I still own a volleyball, a Frisbee, a tennis racket, a backpack, hiking boots, running shoes, a Mercedes 240 Diesel, and a home burglar alarm system. But I cannot say that I am satisfied.

3   I live in Venice, California. Venice is the closest place to downtown Los Angeles where it is possible to live by the water. Because of the breezes, it is relatively free of smog. It is also the only place in Los Angeles where there is street life: You are guaranteed to see people outside their cars.

4   A boardwalk, which isn't exactly a boardwalk but an asphalt path called Ocean Front Walk, runs the length of the beach. Alongside the boardwalk is a bike path, and beside it, the sand and sea. On the other side of the boardwalk are crumbling houses, new apartments, and condominiums packed tightly together. A real estate boom of such proportions has swept through here in the past five years that anyone who bought the

most miserable shack for $30,000 could sell it a few years later for a quarter of a million. And the boom goes on.

5   Living in Venice is like living in a camp for semidemented adults. At every hour, day and night, there are people playing volleyball, running, rolling on skates, riding on bikes, skateboards, or surfboards, flying kites, drinking milk, eating quiche Lorraine. Old people sit under umbrellas playing checkers. Body builders work out in a sandy pen, and crowds line up three deep to perform on the paddle tennis courts. When do these people work? I used to wonder.

6   The residents of Venice fall into two groups: those who work and those who don't. The latter includes senior citizens, drifters, drug addicts, would-be moviemakers, and aging hippies and surfers who have made a cult of idleness and pleasure. The other group includes lawyers, dentists, real estate brokers, accountants. Many are workaholics, attached to their jobs as they are to nothing else. They work nights and weekends, eat fast food while driving to and from their work, and live alone, longing, in the silence before falling asleep, for connection.

7   Everyone comes together on the boardwalk. The natives own their own skates, and the tourists rent them from places like "Cheapskates" and "United Skates of America." Those who have been at it awhile can dance and twirl to music piped in their ears from radio headphones with antennae. The girls are dressed up in costumes like circus performers: sequined tube tops, feathers in their hair, and leotards so skimpy that the nipples show and the cheeks of the buttocks hang out. The men wear shorts and vinyl racing jackets unzipped to the waist.

8   "Hey, that's radical," they call.

9   "Bad ass!"

10   Who are these people? Brown-skinned and lax, they sit around the floors of apartments, eating salads, walking out on balconies to smile and shake their towels. They are waging some kind of sexual competition through T-shirts and bumper stickers:

11   "I'm ripe—eat me."

12   "Sit on my face and I'll guess your weight."

13   "Skin divers do it deeper."

14   "Body builders pump harder."

15   "Plumbers have bigger tools."

16   "Worm fishermen have stiffer rods!"

17   A high school cruising mentality prevails. A girl skates by wearing nothing but a body stocking and a silver G-string, but when two men stop and say, "That's some outfit. Where's the party?" her face turns to ice, and she skates away.

18   Rolling, Rolling. The wind is blowing, the palms are blowing, and people are blowing every which way. I cannot walk on the boardwalk these days

without feeling it in my stomach: Something is wrong. There are too many people on wheels. The skaters will fall, the bikers will crash, they will fly out of control, and there is nothing to hold on to.

19   I retreat to my house and remain indoors all weekend. Venice is odd, unique, and yet I see among the crowds on the boardwalk an exaggeration of common symptoms: the worship of wealth; the insatiable partying; the loss of commitment and ideals; the cult of the body; the wandering of children in a sexual wilderness.

20   What does it mean, I ask myself, to be dressed as a striptease artist on skates?

21   What does it mean to pay half a million dollars for a tacky two-bedroom condo on the sand?

22   What does it mean that everyone I know is looking to make some kind of "killing"?

23   It means, I think, that we are in far deeper than we know.

24   In 1904, Abbot Kinney, who had made a fortune on Sweet Caporal cigarettes, traveled to Europe and so loved what he saw that he conceived of building a replica of Venice in southern California. Kinney raised the money to build canals, lagoons, roller coasters, bathhouses and bridges of fake Italian design, and cottages with docks so people could visit one another by gondola. The idea caught on: "Venice of America" became a fashionable resort. Douglas Fairbanks and Mary Pickford, Charlie Chaplin and Paulette Goddard, kept hideaways on the canals or beach front.

25   In time, the novelty wore off and the resort went to seed. The canals turned stagnant, and the unheated cottages became substandard housing for the poor. In the Sixties, Venice became one of the few places in Los Angeles where numbers of hippies and radicals lived. It was an outlaw gulch—a haven for draft resisters, artists, and drug addicts. At the same time, a real estate development was under way that threatened to alter permanently the character of Venice.

26   The new development was Marina del Rey, which means "the king's boat basin." The Marina, just to the south of Venice, is a modern reworking of Abbot Kinney's dream. The Marina is the largest man-made harbor for small pleasure boats in the world; a system of channels and piers on which there are restaurants, bars, discos, shops, and acres of condominiums. The streets leading to the oceanfront have nautical names in alphabetical order: Anchorage, Buccaneer, Catamaran, Driftwood, Eastwind, Fleet . . . When I first moved to Venice, I used to put myself to sleep by memorizing the streets in the Marina.

27   Once completed, the Marina became one of the fastest-appreciating real estate markets in Los Angeles. Everyone wanted to live by the sea

and still be close to work. The Marina was especially popular with the newly divorced. It was a playland: Almost every condo had a wet bar, a gas barbecue, a water bed, and a fireplace that sprang on at the push of a button. The tenants could use a community sauna, Jacuzzi, pool, and gym. People filled their apartments with fish tanks and telescopes and oars and shells and hammocks and, in the bathroom, stacks of flying magazines.

28   Those who could not afford the rents in the Marina began spilling over into Venice. Prices jumped overnight. Speculators bought up shacks, remodeled them, and sold them for triple what they had paid. Plans were announced to "clean up the canals," and Venice became a "neighborhood in transition." The poor and the hippies who could not adjust were forced to move east.

29   I arrived in Venice in 1974, with my own dream. I wanted to do what Don Juan had advised Castaneda to do: Erase personal history. I was a refugee from the East, from a tumultuous marriage, and from the revolutions of the Sixties. I wanted to begin life again in a place with good weather, a place where I could work, and I wanted to find, if such a creature existed, an unscarred man.

30   It was not long before I met such a person in Venice. His name was Bruce; he was twenty-six and chief of research at a botanical laboratory. He loved his work, but he also loved to be outdoors, to dance and listen to rock'n'roll. Even his handwriting was happy—he drew little circles over his *i*'s. He cooked and kept his house clean. He had no sexual problems. He had made love with his last girl friend every day, "at least once," for four years, and he promised to do the same with me, "as long as we love each other."

31   Being with Bruce was like a happy retrogression to teenage years. We drove around in his car with the top down, ate hamburgers and drank milk shakes, watched kung fu movies, and spent whole weekends at the beach. There was a volleyball net by Bruce's house, and every weekend the same crowd appeared. The men reminded me of fraternity boys who had never grown up. They had their own businesses now, things like parking lots and vending machine companies, but they still drank beer and made jokes about fags and big boobs, jokes at which Bruce, to my relief, did not laugh.

32   The people on the beach played two-man volleyball, a different game entirely from the social volleyball I had played through the years. This volleyball was hard-core stuff. There were two people on a side; they played fast and savagely and were constantly diving in the sand. Bruce showed me the basic hits—bump, set, and spike—but as a beginner, I could not keep up with their games. I was walking on the beach by myself one day when I spotted one of the regulars. This man was unfor-

gettable: He had a head shaped like a pineapple. He must have been working out with weights, for the muscles on his arms and legs popped out, and he even had small breasts. I told him, hopefully, how much I wanted to learn to play volleyball and how nice it would be if I could find someone who would play with me.

33   "You got a problem," he said in a duncelike voice. "The good people want to play with other good people. What you should do is take a class."

34   "A volleyball class?"

35   "Yeah."

36   "Where do you suppose I could find a volleyball class?"

37   "At the junior college."

38   Oh. I found out that Santa Monica College indeed had a volleyball class, and in the following months, my life had a wonderful rhythm. I would wake up, put on a pair of orange shorts that said "SMC," drive to school, and play volleyball. Then I would come home, work, go for a swim, work some more, run on the beach, work again, fix dinner with Bruce, and go to sleep.

39   We were the only couple to reappear together at the volleyball net, week after week. The others were constantly shifting partners, and as one player said, five days with the same woman was "the same as five years." I thought Bruce and I were an island of sanity on this beach, but as the summer progressed, I began to understand why he was not scarred. He had very little compassion for people in trouble. "There's nothing in life that's worth being unhappy about," he used to say. "You choose to feel pain. You can choose, just as easily, not to feel it."

40   "What if someone dies?" I said.

41   "I wouldn't mind dying. And I wouldn't be sad if you died."

42   He did not want to hear about frustration. He did not want to know about writer's block. He did not think I should feel jealous if he dated other women, and he did not believe a relationship should be work.

43   "I think we do too much talking," he said.

44   "That's funny. I think we don't do enough."

45   In the fall I went to New York, and in my absence Bruce took est and fell in love with one of the women at the volleyball net. When I returned, he told me it was time for us to break up because there was "no more cheese in the relationship."

46   I moved to a different part of the beach. A month later, I ran into Bruce with still another woman, whom he introduced as "the love of my life."

47   So much for that dream.

What marijuana was to the Sixties, real estate is to the Seventies.
                                                                    —Ron Koslow, 1978

My mother sells real estate in Los Angeles. So do my aunt and three of my mother's closest friends. The real estate business has always been appealing to women because there are no prerequisites except passing a test. You can start at any point in life, you can set your own hours, and you have the potential to earn far more than was possible for women, until recently, in other fields.

48 My sister and I grew up with an aversion to the phrase "real estate." It meant my mother was never around on Sunday because she was "sitting on a house." It meant violent swings in her mood and our fortunes. Often, she would dash out of the house on a moment's notice to show property, canceling a date to take us to the movies. We never knew if she would return in a terrible mood or with an exultant "I made my deal!"

49 At seventeen, I left Los Angeles and did not return until I was thirty. During the interim years, I grew to have contempt for people who spent money on houses and furniture, expensive cars, and first-class airline tickets. I thought it was more interesting and adventurous to travel second-class if not to hitchhike.

50 I visited and wrote about communes, where "free land" was the ideology. It sounded right: No one should be able to own the land, any more than people could own the sky or the sea. One of my friends refused to buy a country house offered to him at a very low price because, he said, "owning property is theft, and in any case, it would put us in the camp of the ruling class." Another friend gave away her $50,000 inheritance. She believed that God would provide.

51 My sister, after college, became a gym teacher and lived communally in the San Fernando Valley. She ate only vegetables, practiced yoga, made God's-eyes out of yarn and sticks, and rode buses long distances to march in peace demonstrations. She found, very quickly, that she didn't like teaching because it put her in a position of authority over children. So she quit her job, sold all her belongings, and bought a one-way ticket to the South Seas.

52 In 1978, my sister began selling real estate in Hawaii. Her guru was a Chinese broker who gave her the following life plan: Use the commissions you make on sales to acquire one piece of property a year for ten years; then sell half the properties, pay off the mortgages on the rest, retire, and live off the income. In her office at home, in what used to be a sewing and pottery room, was a sign: Y.C.S.A.S.O.Y.A.

53 "What does that mean?" I said.

54 "You can't sell anything sitting on your ass."

55 When I visited her last year, we spent half of our vacation time driving around Oahu, looking at homes. The irony was so overpowering that we did not speak about it.

56 My own interest in real estate had begun the year I moved to

Venice. In the previous twelve months, I had moved three times. I was recently divorced, writing a book, and free to live anywhere. I tried Bridgehampton, Santa Fe, Berkeley, Mill Valley, the Hollywood hills, until the cycle of searching for the perfect place, packing, moving, unpacking, installing phones, and setting up bank accounts became cumulatively so unbearable that I didn't care where I landed so long as I didn't have to move again.

57   The way to ensure this rootedness, I thought, was to buy a house of my own. For a year, I walked up and down the lanes of Venice. I, who had always disparaged the acquisition of property, was spending days with a broker named Milt, who was twenty-seven, had a coarse moustache, and a winner's instinct for beach real estate.

58   Everything we looked at was old, dark, cramped, in terrible condition, and ridiculously expensive. If they had not been so close to the beach, the same houses would have been considered unhabitable. I was about to give up when I went to see a two-story Victorian house, and the minute I stepped in the living room, my heart began to race. Sunlight was pouring in through tall, many-paned windows. The house had a Franklin stove, a large kitchen that needed remodeling, two primitive bathrooms, and three eccentric bedrooms. I looked at Milt and said, "I want it."

59   "Keep your pants on," he said.

60   We made an offer, which was rejected. We made another offer—also rejected. "We got no deal," Milt said. "I won't let you pay a dollar more. It's not worth it." For the next two days I was miserable. Every time I drove past the house, I felt a stab of longing and regret. It was a year since I had broken up with Bruce, and I was involved with a ballet dancer named Tommy who had little money himself but whose father owned casinos and land in Las Vegas. When Tommy heard what was happening, he said, "Pay the owner what he wants. Next year, it'll be worth even more."

61   I instructed Milt to make a third offer, which was accepted. "I bought a house!" I told friends, but everyone except Tommy thought I was crazy.

62   My lawyer said, "I'd never pay so much for that piece of junk."

63   My mother said, "You lost your senses. You got so excited, you couldn't *see*." She began to call me every few hours with new objections. "How will you fit your bed in the bedroom? Why should you have to pay for the termite repairs? The seller should pay."

64   By the time the escrow papers arrived, my enthusiasm had reversed itself and I was in a panic. I was sinking my life's savings into an old, broken-down house half eaten by bugs, and I would have to rent out the upstairs to meet the payments. What if the real estate market fell through?

What if the house needed massive repairs? How would it hold up in an earthquake? What if I couldn't find a tenant and couldn't pay the mortgage? Hadn't my parents seen their friends dispossessed in the Great Depression?

65   At night I lay in bed and shook. Tommy said I was having "buyer's remorse." So there was a name for it. I found that comforting. I knew the panic was unrealistic, but I was helpless to stop it. More was at stake than the purchase of a house. It was a statement about myself.

"He used to be a radical leader. Now he's an actor in soap operas."

"She tried to burn down the Bank of America at Isla Vista. Now she's a vice-president at Universal."

It is a cliché, a joke, something we are past feeling anguished about, but the fact is that a considerable number of people have passed through a door and come out wearing different clothes, and this transformation has taken place almost without comment. People who in the flowering of the Sixties gave their children names like Blackberry and Veda-Rama have changed them to Suzy and John. The parents are, they say, "getting our money trip together." The successful ones are buying homes, Calvin Klein suits, and Porsches and sending their kids to private schools to avoid busing.

66   Not all have come through the door, of course. There are still groups of New Age people in places in Berkeley, Oregon, Hawaii, and Vermont. They are still dedicated to social change, still wearing beards and flowing shawls, still holding symposiums where they talk about holistic health care, living closer to the earth, and creating communities where people can love one another and share and cooperate. But their numbers are dwindling, and few young recruits come along.

67   Those who have crossed the threshold cannot help but feel some irony and bafflement about "the people we've become." They retain an awareness, however faintly it is pulsing, that the acquisition of material wealth does not necessarily bring satisfaction, but that awareness seems to be fading rapidly into unconsciousnes

68   On a Sunday in May 1979, I am walking on the boardwalk in Venice with a friend Andy, who is, in fact, a former radical student, now an actor in soap operas. Andy lives next door with his girl friend, Sue, who works as an accountant while Andy tries to find parts. In 1969, Andy had stood in the front lines, arms locked together with other students occupying University Hall at Harvard. Today he could pose for a life insurance ad, but ten years ago he wore a moustache, a torn leather jacket and a headband over thick black hair that fell to his shoulder blades.

69   In 1969, when police broke down the doors of University Hall with a battering ram, Andy was clubbed and carried off in a paddy wagon. The next day, his head wrapped in bandages, he joined the strike that shut down the school. That June, his parents took time off from their jobs in Cocoa, Florida, to drive up north to see their son graduate from Harvard. But ten minutes into the ceremony, Andy walked out with about 300 others to protest the racist imperialist policies of Harvard University.

70   In the years that followed, Andy founded an alternative high school in the ghetto, lived in a therapeutic community for chronic schizophrenics, worked on an organic farm, ran an assembly district for George McGovern, and joined a commune of twelve who were sailing around the world.

71   Somewhere down the line he took an acting class and decided to settle in Los Angeles. Gradually, his appearance and then his values began to change. When I met him in 1976, he was getting ready to break down and buy a suit—a custom-made suit from a tailor on Rodeo Drive, not from Goodwill. He had decided he wanted to star in movies that would "alter the culture." He had also decided he wanted to be richly rewarded by the culture.

72   "Sometimes I lie in bed and think about how I've changed," Andy says. "I wouldn't want to live in or even walk through a ghetto today. And I've become a racist about Arabs. Their oil money flooding in here is driving up the prices of everything—houses, gas. Did we think we wouldn't have to worry about such things?"

73   I feel myself sinking. "I suppose our commitment wasn't that sincere."

74   Andy disagrees. "Mine was. I gave up years of my life working to make society better. Those were years I could have been earning money and advancing in a career."

75   We notice a commotion on the mall in front of the Venice Pavilion. The usual crowds are skating and wheeling, but in the center, twenty people are standing in a circle, holding signs—STOP NUCLEAR POWER. The leader of the group is on skates and has bloody knees. He starts a chant, "Hell no, we won't glow," but the voices barely carry over the roller-disco.

76   A lone TV cameraman is photographing the group. Some of the spectators are laughing and calling insults. "Smoke a joint guys, and mellow out." I feel embarrassed, the demonstrators look so silly and ineffectual; and yet I know that this is how things begin.

77   Andy says, "What is the point? Who are they reaching here?"

78   We turn and walk away in troubled silence.

79   The window of my study in Venice looks out on a building of single apartments. The average tenant stays six months, and I can tell where he or she is in the cycle by the state of the front yard. If there is a new resident in the building, the yard is full of young plants. They are carefully watered and begin to flower, and then suddenly everything turns brown. Weeds spring up, until the ground is so dry that nothing will grow on it and people throw beer cans and trash on the lot. The old tenants leave without saying good-bye, and new ones arrive and begin to clean up. I watch them installing stereos, hanging wind chimes, and putting out lawn furniture. Home at last: the good life by the beach.

80   One of the tenants this year was a man of thirty, Don, who taught phys ed at a junior high school. After weeks of nodding to each other across the lane, we struck up an acquaintance. Sometimes we would sit on the beach together or have a quick dinner on the Venice pier. Don was exceedingly attractive in a California way: blond hair, blue eyes, a pleasingly symmetrical if not terribly interesting face, and a body kept in wondrous shape. Every so often, preteen girls who had followed him home from school would tiptoe up to his door, ring the bell, and, squealing with laughter, run away.

81   I liked to hear Don talk about teaching. He said the seventh graders need to be disciplined "or else it's *Lord of the Flies*. The kids are confused and can't keep things organized. They're always losing stuff. After a seventh-grade period, we have to go through the locker room and collect their junk in boxes." The eighth graders, he said, are gaining confidence and want to test their limits. "They need to be smashed down." The ninth graders "know what they can get away with, and you can actually teach them stuff."

82   A few months went by in which I didn't see Don, until one Sunday night when he appeared with a bottle of tequila. "I'm glad you were home," he said.

83   "Why?"

84   "I've been alone all week. I went skiing by myself. Every night I just sat and read or daydreamed. I drove back today, and I thought I'd stop at Death Valley and take pictures of wild flowers, but there weren't any. So I came on in." He was staring at his lap. "I didn't want to be alone."

85   "I know what you mean."

86   "Do you?" He looked surprised.

87   I nodded.

88   "I'm in pain. Do you believe me?"

89   I realized, from the question, that people do not tend to take very seriously the pain of a blond gym teacher. "Yes," I said. "You want a close relationship with someone, and you can't have it."

90   He let out a sigh.

91   I said, "It's been six months or so since I was close with anyone."

92   Don said, "It's been three or four years for me. And I have this fantasy—of having a home, a wife and kids. It's very strong. But it's not happening."

93   I said it seemed puzzling: He's so attractive, warm, and good-humored. He meets and dates so many women.

94   He shrugged. "I could say the same about you."

95   Being unattached these days can be such a maddening business. You will have what feels to be the most intimate encounter: There is dazzling promise, blunt truth spoken, laughter and wonderful communication and you will never see the person again. Sometimes it lasts a few weeks, then one or the other calls in sick. I have observed the pattern in myself: Infatuation turns suddenly and without warning to aversion. A friend said it comes over her in waves. "I hate the way he walks, the way he chews. I can't wait to be alone, but in a few days I'll get lonely again." It is nothing short of a disease, and those who have it tend to gravitate toward others with the same affliction.

96   On a weekend in July, I sat out by the lifeguard tower with Don, the gym teacher, and two of his friends. All three had been married and divorced, and every week, they would get together and recount their little disaster stories.

97   David, who is a doctor, described spending the night with a woman who turned out to have silicone breasts. "When she lay down on her back, the breasts didn't move. They felt like Silly Putty. It stopped me cold, man. It was like making love to a goddamned lamp or something."

98   The others howled with laughter.

99   Don reported that a teacher he'd been dating had just told him she wouldn't be seeing him as often. She was starting a new job and giving first priority to her career. Don said, "I grew up thinking my wife would cook while I was out running the school district. It's sad to think I probably won't have kids now."

100   "What makes you so sure?" I said.

101   "Who's going to raise them?"

102   I said there must be women who would want to stay home with children, at least part of the time. But Don disagreed. "Women who are interested in raising kids are dog shit."

103   I looked at the other men. Was this serious? Allan, a lawyer with an Afro, did not seem to be listening.

104   "Hey, Al," Don said. "Where are ya?"

105   Allan said he had been thinking about a woman he'd met at a dinner party. "At first I didn't think much of her, but as the evening pro-

gressed, she became more beautiful. She had a real nice smile, which turns me on. There was a gentleness about her. I liked her voice, and I liked what she was doing. I've been thinking about her all day."

106 "You gonna call her?" Don said.

107 Allan thought a moment. To my surprise, he said no.

108 "Why wouldn't you call her?" I said.

109 He tipped his head from side to side. "Just because I like someone doesn't mean I want to get into a scene."

110 I had a fleeting urge to have at him. What is wrong with these men? But David and Don seemed to empathize with their friend. David said, "You can't satisfy the women out there. No point trying. Anything you do will be criticized."

111 Once, when I was doing research for a film, I spent a day with David on his rounds at the hospital. He has a sensitive face, blue eyes, and dark hair that looks black against the white doctor's coat. David treats very sick people—many are terminally ill—with kindness and concern. He is always overscheduled and yet remains cheerful. Every case requires him to make decisions that will prolong or curtail life. He works grueling shifts with no relief and often goes home and falls asleep in his clothes with the lights on.

112 In his free time, he goes to singles bars. He is adept at one-night stands. While we sat by the lifeguard tower, he described his operating procedure. "The first thing is the preening—you've got to do everything you can to make yourself look great. Because it's real competitive. Make sure you smell good. Blow your hair dry. Your clothes should be casual but stylish.

113 "How long does it take you to get ready?" I said.

114 "About an hour. That includes shaving. I have to put in my contact lenses. Take a shower. Powder my balls."

115 "Come on."

116 "I have to—Johnson's baby powder—otherwise I get a rash from my bikini underwear."

117 When he leaves the house, he takes a leather shaving kit in which he has packed a razor, contact lens solution, K-Y jelly, aspirin, a rubber ("in case the bubblehead forgot to take her pill"), and an address book.

118 You always go to her place if you can. Then you control when you leave. You don't get stuck with her all weekend." He said the first moves in the bar are most important. "You have to feel the woman out, learn what her fantasies are. The best approach is to ask a lot of personal questions without giving her a chance to know that much about you. Let her talk about her problems and nod understandingly. Because really, people love to talk about themselves."

119   Don said, "What if she starts to get upset about her problems?"

120   David: "At this point, it's a good idea to commiserate; either share or manufacture some sort of similar experience."

121   "You're good at this, aren't you?" I said.

122   David: "I'm pretty good at being understanding."

123   "Do you ever make it clear you just want to—?"

124   "Not really, no."

125   "Why?"

126   "It's never worked for me. My basic assumption is that a woman doesn't want one-night stands. She wants an emotional experience. So I make her feel like she's the most fascinating and unique person I've ever met."

127   "What if she is a fascinating person," I said. "What do you do then?"

128   "Either fall in love . . . or run."

129   Don and Allan started hooting and slapping their legs. "Run like hell!"

> Now you rich people listen to me,
> Weep and wail over the miseries
> That are coming, coming up on you . . .
> Your life here on earth has been filled
> With luxury and pleasure,
> You have made yourself fat
> For the day of slaughter.

—From "Warning, Warning,"
by Max Romeo

The only music I follow with any excitement these days is reggae from Jamaica. I cannot abide the monotony of disco, and I'm tired of listening to albums from the Sixties. Reggae music is alive; it has melody, wit, a hypnotic jungle beat, and lyrics that burn with righteous fire.

130   Most reggae singers are Rastafarians—members of a mystic religion; they smoke ganja, worship Haile Selassie, and believe that they are the lost children of Israel who will one day return to Zion. On that day, the rich will eat one another alive and the blessed will survive. The Rastafarians sing about Jerusalem lost and the temptations of dwelling in Babylon. The imagery seems relevant to me and became even more relevant after I visited the actual Jerusalem in 1976.

131   In recent years, I have traveled to Israel so often that people have begun to think me odd. I keep returning for many reasons, one of which is that I find in Israel a sense of belonging to a family—the ancient family

of Jews. To achieve this feeling in America, I would probably have to join a synagogue and come to some decision about observing the orthodox laws. But in Israel, all one has to do is be present. Hebrew is spoken. Everywhere one is reminded of the biblical past. On Friday afternoon, a quiet descends on the cities. Buses stop running, shops close. No newspaper comes out. Nobody works. Everyone, even the most irreligious person, has to be aware that the Sabbath has arrived and that this day will be different.

132   Life in Israel is in diametric contrast to life in southern California. Israelis who are my age have fought and survived two wars. They still serve in the reserves. They know how to handle a gun, fix a Jeep, find water in the desert, and apply first aid to someone with a chest wound. Most of them had married in their early twenties, had had at least two children, and had stayed married.

133   Israel is beset with internal problems and in no way a paradise, but life there has an intensity and meaning, derived from having a common enemy and a sense of purpose in history. The most radical critics of the government will have no qualms about serving as officers in the reserves. There is no contradiction in being a left-wing pacifist and a soldier, because if people fight, it is to protect their homes and friends.

134   Israelis are reminded, almost daily, that human life is transient and relationships are not replaceable. Having a family becomes a matter of critical importance. I never ceased to be moved by the sight of muscular Israeli men playing with their children. One I knew, Gidon, was a commando in the navy and drove heavy machinery on his kibbutz. He had spent a year in New York and told me he was puzzled by the attitude of people there. "All the men and women are interested only in their own careers," he said. "They don't want children." Gidon, who is twenty-eight, has two daughters and a newborn son. "Who says children take away your freedom? I have my family and my work, and tell me, what is a career," he said as he held up his baby son, "compared to this?"

> Have a good tomorrow. Buy real estate today.
> —*A billboard in Marina del Rey*

Six months after I moved into my house in Venice—the house for which everyone thought I had paid too much—realtors began to knock on the door and ask if I wanted to sell. The longer I stayed, the more they offered. After a year, the price of the house had doubled, and after two years, I had earned more money just by living there than I had in my entire writing career.

135   It was phenomenal. The money was insurance for the future, and I wanted more. I began looking in the Marina Peninsula at condominiums on the sand. My house was a short walk from the beach, but, as Bruce Jay

Friedman wrote about such homes "it's either on the beach or it isn't. . . . The fella who is 'a short jog away' is in the same boat as someone who has to be brought in by Concorde."

136   What I saw on the Marina Peninsula was shocking. The condominiums had been built with no concern for aesthetics or quality. They were like shoe boxes, long and narrow, with thin walls and sprayed acoustic ceilings aptly called "cottage cheese." The selling feature, of course, was that the front windows opened onto the surf. If you faced the ocean and forgot about the apartment, it was fine, but the apartments themselves were abysmal.

137   The price of one of these two-bedroom boxes was $400,000 and up—the price you would pay for a nine-room house with a pool and tennis court in another part of the city. The realtors insisted, however, that the prices, outrageous as they were, would only go up. "Beach property is better than gold. They can mine more gold, but they're never going to make any more oceanfront."

138   I saw nothing that I would not have been embarrassed to own, and in any case, I came to the conclusion that I could not afford to move. That is the catch 22 about real estate: The price of your house has gone up, but if you sell it, where are you going to live? If you buy another house, it will cost far more than what you received for your old house, the interest rate will be higher, and you'll be stuck with a whopping overhead. So people tend to stay where they are and remodel. But they cannot stand being left out of the game, so they refinance their homes and use the cash to purchase income units, or they join limited partnerships or get together with three friends and buy a house for speculation.

139   What has resulted is a feeding frenzy. Policemen, plumbers, film directors—everyone is making more in real estate than in the profession he was trained for. When a new "For Sale" sign is posted on Pacific Avenue, cars screech to a halt. I am no less guilty than the others: I am tempted to quit work, cancel dates, and run out if a broker calls to tell me about a "great deal." What is fueling this madness is anxiety about the future and the wish for tangible security. Marriages may not last; political movements come and go; even money loses its value, but the land gains. A woman I know who recently quit her job as a public defender to become a realtor put it this way: "I'll tell you what I'm looking for in real estate: freedom." The only problem with this kind of freedom, of course, is that you can never have enough.

> I think there's going to have to be a reorientation of what people value in their own lives.
>
> —*Jimmy Carter,*
> *Camp David summit,1979*

"I just made a major purchase," Andy told me on the phone. "I just bought some roller skates."

140   "You didn't."

141   "Ninety-five dollars." He laughed sheepishly. "Now I can float along with the rest of the flakes."

142   Once Andy had succumbed, it was only weeks before I followed. I had seen beginning skaters hobbling along the bike path and falling into trash cans, but I figured they had never skated before. When I was eight, I had lived with a skate key around my neck and had been particularly skilled at taking the steep driveways on our block. But a long time had elapsed since I was eight.

143   I rented a pair, laced them on, stood up, and rolled away. Just like that. I could not do tricks, but I could move right along. I thought I had discovered a new and delightful way to keep in shape and promptly bought myself some Roadskates.

144   The next Saturday, Andy and I left our homes in the morning and rolled five miles down the bike path. Despite the claims we had heard that skating is good for the legs, I did not find it strenuous. Andy agreed: "I'm not even sweating." The sensation was more of dawdling: mindless, effortless. It was pleasant, with the surf shooting in the air and gulls flapping overhead. We decided to skate back to Venice and have lunch at the Meatless Mess Hall.

145   The crowds on Ocean Front Walk were thicker than I had ever seen. People were skating down slalom courses marked by beer cans. A man crashed into a tree. A girl on a bike hit a boy on a skateboard. Bums and shopping-cart people were rummaging through the trash cans. A woman had ignored the "Motor Vehicles Prohibited" signs and driven onto the boardwalk. The license plate on her car said, "Moist 1." A policeman was giving her a ticket. He wore his beach uniform: shorts, a holster with a .38, and a T-shirt that said "L.A.P.D."

146   I saw two women I knew from the movie business, Sandy, a producer, and Lois, the token female vice-president at a studio. Both are paid more than $60,000 a year. Sandy was wearing shorts, platform shoes, and a blouse so low-cut that her breasts were spilling out. She said to me, "How's your life? Are you in love?"

147   "No, are you?"

148   "Are you kidding? I can't even get laid."

149   Lois said, "Forget it, you can't get laid in this town. I go to parties and take home phone numbers of women. I may have a guy for you, though, Sandy. He's an old friend."

150   "Yeah?"

151   "He's not that smart."

152   Sandy: "Can he move it in and out?"

153   Lois made a so-so gesture.

154   "Screw it," Sandy said. "If this goes on much longer, I'll die of vaginal atrophy. Give me his number."

155   We said good-bye, laughing, and I looked around for Andy. He was talking with a tall redhead, whom he introduced as Carl—"We used to be roommates at Harvard."

156   Carl was saying, "I'm playing the game of the Seventies: corporate executive."

157   Andy laughed. Carl explained that he had formed a production company and just finished shooting a movie for television.

158   "Great," Andy said, sounding not all that happy.

159   Carl: "I'm going to Cannes next week."

160   "That is fantastic," Andy said, but the word "Cannes" had struck him like a body blow.

161   Carl said, "Look, I spent ten years starving. Now I want to get even."

162   Andy: "I know the feeling."

163   Carl said, "Hey, let's have lunch. Keep in touch."

164   "Sure," Andy said. "And, uh . . . congratulations on your success."

165   As we began to skate away, I could tell Andy was upset. He was racing, making quick turns and plowing through groups of people. I let him move ahead. Just before the Meatless Mess Hall, I saw a bump in the asphalt. I thought I could take it the way you take a wave in water skiing. I rolled up the rise, but at the top, my skates continued flying upward instead of down the other side. Before I could think, my feet were in the air and my back hit the concrete, four feet down, smack! I blacked out for a second, and when I came to, I could feel the impact in my chest, head, teeth.

166   "Are you all right?" someone was asking.

167   "I don't know." I had no wind. I was afraid to move, afraid I had crippled myself. Was this dumb, I thought. What a price you're going to pay. Andy had to half-carry me home and then drive me to the hospital emergency room, but the X rays showed nothing broken. I had bruised and badly swollen tissue, but with ice packs followed by heat, I was told, I would recover.

168   For the next two weeks, I minced around painfully, unable to stand upright. I began to notice people on the boardwalk wearing casts on their arms and legs. One retired surfer on our block took a terrible spill and dislocated his shoulder. Still he went skating, wearing a brace. "Why?" I said. "Anytime you fall, you hit concrete." He shrugged. "What else is there to do?"

169   Every day, there was at least one call for an ambulance and somebody was carried off on a stretcher. Then in June, an eighty-six-year-old

woman, Ann Gerber, was killed on the boardwalk when she was run over by a twenty-five-year-old bicyclist, who explained later, "She got in my way."

170   The Los Angeles City Council called a meeting to consider the situation. On the boardwalk, it was war on wheels: Shouting and pushing erupted between skaters and bicyclists and joggers and senior citizens over who had the right-of-way. The skaters had the numbers and were gaining each day. People were skating to the bank, to the laundromat, to restaurants, to walk their dogs.

171   The City Council voted to ban skating on parts of the boardwalk, but people disobeyed.

172   "No skating on the boardwalk!"

173   "Up yours, ya jerk!"

174   A ninety-two-year-old woman struck a skater with her cane when he cut in front of her. "I'm living here twenty-five years," she shouted. "You should be ashamed."

175   I was driving home from the doctor's. I stopped at the light on Venice Boulevard and Pacific Avenue. A girl was waiting for the bus—and Oriental girl wearing a leopard skin bikini and thin high heels. She was carrying two electric guitars. Where could she be going on the bus? The light changed. As I started to move, a man who had a beard on one side of his face and was clean-shaven on the other stepped off the curb. I hit the brakes. I nearly ran him over. You're going to have to be more alert, I thought. There are crazy people, and wouldn't it be terrible to hit someone. I saw a picture in my mind of the man lying under my car. If it had happened, if he was actually under the car, I thought, what should I do? Drive forward or backward or leave it there and try to jack it up? My thoughts drifted on, and soon it was time to pull into my carport.

176   The space is narrow, so I made a wide arc, glided through the turn, and was coming to a stop when, clunk, I felt the car roll over something that sounded like a metal trash can. What was it? Why hadn't I seen it?

177   I stepped out of the car and got down on my knees. A man was lying under the car. A wino, flat on his back, dressed in a green-plaid shirt and woolen cap and brown shoes. I screamed. Should I drive forward, or backward . . . His legs were behind the rear wheels, extending out across the driveway. I had to have driven over his legs. I looked for blood.

178   "Are you all right?" My voice was high, like a shriek. "Did I hurt you?"

179   "No," he said fuzzily. He seemed to have been in a drunken sleep.

180   "You must be hurt."

181   "No, I'm not."

182   "But my car—"

183   "Nahhh," he said in the slurred, combative manner of drunks. "If I was hurt, I'd know it."

184   He was struggling to raise himself. "I wanted to sit down here . . . think about shit."

185   Suddenly he jumped to his feet. I jumped back and screamed.

186   Andy, who had heard the commotion from next door, came running over.

187   The wino said, "What do you know, goddamnit! I been in Venice longer'n you. This is my home."

188   Andy said, sounding friendly, "You like it here, huh?"

189   "Yeah. I got shit on my mind. I wanna sit down, nobody's gonna stop me."

190   I said, "I'm just glad you weren't hurt. It scared the . . . life out of me."

191   The drunk swayed in my direction. "Awww, look, I'm really sorry, Miss, I didn't mean to bother you."

192   An urge to laugh came over me. This made the drunk laugh too.

193   "What's your name?" he said.

194   Pause. "Sharon," I lied.

195   "Okay, Sherry. Take it easy." He pulled his cap down and started to walk away, without apparent limp or pain.

196   "How could this be?" I said to Andy.

197   "I don't know."

198   "I must have driven over him."

199   "You did. I saw it from my window."

200   The drunk reached the corner, turned, and disappeared. As I stood there, I realized that I was thirty-five and I was still waiting, expecting I would soon wake up from all of this.

TO THINK ABOUT

1. Imagine yourself talking with Sara Davidson. Where would the conversation take place? What sort of dynamics would prevail? How would you feel about speaking with this narrator?
2. The essay is a collage, a series of sections separated by white space. How does this arrangement affect the piece?
3. What is the theme of this essay? Is it stated explicitly or simply implied?
4. Davidson writes of visiting Israel "so often that people have begun to think me odd." In an essay about Venice, California, what is the purpose of including a few paragraphs about Israel?

TO DO

1. Write an essay in which you capture the essence of your time, your place. You may choose your college community, your hometown, or any other place where you have spent a considerable amount of time lately. You might begin by making a list of episodes, incidents, and bits of dialogue that, together, will constitute a portrait of the time, the place.
2. Write a letter to Sara Davidson in which you compare your time, your place, with hers. (This may turn out to be another essay.)

TIP

Start with the good stuff. Don't worry about chronology; start in the middle, if you like. Or at the end. One of the nice things about writing an essay in the form of a collage is that it doesn't matter where you start; your first draft will consist of a pile of separate chunks. It does not matter in what order you write the chunks, because you will be able to shuffle them, rearrange them, until they form a whole.

9

Write Till You Drop
Annie Dillard

I have heard that Annie Dillard plays softball with the same intensity she brings to her writing. This would make her the Ty Cobb of softball, or maybe of writing, except that where Cobb was petty and selfish, Dillard is blessed with a ferocious generosity of spirit that appears to encompass every living thing. In 1974 the publication of Pilgrim at Tinker Creek, *a memoir of a single year's explorations of a valley near her home in Virginia's Blue Ridge, brought her instant recognition as an extraordinarily gifted writer. Since then she has written essays, poetry, an autobiography, and a novel, and neither her skill nor her hunger for discovery has waned. It is that hunger, and Dillard's eagerness to share it, that make her writing irresistible.*

Now she will tell you how to write. Like the wedding guest transfixed by Coleridge's Ancient Mariner, you have no choice. Listen while you can.

1   People love pretty much the same things best. A writer looking for subjects inquires not after what he loves best, but after what he alone loves at all. Strange seizures beset us. Frank Conroy loves his yo-yo tricks. Emily Dickinson her slant of light; Richard Selzer loves the glistening peritoneum, Faulkner the muddy bottom of a little girl's drawers visible when she's up a pear tree. "Each student of the ferns," I once read, "will have his own list of plants that for some reason or another stir his emotions."

2   Why do you never find anything written about that idiosyncratic thought you advert to, about your fascination with something no one else understands? Because it is up to you. There is something you find interesting, for a reason hard to explain. It is hard to explain because you have never read it on any page; there you begin. You were made and set here to give voice to this, your own astonishment. "The most demanding

part of living a lifetime as an artist is the strict discipline of forcing one-self to work steadfastly along the nerve of one's own most intimate sensitivity." Anne Truitt, the sculptor, said this. Thoreau said it another way: know your own bone. "Pursue, keep up with, circle round and round your life. . . . Know your own bone: gnaw at it, bury it, unearth it, and gnaw at it still."

3   Write as if you were dying. At the same time, assume you write for an audience consisting solely of terminal patients. That is, after all, the case. What would you begin writing if you knew you would die soon? What could you say to a dying person that would not enrage by its triviality?

4   Write about winter in the summer. Describe Norway as Ibsen did, from a desk in Italy; describe Dublin as James Joyce did, from a desk in Paris. Willa Cather wrote her prairie novels in New York City; Mark Twain wrote *Huckleberry Finn* in Hartford. Recently, scholars learned that Walt Whitman rarely left his room.

5   The writer studies literature, not the world. He lives in the world; he cannot miss it. If he has ever bought a hamburger, or taken a commercial airplane flight, he spares his readers a report of experience. He is careful of what he reads, for that is what he will write. He is careful of what he learns, because that is what he will know.

6   The writer knows his field—what has been done, what could be done, the limits—the way a tennis player knows the court. And like that expert, he, too, plays the edges. That is where the exhilaration is. He hits up the line. In writing, he can push the edges. Beyond this limit, here, the reader must recoil. Reason balks, poetry snaps; some madness enters, or strain. Now gingerly, can he enlarge it, can he nudge the bounds? And enclose what wild power?

7   The body of literature, with its limits and edges, exists outside some people and inside others. Only after the writer lets literature shape her can she perhaps shape literature. In working-class France, when an apprentice got hurt, or when he got tired, the experienced workers said, "It is the trade entering his body." The art must enter the body, too. A painter cannot use paint like glue or screws to fasten down the world. The tubes of paint are like fingers; they work only if, inside the painter, the neural pathways are wide and clear to the brain. Cell by cell, molecule by molecule, atom by atom, part of the brain changes physical shape to accommodate and fit paint.

8   You adapt your self, Paul Klee said, to the contents of the paintbox. Adapting yourself to the contents of the paintbox, he said, is more important than nature and its study. The painter, in other words, does not fit the paints to the world. He most certainly does not fit the world to

himself. He fits himself to the paint. The self is the servant who bears the paintbox and its inherited contents. Klee called this insight, quite rightly, "an altogether revolutionary new discovery."

9   A well-known writer got collared by a university student who asked, "Do you think I could be a writer?"

10   "Well," the writer said, "I don't know. . . . Do you like sentences?"

11   The writer could see the student's amazement. Sentences? Do I like sentences? I am 20 years old and do I like sentences? If he had liked sentences, of course, he could begin, like a joyful painter I knew. I asked him how he came to be a painter. He said, "I liked the smell of the paint."

12   Hemingway studied, as models, the novels of Knut Hamsun and Ivan Turgenev. Isaac Bashevis Singer, as it happened, also chose Hamsun and Turgenev as models. Ralph Ellison studied Hemingway and Gertrude Stein. Thoreau loved Homer; Eudora Welty loved Chekhov. Faulkner described his debt to Sherwood Anderson and Joyce; E. M. Forster, his debt to Jane Austen and Proust. By contrast, if you ask a 21-year-old poet whose poetry he likes, he might say, unblushing, "Nobody's." In his youth, he has not yet understood that poets like poetry, and novelists like novels; he himself likes only the role, the thought of himself in a hat. Rembrandt and Shakespeare, Tolstoy and Gauguin, possessed, I believe, powerful hearts, not powerful wills. They loved the range of materials they used. The work's possibilities excited them; the field's complexities fired their imaginations. The caring suggested the tasks; the tasks suggested the schedules. They learned their fields and then loved them. They worked, respectfully, out of their love and knowledge, and they produced complex bodies of work that endure. Then, and only then, the world flapped at them some sort of hat, which, if they were still living, they knocked away as well as they could, to keep at their tasks.

13   It makes more sense to write one big book—a novel or nonfiction narrative—than to write many stories or essays. Into a long, ambitious project you can fit or pour all you possess and learn. A project that takes five years will accumulate those years' inventions and richnesses. Much of those years' reading will feed the work. Further, writing sentences is difficult whatever their subject. It is no less difficult to write sentences in a recipe than sentences in *Moby-Dick*. So you might as well write *Moby-Dick*. Similarly, since every original work requires a unique form, it is more prudent to struggle with the outcome of only one form—that of a long work—than to struggle with the many forms of a collection. Each chapter of a prolonged narrative is problematic too, of course, and

the writer undergoes trials as the structure collapses and coheres by turns—but at least the labor is not all on spec. The chapter already has a context: a tone, setting, characters. The work is already off the ground. You must carry the reader along, but you need not, after the first chapters, bear him aloft while performing a series of tricky introductions.

14   Writing every book, the writer must solve two problems: Can it be done? and, Can I do it? Every book has an intrinsic impossibility, which its writer discovers as soon as his first excitement dwindles. The problem is structural; it is insoluble; it is why no one can ever write this book. Complex stories, essays, and poems have this problem, too—the prohibitive structural defect the writer wishes he had never noticed. He writes it in spite that. He finds ways to minimize the difficulty; he strengthens other virtues; he cantilvers the whole narrative out into thin air and it holds. And if it can be done, then he can do it, and only he. For there is nothing in the material for this book that suggests to anyone but him alone its possibilities for meaning and feeling.

15   Why are we reading, if not in hope of beauty laid bare, life heightened and its deepest mystery probed? Can the writer isolate and vivify all in experience that most deeply engages our intellects and our hearts? Can the writer renew our hope for literary forms? Why are we reading if not in hope that the writer will magnify and dramatize our days, will illuminate and inspire us with wisdom, courage, and the possibility of meaningfulness, and press upon our minds the deepest mysteries, so we may feel again their majesty and power? What do we ever know that is higher than that power which, from time to time, seizes our lives, and which reveals us startlingly to ourselves as creatures set down here bewildered? Why does death so catch us by surprise, and why love? We still and always want waking. We should amass half-dressed in long lines like tribesmen and shake gourds at each other, to wake up; instead we watch television and miss the show.

16   And if we are reading for these things, why would anyone read books with advertising slogans and brand names in them? Why would anyone write such books? Commercial intrusion has overrun and crushed, like the last glaciation, a humane landscape. The new landscape and its climate put metaphysics on the run. Must writers collaborate? Well, in fact, the novel as a form has only rarely been metaphysical; it usually presents society. The novel often aims to fasten down the spirit of its time, to make a heightened simulacrum of our recognizable world in order to present it shaped and analyzed. This has never seemed to me worth doing, but it is certainly one thing literature has always done. (Any writer draws idiosyncratic boundaries in the field.) Writers at-

tracted to metaphysics can simply ignore the commercial blare, as if it were a radio, or use historical settings, or flee to nonfiction or poetry. Writers might even, with their eyes wide open, redeem the commercial claptrap from within the novel, using it not just as a quick, cheap, and perfunctory background but—as Updike did in *Rabbit Is Rich*—as part of the world subject to a broad and sanctifying vision.

17   The sensation of writing a book is the sensation of spinning, blinded by love and daring. It is the sensation of rearing and peering from the bent tip of a grassblade, looking for a route. At its absurd worst, it feels like what mad Jacob Boehme, the German mystic, described in his first book. He was writing, incoherently as usual, about the source of evil. The passage will serve as well for the source of books.

18   "The whole Deity has in its innermost or beginning Birth, in the Pith or Kernel, a very tart, terrible *Sharpness*, in which the astringent Quality is very horrible, tart, hard, dark and cold Attraction or Drawing together, like *Winter*, when there is a fierce, bitter cold Frost, when Water is frozen into Ice, and besides is very intolerable."

19   If you can dissect out the very intolerable, tart, hard, terribly sharp Pith or Kernel, and begin writing the book compressed therein, the sensation changes. Now it feels like alligator wrestling, at the level of the sentence.

20   This is your life. You are a Seminole alligator wrestler. Half naked, with your two bare hands, you hold and fight a sentence's head while its tail tries to knock you over. Several years ago in Florida, an alligator wrestler lost. He was grappling with an alligator in a lagoon in front of a paying crowd. The crowd watched the young Indian and the alligator twist belly to belly in and out of the water; after one plunge, they failed to rise. A young writer named Lorne Ladner described it. Bubbles came up on the water. Then blood came up, and the water stilled. As the minutes elapsed, the people in the crowd exchanged glances; silent, helpless, they quit the stands. It took the Indians a week to find the man's remains.

21   At its best, the sensation of writing is that of any unmerited grace. It is handed to you but only if you look for it. You search, you break your heart, your back, your brain, and then—and only then—it is handed to you. From the corner of your eye you see motion. Something is moving through the air and headed your way. It is a parcel bound in ribbons and bows; it has two white wings. It flies directly at you; you can read your name on it. If it were a baseball, you would hit it out of the park. It is that one pitch in a thousand you see in slow motion; its wings beat slowly as a hawk's.

22   One line of a poem, the poet said—only one line, but thank God for that one line—drops from the ceiling. Thornton Wilder cited this unnamed writer of sonnets: one line of a sonnet falls from the ceiling, and

you tap in the others around it with a jeweler's hammer. Nobody whispers it in your ear. It is like something you memorized once and forgot. Now it comes back and rips away your breath. You find and finger a phrase at a time; you lay it down cautiously as if with tongs, and wait suspended until the next one finds you: Ah yes, then this and yes; praise be, and yes, then this.

23   Einstein likened the generation of a new idea to a chicken's laying an egg. *"Kieks—auf einmal ist es da."* Cheep—and all at once there it is. Of course, Einstein was not above playing to the crowd.

24   One January day, working alone in that freezing borrowed cabin I used for a study on Puget Sound—heated not at all by the alder I chopped every morning—I wrote one of the final passages of a short, difficult book. It was a wildish passage in which the narrator, I, came upon the baptism of Christ in the water of the bay in front of the house. There was a northeaster on—as I wrote. The stormy salt water I saw from the cabin window looked dark as ink. The parallel rows of breakers made lively, broken lines, closely spaced row on row, moving fast and pulling the eyes; they reproduced the sensation of reading exactly, but without reading's sense. Mostly I shut my eyes. I have never been in so trancelike a state, and in fact I dislike, as romantic, the suggestion that any writer works in any peculiar state. I sat motionless with my eyes shut, like a Greek funerary marble.

25   The writing was simple yet graceless; it surprised me. It was arrhythmical, nonvisual, clunky. It was halting, as if there were no use trying to invoke beauty or power. It was plain and ugly, urgent, like child's talk. "He led him into the water," it said, without antecedents. It read like a translation from the *Gallic Wars*.

26   Once when I opened my eyes the page seemed bright. The windows were steamed and the sun had gone behind the firs on the bluff. I must have had my eyes closed long. I had been repeating to myself, for hours, like a song, "It is the grave of Jesus, where he lay." From Wallace Stevens' poem, "Sunday Morning." It was three o'clock then; I heated some soup. By the time I left, I was scarcely alive. The way home was along the beach. The beach was bright and distinct. The storm still blew. I was light, dizzy, barely there. I remembered some legendary lamas, who were chains to keep from floating away. Walking itself seemed to be a stunt; I could not tell whether I was walking fast or slowly. My thighs felt as if they had been reamed.

27   And I have remembered it often, later, waking up in that cabin to windows steamed blue and the sun gone around the island; remembered putting down those queer, stark sentences half blind or yellow paper; remembered walking ensorcerized, tethered, down the gray cobble beach like an aisle. Evelyn Underhill describes another life, and a better one, in

words that recall to me that day, and many another day, at this queer task: "He goes because he must, as Galahad went towards the Grail: knowing that for those who can live it, this alone is life."

28   Push it. Examine all things intensely and relentlessly. Probe and search each object in a piece of art. Do not leave it, do not course over it, as if it were understood, but instead follow it down until you see it in the mystery of its own specificity and strength. Giacometti's drawings and paintings show his bewilderment and persistence. If he had not acknowledged his bewilderment, he would not have persisted. A twentieth-century master of drawing, Rico Lebrun, taught that "the draftsman must aggress; only by persistent assault will the live image capitulate and give up its secret to an unrelenting line." Who but an artist fierce to know—not fierce to seem to know—would suppose that a live image possessed a secret? The artist is willing to give all his or her strength and life to probing with blunt instruments those same secrets no one can describe in any way but with those instruments' faint tracks.

29   Admire the world for never ending on you—as you would admire an opponent, without taking your eyes from him, or walking away.

30   One of the few things I know about writing is this: spend it all, shoot it, play it, lose it, all, right away, every time. Do not hoard what seems good for a later place in the book, or for another book; give it, give it all, give it now. The impulse to save something good for a better place later is the signal to spend it now. Something more will arise for later, something better. These things fill from behind, from beneath, like well water. Similarly, the impulse to keep to yourself what you have learned is not only shameful, it is destructive. Anything you do not give freely and abundantly becomes lost to you. You open your safe and find ashes.

31   After Michelangelo died, someone found in his studio a piece of paper on which he had written a note to his apprentice, in the handwriting of his old age: "Draw, Antonio, draw, Antonio, draw and do not waste time."

TO THINK ABOUT

1. What is the persona of this narrator? What is her attitude toward her subject, writing? What is the nature of the relationship she forms with you?
2. Dillard says: "One of the few things I know about writing is this: spend it all, shoot it, play it, lose it, all, right away, every time." Compare this with your own approach to writing.

3. Dillard says it is important to like sentences. Do you like sentences? Are you selective about the sentences you like? Do you like your own sentences? Which ones? What is the difference between the ones you like and the ones you don't?
4. Dillard describes a student who "likes only the role [of a poet], the thought of himself in a hat." Think of your own aspirations. On close examination, which are simply roles to play? And which are the real things?
5. Compare "Write Till You Drop" with Natalie Goldberg's "Obsessions" (Chapter 16). How does each essay affect you?

TO DO

1. Read the last two paragraphs of "Write Till You Drop" aloud, in the voice you think Dillard intended.
2. "Write as if you were dying," says Dillard. What would you write if you were dying? Why? Make a list. Then choose an item from the list and start writing. Try imitating Dillard's voice.
3. Have you ever experienced what Dillard might describe as "unmerited grace"? List the moments in your life that might qualify. Do they have anything in common, beyond the feeling of grace itself? Were they truly unmerited? Write about one or more of them.

TIP

Dillard writes of the tennis player who plays the edges, the writer who pushes the limits. The tennis player starts with the basics, the ground strokes. The writer starts with the basic building block, the simple declarative sentence. The tennis player scores with an occasional spectacular lob or smash, but it is the accumulation of flawless ground-strokes that wins the match. And so it is with the writer. An occasional metaphor may astonish the readers, an occasional compound or complex sentence may dazzle them, but only the accumulation of simple crystalline sentences will carry them through the piece.

10

'So long 4 ever'
Elissa Ely

Elissa Ely is a Boston psychiatrist and a frequent contributor to the op-ed page of the Boston Globe. *She is an expert at putting complex problems into concrete, tangible terms. In this piece about a young girl who has run away after threatening suicide, Ely lays out the problem, then turns directly to her readers and asks for advice. It is as though the action in a stage play were frozen while one of the characters comes forward and asks the audience:* **What would you do next if you were me?**

The writer does not have all the answers. Nevertheless, her voice rings with urgency and authority.

1   "Gudby 4 now," the note (edited for anonymity) begins.

2   "I run away. I mean to kilt myself. It not you falt. I can't trust no-one. Don't luk 4 me. I will kilt myself. So long 4 ever."

3   The writer is sitting in a bare room, her feet dangling over the chair.

4   A game of Go Fish laid out on the table in front of her has been interrupted by the appearance of a meatball sub. The sub is disappearing fast. "I like burritos better," says the writer, her mouth full.

5   Her foster mother describes the past few weeks: restless sleep, school fights, downward grades. She began to lie to her foster parents. She hit her younger brother ("I only told him to take a hike," she says). She threatened to run away. She threatened to "kilt" herself. She wept.

6   She wrote the note and disappeared the day after the court hearing, when a judge reinstated weekly visits with her biological mother. In psychiatry, all truth has two sides. On the one, a woman petitioned to regain custody, claiming noninvolvement with her daughter's many injuries and pediatric Emergency Room appearances. On the other, less was clear, for the writer wasn't telling.

7   She was missing overnight, and discovered the next morning, unrepentant and ravenous. She wanted to go home ("or to Friendly's") but her foster mother, frantic, brought her here, instead.

8   She has been in the room several hours now, interviewed by a panel of increasingly specialized psychiatric staff; they have also taken turns running to the cafeteria vending machines for the courses of her meal: meatball sub, two kinds of chips, orange juice, Sports bar, and a soggy piece of coconut cake viewed by all with suspicion.

9   The reason it is taking so long is not that the problem is unclear. It is a solution that is missing.

10   Now I ask you—doctors, armchair analysts, coffee-table psychotherapists, all who think this business requires no more than two friendly, unclogged ears and a listening outlook—what should we do? Here is a young woman who wishes to die. It is a threat that must be taken seriously.

11   A court that seems not to hear. A mother who claims the right to make amends. A frantic foster family. Many facts and no truth. What would you do?

12   Here is a hint: the necessary decision won't make anyone happy. You, in particular, will not sleep soundly tonight. There is no other decision to reach, and yet it does not feel like the right one—the writer must go where she can be safe. Her despair must be believed, even if it seems to have disappeared, digested somewhere between the sub and Sports bar.

13   She cannot be safe at home, and so she must be hospitalized. She does not have insurance, and so it must be a state hospital. She will not go voluntarily, and so she must be committed.

14   She will not stay, and so she must be placed on a locked ward. The Go Fish cards will be hurled to the floor and she will need to be carried to the ambulance. She will scream that locking her away won't change the way she feels. (This is true). She will see the necessary decision as a punishment (it will feel this way to you, too). It will be impossible to convince her otherwise. She will be removed from your sight, but not from your mind's eye.

15   Then strange things will happen. Though she is gone, she will remain, crouched over your retina, blocking your view. You will find you can't stop rubbing your eyes. Your vision is blurry. You feel shortsighted. You can't forget her.

16   And this is why: the Necessary Decision you made is right, but it is not just. She has been sent away for crimes very likely committed to her, not by her.

17   Your decision did not begin to solve the problems that brought her to your room. You are a specialist in the field, all unclogged ears and

listening outlook, but you have no answer for these problems. There may not be one.

18   Only one thing is clear. In this book of colliding stories and many-sided truth—written, for so many years without the subject's consent—there will be a next chapter. You have kept this young writer, for now, from "kilting" herself. But sending her away does not mean she is gone "4 ever."

19   Make no mistake. Her time with you is just beginning.

TO THINK ABOUT

1. What is the theme of this piece? How does it transcend the specific situation in question?
2. In this piece readers are directly invited to participate in the process of decision making. The writer says the "Necessary Decision . . . is right, but it is not just." How is this possible? Imagine other possibilities: a solution that would have been both right and just, for example. Or one that would have been just but not right.
3. What is the effect of the tenth paragraph of the piece ("Now I ask you—doctors, armchair analysts, coffee-table psychotherapists. . . ") on you? What is the effect of the last paragraph?

TO DO

1. Make a list of areas in which you are an authority. (You do not necessarily need formal training to be an authority on something. You *do* need experience.) Then select from the list an item that you have both the desire and the expertise to write about.
2. Write an essay about the item you have chosen, using experiences you have had. Try consulting readers directly about a difficult problem, as Elissa Ely does.

TIP

When we write about our own areas of expertise it is easy to forget that our readers are *not* experts. This kind of forgetting often results in one or both of the following writing errors: (1) We assume the readers know more than they do about the subject, and we fail to provide enough information; or (2) we use a voice that condescends to nonexperts. In either case, we lose our readers.

Be inclusive. Be aware that your readers don't know as much as you do about your subject, and use a voice that invites them to share your expertise.

11

A Few Words About Breasts: Shaping Up Absurd

Nora Ephron

Come here. Closer. Let me tell you why I've always loved Nora Ephron's stuff. It's because everything she writes holds the promise of something naughty, something sexy, or mean, or outrageous—something Ephron intends to share with only the privileged few. Me, for instance. Reading an Ephron piece is like sitting in an elegant little restaurant with the narrator, sipping coffee and sharing wonderful, juicy gossip. She is, by turns, catty, remorseful, spiteful, sweet, and self-mocking. There is a breathy quality here; the sentences are quick and furtive. ("Buster Klepper was the first boy who ever touched them. He was my boyfriend my senior year of high school.") When she really gets rolling—for example, in the section below in which she talks about the mother of her fiance telling her she should take the top position in lovemaking to minimize the smallness of her breasts—her voice contains a mixture of contempt and incredulity which is as delicious and sharp as fine old cheddar.

The other thing I love about Nora Ephron is that she is full of surprises, and sometimes they come at the end. That is all I will tell you.

1   I have to begin with a few words about androgyny. In grammar school, in the fifth and sixth grades, we were all tyrannized by a rigid set of rules that supposedly determined whether we were boys or girls. The episode in *Huckleberry Finn* where Huck is disguised as a girl and gives himself away by the way he threads a needle and catches a ball—that kind of thing. We learned that the way you sat, crossed your legs, held a cigarette and looked at your nails, your wristwatch, the way you did these things instinctively was absolute proof of your sex. Now obviously most children did not take this literally, but I did. I thought that just one slip, just one incorrect cross of my legs or flick of an imaginary cigarette

ash would turn me from whatever I was into the other thing; that would be all it took, really. Even though I was outwardly a girl and had many of the trappings generally associated with the field of girldom—a girl's name, for example, and dresses, my own telephone, an autograph book—I spent the early years of my adolescence absolutely certain that I might at any point gum it up. I did not feel at all like a girl. I was boyish. I was athletic, ambitious, outspoken, competitive, noisy, rambunctious. I had scabs on my knees and my socks slid into my loafers and I could throw a football. I wanted desperately not to be that way, not to be a mixture of both things but instead just one, a girl, a definite indisputable girl. As soft and as pink as a nursery. And nothing would do that for me, I felt, but breasts.

2   I was about six months younger than everyone in my class, and so for about six months after it began, for six months after my friends had begun to develop—that was the word we used, develop—I was not particularly worried. I would sit in the bathtub and look down at my breasts and know that any day now, any second now, they would start growing like everyone else's. They didn't. "I want to buy a bra," I said to my mother one night. "What for?" she said. My mother was really hateful about bras, and by the time my third sister had gotten to the point where she was ready to want one, my mother had worked the whole business into a comedy routine. "Why not use a Band-Aid instead?" she would say. It was a source of great pride to my mother that she had never even had to wear a brassiere until she had her fourth child, and then only because her gynecologist made her. It was incomprehensible to me that anyone would ever be proud of something like that. It was the 1950s, for God's sake. Jane Russell. Cashmere sweaters. Couldn't my mother see that? *"I am too old to wear an undershirt."* Screaming. Weeping. Shouting. "Then don't wear an undershirt," said my mother. "But I want to buy a bra," "What for?"

3   I suppose that for most girls, breasts, brassieres, that entire thing, has more trauma, more to do with the coming of adolescence, of becoming a woman, than anything else. Certainly more than getting your period, although that too was traumatic, symbolic. But you could *see* breasts; they were there; they were visible. Whereas a girl could claim to have her period for months before she actually got it and nobody would ever know the difference. Which is exactly what I did. All you had to do was make a great fuss over having enough nickels for the Kotex machine and walk around clutching your stomach and moaning for three to five days a month about The Curse and you could convince anybody. There is a school of thought somewhere in the women's lib/women's mag/gynecology establishment that claims that menstrual cramps are purely psychological, and I lean toward it. Not that I didn't have them finally.

Agonizing cramps, heating-pad cramps, go-down-to-the-school-nurse-and-lie-on-the-cot cramps. But unlike any pain I have ever suffered, I adored the pain of cramps, welcomed it, wallowed in it, bragged about it. "I can't go. I have cramps." "I can't do that. I have cramps." And most of all, gigglingly, blushingly: "I can't swim. I have cramps." Nobody ever used the hard-core word. Menstruation. God, what an awful word. Never that. "I have cramps."

4   The morning I first got my period, I went into my mother's bedroom to tell her. And my mother, my utterly-hateful-about-bras mother, burst into tears. It was really a lovely moment, and I remember it so clearly not just because it was one of the two times I ever saw my mother cry on my account (the other was when I was caught being a six-year-old kleptomaniac), but also because the incident did not mean to me what it meant to her. Her little girl, her firstborn, had finally become a woman. That was what she was crying about. My reaction to the event, however, was that I might well be a woman in some scientific, textbook sense (and could at least stop faking every month and stop wasting all those nickels). But in another sense—in a visible sense—I was as androgynous and as liable to tip over into boyhood as ever.

5   I started with a 28AA bra. I don't think they made them any smaller in those days, although I gather that now you can buy bras for five year olds that don't have any cups whatsoever in them; trainer bras they are called. My first brassiere came from Robinson's Department Store in Beverly Hills. I went there alone, shaking, positive they would look me over and smile and tell me to come back next year. An actual fitter took me into the dressing room and stood over me while I took off my blouse and tried the first one on. The little puffs stood out on my chest. "Lean over," said the fitter (to this day I am not sure what fitters in bra departments do except to tell you to lean over). I leaned over, with the fleeing hope that my breasts would miraculously fall out of my body and into the puffs. Nothing.

6   "Don't worry about it," said my friend Libby some months later, when things had not improved. "You'll get them after you're married."

7   "What are you talking about?" I said.

8   "When you get married," Libby explained, "your husband will touch your breasts and rub them and kiss them and they'll grow."

9   That was the killer. Necking I could deal with. Intercourse I could deal with. But it had never crossed my mind that a man was going to touch my breasts, that breasts had something to do with all that, petting, my God they never mentioned petting in my little sex manual about fertilization of the ovum. I became dizzy. For I knew instantly—as naïve as I had been only a moment before—that only part of what she was saying was true: the touching, rubbing, kissing part, not the growing part. And I

knew that no one would ever want to marry me. I had no breasts. I would never have breasts.

10   My best friend in school was Diana Raskob. She lived a block from me in a house full of wonders. English muffins, for instance. The Raskobs were the first people in Beverly Hills to have English muffins for breakfast. They also had an apricot tree in the back, and a badminton court, and a subscription to *Seventeen* magazine, and hundreds of games like Sorry and Parcheesi and Treasure Hunt and Anagrams. Diana and I spent three or four afternoons a week in their den reading and playing and eating. Diana's mother's kitchen was full of the most colossal assortment of junk food I have ever been exposed to. My house was full of apples and peaches and milk and homemade chocolate-chip cookies—which were nice, and good for you, but-not-right-before-dinner-or-you'll-spoil-your-appetite. Diana's house had nothing in it that was good for you, and what's more, you could stuff it in right up until dinner and nobody cared. Bar-B-Q potato chips (they were the first in them, too), giant bottles of ginger ale, fresh popcorn with melted butter, hot fudge sauce on Baskin-Robbins jamoca ice cream, powdered-sugar doughnuts from Van de Kamps. Diana and I had been best friends since we were seven; we were about equally popular in school (which is to say, not particularly), we had about the same success with boys (extremely intermittent) and we looked much the same. Dark. Tall. Gangly.

11   It is September, just before school begins. I am eleven years old, about to enter the seventh grade, and Diana and I have not seen each other all summer. I have been to camp and she has been somewhere like Banff with her parents. We are meeting, as we often do, on the street midway between out two houses and will walk back to Diana's and eat junk and talk about what has happened to each of us that summer. I am walking down Walden Drive in my jeans and my father's shirt hanging out and my old red loafers with the socks falling into them and coming toward me is . . . I take a deep breath . . . a young woman. Diana. Her hair is curled and she has a waist and hips and a bust and she is wearing a straight skirt, an article of clothing I have been repeatedly told that I will be unable to wear until I have the hips to hold it up. My jaw drops, and suddenly I am crying, crying hysterically, can't catch my breath sobbing. My best friend has betrayed me. She has gone ahead without me and done it. She has shaped up.

12   Here are some things I did to help:

13   Bought a Mark Eden Bust Developer.

14   Slept on my back for four years.

15   Splashed cold water on them every night because some French actress said in *Life* magazine that that was what *she* did for her perfect bustline.

16   Ultimately, I resigned myself to a bad toss and began to wear padded bras. I think about them now, think about all those years in high school I went around in them, my three padded bras, every single one of them with different sized breasts. Each time I changed bras I changed sizes: one week nice perky but not too obtrusive breasts, the next medium-sized slightly pointed ones, the next week knockers, true knockers; all the time, whatever size I was, carrying around this rubberized appendage on my chest that occasionally crashed into a wall and was poked inward and had to be poked outward—I think about all that and wonder how anyone kept a straight face through it. My parents, who normally had no restraints about needling me—why did they say nothing as they watched my chest go up and down? My friends, who would periodically inspect my breasts for signs of growth and reassure me—why didn't they at least counsel consistency?

17   And the bathing suits. I die when I think about the bathing suits. That was the era when you could lay an uninhabited bathing suit on the beach and someone would make a pass at it. I would put one on, an absurd swimsuit with its enormous bust built into it, the bones from the suit stabbing me in the rib cage and leaving little red welts on my body, and there I would be, my chest plunging straight downward absolutely vertically from my collarbone to the top of my suit and then suddenly, wham, out came all that padding and material and wiring absolutely horizontally.

18   Buster Klepper was the first boy who ever touched them. He was my boyfriend my senior year of high school. There is a picture of him in my high-school yearbook that makes him look quite attractive in a Jewish, horn-rimmed glasses sort of way, but the picture does not show the pimples, which were air-brushed out, or the dumbness. Well, that isn't really fair. He wasn't dumb. He just wasn't terribly bright. His mother refused to accept it, refused to accept the relentlessly average report cards, refused to deal with her son's inevitable destiny in some junior college or other. "He was tested," she would say to me, apropos of nothing, "and it came out 145. That's near-genius." Had the word underachiever been coined, she probably would have lobbed that one at me, too. Anyway, Buster was really very sweet—which is, I know, damning with faint praise, but there it is. I was the editor of the front page of the high-school newspaper and he was editor of the back page; we had to work together, side by side, in the print shop, and that was how it started. On our first date, we went to see *April Love* starring Pat Boone. Then we started going together. Buster had a green coupe, a 1950 Ford with an engine he had handchromed until it shone, dazzled, reflected the image of anyone who looked into it, anyone usually being Buster polishing it or the gas-station attendants he constantly asked to check the oil

in order for them to be overwhelmed by the sparkle on the valves. The car also had a boot stretched over the back seat for reasons I never understood; hanging from the rearview mirror, as was the custom, was a pair of angora dice. A previous girl friend named Solange who was famous throughout Beverly Hills High School for having no pigment in her right eyebrow had knitted them for him. Buster and I would ride around town, the two of us seated to the left of the steering wheel. I would shift gears. It was nice.

19   There was necking. Terrific necking. First in the car, overlooking Los Angeles from what is now the Trousdale Estates. Then on the bed of his parents' cabana at Ocean House. Incredibly wonderful, frustrating necking, I loved it, really, but no further than necking, please don't, please, because there I was absolutely terrified of the general implications of going-a-step-further with a near-dummy and also terrified of his finding out there was next to nothing there (which he knew, of course; he wasn't that dumb).

20   I broke up with him at one point. I think we were apart for about two weeks. At the end of that time I drove down to see a friend at a boarding school in Palos Verdes Estates and a disc jockey played *April Love* on the radio four times during the trip. I took it as a sign. I drove straight back to Griffith Park to a golf tournament Buster was playing in (he was the sixth-seeded teen-age golf player in Southern California) and presented myself back to him on the green of the 18th hole. It was all very dramatic. That night we went to a drive-in and I let him get his hand under my protuberances and onto my breasts. He really didn't seem to mind at all.

21   *"Do you want to marry my son?" the woman asked me.*

22   *"Yes," I said.*

23   *I was nineteen years old, a virgin, going with this woman's son, this big strange woman who was married to a Lutheran minister in New Hampshire and pretended she was Gentile and had this son, by her first husband, this total fool of a son who ran the hero-sandwich concession at Harvard Business School and whom for one moment one December in New Hampshire I said—as much out of politeness as anything else— that I wanted to marry.*

24   *"Fine," she said. "Now, here's what you do. Always make sure you're on top of him so you won't seem so small. My bust is very large, you see, so I always lie on my back to make it look smaller, but you'll have to be on top most of the time."*

25   *I nodded. "Thank you," I said.*

26   *"I have a book for you to read," she went on. "Take it with you when you leave. Keep it." She went to the bookshelf, found it, and gave it to me. It was a book on frigidity.*

27   *"Thank you," I said.*

28   That is a true story. Everything in this article is a true story, but I feel I have to point out that that story in particular is true. It happened on December 30, 1960. I think about it often. When it first happened, I naturally assumed that the woman's son, my boyfriend, was responsible. I invented a scenario where he had had a little heart-to-heart with his mother and had confessed that his only objection to me was that my breasts were small; his mother then took it upon herself to help out. Now I think I was wrong about the incident. The mother was acting on her own, I think: that was her way of being cruel and competitive under the guise of being helpful and maternal. You have small breasts, she was saying; therefore you will never make him as happy as I have. Or you have small breasts; therefore you will doubtless have sexual problems. Or you have small breasts; therefore you are less woman than I am. She was, as it happens, only the first of what seems to me to be a never-ending string of women who have made competitive remarks to me about breast size. "I would love to wear a dress like that," my friend Emily says to me, "but my bust is too big." Like that. Why do women say these things to me? Do I attract these remarks the way other women attract married men or alcoholics or homosexuals? This summer, for example. I am at a party in East Hampton and I am introduced to a woman from Washington. She is a minor celebrity, very pretty and Southern and blonde and outspoken and I am flattered because she has read something I have written. We are talking animatedly, we have been talking no more than five minutes, when a man comes up to join us. "Look at the two of us," the woman says to the man, indicating me and her. "The two of us together couldn't fill an A cup." Why does she say that? It isn't even true, dammit, so why? Is she even more addled than I am on this subject? Does she honestly believe there is something wrong with her size breasts, which, it seems to me, now that I look hard at them, are just right. Do I unconsciously bring out competitiveness in women? In that form? What did I do to deserve it?

29   As for men.

30   There were men who minded and let me know they minded. There were men who did not mind. In any case, I always minded.

31   And even now, now that I have been countlessly reassured that my figure is a good one, now that I am grown up enough to understand that most of my feelings have very little to do with the reality of my shape, I am nonetheless obsessed by breasts. I cannot help it. I grew up in the terrible Fifties—with rigid stereotypical sex roles, the insistence that men be men and dress like men and women be women and dress like women, the intolerance of androgyny—and I cannot shake it, cannot shake my feelings of inadequacy. Well, that time is gone, right? All those exagger-

ated examples of breast worship are gone, right? Those women were freaks, right? I know all that. And yet, here I am, stuck with the psychological remains of it all, stuck with my own peculiar version of breast worship. You probably think I am crazy to go on like this: here I have set out to write a confession that is meant to hit you with the shock of recognition and instead you are sitting there thinking I am thoroughly warped. Well, what can I tell you? If I had had them, I would have been a completely different person. I honestly believe that.

32   After I went into therapy, a process that made it possible for me to tell total strangers at cocktail parties that breasts were the hang-up of my life, I was often told that I was insane to have been bothered by my condition. I was also frequently told, by close friends, that I was extremely boring on the subject. And my girl friends, the ones with nice big breasts, would go on endlessly about how their lives had been far more miserable than mine. Their bra straps were snapped in class. They couldn't sleep on their stomachs. They were stared at whenever the word "mountain" cropped up in geography. And *Evangeline*, good God what they went through every time someone had to stand up and recite the Prologue to Longfellow's *Evangeline*: "*. . . stand like druids of eld . . . /With beards that rest on their bosoms.*" It was much worse for them, they tell me. They had a terrible time of it, they assure me. I don't know how lucky I was, they say.

33   I have thought about their remarks, tried to put myself in their place, considered their point of view. I think they are full of shit.

TO THINK ABOUT

1. Ephron deals casually with what many would consider a taboo subject. What is the effect of this relaxed approach?
2. Ephron opens the piece with a discussion of "a rigid set of rules that supposedly determined whether we were boys or girls." What accounts for the existence of unwritten, yet often tyrannical, codes of conduct?
3. Ephron writes that she bought a bust developer, slept on her back, and splashed cold water on her breasts in order to stimulate growth. Why would an intelligent young woman try such clearly bogus methods?
4. Compare "A Few Words About Breasts" with "High Heels" by Caryl Rivers (Chapter 39). What are the similarities between the two pieces? What are the differences?

TO DO

1. Imagine that the narrator of this essay is *speaking* it to you over a drink. What would *your* side of the conversation be like? Select a passage and, where appropriate, respond to the narrator.
2. Make a list (privately) of your own physical characteristics. Write about the one which preoccupies you the most, and about how you think it affects your interaction with others. Try imitating Nora Ephron's voice.
3. Write about someone you know who is inordinately preoccupied with physical appearance. Do it sympathetically. Get beyond the *what* of the situation and concentrate on the *why*.

TIP

When we read or write about matters as intimate as the importance of physical characteristics we may become embarrassed or defensive. Sometimes we mask these feelings with braggadocio or ridicule. If you find yourself writing in either of these modes, stop; think, for a moment, of the effect these voices have on your readers, and on your readers' perception of you, the narrator. Now try another voice.

12

Handicapped
Judy Foreman

We find much raw material for writing in the events taking place in the natural course of our lives. But sometimes we become curious about experiences we have not had, and are not likely to have—unless we deliberately go about setting them up. George Plimpton, the gangly editor of the Paris Review, *popularized this form of journalism in* Paper Lion, *the book that recounted his adventures in the training camp of the Detroit Lions of the National Football League. Ever since, journalists have been finding out first hand about everything from bullfighting to skydiving. But the form is not restricted to sports.*

Can an able-bodied person write knowledgeably about what it is like to be a quadriplegic? Boston Globe reporter Judy Foreman sought to find out by spending a day in a wheelchair, in the company of a genuine "quad." She learned much about being handicapped—but even more about herself.

1   It is 8:15 A.M. Marc Fiedler's Brookline apartment. No way to stall any longer. I park outside.

2   He is at the doorway of his apartment, reaching onto the floor of the hallway for the New York Times. He sees me, and a bit shakily, extends his right hand, though his fingers don't seem to work. But thank God. We can shake hands. Literally, a touch of normality.

3   He begins chatting easily. He is good-looking, with black hair, glasses and a mustache, a little pale, perhaps, but dressed neatly in a business suit and not at all slumping in his chair. Maybe this won't be so bad.

4   I am, unlike an estimated 3 to 7 percent of the American population, totally able-bodied.

5   But Marc, 24, is a "quad" (quadriplegic) who broke his neck in a car accident four years ago, one of approximately 400,000 Americans suffering paralysis from spinal cord injuries.

6   I see the wheelchair waiting for me in the corner of his living room. I avoid it. Instead, I sit on the arm of the couch and say that when we go downstairs to get into the handicapped people's van, I'll zip over and roll up my car windows.

7   "I think you'd better go down now and do that before we start," Marc says firmly. We have made a bargain. I want to know what life is like in a wheelchair, what things look like from a permanent sitting position three feet below everybody else's eye level.

8   Marc is the deputy director of the new state Office of Handicapped Affairs and has agreed to squire me around, letting me borrow a friend's wheelchair, but I have to behave handicapped all day. No getting out to stretch. No telling people I'm faking it. No cheating. I wonder if people will treat me differently just because my legs are hanging apparently useless from this ugly, metal contraption which seems to have STIGMA written all over it.

9   I run down to roll up the windows and return. Marc wheels into his room to get his briefcase, leaving me alone to face the chair.

10   I go over to it, fix the foam cushion and stare. Finally I sit. I immediately feel ugly and awkward, and I haven't even tried to move it. This is going to be awful. I hate it already.

11   There are books in his bookcase, including one right at my eye level which is one of my favorites, Jim Fixx's book on running. (I am a jogger.) The coffee table is between me and the book. I'll leaf through it some other day.

12   Marc's roommate Cliff bustles around, a strong-looking black man I later find out is Marc's "personal care attendant," paid for by public funds, but by now a friend.

13   The running book must be his, lucky guy. Probably doesn't even realize how lucky he is to be able to walk, let alone run.

14   I practice a little before we attempt the elevator and, in a few minutes, the van. Steering is not so bad; in fact, a lot like turning a canoe, by moving one wheel backward and the other forward. But the huge wheels keep sticking out farther than I think. I bang into the doorway. I feel like a klutz.

15   On the way out, I see a six-pack of Molson's ale on the kitchen counter. For some reason, it cheers me up immensely. Life can't be that difficult if you can still come home after work and have a good beer.

16   Marc follows me into the hallway. I get to the elevator first and try to reach the button. After all, I am the able-bodied one. But to my surprise, I can't do it. Marc, who has to use a kind of throwing motion to bang his forefinger knuckle against the button succeeds.

17   I start in first.

18   "Can you manage by yourself? It only will fit one of us," says Marc.

19   The elevator didn't even look small to me on my trip up.

20   Inside, I am faced all wrong, with my back to the door through which I will have to exit. I sit through the ride with my finger on the Door Open button, afraid of getting stuck part way out when the door opens. I make it, wheeling out backwards.

21   All right! Triumph! I'm pretty good at this!

22   Then it hits: has my world shrunk so much already that, in just five minutes, successfully negotiating a lousy elevator has become a big deal?

23   Outside, I let Marc show me how to get onto the mechanized ramp to the van. But when it's my turn, I forget to lock my wheels and start to slide down. The driver-attendant has opened the side door of the van, I bang my elbow trying to back into my place along the van wall. I get my small front wheels, which keep going their own way, tangled with Marc's. I feel so frustrated. Again the driver has to do it for me.

24   As Marc rips off two 75-cent MBTA van tickets from his booklet by using his hands and his teeth, I see a woman bicycling and a man jogging. Don't they see me in here and know that I'm really one of them? How can I let them know I'm not really in this wheelchair in this van?

25   We arrive at the McCormack building and the van driver wheels me up the twisty ramp. I don't care. It must be close to 90 degrees today. Why should I push myself up? I feel embarassed and helpless to be pushed like a baby in a carriage. But I don't have any good choices. I am in a stupid wheelchair.

26   Marc is wheeling himself up the ramp and it takes him several minutes. Well, let him do it the hard way.

27   I see a man in a wheelchair outside the building. I'm not like him. Can't he see there's really nothing wrong with me? He doesn't even seem very disabled, because I can see him stretching his legs. He smiles.

28   As Marc rolls up, I see the revolving doors. How in heaven's name am I going to be able to push the wheelchair and the doors at the same time? It's hard enough to deal with revolving doors on foot without getting your heels mashed. Marc points out the side door, a regular push door with round doorknob.

29   "Revolving doors are impossible," says Marc, "but you'll get to love the sliding doors like they have in supermarkets." He makes me look closely at the doorknob of the door we'll go through, a normal, everyday doorknob.

30   "If they put levers on these doors instead of round knobs, handicapped people who can't grasp things could open them easily. So could people carrying bundles. You could even open them with your elbow."

31   Marc cannot really grip the handle, but using gravity and the weight of his hand, opens the door anyway and wheels through. I can't reach far enough out from my sitting position to push the door with one hand and

move my wheelchair forward with the other. Among other things, wheeling only one wheel turns the chair. My foot pedals clang into the door jam. Finally, someone holds the door for me.

32   We reach Marc's office.

33   His boss and office mate, Michael Robson, able-bodied, comes in and asks if I could please open the blinds to let in some early morning, not yet-scorching sunshine.

34   Why doesn't he do it himself? He has legs and arms that work. But I am secretly pleased to be treated normally.

35   Getting my wheelchair where I want it in that cramped office is like spending all day parking a car, making little K-turn, backing and turning. It takes me several minutes to get close enough to reach the pullchords for the blinds and then I can only barely reach over the wide window sill to do it. The venetianlike blinds jam up on themselves and I can't reach far enough to straighten them out. So we won't have sunshine. I don't care. Maybe someone else will come along and open them. The effort-to reward ratio in a wheelchair seems like 100 to one against me.

36   Just before 10 A.M., Marc and I start upstairs to a conference room where he will address a group of handicapped Boston high school students from a vocational education summer program.

37   We both fit onto the same elevator, but it is hell.

38   A very good-looking blond man in a three-piece suit attracts my attention. Normally, there would be that momentarily-held eye contact, the flicker of a small smile, one of the safe elevator flirtations of everyday life.

39   But he is looking right over me. My eyes are easily three feet lower than his. I feel unpretty, unnoticed and furious. How are you supposed to deal with the world when everybody is literally looking down at you or not seeing you at all? How can you possibly feel equal and dignified like this? How are you supposed to feel pretty and flirty in this dumb chair?

40   At each floor, people from the back of the elevator have to stumble and climb over our wheels, muttering "I'm sorry" or "Excuse me." They are very nice about it. But I don't want to be in their way. I hate being an obstacle, causing them inconvenience.

41   Marc nicely and assertively asks someone to push the button for our floor. I feel I could never do that. Ask for help with that kind of dignity.

42   We wheel into the conference room, and my heart sinks. I feel humiliated enough being in a wheelchair. But some of these kids are in wheelchairs and look retarded besides. To make matters worse, they seem to think I'm one of them. Can't they see I'm normal except for the wheelchair? My rush to distance myself emotionally from them appalls

me. I am supposed to be tolerant and respectful but all I can think is, "Don't let anybody see me with them."

43   We all go on a tour of the State House, no easy trick for us "crips" because we have to push our wheelchairs or limp along on crutches up-hill from the McCormack building to the golden dome.

44   The potholes are impossible. The sun is beating down and the traffic is terrifying.

45   I really don't care enough about a State House tour to push myself up the hill.

46   But one of the kids' teachers walks along beside me and, very nicely but with complete respect, asks if I'd like a push. I accept, as grateful for the fact that he can help me with respect as for the push itself.

47   My values take a turn. Normally, in a busy street scene like this, I'd look at the faces of people scurrying by and wonder about their destinations, their hurry, their lives, their successes. Suddenly, kindness zooms to the top of my priority list, along with being looked at as though I were really a normal person. As though. Aren't I still? And what about the others in their chairs—are they, too?

48   The tour lady explains the marble, murals, domes and inscriptions. So what? History was not made by people in wheelchairs, with a few notable exceptions. Our chairs are awkward, making it hard to jockey for a good enough position to see what the tour guide is gesturing toward. I don't bother.

49   But as I start wheeling up the ramp to the House of Representatives chamber, something happens. Without conscious mental effort, I feel my attitude changing—though I can't pinpoint why I try to make it alone. It is much too steep and I slide backward and nearly fall over. But I feel like fighting the ramp. I bull my way up, rescued from tipping over by the tour lady. But her help seems now more like an assist. I almost did it myself.

50   The kids are all excited because Gov. King has decided to come out to greet us for a moment.

51   Maybe it's just the perspective from a wheelchair, but King looks more the hefty linebacker than ever to me, towering over us. He shakes hands with Marc and the rest of us and rarely makes eye contact. Marc winks to me as King proceeds down the line.

52   Marc quietly and firmly backs his wheelchair into a position where King will have to talk to him on the way back into the governor's office. Lobbying for a moment's contact with the governor, jockeying for position is a fine art in government and politics—and a wheelchair seems an impossible, unfair handicap. But Marc is determined, and in a few minutes, he succeeds.

53   King's voice booms out pleasantries as his eyes look right over us,

scanning the small crowd beyond. One retarded boy looks right at him and asks, "Where is Gov. Dukakis?" A wheelchair-ridden girl blurts out, "I like Gov. Dukakis (who signed the executive order which set up the new Office of Handicapped Affairs)." King seems not to notice.

54   The tour guide takes Marc aside to explain that, normally, the tour includes a visit to the state archives. But it is inaccessible to wheelchairs.

55   "That's really a shame," Marc says to her, locking her eyes for a minute, waiting for his message to sink in. It seems to.

56   Outside again in the blistering sun, our motley crew faces the hill from the parking lot back up to the street. The grade can't be more than a few degrees. In fact, I would never even have noticed it was a hill at all until today. But it feels like a summit expedition.

57   This time, though, I am off and rolling, slowly, thumbs getting mashed with each push of the wheels, but I make it easily, and more or less cheerfully, to the top.

58   It's not such a big deal. The kids cheer me on warmly now.

59   I have had to tell them that I am a reporter. When one of their teachers, himself wheelchair-bound because of MS (multiple sclerosis) inquired about my "disability," I had begun to fabricate a story, which ended with a vague assertion that I probably wouldn't be in a wheelchair forever.

60   I wanted to stick to the no-telling bargain I had made with Marc. But the teacher shook my hand warmly, saying he hoped and prayed I would make it out of the wheelchair. It became impossible to keep my cover and accept such kindness, and I decided to let the kids and their teachers in on our experiment.

61   Instead of feeling betrayed or bitter that my "handicap" was fake, while theirs were real, they were delighted with the idea of the experiment and glad for me that my wheelchair was not forever. What kind of people are these who would welcome me as one of them—and be so pleased for me that I am not?

62   At the top of the hill, we gather at a nice curb cut for wheelchairs. But a huge gas guzzler is parked right across it, and the curb is too high to ease a clumsy wheelchair down.

63   Marc, who has spent all morning telling the kids of their legal rights of access to public buildings and to jobs and to housing and to life itself, flags down a passing young woman and asks her to find a Capitol police officer to have the car towed.

64   "You know," he tells the kids," you are entitled to have the police move that car. And if you don't, no one else will."

65   "People don't believe that, with all disabilities lumped together, 7 percent of Americans are handicapped," he says. "That's because of

things like this, cars blocking curb cuts, elevator buttons which aren't raised so the blind can feel them, doorknobs, things like that. The handicapped are there—they just end up staying home because it gets to be too much trouble to go out."

66   Marc and I wheel back to the State House for the rest of the afternoon.

67   Laughing, I announce there is a problem I can't put off any longer.

68   I find a ladies' room, but it is not equipped for the handicapped. I can't face another wrestling match between me, my chair and the elevator which could take me to a restroom for the handicapped, so I attempt to use the one where I am.

69   First comes the huge, beautiful, heavy door with the ubiquitous round doorknob. I get it open about six inches, but keep steering my chair into the doorjam. A man finally comes by and holds the door for me. This has to be a first in chivalry, a man holding the door to the ladies' room and it feels odd.

70   The ladies' room is small, only two stalls, and I try to aim the wheelchair toward the closest one. It won't fit, which means when I try to transfer my weight (one hand on the none-too-sturdy toilet paper dispenser and the other on the seat), I am frightened I will be way off balance.

71   I succeed, but the bottom of my skirt falls in and gets soaked.

72   Transferring back to the chair is even harder, but thank God I thought to lock the brakes to prevent the chair from rolling away as I transfer my weight into it. (Marc later jokes with me that all of such possible disasters do happen to people in wheelchairs.)

73   But in the ladies' room, a pleasant surprise, the sink is high enough for my wheelchair to slip under and I can wash my hands easily. So what if the mirror is so high that I can't even see the top of my head, let alone comb my hair?

74   My mood is definitely changing, when I return to the hall where Marc waits for me, I have conquered something.

75   He smiles, and compares life now to his pre-accident days when he was planning an academic and research career at Harvard in psychology.

76   "Now, I'm much more assertive," he says. "And now, paradoxically enough. I am a man of action, not a man of the mind."

77   Shunning the more sheltered academic world for the State House and politics, he says, "I guess it's a human rights thing for me, a political thing, doing something because the world is so grossly unfair for handicapped people. It's not even so much the architectural barriers or lack of money—it's attitudinal barriers that are the worst. I know I'll be in a wheelchair forever, but that's not so bad. And it's no reason for society to exclude you from things."

78   Marc leaves for a few minutes and I sit watching the people go by. Without Marc as a buffer, I slowly become aware of an odd observation: The men rush by, busy, preoccupied, glancing quickly away once they see me. The women make eye contact and smile, and sometimes even say hello. Do the men simply not want to deal with afflictions? Are they uninterested in a woman sitting in a wheelchair?

79   A 60-ish black janitor with white hair pauses on his rounds. With utter kindness, he says, "It's amazing how you people get around." I realize he is the only one who has really noticed me, the only one who has spoken more than a "hello." He has the time to talk and the openness to make contact. Is he just a nice human being? Or do we both feel we are society's outcasts?

80   Marc returns and gives me the names of some "quads" who are friends of his.

81   On subsequent days, I will hear their stories. The man, paralyzed from the neck down, who has to get up an hour or two earlier than everybody else in hopes that the body over which he has no bladder and bowel control will do its thing in the privacy of his home, not his office. The man who has learned to deal with accidents by telling himself, "Okay, I had an accident. It's embarrassing. Tough. So what?" And continuing on with dignity.

82   And the man, paralyzed at age 16 many years ago, who couldn't find a doctor who could tell him whether or not he'd be capable of sex and reproduction. Of his visit to one doctor who gave then-radical advice: 'find a partner and experiment. Maybe it can work.' Of his joy when it did, including genital sensation. And his even greater joy, years later, when he and his wife produced a child, now a robust 11-year-old.

83   Another man, now the father of two, who has made himself an apparent professional success.

84   And the woman, paralyzed from the waist down, whose pregnancy was normal and who was delighted to discover that her labor—perhaps because of the diminished ability to feel pain—lasted only 15 minutes.

85   Suddenly, I realize that this day—which I had thought would never end, is nearly over. I have passed through in compressed form, many of the emotions that Marc, his friends and thousands of others feel forever, for real, every day.

86   Initial feelings of depression, frustration and a profound sense of shame and humiliation have turned slowly to more acceptance and the discovery that life in a wheelchair would be hard, but livable.

87   Passive, self-pitying acceptance of every push uphill, no matter how humiliating the help, has turned to making most hills and ramps an athletic contest, my own marathon, the hill against me, with me the winner.

88   I have learned—to my embarrassment and surprise—how hair-fine but crucial are the different shades of stigma in our society, how looking normal except for the wheelchair (the "clean cut quad look," as one disabled person later put it) seemed so much desperately "better" than being lumped with those who looked "worse off," particularly the retarded.

89   Marc and I end the day in the Boston office of a friend of his, where the three of us, all in wheelchairs, chat with the friend's secretary, an open, middle-aged, abled-bodied woman.

90   Marc's friend, who knows of our experiment, discusses the merits of his motorized wheelchair. The secretary—who is unaware of the experiment—is listening.

91   The time has come. I am almost—but not quite—reluctant to get out of the chair. It still shouts STIGMA to me, but that seems more like the world's problem, not mine.

92   I stir. My legs feel pins and needles. I stand up, stretching luxuriously, and begin to walk away from the chair.

93   By accident, I catch the secretary's eye. She is completely dumbfounded, her jaw as wide open as her eyes.

94   In an instant, the stunning effect of what I've just done hits us all.

95   Marc roars and cracks to his friend, "Hey, not bad. I guess our miracle cure is really coming along. Maybe you're next."

TO THINK ABOUT

1. What is the effect of Foreman's first paragraph on you, the reader?
2. How does the piece keep you engaged emotionally?
3. What is the turning point of the piece?
4. What is the significance of the narrator's encounter with the black janitor toward the end of the piece?

TO DO

1. Read "On Being a Cripple" by Nancy Mairs (Chapter 31). Compare and contrast the perspectives and insights of Mairs and Judy Foreman.
2. Make a list of things you've always wanted to do but have never done. Choose one and arrange to do it. The activity should be (a) within the realm of possibility; (b) inherently interesting to a general readership; (c) legal; (d) reversible (one of my students went out and got herself a tatoo); and (e) reasonably safe. (I do not want calls from parents who report that the last thing little Johnny said before attempting to jump thirty buses on his motorcycle was that he got the

idea from my book.) The activity need not be spectacular; one of the best pieces of this kind that I've seen is by a patrician sort of fellow who apprenticed himself to a garbage collector in the fishing city of Gloucester, Massachusetts.
3. Engage in your chosen activity.
4. Write a piece about it.

TIPS

1. You will probably need a mentor. When you try something for the first time, you need someone to guide you. A cooperative and articulate mentor, like Foreman's Marc Fiedler, is often critical to the success of such an endeavor.
2. Be sure to write about your feelings. It is not enough to give a blow-by-blow account of the mechanical aspects of your adventure. Readers want to experience the event vicariously through you, and to do that, they require access to your emotions. It is Judy Foreman's running account of what goes on *inside her head* that makes her piece a success.
3. Don't worry about showing your weaknesses and mistakes. A reader is much more likely to identify with, and empathize with, a vulnerable narrator than with one who insists on seeming flawless.

13

Bureaucracy/2
Bureaucracy/3
Eduardo Galeano

Eduardo Galeano was born in Montevideo, Uruguay, in 1940. He became a journalist and edited a series of daily and weekly newspapers. In 1973 he went into exile in Argentina to escape the dictatorship in Uruguay; from 1976 to 1984 he lived in Spain. In 1989 he published The Book of Embraces, *a series of brief essays, many of which address the conditions in Uruguay during the dictatorship. Galeano's voice in the following brief essays is intentionally flat, toneless, like an official report. The voice is in stark contrast to the material it conveys.*

Bureaucracy/2

1   Tito Sclavo managed to see and transcribe some official documents in the prison called Liberty during the years of the Uruguayan dictatorship. They were rules for punishment: prisoners committing the crime of drawing birds or couples or pregnant women, or those caught using flowered towels, were sentenced to solitary confinement. One prisoner, who like everyone else had his head shaved clean, was punished *"for entering the dining room uncombed."* Another *"for sticking his head under the door"*—though one millimeter of light passed beneath the door. Solitary confinement also awaited the prisoner who *"tried to befriend a military dog"* and another who *"insulted a dog who was a member of the Armed*

Forces." Another earned the same reward for *"barking like a dog for no good reason."*

Bureaucracy/3

1   Sixto Martínez completed his military service at a barracks in Seville.

2   In the middle of the courtyard of that barracks was a small bench. Next to the small bench, a soldier stood guard. No one knew why the bench had to be guarded. The bench was guarded around the clock, just because: every day, every night, and from one generation of officers to the next the order was passed on and the soldiers obeyed it. No one expressed any doubts or ever asked why. If that's how it was done, and that's how it had always been done, there had to be a reason.

3   And so it continued until someone, some general or colonel, wanted to look at the original order. He had to rummage through all the files. After a good deal of poking around, he found the answer. Thirty-one years, two months and four days ago, an officer had ordered a guard to be stationed beside the small bench, which had just been painted, so that no one would think of sitting on the wet paint.

TO THINK ABOUT

1. Imagine the voice you use reflexively when you are outraged. If you are like most of us, this voice is loud, angry, aggressive. And the material it conveys is general and vague, rather than specific. This is true in writing as well as speaking, and it is true in public discourse as well as private communication. Political rhetoric and letters to former lovers can be equally harsh. Consider the effect of such harsh rhetoric. How persuasive is it?
2. Imagine how Eduardo Galeano might have conveyed the information in "Bureaucracy/2" and "Bureaucracy/3" had he succumbed to the temptation to vent his anger in the conventional manner. How might such a tirade have sounded?
3. Now compare the effects of the two voices, the calm and the strident. Which is more effective? Why?

TO DO

1. Think of whatever makes you angry these days. Write about it non-stop, as fast as you can, for about fifteen minutes.
2. Take a careful look at what you have just written. Is it general or specific? Angry or calm?
3. Write the piece again, this time approaching the subject the way Galeano would. Simply convey the specifics of the situation in a flat voice, with little or no commentary.
4. Now compare the two pieces. Which do you think is more persuasive?

TIP

As a rule, anger in a piece of writing works only if the cause of the anger is sufficient to move your readers to anger as well. War, hunger, racism, sexism, injustice on a major scale—these are worth your anger. The quality of the food in the college dining hall is not. Neither is the length of the line at the registrar's office. These are annoyances, probably not worth your writing time and energy. Before you start writing, think: Is there an audience out there for this piece?

14

38 Who Saw Murder Didn't Call the Police

Martin Gansberg

A murder that takes place in a small town is big news. A murder that takes place in a big city is not, unless there is something exceptional about it: the murder of a prominent citizen, for example, or a gangland killing. The murder of Kitty Genovese in March 1964 was neither of these. Sadly, it was not an unusual murder. But because of certain circumstances, and because of reporter Martin Gansberg's account of those circumstances, the Genovese murder will always be remembered as one of the most shameful examples of citizen apathy in the history of New York City and, perhaps, the entire country. Gansberg's piece appeared in The New York Times, *March 27, 1964. His voice is calm. He lets the facts speak for themselves.*

1   For more than half an hour 38 respectable, law-abiding citizens in Queens watched a killer stalk and stab a woman in three separate attacks in Kew Gardens.

2   Twice their chatter and the sudden glow of their bedroom lights interrupted him and frightened him off. Each time he returned, sought her out, and stabbed her again. Not one person telephoned the police during the assault; one witness called after the woman was dead.

3   That was two weeks ago today.

4   Still shocked is Assistant Chief Inspector Frederick M. Lussen, in charge of the borough's detectives and a veteran of 25 years of homicide investigations. He can give a matter-of-fact recitation on many murders. But the Kew Gardens slaying baffles him—not because it is a murder, but because the "good people" failed to call the police.

5   "As we have reconstructed the crime," he said, "the assailant had three chances to kill this woman during a 35-minute period. He returned

twice to complete the job. If we had been called when he first attacked, the woman might not be dead now."

6   This is what the police say happened beginning at 3:20 A.M. in the staid, middle-class, tree-lined Austin Street area:

7   Twenty-eight-year-old Catherine Genovese, who was called Kitty by almost everyone in the neighborhood, was returning home from her job as manager of a bar in Hollis. She parked her red Fiat in a lot adjacent to the Kew Gardens Long Island Rail Road Station, facing Mowbray Place. Like many residents of the neighborhood, she had parked there day after day since her arrival from Connecticut a year ago, although the railroad frowns on the practice.

8   She turned off the lights of her car, locked the door, and started to walk the 100 feet to the entrance of her apartment at 82–70 Austin Street, which is in a Tudor building, with stores in the first floor and apartments on the second.

9   The entrance to the apartment is in the rear of the building because the front is rented to retail stores. At night the quiet neighborhood is shrouded in the slumbering darkness that marks most residential areas.

10   Miss Genovese noticed a man at the far end of the lot, near a seven-story apartment house at 82–40 Austin Street. She halted. Then nervously, she headed up Austin Street toward Lefferts Boulevard, where there is a call box to the 102nd Police Precinct in nearby Richmond Hill.

11   She got as far as a street light in front of a bookstore before the man grabbed her. She screamed. Lights went on in the 10-story apartment house at 82–67 Austin Street, which faces the bookstore. Windows slid open and voices punctuated the early-morning stillness.

12   Miss Genovese screamed: "Oh, my God, he stabbed me! Please help me! Please help me!"

13   From one of the upper windows in the apartment house, a man called down: "Let that girl alone!"

14   The assailant looked up at him, shrugged and walked down Austin Street toward a white sedan parked a short distance away. Miss Genovese struggled to her feet.

15   Lights went out. The killer returned to Miss Genovese, now trying to make her way around the side of the building by her parking lot to get to her apartment. The assailant stabbed her again.

16   "I'm dying!" she shrieked. "I'm dying!"

17   Windows were opened again, and lights went on in many apartments. The assailant got into his car and drove away. Miss Genovese staggered to her feet. A city bus, O–10, the Lefferts Boulevard line to Kennedy International Airport, passed. It was 3:35 A.M.

18   The assailant returned. By then, Miss Genovese had crawled to the back of the building where the freshly painted brown doors to the

apartment house held out hope for safety. The killer tried the first door; she wasn't there. At the second door, 82–62 Austin Street, he saw her slumped on the floor at the foot of the stairs. He stabbed her a third time—fatally.

19   It was 3:50 by the time the police received their first call, from a man who was a neighbor of Miss Genovese. In two minutes they were at the scene. The neighbor, a 70-year-old woman, and another woman were the only persons on the street. Nobody else came forward.

20   The man explained that he had called the police after much deliberation. He had phoned a friend in Nassau County for advice and then he had crossed the roof of the building to the apartment of the elderly woman to get her to make the call.

21   "I didn't want to get involved," he sheepishly told the police.

22   Six days later, the police arrested Winston Moseley, a 29-year-old business-machine operator, and charged him with homicide. Moseley had no previous record. He is married, has two children and owns a home at 133–19 Sutter Avenue, South Ozone Park, Queens. On Wednesday, a court committed him to Kings County Hospital for psychiatric observation.

23   When questioned by the police, Moseley also said that he had slain Mrs. Annie May Johnson, 24, of 146–12 133rd Avenue, Jamaica, on Feb. 29 and Barbara Kralik, 15, of 174–17 140th Avenue, Springfield Gardens, last July. In the Kralik case, the police are holding Alvin L. Mitchell, who is said to have confessed that slaying.

24   The police stressed how simple it would have been to have gotten in touch with them. "A phone call," said one of the detectives, "would have done it." The police may be reached by dialing "O" for operator or SPring 7–3100.

25   Today witnesses from the neighborhood, which is made up of one-family homes in the $35,000 to $60,000 range with the exception of the two apartment houses near the railroad station, find it difficult to explain why they didn't call the police.

26   A housewife, knowingly if quite casually, said, "We thought it was a lover's quarrel." A husband and wife both said, "Frankly, we were afraid." They seemed aware of the fact that events might have been different. A distraught woman, wiping her hands on her apron, said, "I didn't want my husband to get involved."

27   One couple, now willing to talk about that night, said they heard the first screams. The husband looked thoughtfully at the bookstore where the killer first grabbed Miss Genovese.

28   "We went to the window to see what was happening," he said, "but the light from our bedroom made it difficult to see the street." The wife, still apprehensive, added: "I put out the light and we were able to see better."

29   Asked why they hadn't called the police, she shrugged and replied: "I don't know."

30   A man peeked out from a light opening in the doorway to his apartment and rattled off an account of the killer's second attack. Why hadn't he called the police at the time? "I was tired," he said without emotion. "I went back to bed."

31   It was 4:25 A.M. when the ambulance arrived to take the body of Miss Genovese. It drove off. "Then," a solemn police detective said, "the people came out."

TO THINK ABOUT

1. Martin Gansberg takes no overt position on the events he describes. What is the theme of the piece? How is it implied?
2. In what position does Gansberg place the reader?
3. What is the structure of this piece?
4. If a similar incident were to take place in your hometown, would witnesses call the police or do nothing for fear of "getting involved"? What would *you* do?

TO DO

1. Make a list of incidents in which timely intervention by you or someone you know prevented an injustice. Make another list of incidents in which intervention never came. Write an essay about one or more of these incidents.
2. Write a similar essay about *inappropriate* intervention: there are times when no action is the best alternative.
3. Combine the two essays into one.

TIP

The strength of an essay of this kind lies in the details. It is one thing to rail on, in general terms, against apathy; it is another to show the results of one instance of apathy in chilling detail. This principle applies to nearly all good writing.

If you think a piece of writing is weak, but are not sure why, try this: read each paragraph separately. If the paragraph is general in nature, mark it with a *G*. If it is filled with specifics, mark it with an *S*. In most strong essays, the *S*'s will outnumber the *G*'s.

15

Canon Confidential: A Sam Slade Caper

Henry Louis Gates

*Have you ever wondered why certain books are required read-
ing in high school and college English classes, while others are not?
In fact, the lists are not as immutable as they may appear. One
decade's must-read is another's forgotten remainder. And the business of who is on the list and who is off is serious stuff, the subject
of heated (and sometimes stuffy) debate among literary critics of
different stripes: Marxists, feminists, deconstructionists, Lacanians,
and many others.*

*Here Henry Louis Gates, director of African American studies
at Harvard University, general editor of* The Norton Anthology of
African-American Literature, *and himself one of the most prominent
and respected critics in America, lets us in on the bizarre dynamics
of the keeping of the Canon. To unravel the mystery he uses the
voice and the persona of Dashiel Hammett's classic private eye,
Sam Spade.*

1   Her name was Estelle. I should have known the broad spelled trouble when she came into my office and started talking about the canon.
The literary canon.

2   I stubbed out my Lucky Strike and glanced up at her, taking in her
brass-blond hair, all curled and stiff with spray. Like she had a still of
Betty Grable taped to the corner of her mirror.

3   Turned out she'd been peddling her story for the past couple of
years. Nobody would take it on; I shouldn't have either. But when I was a
kid I used to write doggerel. Maybe that's why I didn't throw the babe
out of my office.

4   "Tell me what I need to know, sugar." I splashed some bourbon in
my coffee mug, put my feet on my desk, and listened.

5   Seemed there was some kind of a setup that determined which authors get on this A list of great literature. Payout was all perks, so far as I could make out. If you're on this list, they teach your work in school and write critical essays on you. Waldenbooks moves you from the Fiction section to the Literature section. I couldn't figure where the percentage was, unless some big shot was getting a cut of the reprint royalties, but she didn't think that was it.

6   "So what are you saying? You want me to shut down this operation? Round up the bad guys?"

7   "Nothing like that," she said huskily. "I got no beef with the canon as such. It serves a legit purpose." She looked around nervously and lowered her voice. "What I'm telling you is, it's fixed. It's not on the level." She paused. "What I'm telling you is, this is the biggest scam since the 1919 World Series."

8   I whistled softly. "We're talking thousands of books, right? The jewels of Western culture, right?"

9   She nodded. "You'll be going up against the big boys. Does that scare you?"

10   I patted my shoulder holster. "I'm prepared."

11   "You get twenty-five a day plus expenses," she said.

12   I said, "Fair enough." It was all Philip Marlowe got in *Trouble Is My Business.*

· · ·

13   The first person I spoke to was Helen Vendler, and all she was sure of was I was wasting my time.

14   I found her at the Harvard Club, on Forty-fourth Street off Fifth Avenue, eating alone. She swore up and down I was being snookered.

15   "Oh, I hear the talk. But it's just a tabloid fantasy," she assured me, fastidiously squeezing a lemon section over her oysters. "There is no overlord, Slade. Nobody's fixing what we read—the whole idea's preposterous. If a book's good, people read it. If it's bad, people won't."

16   She was smug about it. Too smug.

17   "They've got something on you, don't they?" I said, thinking hard. "That's why they let you edit *The Harvard Book of Contemporary American Poetry*—because they knew you'd do their dirty work for them."

18   She wasn't smiling anymore. "You won't get a thing out of me," she said. Then I saw her make eye contact with the bouncer. All three hundred pounds of him. "Malloy," she said quietly, "get him out of here."

19   Figured a walk would do me good anyway.

20   I looked up a few of the writers I knew, but I didn't fare much better. It was like somebody had gotten to them first. Harold Brodkey

told me he'd like to talk about it, only he'd grown too fond of his kneecaps. Toni Morrison was hiding out in Key West. And Cynthia Ozick slammed her front door on my thumb.

21   I was making the rounds at Columbia when a black Cadillac with tinted windows pulled up alongside me on Broadway at 115th Street. Two pugs came out and threw me in the back seat like a sack of potatoes.

22   "Let me be blunt, Mr. Slade. Do you know what happens to people who stick their noses into other people's business?"

23   On my left, Elizabeth Hardwick. On my right, one of her gorillas. I turned to the lady.

24   "I seen *Chinatown*," I murmured.

25   "A good film," she said. "But not a great one. The great ones are those taught in film classes, in universities around the country. For example, anything by Eisenstein."

26   "I saw one of his films once. Bored me stiff."

27   "As it does avid film students around the world. But that, my friend, is how canonization works. All the films you'd never see if it were up to you, all the books you'd never read if you really had a choice—they are the very lifeblood of the canon."

28   "You're losing me, Lizzy."

29   "Come, come. The nineteenth-century American novels that go on for hundreds of mind-numbing pages about cetaceans. The endless Russian novels about theodicy, suffering, and salvation, with an unpronounceable cast of thousands. Where would they be without the required reading list?"

30   "Out of print?" I hazarded.

31   "You see why we can't let you continue, then." She patted my knee consolingly. "There's simply too much at stake."

32   The car probably wasn't going much more than twenty miles an hour when they threw me out.

33   Fact was, I didn't much like being manhandled by literary mandarins. But now I had a pretty good hunch about where to look next.

34   I caught up with Alfred Kazin in the New York Public Library; I figured he had to know something. Maybe he did, but when I mentioned the canon, he turned nasty.

35   "Beat it," he growled. "I've got nothing to say to you."

36   I grabbed him by the collar, lifted him a few inches off the floor, and brought his face real close to mine. "Are we having a communication problem?"

37   "Please," he murmured, his head lolling against Edmund Wilson's *Letters on Literature and Politics.* "You know I don't make the decisions."

38 "I've heard that tune more often than Pachelbel's Canon. Don't sweet-talk me, punk. Who's in on it?"

39 His eyes glinted. "Look, it's an institutional configuration. It's societal. *Everybody*'s in on it."

40 "Oh, get off it," I snapped. "Try telling that to the gals who never made it into the great American procession. Try telling that to Phillis Wheatley. Or Zora Neale Hurston. Or Charlotte Perkins Gilman." I poked him in the chest. "You guys really did a job on them. Kept them out in the cold."

41 "You still mad about that?" He rolled his eyes. "Hell, we made it up to them. Everybody's reading those broads today. Take a look at any freshman syllabus; they're practically compulsory." He mopped the sweat off his brow. "Look, better late than never, right?"

42 "That's not the point and you know it. Now tell me who supplies you."

43 His eyes darted around the stacks, and then he loosened up. That's when I knew something was wrong.

44 "I believe the person you want is right behind you," he smirked.

45 Something hard jabbed into my back.

46 I turned around slowly, my hands held high.

47 It was Jacques Barzun, a .38 Beretta resting comfortably in one hand. He was in black tie, looking like he'd just stepped out of a cocktail party.

48 "Big surprise," I said, trying to look more relaxed than I was. "Shoulda figured this one out myself."

49 "There are a great many things you should have figured out, Mr. Slade."

50 "Yeah? Gimme a for instance."

51 "Standards, Mr. Slade. Do you know what standards are?" His menacing smile was perfect—probably practiced it in front of a mirror.

52 "No culture without norms, Mr. Slade. It's an elementary principle. History gives us no reason for optimism about the triumph of civilization over barbarity. Where we do not move forward, we regress. To be sure, it begins with slight lapses. Errors of usage—confusing *disinterest* with *uninterest*, using *hopefully* for *it is to be hoped*. And then, with astonishing swiftness, the rot sets in. With our sense of language dulled, who can appreciate the exquisite verbal precision of the very finest literature? We cease to judge, we join the relativist's party of mindless tolerance, we descend into the torpor of cultural egalitarianism."

53 "Sounds ugly," I said.

54 "It is."

55 "Even so," I said levelly, "you wouldn't shoot me."

56 "Wouldn't I?" He raised an eyebrow.

57   "You don't have a silencer," I pointed out, "and the sign says to be quiet in the library."

58   I knew I had him there.

. . .

59   There was one more lead I had to check out. Word on the street had it that a certain Harold Bloom was deeply involved in the whole business. He was a critic who taught at Yale and moonlighted at City College. I figured the time might be right to pay him a visit. I didn't talk conspiracy with him. Just said people around town thought he knew a lot about canon formation. Maybe even had something to do with it himself.

60   Bloom folded his hands together under his chin. "My dear, the strong poet will abide. The weak will not. All else is commentary. Politics has nothing to do with it."

61   Something else was bothering me, and I decided to be up-front. "I noticed the cops paid you a visit before I came by. What'd they want?"

62   "I'm a suspect, if you can believe it." He looked at me wide-eyed. "Somebody killed off Thomas Stearns Eliot, and they think I had something to do with it. Imagine that. Little old me." Then he grinned, and I saw he could be a very dangerous man.

63   So Tommy was dead. That should have cheered me up, but it didn't. From a pay phone on the corner, I made a quick call to an old friend in the NYPD. Turned out Bloom had a rap sheet longer than a three-part *New Yorker* profile. They were after him for a whole series of murders, from Matthew Arnold to Robert Lowell. All of them savaged with bloody dispatch, often in a paragraph or less. So far, they couldn't pin anything on him.

64   The police were biding their time. Seems they had a decoy all set up. A young policewoman who wrote poetry in the style of Sylvia Plath, working undercover at *The New York Review of Books.* But that wasn't going to do me any good. Bloom was a small fish. I was angling for the biggest one of all.

65   Problem was, I was banging my head against a brick wall and it wasn't for sure which was going to give first. I didn't like to call in debts, but I couldn't put it off any longer. It was time to look up my old friend Jason Epstein. These days he was a big cheese at Random House, but I knew him back when he was a gumshoe at Pinkerton's.

66   When he showed up at the Royalton on West Forty-fourth Street, I could tell something was wrong.

67   They had got to him.

68   "You too, Jason?" It hurt; I couldn't hide that. "Just tell me why. What's in it for you?"

69   In reply, he dropped a book on my lap that made the Manhattan phone directory look like a pocket diary. "It's called *The Reader's Catalog*," he said, "and it's my baby. It lists every book worth reading."

70   I was beginning to understand.

71   He wouldn't meet my eyes. "Look, Slade, I can't afford to make up the *Catalog* from scratch every week. We're talking stability. Critics talk about the literary canon, publishers talk about the importance of a strong backlist, but it comes to the same."

72   With the help of two waiters, I lifted *The Reader's Catalog* back onto the table. I thought about all the lives that had been ruined to make it possible. I thought about the most respected writers of our time acting like citizens of the Town That Dreaded Sundown. "You've got to give me a name, Jason," I said. There was anger in my voice; fear, too. I didn't care what they'd done to him, didn't care about the things he'd done. I just had to reach him somehow.

73   Jason didn't say anything for a long while, just watched the ice cubes dissolve in his Aqua Libra.

74   "I'm taking a big risk just being seen with you," he said, massaging his temples.

75   But in the end, he came through.

· · ·

76   So that's what I was doing at ten o'clock in the morning, my trench coat hunched over my head, tailing Susan Sontag down the rainy streets. Epstein told me she was scheduled to make a pickup that morning. If so, she'd lead me where I wanted to go.

77   My confidence was growing, and I didn't think twice when she strode under the Thirty-eighth Street overpass on the East Side. Vandals had knocked out most of the lights. The darkness protected me, but I had a hard time making her out in the gloom.

78   Then somebody laid a blackjack to the back of my head and the lights went out completely.

· · ·

79   When I came to, my head was throbbing and my eyes didn't want to focus. I made them.

80   Something told me I'd arrived at my destination. I was seated before an enormous desk, ornately carved with claw-and-ball feet. And an enormous tufted leather chair with its back to me.

81   Slowly, it swiveled around.

82   The old man was small, and the huge chair made him seem tiny. He winked at me.

83   "Who are you?" I said. It came out like a croak.

84   "It's not important," he said blandly. "The organization is what's important."

85   "Organization?" I was dimly aware of the floor vibrating beneath my feet. Meant we were probably in a factory of some sort.

86   "The literary canon—now that ain't chopped liver. Could be you don't understand how big this thing is. We've got people all over, wouldn't work otherwise. We've got the daily reviewers, we've got the head of the teachers' union. . . ."

87   "Al Shanker? He's with you?"

88   He seemed amused by my naïveté. "We've got people in the teacher's training colleges. We got the literature profs at your colleges, they're all in on it. The guys who edit the anthologies—Norton, Oxford, you name it—they all work for us. Ever hear about the Trilateral Commission?"

89   "Something to do with international trade?"

90   His cheeks dimpled when he smiled. "That's the front. It's really about the literary canon. The usual hustle: we'll read Lady Murasaki if they let in James and Emerson. It's a tricky business, though, when you get into fair-trade issues. We got reports that the English are *dumping*. Some of our guys wanted to use the farm parity system for Anthony Burgess—you know, pay him not to write novels." He rolled his eyes. "Never works. They tried it over here with Joyce Carol Oates. She just sold the overage under a bunch of pseudonyms."

91   I tried to cluck sympathetically, but it caught in my throat.

92   "Sooner or later they'll come to me," he said. "And I'll take care of it, like I always do."

93   "Sounds like a lot of responsibility."

94   "You see why my boys didn't appreciate your sniffing around. There's too much at stake. You gotta play by the rules." He spread his brown-spotted hands on the desk. "Our rules."

95   "Who would've thought it? Literary immortality a protection racket."

96   He mouthed his cigar obscenely. "Come off it, kid. There's no immortality in this business. You want twenty years, even forty, we can arrange it. Beyond that, we'll have to renegotiate terms at the end of the period. Sooner or later there's going to be a, whaddaya call it, reassessment. We send a guy down, he does an appraisal, figures the reputation's not really earned, and bingo, you're out. Maybe you'll get a callback in fifty years or so. Maybe not."

97   I shook my head. "You guys play hardball." I laughed, but I was scared.

98   "You see what we did with James Gould Cozzens?"

99   "Who?"

100 "Exactly. And thirty years ago, he was the hottest thing around. Then somebody got a little greedy, figured they could cut their own deal. . . ." The old man laughed, showed teeth like little yellow nubbins. "Something I want you to see."

101 He led me out of his office and onto an inside balcony overlooking a vast industrial atrium. I heard the din of machinery, felt the blast of hot factory air. And I saw the automatic conveyor belt below. At first I thought it was a moving slag heap, but it wasn't. All at once I felt sick and dizzy.

102 Heaped high on the conveyor belt, thousands and thousands of books were being fed into a belching, grinding mechanical maw.

103 Turned into pulp.

104 I could make out only some of the titles. There were fat novels by James Jones and Erskine Caldwell and Thomas Wolfe and James T. Farrell and Pearl Buck. Thin novels by Nelson Algren and William Saroyan. The old Brooks and Warren *Understanding Poetry* nestled beside the collected plays of Clifford Odets. I tried to look away, but my eyes were held by a sick fascination. *Butterfield* 8 and *The Big Sky*, *Young Lonigan* and *Manhattan Transfer*, *Darkness at Noon* and *On the Road*—the literary has-beens of our age, together at last, blended into a high-fiber gruel.

105 The old man led me back into his office and closed the door.

106 "Beginning to get the picture? You want to take care you don't end up on that pile, Mr. Slade." He squeezed my shoulder and said, "Of course there might be another way."

107 I shook my head. "You're going to have to kill me," I said.

108 He opened the left-hand drawer of his desk, removed a dog-eared copy of a journal. "My boys came up with something interesting." It was in *The Dalhousie Review*, Spring 1947. He looked triumphant. "A sestina called 'Cadences of Flight.' Makes you a published poet yourself, doesn't it?"

109 "Jeepers," I said. My face was hot with embarrassment. "I was in high school."

110 That's when he made his proposal. I know, Dwight Macdonald said that people who sell out never really had anything to sell, but what did I care? Turned out Dwight was on their payroll from the beginning. Listening to the sound of untold literary tonnage being pulped, I had to admit there were worse things than being co-opted.

. . .

111 When I got to my apartment, I dialed Estelle's number and told her she might as well come over. She was at my door in a quarter of an hour, wearing a long gray trench coat with a belt, as heavily made-up as ever.

112   "Estelle," I said, "I'm off the case." I peeled twenty-five dollars off my billfold. "You can have your money back."

113   "They turned you, didn't they?" she said, scarlet suffusing her beige pancake foundation.

114   I looked at her wistfully. The gal had spunk, and I admired that. I felt a sudden rush of warmth toward her. All these years of kicking around the city alone—maybe it was time to settle down with somebody. Sure, her cockamamie assignment had turned my life upside down, but right then her body looked inviting to my tired eyes. Maybe it was fate that brought us together. I was thinking. Maybe.

115   I said, "Lookit, everyone's got a price."

116   "Yeah? What was yours?"

117   "I'm in, sugar," I blurted. "You understand what I'm saying? They're going to put 'Cadences of Flight' in *The Norton Anthology of Poetry*, fourth edition. It's gonna be deconstructed, reconstructed, and historicized in *PMLA*. And there's going to be a couple of questions about it on the New York State Regents exam in English. It was a take-it-or-leave-it proposition, baby. How could I say no?"

118   "You were going to blow the whistle on the whole outfit."

119   "And they were going to feed me into a paper mill. Sometimes you don't know what's in your best interest till someone points it out to you."

120   The look she gave me was smoldering, and not with passion.

121   "But Estelle"—and I gazed into her eyes soulfully—"I been thinking maybe we have the rest of our lives together for explanations."

122   Estelle stared at me for what seemed like a long time. Then she worked her fingers into her hair and started working it free. It was a wig. The eyelashes went next, then she ran a towel under the tap and scrubbed off her makeup. She fished out the stuffed brassiere last of all.

123   The transformation was astonishing. Before me stood a perfectly ordinary-looking man in his early fifties, his dark hair beginning to gray.

124   I began to shake. "You're—you're. . . ."

125   "Thomas Pynchon," he said in a baritone. Pulled off the white gloves and extended a meaty paw.

126   Thomas Pynchon. Now there was someone you never saw on "Oprah Winfrey."

127   My mind wanted to reel, but I pulled it in sharp. "So that's why you sent me on this mission impossible."

128   "I knew you'd never take the case if you knew who I was."

129   Mists were clearing. "Damn right I wouldn't. Being a famous recluse wasn't good enough for you. It was anonymity you were after. You didn't care if you had to bring down the whole system of dispensation to get it." I paused for breath. "I've got it right, haven't I? That's why you set me up, with this despicable Estelle act."

130   Pynchon only shrugged.

131   "So," I said, "you wanted out." The words came out through gritted teeth: "Out of the canon."

132   "Can you blame a guy for trying?" he asked, and walked out of my life.

133   Alone in my apartment, I poured myself a couple of fingers of Jack Daniels and tried to make room on my shelves for the critical essays and Ph.D. dissertations about me they said would come flooding in. I was going to be explicated, which was good. I was going to be deconstructed, which wasn't so good. It was a tough job, being a canonical author.

134   But somebody had to do it.

TO THINK ABOUT

1. What is the effect of Gates's use of pulp novel prose to unravel an academic mystery?
2. Why do you think Gates, a serious scholar himself, wrote the piece? What is the theme, the underlying message?
3. Think of the literature you have been required to read in high school and college. Which books did you appreciate and learn from? Which did you consider a waste of time? Why? Have you revised your original opinions about any of these books?
4. What are your own standards for judging literature? Think of specific texts to illustrate your answer.

TO DO

1. Make a list of serious subjects. (Maybe *too* serious.)
2. Make a list of less-than-deadly-serious genres. (Pulp mystery, light science fiction, romance novels, sports biographies, etc.)
3. Then choose one from column A and one from column B. Write about the subject of your choice, using the voice of your choice.
4. You can also reverse the process, using a serious voice to write about a less-than-serious subject.

TIP

Remember that whatever voice you choose, your own sensibilities will always lurk near the surface of your writing. Underneath Henry Louis Gates's putdown of the literary/academic establishment lies a deep affection for literature, literary criticism, and the give and take of fierce debate over the canon. (Note that in the end, Gates allows his alter ego, the narrator, to be co-opted by the system.) It is this affection which allows him to criticize without coming across as mean or petty.

16

Obsessions

Natalie Goldberg

My favorite book about writing is Writing Down the Bones by Natalie Goldberg. When I want to be inspired, awe-struck, I read Annie Dillard (see Chapter 9). But when I want to write, I read Goldberg. She is a poet and a teacher who de-mystifies writing without removing the magic. She combines the voice of a Jewish mother with the approach of a Zen master. So, nu, writing is a way of being. The sentences move with the rhythm of the deli, the kitchen table, and this *Jewish mother tells you you're allowed to do so much more, not less, than what you're doing now.*

Here, relax, have a bagel. Do some writing.

1   Every once in a while I make a list of my obsessions. Some obsessions change and there are always more. Some are thankfully forgotten.

2   Writers end up writing about their obsessions. Things that haunt them; things they can't forget; stories they carry in their bodies waiting to be released.

3   I have my writing groups make lists of their obsessions so that they can see what they unconsciously (and consciously) spend their waking hours thinking about. After you write them down you can put them to good use. You have a list of things to write about. And your main obsessions have power; they are what you will come back to in your writing over and over again. And you'll create new stories around them. So you might as well give in to them. They probably take over your life whether you want them to or not, so you ought to get them to work for you.

4   One of my obsessions is my Jewish family. Every once in a while I decide I've written enough about them. I don't want to sound like a momma's girl. There are other things in the world to write about. It is true that there are other topics and they do come up naturally, but when

I have made a conscious decision to not write about my family, the act of repressing it seems to repress everything else too, simply because I am spending a lot of energy avoiding something.

5   It's like when I decide to go on a diet. Right after I make that decision, food seems to be the only real thing on earth, and as I drive the car, run down the block, write in my journal—all these actions become ways of avoiding the one thing I suddenly really want. For me, it works better to give food and hunger a space in my life, but in a friendly way so that I don't destructively devour twelve cookies at a time.

6   Just so with writing about my family. Give them a few pages and they will take their place in the Hall of Obsessions and allow me space for other topics. Try to squelch them and they turn the corner in every one-horse-town poem I've ever written—even an Iowa farm wife begins to sound like she's about to make blintzes.

7   I learned once from a recovering alcoholic that at parties alcoholics always know where the liquor is, how much there is, how much they've drunk, and where they are going to get their next drink. I have never cared that much about liquor, but I know I love chocolate. After hearing about an alcoholic's behavior, I watched myself. The next day I was at a friend's. His roommate was making brownies. We had to go to a show before the brownies were out of the oven. I was aware that subtly throughout the whole movie I was thinking about those brownies. I couldn't wait to get back and have one. When the show was finished, we coincidentally met some friends who suggested that we go out some place to talk. I saw myself get panicky: I wanted those brownies. I made up a quick excuse why we had to return to my friend's house before we went on with the evening.

8   We are run by our compulsions. Maybe it's just me. But it seems that obsessions have power. Harness that power. I know most of my writing friends are obsessed with writing. It works in the same way as chocolate does. We're always thinking we should be writing no matter what else we might be doing. It's not fun. The life of an artist isn't easy. You're never free unless you are doing your art. But I guess doing art is better than drinking a lot or filling up with chocolate. I often wonder if all the writers who are alcoholics drink a lot because they aren't writing or are having trouble writing. It is not because they are writers that they are drinking, but because they are writers who are not writing.

9   There is freedom in being a writer and writing. It is fulfilling your function. I used to think freedom meant doing whatever you want. It means knowing who you are, what you are supposed to be doing on this earth, and then simply doing it. It is not getting sidetracked, thinking you shouldn't write any more about your Jewish family when that's your role in life: to record their history, who they were in Brooklyn, on Long

Island, at Miami Beach—the first generation of American Goldbergs—before it all passes and is gone.

10   Katagiri Roshi says: "Poor artists. They suffer very much. They finish a masterpiece and they are not satisfied. They want to go on and do another." Yes, but it's better to go on and do another if you have the urge than to start drinking and become an alcoholic or eat a pound of good fudge and get fat.

11   So perhaps not all obsessions are bad. An obsession for peace is good. But then be peaceful. Don't just think about it. An obsession for writing is good. But then write. Don't let it get twisted into drinking. An obsession for chocolate is not good. I know. It's unhealthy and doesn't help the world the way peace and writing do.

12   Carolyn Forché, a poet who won the Lamont Poetry Award for her book *The Country Between Us*, about El Salvador, said, "Change your innermost obsessions to become a political writer." That makes sense. You don't write about politics by *thinking* you should. That will become doggerel. Start caring about politics, reading about it, talking about it, and don't worry about what it will do to your writing. When it becomes an obsession, you will naturally write about it.

TO THINK ABOUT

1. In "Obsessions," what is Golberg's theme? Read Annie Dillard's "Write Till You Drop" (Chapter 9) and compare the themes.
2. Imagine a conversation between Natalie Golberg and Annie Dillard. Then imagine yourself joining the discussion.
3. Golberg says, "There is freedom in being a writer and writing. I used to think freedom meant doing whatever you want." What *does* freedom mean to her? To you?
4. Golberg quotes poet Carolyn Forché: "Change your innermost obsessions to become a political writer." Is it possible to cultivate an obsession? How might you go about it? What would you *like* to be obsessed about?

TO DO

1. Make a list of the things you are thinking about that are getting in the way of your writing (i.e. your love life; your financial situation; your relationship with your parents; your concern about a political, religious, philosophical, or moral issue). Identify the items on the

list that qualify as obsessions. Free-write about the item you are most obsessed about now.
2. Write ten questions about the piece of free-writing you have just produced. Go to the library. Find answers to the questions. Now write an informed piece about your obsession.

TIP

The good news about obsessions is that they are full of psychic energy that is ready to come pouring out on the page. Getting a first draft is easy. The bad news is that sometimes it is difficult to distance oneself sufficiently to write about an obsession in a way that will be meaningful and engaging to an audience. Sometimes it helps to write about your obsession in the third person (see Ellen Goodman's "Rating the Kids," Chapter 18) or to discuss it with yourself in an internal dialogue, using two different voices (see A. G. Mojtabai's "On Wearing the Chador," Chapter 36).

17

Dick and Jane Play Tennis

Ellen Goodman

Ellen Goodman writes columns. She writes for the Boston Globe. *Mostly she writes like a grownup. But sometimes the grownups don't act grown up. Then Goodman writes like a first grader. She does this to make a point.*

1. Dick and Jane play middle-aged tennis.
2. See the brace Dick puts on his right arm to protect his tennis elbow.
3. See the high-top shoes he ties to support the foot which he broke playing middle-aged squash.
4. See the double socks he wears to shield the bone spur on the other foot.
5. See Jane's orthopedic lifts, specially made for her tennis shoes.
6. See the elastic support on her right knee.
7. See the X rays of her back.
8. This is how Dick and Jane prepare to play middle-aged tennis this morning.
9. Dick stretches his hamstrings.
10. Jane stretches her back.
11. Dick takes aspirin.
12. Jane takes calcium.
13. Dick drives to the tennis court to save wear and tear on his bone spur.
14. Jane walks to the tennis court to warm up her spine.
15. Dick and Jane take out their middle-aged, mid-sized racquets, their sun block, their yellow balls, and play.
16. Look at Jane lunge.
17. See how she winces.
18. Look at Dick hitting a backhand.
19. See how he twitches.

20   Dick and Jane are playing middle-aged tennis to stay in shape. The shape of a pretzel.

21   Dick and Jane have two friends. They are Jack and Jill. These two do not play tennis. Nor do they run. Nor do they ache.

22   But Dick and Jane worry about their friends' health. "What will become of Jack?" frowns Dick at times. He sends Jack articles about exercise and blood pressure. "What will become of Jill?" frets Jane. She sends Jill research about aerobics and heart disease.

23   Right before Dick's fortieth birthday, he and Jane began to read about health. They read that exercise was an antidepressant. They read that exercise promoted a longer life. They read that exercise helped the cardiovascular system.

24   Right before Jane's fortieth birthday, they began to notice wear and tear among their athletic friends. They saw their casts and crutches. They saw their X rays and membership cards at sports medicine clinics.

25   Dick and Jane decided that there were two choices for middle age. They could be depressed or broken. They could strain their hearts or their backs. They could choose between cardiologists or orthopedists. They could live a shorter life of leisure or a longer life of injury. They could be Jack and Jill or Dick and Jane. They decided to play for the long run.

26   See Dick and Jane now as they finish their game of middle-aged tennis.

27   Off goes his elbow brace.

28   Off goes her knee support.

29   Dick stretches out his hamstrings.

30   Jane stretches out her back.

31   Dick drives home to save wear and tear on his foot.

32   Jane walks home to cool down her vertebrae.

33   Listen to Dick as he puts the flexible cold pack on his toe: "I feel great!"

34   Listen to Jane as she puts the flexible cold pack on her sacroiliac: "Fit as a fiddle!"

35   Dick and Jane are willing to sacrifice every bone in their body in order to stay healthy.

TO THINK ABOUT

1. What is the effect of Goodman's use of the first-grade primer voice in this essay? What is the nature of the relationship she establishes with you, the reader?
2. What is Goodman's attitude toward her subjects?

3. Compare Goodman's voice in "Dick and Jane Play Tennis" to the voices in two other Goodman essays: "Rating the Kids" (Chapter 18) and "Real Foes, False Foes" (Chapter 19). How do they differ? Is there a common thread among them?
4. Goodman writes: "Dick and Jane decided that there were two choices for middle age. They could be depressed or broken. They could strain their hearts or their backs." Does Goodman agree with this point of view? Are there other choices?

TO DO

1. Make a list of trendy behavior patterns engaged in by you, your friends, or other people you know. Pick a fad that seems silly or overrated. Write an essay about it, focusing on people who are particularly fanatical about it. Try writing the piece Dick-and-Jane style if it seems appropriate; if not, select a voice that is.
2. Write about a trend or fad you were once caught up in, but have since rejected. Write it as a before-and-after piece. Pay particular attention to the turning point or points—the moment or period when you realized the fad was not for you.

TIP

I suspect that Goodman's Dick and Jane are not precisely true-to-life; they are either caricatures of real people or they are composites invented by Goodman for the purpose of making a point. While ordinarily it is best to write about real people, caricatures of this sort are useful when the writer wishes to ridicule a type of behavior without ridiculing specific individuals.

18

Rating the Kids

Ellen Goodman

There are times when we want to write about something that is going on in our lives, want badly to write about it, but can't find our way into the subject. Often this is because we are simply too close to it. Maybe we are too emotionally involved to find a reasonable perspective from which to work. Maybe an episode we wish to write about has not receded sufficiently into the past to allow us to see it clearly. In these situations, sometimes it helps to imagine an out-of-body experience—that is, to leave one's body, look over one's own shoulders, and write about oneself in the third person.

Here, Boston Globe *columnist Ellen Goodman writes about the habit parents have of comparing their children unfavorably with other children. Goodman is a mother. The "She" in this piece is herself.*

1   The problem was that she had been visiting New York children.

2   Not that they looked different from other people's children. They didn't. They were even disguised in blue jeans so that they could pass in Des Moines or Tuscaloosa. Yet the New York children she met always reminded her of exotic plants encouraged to blossom early by an impatient owner.

3   She had spent one night with two thirteen-year-old girls who went to a school where they learned calculus in French. The next night she met a boy who had begged his parents for a Greek tutor so he could read the *Iliad.* He was nine.

4   This same boy came downstairs to announce that the Ayatollah Khomeini had just come to power. What, he wondered, would happen to Bakhtiar? Or oil imports?

5   She wondered for a moment whether this person wasn't simply short for his real age, say, thirty-two. But no, he was a New York child. She'd known many of them at camp and college. They wrote novels at

twelve, had piano debuts at fourteen, impressed M.I.T. professors at sixteen. (She was, of course, exaggerating.)

6   The woman was thinking about all this on the plane. She was flying her flu home to bed. Sitting at 16,000 feet, enjoying ill health, it occurred to her that she was guilty of the sin of child rating.

7   It wasn't New York children; it was other people's children. It wasn't awe, she knew deep in her squirming soul; it was the spoilsport of parenting—comparing.

8   Her own daughter was reading *My Friend Flicka* while this boy was reading the *Iliad.* Her daughter regarded math as a creation of the marquis de Sade, and she was taught in English.

9   The girl could plot the social relations of every member of Class 5-C with precision, but she couldn't pronounce the Ayatollah to save her gas tank. At ten, she was every inch a ten year old.

10   The woman hunched down in her seat, wrapping her germs around her like a scarf. When her child was little, the woman had refused to participate in playground competitiveness, refused to note down which child said the first word, rode the first bike. She thought it inane when parents basked in reflected "A's" and arabesques and athletics.

11   Now she wondered whether it was possible for parents not to compare their children with The Others. Didn't we all do it, at least covertly?

12   In some corner of our souls, we all want the child we consider so extraordinary to be obviously extraordinary. While we can accept much less, at some point we have all wanted ours to be first, the best, the greatest.

13   So, we rank them here and there. But we are more likely to notice their relative competence than their relative kindness. More likely to worry about whether they are strong and smart enough, talented enough, to succeed in the world. We are more likely to compare their statistics than their pleasures.

14   And we are always more likely to worry. She had often laughed at the way parents all seek out new worry opportunities. If our kids are athletic, we compare them to the best students. If they are studious, we worry that they won't get chosen for a team. If they are musical, we worry about their science tests.

15   If they are diligent, we compare them to someone who is easygoing. And if they are happy, we worry about whether they are serious enough. Perhaps the boy's parents wish he could ski.

16   We compare our kids to the ace, the star. We always notice, even against our will, what is missing, what is the problem. We often think more about their flaws than their strengths. We worry about improving them, instead of just enjoying them.

17   She thought about how many parents are disappointed in some part of their children, when they should fault their own absurd expectations.

18   The woman got off the plane in the grip of the grippe. She got home and crawled into bed. The same daughter who cannot understand why anyone would even want to reduce a fraction brought her soup and sympathy. Sitting at the edge of the bed, the girl read her homework to her mother. She had written a long travel brochure extolling the vacation opportunities of a week in that winter wonderland, the Arctic Circle.

19   The mother laughed, and felt only two degrees above normal. She remembered that Urie Bronfenbrenner, the family expert, had once written that every child needed somebody who was "just crazy" about him or her. He said, "I mean there has to be at least one person who has an irrational involvement with that child, someone who thinks that kid is more important than other people's kids."

20   Well, she thought, most of us are crazy about our kids. Certifiably.

TO THINK ABOUT

1. Why did Goodman write this narrative in the third person rather than in the first person? Would a first-person approach have changed the piece significantly?
2. For the first half of the piece, Goodman the narrator is off-stage, writing about Goodman the mother. Then the narrator appears, third-person plural: "In some corner of our souls, we all want the child we consider so extraordinary to be obviously extraordinary." How does this development affect the reader?
3. Goodman writes about the habit parents have of comparing their children to the children of others. But the reverse is true as well. How do children go about rating their parents?

TO DO

1. Write a quick profile of one of your parents. Compare this parent to the parents of your friends. Is your perspective now the same as it was five years ago? Ten years ago?
2. Write about yourself in the third person. For best results, choose an episode or series of episodes which you feel strongly about. Be as specific as possible.

TIP

Sometimes the technique of writing about ourselves in the third person serves us admirably in a first draft—and then, having achieved the distance we were seeking, we are able to convert the piece back into the first person in subsequent drafts. As is often the case, there are no rules about this. Experiment. Do what is comfortable, and what works.

19

Real Foes, False Foes

Ellen Goodman

*The time was May 1991. Soldiers, sailors, and fliers were re-
turning to the United States after driving the Iraqi Army out of
Kuwait. Boston Globe columnist Ellen Goodman was on vacation in
Casco Bay, Maine, when she observed a male cardinal engaged in
self-destructive behavior. And she made a connection.*

*It is not a perfect connection, however. Goodman has a point
to make, but she makes it cautiously, with qualifications. Here is a
voice of concern and frustration, with a touch of self-mockery
thrown in.*

1   I am in the bushes, digging out the bittersweet vines wrapped mur-
derously around a tree, when the cardinal comes back into view. The
bird in all his finery, flies across the lawn, undulating in great long crim-
son loops. And then ends his elegant flight pattern by crashing into the
barn window.

2   Mission accomplished, he retreats to a bush. From this launching
pad, he commences his afternoon of battering. The bird I have come to
call Knocko attacks the glass once, twice, a dozen times, before he takes
off to fight another time.

3   I have been watching this routine for weeks. The first time I saw
him perform his Great Window Crash, I felt like the audience at an air
show when the careful choreography of the planes suddenly turns into a
midair collision.

4   Like any guilt-ridden eco-worrier, I assumed it was my fault. Last
year some cardinals had nested in the barn; this year, we replaced the
window. Was the bird trying merely to get home through the pane?

5   But as Knocko went another and then another round with the window, it occurred to me that he must be fighting. With his own mirror image.

6   Did this splendid and bird-brained creature see an enemy in the reflection of the window pane? Did he come out attacking—day three, round twelve—an imagined rival? Himself?

7   Watching Knocko knock out his brains and aware that I am no naturalist, I call the Audubon Society, where a field ornithologist confirms my own mischievous diagnosis of Knocko's behavior. The cause, admits Simon Perkins, is testosterone.

8   At this time of year, Perkins tells me that males often smash themselves against windows, hubcaps, even rear-view mirrors. "What they see in their reflection is an intruder in their territory and they attack it. They won't give up as long as their hormone level is up."

9   Lest he be guilty of stereotypes, Perkins adds that occasionally a female will do it as well. But by and large, banging your head against a wall is a male activity. Testosterone, he adds traitorously to his sex, "is a universal hormone that makes all males do very strange things."

10   This sort of behavior, built into their systems long before there were windows or hubcaps in the world, is now entirely unfit for the rigors and traps of modern civilization. "Even if they don't injure or blow themselves out immediately, they only have a certain amount of energy in their short lives," says Perkins. "It's like a gas tank. What you use now you won't have later."

11   Knocko and his like not only harm themselves, but their families. "Raising young is an extremely expensive task. To have to expend more energy on an imagined foe is," he says conclusively, "not good."

12   Simon Perkins is no sociobiologist. Nor am I. Leaping from birds to humans or from cardinals to generals is a risky business. Furthermore, neither of us wants to be accused of male-bashing. After all, the cardinal is doing quite enough male-bashing for both of us.

13   But this week at least, even in Knocko's territory, people are asking whether George Bush's decision to fight in the Gulf was the product of thought or a hyperactive thyroid. So we're entitled to worry a bit about nature, nurture and warfare.

14   In the aftermath of the Cold War as well, men and women are wondering if Russia was ever the real threat. Which of today's enemies are a figment of our imagination? A mirror image?

15   And while we are on the subject, it isn't just ornithologists who notice that "raising young is an extremely expensive task." Nor is it just environmentalists calculating how much money has gone to fools' fights instead of children. The task of separating real and false foes is a central one for any life built on instinct but dependent on reason.

16   Ah, but for Knocko at least, there is good news, a cure. His hormone level will be down in another week or two. In the meantime I am instructed to cover the window. With one blanket, carefully placed, I can wipe out an enemy and save a small friend.

17   What is this? Think globally, act locally? Today, with a punch-drunk cardinal at my window, he makes it sound so easy.

TO THINK ABOUT

1. Goodman suggests carefully that the male hormone testosterone may contribute to the tendency of powerful men to focus their energy on "fools' fights instead of children." Is it a fair implication? If you were in conversation with Goodman, how would you respond?
2. Goodman writes: "Simon Perkins is no sociobiologist. Nor am I. Leaping from birds to humans or from cardinals to generals is a risky business." Has she covered herself sufficiently to make the leap? Who else besides Perkins might she have consulted?
3. The piece ends: "What is this? Think globally, act locally? Today, with a punch-drunk cardinal at my window, he makes it sound so easy." What is the effect of this final paragraph on the overall message of the essay?

TO DO

1. Make a list of "real foes, false foes" in your life. You may discover an essay.
2. Make a list of all the clichés you can think of. Vow never to use them again—at least, not without a new twist.
3. Take a walk. Bring a notebook. Jot down images, incidents, bits of overheard dialogue that interest you. (Don't worry, just yet, about *why* they interest you.) When you return to your room, read your notes. Then put them away. There are no guarantees, but the next time you write an essay, something from your list of literal observations may emerge in figurative form. (The more observing you do, the better are the odds of this happening.)

TIP

Old metaphors, analogies, and similes are clichés. Avoid them, for they are stale and often meaningless. (Selling like hotcakes? How do hotcakes sell?)

An original metaphor is like a butterfly: it does not start out life that way. A metaphor begins as something literal—a cardinal attacking its reflection in a barn window, for example. The metamorphosis takes place in the writer's brain—in this case, the connection between the cardinal's behavior and the behavior of male human beings.

Original metaphors and similes are all around you—in your room, on the street, in the behavior of your friends and classmates. Eventually you will find them.

20

On Free Speech
Lois Gould

Sometimes we feel strongly about an issue: we favor both sides. This state of affairs has its advantages; we can, for example, take either side in an argument and present a convincing case. And we can mediate between two people whose friendship is threatened by their difference of opinion over the issue.

But eventually, something happens forcing us to make a choice. And so we make it.

Here novelist Lois Gould, whose own works (for example, Waiting for Mr. Goodbar) contain some racy material, is asked to sign a petition protesting the jailing of a publisher of pornography. She is strongly inclined to sign. She is strongly inclined not to sign. She weighs the arguments for each course of action. Her voice wavers between certainty and doubt. Then she makes up her mind.

1   My friend Pamela confesses she is no longer big on freedom of expression. In fact, when a man in her life recently mentioned, in a dismayed tone, that some misguided judge in Ohio had thrown a man in jail for seven to twenty-five years, just for publishing a "girlie" magazine, Pamela smiled one of her most delightful smiles and said softly, "Oh, that's wonderful."

2   I guess I have never gone quite so far as Pamela. But then, neither have I gone quite so far the other way as my friend Nancy the devout civil libertarian, who swears she would, if pushed to the typewriter, force herself to defend that publisher's right to air his disgusting magazine live and in color on prime-time TV, or on the 59th Street Bridge during rush hour.

3   Nancy also insists she would defend outrageous lies in advertising (even if the slogan went: "Ask Mommy to buy Old Tar cigarettes— they're good for kids!") and catchy racist epithets on the evening news,

133

and free demonstrations of sado-masochism in front of Robert Wagner Junior High School, if not right in the science lab.

4   In the name of our First Amendment, Nancy says, we must simply learn—and teach our children—to avert the eyes, ears and nose, much as we acquire, and instruct the young in, the useful habit of stepping nimbly around other public nuisances that litter the crosswalks of life in a free country.

5   While I was pondering that, my telephone rang, and it was a pleasant young man calling on behalf of the very magazine whose publisher had just been thrown in jail. For a brief, crazy minute, I wondered if he was going to offer me one of their million-dollar "modeling" fees that went begging last year after Barbara Walters, Gloria Steinem, Caroline Kennedy, Patty Hearst and other selected targets declined to answer the call. I remembered wishing at the time that they had all accepted—and then used the proceeds to buy the magazine and tear it up.

6   But that was not the subject of the young man's call. All he wanted was my name. Specifically, he wanted it on a petition expressing my concern at the jailing of his publisher. He assumed that no matter what I as a woman think of his product, I as a writer would force myself, like Nancy, to take up arms against his suppressors, lest they light out next week after Kay Graham or Adrienne Rich—or me. In other words, all us free-press persons should hold our averted noses and step in this public nuisance together.

7   By now I was feeling acutely uncomfortable. What if the fellow is right? What if they're *all* right? Pamela had to be right, because she knows that the magazine is much more than merely disgusting: it is also potent—a weapon and a textbook, not only for the very young, but also for the older and more dangerous. She knows that the thing it does is teach people that women are consumer goods—silly putty toys with replaceable parts, or snack foods with flavors enhanced by artificial spice and color.

8   On the other hand, Nancy had to be right, too, because she knows that the opposite of absolute freedom is, at least potentially, absolute tyranny, and because she has lived in the Soviet Union, where there is no porn to speak of, and where all sorts of writers are routinely thrown into jail.

9   Finally, I had to concede, the man from the magazine was right, because he knows that he's got us where we live—and what he sees fit to print has nothing at all to do with it.

10   Hmm, yes, well, I let my anxiety marinate overnight, and the next day I talked to my friend Charles Rembar, the attorney who escorted both Lady Chatterley and Fanny Hill to their triumphant American de-

buts, thereby spreading his cloak—and ours—in the mud puddle for a pack of porn hustlers. And I told him what was bothering me. I said that as a feminist I stood with Pamela all the way. But that as an American and a liberal, I stood with Nancy. And that as a writer, there seemed no place for me to stand but in the arms of a man who publishes a disgusting magazine.

11   "Uh-huh," said my friend, the libertarian attorney. "The First Amendment junkies are out pushing again." Junkies? I echoed. But I already knew what he meant. If the junkies really had their way, we would all O.D. on free expression—because there would be no stopping even the classic mad false-alarmist who yells "Fire!" in a crowded theater. But the junkies can give you their solemn word that they'd put up with anyone saying or writing or advertising anything they know they'll never have to make good on.

12   The minute our friend the publisher tried to unstaple his centerfold on TV, the network would bleep it—for fear of losing its license. And the minute he tried staging it on the 59th Street Bridge, he'd be safely hauled away for disrupting traffic. We've got the Federal Trade Commission and the Food and Drug Administration "censoring" the man who would say cigarettes are good for kids. And public nuisance laws keeping Lady Godiva from prancing through the midtown area, or Peeping Tom from gluing his eye to the keyholes in the Plaza Hotel. And the First Amendment junkies haven't been out waving their protest petitions to put a stop to any of it.

13   The truth is that we are already up to our averted eyes and ears in ifs and buts that stop us from expressing ourselves in a thousand disruptive or offensive ways. We are, after all, only relatively free. Which means that the rules can change as fast, or as slowly, as you can invent a newly printable four-letter word for a Supreme Court decision—or a disgusting magazine.

14   So there it was. Neither Nancy nor the magazine man could hold their freedom guns to my writer's head, and force me to embrace that publisher—or else. When my friend the attorney saved Fanny Hill from a fate worse than publishing death, he predicted that we would have to put up with a lot of bad things. But not with *everything*.

15   I just wanted Pamela to know that I'm not signing the 5/6¶&5/6! petition. And I wanted Nancy to know that my $c&! conscience is clear.

TO THINK ABOUT

1. Gould rejects two extremes in the argument of censorship versus absolute free speech in order to stake out a middle ground. What strategy does she use to establish her opening position?

2. Compare Gould's essay with Kurt Vonnegut's "The First Amendment" (Chapter 50). How do you think Vonnegut would react to Gould's conclusion? How do the arguments of these two writers differ in emphasis? Imagine a conversation between Gould and Vonnegut. See if you can replay each of their voices in your head.

3. Gould notes that some speech is not protected by the First Amendment, and cites the classic example, yelling "Fire" in a crowded theater. Her essay implicitly straddles the line between protected and unprotected speech. Think about that line, and define it for yourself.

TO DO

1. Make a list of issues about which you feel ambivalent. Pick the one that intrigues you most. Write about it in specific terms, incorporating research material with personal experience.

2. Lois Gould brings the issue of free speech to life by presenting friends of hers with extreme, opposing views. Then she introduces a third friend, one with moderate views, and takes her cue from him. Try writing an essay in which you present the various sides of a controversial issue in this manner.

TIP

Know your audience and write accordingly. Different voices are appropriate for different audiences. Kurt Vonnegut's defense of the First Amendment is a wake-up call for those who already agree with him, at least in theory, but it is not likely to win any converts. By contrast, Gould's measured approach is likely to appeal to a broader audience. Each piece is effective, because these writers know their audiences.

21

The Streak of Streaks

Stephen J. Gould

There are times when it is useful to approach a serious, formal subject in a light, informal manner. But there are also times when the opposite is true. Stephen J. Gould, scientist, writer, and baseball aficionado, has treated subjects as diverse as Mickey Mouse, Alexander Doubleday, and the opposable thumb with equal gravity and respect. Here he turns his attention to Joe DiMaggio's 56-game hitting streak, which, he contends, is the single most remarkable feat in the history of sports. To make his case he draws from the disciplines of theology, literature, and psychology, as well as the science of probability. In the process, he condemns stereotyping as a morally repugnant, statistically invalid means of judging people. He writes in the voice of a professor—a good professor, one who has no trouble keeping his 8 A.M. class awake and engaged.

1   My father was a court stenographer. At his less than princely salary, we watched Yankee games from the bleachers or high in the third deck. But one of the judges had season tickets, so we occasionally sat in the lower boxes when hizzoner couldn't attend. One afternoon, while DiMaggio was going 0 for 4 against, of all people, the lowly St. Louis Browns, the great man fouled one in our direction. "Catch it, Dad," I screamed. "You never get them," he replied, but stuck up his hand like the Statue of Liberty—and the ball fell right in. I mailed it to DiMaggio, and, bless him, he actually sent the ball back, signed and in a box marked "insured." Insured, that is, to make me the envy of the neighborhood, and DiMaggio the model and hero of my life.

2   I met DiMaggio a few years ago on a small playing field at the Presidio of San Francisco. My son, wearing DiMaggio's old number 5 on his Little League jersey, accompanied me, exactly one generation after my father caught that ball. DiMaggio gave him a pointer or two on batting and then signed a baseball for him. One generation passeth away, and another generation cometh: But the earth abideth forever.

3   My son, uncoached by Dad, and given the chance that comes but once in a lifetime, asked DiMaggio as his only query about life and career: "Suppose you had walked every time up during one game of your 56-game hitting streak? Would the streak have been over?" DiMaggio replied that, under 1941 rules, the streak would have ended, but that this unfair statute has since been revised, and such a game would not count today.

4   My son's choice for a single question tells us something vital about the nature of legend. A man may labor for a professional lifetime, especially in sport or in battle, but posterity needs a single transcendent event to fix him in permanent memory. Every hero must be a Wellington on the right side of his personal Waterloo; generality of excellence is too diffuse. The unambiguous factuality of a single achievement is adamantine. Detractors can argue forever about the general tenor of your life and works, but they can never erase a great event.

5   In 1941, as I gestated in my mother's womb, Joe DiMaggio got at least one hit in each of 56 successive games. Most records are only incrementally superior to runners-up; Roger Maris hit 61 homers in 1961, but Babe Ruth hit 60 in 1927 and 59 in 1921, while Hank Greenberg (1938) and Jimmy Foxx (1932) both hit 58. But DiMaggio's 56-game hitting streak is ridiculously, almost unreachably far from all challengers (Wee Willie Keeler and Pete Rose, both with 44, come second). Among sabermetricians (a happy neologism based on an acronym for members of the Society for American Baseball Research, and referring to the statistical mavens of the sport)—a contentious lot not known for agreement about anything—we find virtual consensus that DiMaggio's 56-game hitting streak is the greatest accomplishment in the history of baseball, if not all modern sport.

6   The reasons for this respect are not far to seek. Single moments of unexpected supremacy—Johnny Vander Meer's back-to-back no-hitters in 1938, Don Larsen's perfect game in the 1956 World Series—can occur at any time to almost anybody, and have an irreducibly capricious character. Achievements of a full season—such as Maris's 61 homers in 1961 and Ted Williams's batting average of .406, also posted in 1941 and not equaled since—have a certain overall majesty, but they don't demand unfailing consistency every single day; you can slump for a while, so long as your average holds. But a streak must be absolutely exceptionless; you are not allowed a single day of subpar play, or even bad luck. You bat only four or five times in an average game. Sometimes two or three of these efforts yield walks, and you get only one or two shots at a hit. Moreover, as tension mounts and notice increases, your life becomes unbearable. Reporters dog your every step; fans are even more intrusive than usual (one stole DiMaggio's favorite bat right in the middle of his streak). You cannot make a single mistake.

7   Thus Joe DiMaggio's 56-game hitting streak is both the greatest factual achievement in the history of baseball and a principal icon of American mythology. What shall we do with such a central item of our cultural history?

8   Statistics and mythology may strike us as the most unlikely of bedfellows. How can we quantify Caruso or measure *Middlemarch?* But if God could mete out heaven with the span (Isaiah 40:12), perhaps we can say something useful about hitting streaks. The statistics of "runs," defined as continuous series of good or bad results (including baseball's streaks and slumps), is a well-developed branch of the profession, and can yield clear—but wildly counterintuitive—results. (The fact that we find these conclusions so surprising is the key to appreciating DiMaggio's achievement, the point of this article, and the gateway to an important insight about the human mind.)

9   Start with a phenomenon that nearly everyone both accepts and considers well understood—"hot hands" in basketball. Now and then, someone just gets hot, and can't be stopped. Basket after basket falls in— or out as with "cold hands," when a man can't buy a bucket for love or money (choose your cliché). The reason for this phenomenon is clear enough: It lies embodied in the maxim, "When you're hot, you're hot; and when you're not, you're not." You get that touch, build confidence; all nervousness fades, you find your rhythm; *swish, swish, swish.* Or you miss a few, get rattled, endure the booing, experience despair; hands start shaking and you realize that you shoulda stood in bed.

10   Everybody knows about hot hands. The only problem is that no such phenomenon exists. Stanford psychologist Amos Tversky studied every basket made by the Philadelphia 76ers for more than a season. He found, first of all, that the probability of making a second basket did not rise following a successful shot. Moreover, the number of "runs," or baskets in succession, was no greater than what a standard random, or coin-tossing, model would predict. (If the chance of making each basket is 0.5, for example, a reasonable value for good shooters, five hits in a row will occur, on average, once in 32 sequences—just as you can expect to toss five successive heads about once in 32 times, or 0.5^5.)

11   Of course Larry Bird, the great forward of the Boston Celtics, will have more sequences of five than Joe Airball—but not because he has greater will or gets in that magic rhythm more often. Larry has longer runs because his average success rate is so much higher, and random models predict more frequent and longer sequences. If Larry shoots field goals at 0.6 probability of success, he will get five in a row about once every 13 sequences (0.6^5). If Joe, by contrast, shoots only 0.3, he will get his five straight only about once in 412 times. In other words, we need no special explanation for the apparent pattern of long runs. There is no ineffable "causality of circumstance" (to coin a phrase), no definite

reason born of the particulars that make for heroic myths—courage in the clinch, strength in adversity, etc. You only have to know a person's ordinary play in order to predict his sequences. (I rather suspect that we are convinced of the contrary not only because we need myths so badly, but also because we remember the successes and simply allow the failures to fade from memory. More on this later.) But how does this revisionist pessimism work for baseball?

12   My colleague Ed Purcell, Nobel laureate in physics but, for purposes of this subject, just another baseball fan, has done a comprehensive study of all baseball streak and slump records. His firm conclusion is easily and swiftly summarized. Nothing ever happened in baseball above and beyond the frequency predicted by coin-tossing models. The longest runs of wins or losses are as long as they should be, and occur about as often as they ought to. Even the hapless Orioles, at 0 and 21 to start the 1988 season, only fell victim to the laws of probability (and not to the vengeful God of racism, out to punish major league baseball's only black manager).

13   But "treasure your exceptions," as the old motto goes. Purcell's rule has but one major exception, one sequence so many standard deviations above the expected distribution that it should never have occurred at all: Joe DiMaggio's 56-game hitting streak in 1941. The intuition of baseball aficionados has been vindicated. Purcell calculated that to make it likely (probability greater than 50 percent) that a run of even 50 games will occur once in the history of baseball up to now (and 56 is a lot more than 50 in this kind of league), baseball's rosters would have to include either four lifetime .400 batters or 52 lifetime .350 batters over careers of 1,000 games. In actuality, only three men have lifetime batting averages in excess of .350, and no one is anywhere near .400 (Ty Cobb at .367, Rogers Hornsby at .358, and Shoeless Joe Jackson at .356). DiMaggio's streak is the most extraordinary thing that ever happened in American sports. He sits on the shoulders of two bearers—mythology and science. For Joe DiMaggio accomplished what no other ballplayer has done. He beat the hardest taskmaster of all, a woman who makes Nolan Ryan's fastball look like a cantaloupe in slow motion—Lady Luck.

14   A larger issue lies behind basic documentation and simple appreciation. For we don't understand the truly special character of DiMaggio's record because we are so poorly equipped, whether by habits of culture or by our modes of cognition, to grasp the workings of random processes and patterning in nature.

15   Omar Khayyám, the old Persian tentmaker, understood the quandary of our livs (*Rubaiyat of Omar Khayyám*, Edward Fitzgerald, trans.):

> Into this Universe, and Why not knowing,
> Nor Whence, like Water willy-nilly flowing;

And out of it, as Wind along the Waste,
I know not Whither, willy-nilly blowing.

But we cannot bear it. We must have comforting answers. We see pattern, for pattern surely exists, even in a purely random world. (Only a highly nonrandom universe could possibly cancel out the clumping that we perceive as pattern. We think we see constellations because stars are dispersed at random in the heavens, and therefore clump in our sight.) Our error lies not in the perception of pattern but in automatically imbuing pattern with meaning, especially with meaning that can bring us comfort, or dispel confusion. Again, Omar took the more honest approach:

Ah, love! could you and I with Fate conspire
To grasp this sorry Scheme of Things entire,
Would not we shatter it to bits—and then
Re-mould it nearer to the Heart's Desire!

We, instead, have tried to impose that "heart's desire" upon the actual earth and its largely random patterns (Alexander Pope, *Essay on Man*, end of Epistle 1):

All Nature is but Art, unknown to thee;
All Chance, Direction, which thou canst not see;
All Discord, Harmony not understood:
All partial Evil, universal Good.

Sorry to wax so poetic and tendentious about something that leads back to DiMaggio's hitting streak, but this broader setting forms the source of our misinterpretation. We believe in "hot hands" because we must impart meaning to a pattern—and we like meanings that tell stories about heroism, valor, and excellence. We believe that long streaks and slumps must have direct causes internal to the sequence itself, and we have no feel for the frequency and length of sequences in random data. Thus, while we understand that DiMaggio's hitting streak was the longest ever, we don't appreciate its truly special character because we view all the others as equally patterned by cause, only a little shorter. We distinguish DiMaggio's feat merely by quantity along a continuum of courage; we should, instead, view his 56-game hitting streak as a unique assault upon the otherwise unblemished record of Dame Probability.

16   Amos Tversky, who studied "hot hands," has performed, with Daniel Kahneman, a series of elegant psychological experiments. These long-term studies have provided our finest insight into "natural reasoning" and its curious departure from logical truth. To cite an example, they construct a fictional description of a young woman: "Linda is 31 years old, single, outspoken, and very bright. She majored in philosophy. As a student, she was deeply concerned with issues of discrimination and social justice, and also participated in anti-nuclear demonstrations."

Subjects are then given a list of hypothetical statements about Linda: They must rank these in order of presumed likelihood, most to least probable. Tversky and Kahneman list eight statements, but five are a blind, and only three make up the true experiment:

> Linda is active in the feminist movement;
> Linda is a bank teller;
> Linda is a bank teller and is active in the feminist movement.

17   Now it simply must be true that the third statement is least likely, since any conjunction has to be less probable than either of its parts considered separately. Everybody can understand this when the principle is explained explicitly and patiently. But all groups of subjects, sophisticated students who have pondered logic and probability as well as folks off the street corner, rank the last statement as more probable than the second. (I am particularly fond of this example because I know that the third statement is least probable, yet a little homunculus in my head continues to jump up and down, shouting at me—"but she can't just be a bank teller; read the description.")

18   Why do we so consistently make this simple logical error? Tversky and Kahneman argue, correctly I think, that our minds are not built (for whatever reason) to work by the rules of probability, though these rules clearly govern our universe. We do something else that usually serves us well, but fails in crucial instances: We "match to type." We abstract what we consider the "essence" of an entity, and then arrange our judgments by their degree of similarity to this assumed type. Since we are given a "type" for Linda that implies feminism, but definitely not a bank job, we rank any statement matching the type as more probable than another that only contains material contrary to the type. This propensity may help us to understand an entire range of human preferences, from Plato's theory of form to modern stereotyping of race or gender.

19   We might also understand the world better, and free ourselves of unseemly prejudice, if we properly grasped the workings of probability and its inexorable hold, through laws of logic, upon much of nature's pattern. "Matching to type" is one common error; failure to understand random patterning in streaks and slumps is another—hence Tversky's study of both the fictional Linda and the 76ers' baskets. Our failure to appreciate the uniqueness of DiMaggio's streak derives from the same unnatural and uncomfortable relationship that we maintain with probability. (If we knew Lady Luck better, Las Vegas might still be a roadstop in the desert.)

20   My favorite illustration of this basic misunderstanding, as applied to DiMaggio's hitting streak, appeared in a recent article by baseball writer John Holway, "A Little Help from His Friends," and subtitled

"Hits or Hype in '41" (*Sports Heritage,* 1987). Holway points out that five of DiMaggio's successes were narrow escapes and lucky breaks. He received two benefits-of-the-doubt from official scorers on plays that might have been judged as errors. In each of two games, his only hit was a cheapie. In game 16, a ball dropped untouched in the outfield and had to be called a hit, even though the ball had been misjudged and could have been caught; in game 54, DiMaggio dribbled one down the third-base line, easily beating the throw because the third baseman, expecting the usual, was playing far back. The fifth incident is an oft-told tale, perhaps the most interesting story of the streak. In game 38, DiMaggio was 0 for 3 going into the last inning. Scheduled to bat fourth, he might have been denied a chance to hit at all. Johnny Sturm popped up to begin the inning, but Red Rolfe then walked. Slugger Tommy Henrich, up next, was suddenly swept with a premonitory fear: Suppose I ground into a double play and end the inning? An elegant solution immediately occurred to him: Why not bunt (an odd strategy for a power hitter). Henrich laid down a beauty; DiMaggio, up next, promptly drilled a double to left.

21   I enjoyed Holway's account, but his premise is entirely, almost preciously, wrong. First of all, none of the five incidents represents an egregious miscall. The two hits were less than elegant, but undoubtedly legitimate; the two boosts from official scorers were close calls on judgment plays, not gifts. As for Henrich, I can only repeat manager Joe McCarthy's comment when Tommy asked him for permission to bunt: "Yeah, that's a good idea." Not a terrible strategy either—to put a man into scoring position for an insurance run when you're up 3–1.

22   But these details do not touch the main point: Holway's premise is false because he accepts the conventional mythology about long sequences. He believes that streaks are unbroken runs of causal courage—so that any prolongation by hook-or-crook becomes an outrage against the deep meaning of the phenomenon. But extended sequences are not pure exercises in valor. Long streaks always are, and must be, a matter of extraordinary luck imposed upon great skill. Please don't make the vulgar mistake of thinking that Purcell or Tversky or I or anyone else would attribute a long streak to "just luck"—as though everyone's chances are exactly the same, and streaks represent nothing more than the lucky atom that kept moving in one direction. Long hitting streaks happen to the greatest players—Sisler, Keeler, DiMaggio, Rose—because their general chance of getting a hit is so much higher than average. Just as Joe Airball cannot match Larry Bird for runs of baskets, Joe's cousin Bill Ofer, with a lifetime batting average of .184, will never have a streak to match DiMaggio's with a lifetime average of .325. The statistics show something else, and something fascinating: There is no "causality of circumstance," no "extra" that the great can draw from the soul of their

valor to extend a streak beyond the ordinary expectation of coin-tossing models for a series of unconnected events, each occurring with a characteristic probability for that particular player. Good players have higher characteristic probabilities, hence longer streaks.

23   Of course DiMaggio had a little luck during his streak. That's what streaks are all about. No long sequence has ever been entirely sustained in any other way (the Orioles almost won several of those 21 games). DiMaggio's remarkable achievement—its uniqueness, in the unvarnished literal sense of that word—lies in whatever he did to extend his success well beyond the reasonable expectations of random models that have governed every other streak or slump in the history of baseball.

24   Probability does pervade the universe—and in this sense, the old chestnut about baseball imitating life really has validity. The statistics of streaks and slumps, properly understood, do teach an important lesson about epistemology, and life in general. The history of a species, or any natural phenomenon that requires unbroken continuity in a world of trouble, works like a batting streak. All are games of a gambler playing with a limited stake against a house with infinite resources. The gambler must eventually go bust. His aim can only be to stick around as long as possible, to have some fun while he's at it, and, if he happens to be a moral agent as well, to worry about staying the course with honor. The best of us will try to live by a few simple rules: Do justly, love mercy, walk humbly with thy God, and never draw to an inside straight.

25   DiMaggio's hitting streak is the finest of legitimate legends because it embodies the essence of the battle that truly defines our lives. DiMaggio activated the greatest and most unattainable dream of all humanity, the hope and chimera of all sages and shamans: He cheated death, at least for a while.

TO THINK ABOUT

1. Gould's argument that DiMaggio's streak transcends all other achievements in sports is based on the laws of probability, yet he uses personal anecdotes and literary allusions as well. How do these nonstatistical components enhance the piece?
2. Gould's argument that streaks are simply random manifestations of mathematical laws clearly has implications that transcend baseball. What are some of these implications?
3. Gould says athletes and other public figures are remembered for specific achievements, rather than overall careers. To some extent, this is true for the rest of us as well. Consider people you know. Can you think of a single, defining episode for each family member, each friend?

4. Have you ever had the "hot hand" in a sporting event, as Gould describes it? Do you accept his argument that such things are simply inevitable manifestations of the laws of probability? Why or why not?

TO DO

1. Make a list of the five greatest achievements in your life. Then rank the items from one to five. Write an essay in which you compare the five, and explain why Number 1 is, indeed, your greatest achievement. Do not rely simply on your own gut feelings to make your case.
2. Make a list of the five greatest achievements in any field that appeals to you—science, art, literature, philosophy, politics, theology, sports. (You may want to narrow the categories further.) Then defend one of the items on your list as the greatest achievement of all in that field.

TIP

The best writers read beyond their own disciplines. Science writers read history. Historians read psychology and geology. Psychologists read Shakespeare. Literary critics read Adam Smith. Business writers read Stephen J. Gould. Gould reads everything. If you are an English major, make a point of reading physics, political science, whatever field you feel inadequate to write about. Engineering majors should try Melville and Toni Morrison. With each new frame of reference, the possibilities for writing increase geometrically.

22

Hello, CIA?

Paul H. Harasim

There are times when we are flummoxed, foiled, stiffed, stymied, stonewalled. We don't get what we want, even though what we want is reasonable and our manner of seeking it is rational. But if we look closely, we may be able to salvage something from the experience—something worth writing about.

In 1983, during the waning years of the Cold War, Paul H. Harasim, a reporter for the Cincinnati Post, *set out to discover the nature and purpose of two Central Intelligence Agency offices located in Cincinnati. He failed. But he did not fail miserably. In fact, he failed gloriously. For although the CIA operatives told him nothing, their secretive manner and the cloak-and-dagger atmosphere in which they worked told him a great deal.*

The voice he uses is straight out of "Dragnet."

1   Gunn sat there in a gray suit. He talked from behind a cloud of cigarette smoke.

2   "I can't tell you," he said, "what else the CIA does in Cincinnati."

3   It was 1345 hours—1:45 P.M. to most Cincinnatians—and Stephen Gunn, an agent of the Central Intelligence Agency in Cincinnati, had clammed up.

4   "How many CIA agents work in Cincinnati?" the visitor asked.

5   "That's privileged."

6   "How many people have you recruited for the CIA from Cincinnati?"

7   "I can't tell you that."

8   "Where were you stationed as an agent overseas?"

9   "That's confidential."

10   "How many people work for the CIA?"

11   "That's classified."

12   "Where is the other CIA office in Cincinnati?"

13   "I can't tell you that."

14   There was a pause, a long pause, as the visitor checked through his notes. Gunn—"yes, that's my real name"—was smiling.

15   "What can you say about what the other CIA agents do in Cincinnati?"

16   "I can tell you they are not engaged in any domestic surveillance."

17   Silence filled the room. Situated downtown on the tenth floor of the Federal building at 550 Main St., the CIA personnel recruiting office had all the warmth that cigarette smoke, a desk, a chair, a phone, and metal walls can bring.

18   To reach this warmth, the visitor had knocked on a door marked only by a number. When there was no answer, a turn of the door handle brought the visitor into a room the size of a jetliner's lavatory.

19   A phone, set at the knees, rang. "Mr. Gunn," a female voice said, "will see you in a moment." Within seconds, following what appeared to be a camera scan from above, a buzzer opened the door to a larger room.

20   That entry, with its high-tech security feel, seemed to force the visitor to pepper Gunn with questions.

21   "Are these offices bugged?"

22   "Not by me or the agency."

23   "Who would then?"

24   "I don't know."

25   "Has the CIA ever set up its own agents to be killed?"

26   "Not that I know of."

27   The conversation with Gunn made it easier for the visitor to find this truth self-evident: the interview—supposedly set up through the CIA's main office in Virginia to discuss the activities of the intelligence agency's two offices in Cincinnati—wasn't operative.

28   Somehow it seemed easier to learn of the CIA's overt covert action in Nicaragua than to find out if the agency had anyone skulking around Westwood or Hyde Park.

29   "Call me," Gunn said as the visitor got up to leave, "if I can be of any more help."

30   A telephone call, 684-3869, was soon dialed, not to Gunn, but to the other local CIA post, a regional field office. The phone book listed no address, just the number.

31   A woman answered.

32   "3-8-6-9," she said.

33   The caller identified himself and asked for the address.

34   A male voice came on the line. He interrupted the question.

35   "I can't tell you where the office is," he said.

36   "To whom am I speaking?"

37   "I can't tell you that."

38   "What are you doing here?"

39   "I can't tell you that . . . Listen, I gave you that number before in Virginia to call. Call that. . . "

40   Dale Peterson, a CIA public affairs officer stationed in Virginia, answered the long-distance call.

41   "I didn't know they had that kind of office in Cincinnati," he said. "I thought they only had the personnel recruiting office."

42   "What does the other CIA office in Cincinnati do?"

43   "I'll call them, find out and call you back . . . no, our phones are not tapped."

44   Trying to hurry the process along, the caller gave Peterson the telephone book listing of the CIA regional field office, 684-3869.

45   A phone rang in The Cincinnati Post newsroom.

46   "Hello, this is Dale Peterson. Is this the CIA regional field office in Cincinnati?"

47   "No, this is The Cincinnati Post."

48   Peterson hung up, no explanation given. Five minutes later he was back on the line.

49   "The location of that CIA office can't be given out," he said. "We have to protect the agents' confidentiality. Their sources have to be protected."

50   CIA agents in Cincinnati, he explained, collect information that is "voluntarily given to them by the local citizenry."

51   "When people go overseas, they may see something that they want to voluntarily pass on to the U.S. government," Peterson said. "It's our job to collect intelligence about foreign countries so our government can make wise decisions."

52   "How many people in Cincinnati, when they get back from Europe or wherever, think of calling the CIA with information?"

53   "Not all the people who call us get their information from overseas," he said. "They may have talked to someone here who was there or they may have found something out in their studies that they want to share."

54   "Doesn't the government ever make the first contact?"

55   "When we know they're going overseas we may make the first move," he said.

56   "How does the CIA know people are going overseas?"

56   "Remember, the information is all voluntarily given," he said, ignoring the question. "We are not talking about asking people to spy or making people paid informants."

58   "We are trying to be much more open with the public now," Peterson said in signing off his long-distance call. "We think it is important that the people understand what is going on."

TO THINK ABOUT

1. What persona does the writer adopt for himself? How does he portray the CIA agent Gunn? What is the nature of the brief relationship between the two?
2. After reading the piece, what are your thoughts about the CIA operation in Cincinnati, and, perhaps, elsewhere?
3. Much of the piece consists of rapid-fire dialogue. What is the effect of this style of writing on you, the reader?
4. The narrator refers to himself only as "the visitor." Why do you think he does this?
5. Compare Harasim's narrator to Henry Louis Gates's narrator in "Canon Confidential: A Sam Slade Caper" (Chapter 15). How do their roles differ?

TO DO

1. For the next 24 hours, pay strict attention to conversations around you, including those in which you take part. Take notes. At the end of the 24-hour period, write a list of the most intriguing conversations you heard. Write a send-up of one of them, slightly exaggerating the nature of the voices.
2. Flip through the yellow pages of your local phone book. Find a business that piques your curiosity—something exotic, strange, mysterious, unexpected. Pay the place a visit. Write about what you find.

TIP

Do not write dialogue simply for the sake of writing dialogue. In both fiction and nonfiction, effective dialogue is meaningful dialogue; every line, every sentence, serves to advance the story. In nonfiction writing, the dialogue on the page must be a faithful reproduction of what the writer heard. However, the writer is free to excise inconsequential chitchat and repetition.

23

Girl
Jamaica Kincaid

Jamaica Kincaid grew up on the island of Jamaica. This piece is about her upbringing. It contains two voices. Although the voices are never identified, it is clear that one is a mother and the other is her daughter. The daughter manages to speak twenty-five words; the mother speaks the rest. The entire piece consists of a single paragraph, which consists of a single sentence. This sentence contains many semicolons, a few dashes, a few commas, three question marks (two of which come at the ends of sentences within the long sentence that is the piece), and no periods. The effect is lilting, rhythmic, insistent. The early reference to benna *(calypso music) resonates throughout.*

1   Wash the white clothes on Monday and put them on the stone heap; wash the color clothes on Tuesday and put them on the clothesline to dry; don't walk barehead in the hot sun; cook pumpkin fritters in very hot sweet oil; soak your little cloths right after you take them off; when buying cotton to make yourself a nice blouse, be sure that it doesn't have gum on it, because that way it won't hold up well after a wash; soak salt fish overnight before you cook it; is it true that you sing benna in Sunday school?; always eat your food in such a way that it won't turn someone else's stomach; on Sundays try to walk like a lady and not like the slut you are so bent on becoming; don't sing benna in Sunday school; you mustn't speak to wharf-rat boys, not even to give directions; don't eat fruits on the street—flies will follow you; *but I don't sing benna on Sundays at all and never in Sunday school;* this is how to sew on a button; this is how to make a buttonhole for the button you have just sewed on; this is how to hem a dress when you see the hem coming down and

so to prevent yourself from looking like the slut I know you are so bent on becoming; this is how you iron your father's khaki shirt so that it doesn't have a crease; this is how you iron your father's khaki pants so that they don't have a crease; this is how you grow okra—far from the house, because okra tree harbors red ants; when you are growing dasheen, make sure it gets plenty of water or else it makes your throat itch when you are eating it; this is how you sweep a corner; this is how you sweep a whole house; this is how you sweep a yard; this is how you smile to someone you don't like too much; this is how you smile to someone you don't like at all; this is how you smile to someone you like completely; this is how you set a table for tea; this is how you set a table for dinner; this is how you set a table for dinner with an important guest; this is how you set a table for lunch; this is how you set a table for breakfast; this is how to behave in the presence of men who don't know you very well, and this way they won't recognize immediately the slut I have warned you against becoming; be sure to wash every day, even if it is with your own spit; don't squat down to play marbles—you are not a boy, you know; don't pick people's flowers—you might catch something; don't throw stones at blackbirds, because it might not be a blackbird at all; this is how to make a bread pudding; this is how to make doukona; this is how to make pepper pot; this is how to make a good medicine for a cold; this is how to make a good medicine to throw away a child before it even becomes a child; this is how to catch a fish; this is how to throw back a fish you don't like, and that way something bad won't fall on you; this is how to bully a man; this is how a man bullies you; this is how to love a man, and if this doesn't work there are other ways, and if they don't work don't feel too bad about giving up; this is how to spit up in the air if you feel like it, and this is how to move quick so that it doesn't fall on you; this is how to make ends meet; always squeeze bread to make sure it's fresh; *but what if the baker won't let me feel the bread?*; you mean to say that after all you are really going to be the kind of woman who the baker won't let near the bread?

TO THINK ABOUT

1. What can you infer about the relationship between the mother and the daughter who speak in this piece?
2. What can you infer about the mores and values of the culture in which they live? About the relative statuses of men and women?
3. Who do you identify with, the mother or the daughter? Why?

TO DO

1. Write a piece in the voice of one of your parents, addressing yourself.
2. Make a list of the rules of work and behavior that shaped your childhood. Be as specific as possible. Write a piece in which the rules are enforced, or not. If the piece is successful it will convey to the reader the world in which you grew up.
3. Make a list of the rules of work and behavior that shape your world now. (It is likely that the rule-makers and enforcers are different now, and the rules themselves more varied, complex, and open to interpretation.) Write the same kind of piece.
4. See if you can combine elements of these two pieces to produce a single essay showing the evolution of rules and values in your life.

TIP

At all costs, avoid the voice of self-pity when you write this sort of piece. If you felt sorry for yourself as a child, show it, but your narrative voice should make it clear that it is not the child speaking now.

24

I Have a Dream

Martin Luther King, Jr.

Let us include a speech, because in a speech, transcribed, the written voice and the spoken voice become one. Let us include an historic speech because it is likely that you, the reader, have heard it on tape or seen it on film, so that its echo is already rumbling in your head. Let us include a speech by a man with a powerful voice, a resonant voice, a rhythmic voice, a voice that has outlived its owner by a quarter of a century and shows no sign of abating. Martin Luther King, Jr., delivered this speech at the Lincoln Memorial in Washington in 1963, at the height of the Civil Rights movement which he led.

1   I am happy to join with you today in what will go down in history as the greatest demonstration for freedom in the history of our nation.

2   Five score years ago, a great American, in whose symbolic shadow we stand today, signed the Emancipation Proclamation. This momentous decree came as a great beacon light of hope to millions of Negro slaves who had been seared in the flames of withering injustice. It came as a joyous daybreak to end the long night of their captivity.

3   But one hundred years later, the Negro still is not free; one hundred years later, the life of the Negro is still sadly crippled by the manacles of segregation and the chains of discrimination; one hundred years later, the Negro lives on a lonely island of poverty in the midst of a vast ocean of material prosperity; one hundred years later, the Negro is still languished in the corners of American society and finds himself in exile in his own land.

4   So we've come here today to dramatize a shameful condition. In a sense we've come to our nation's capital to cash a check. When the architects of our republic wrote the magnificent words of the Constitution and the Declaration of Independence, they were signing a promissory note to which every American was to fall heir. This note was the promise that all men, yes, black men as well as white men, would be

153

guaranteed the unalienable rights of life, liberty, and the pursuit of happiness.

5   It is obvious today that America has defaulted on this promissory note in so far as her citizens of color are concerned. Instead of honoring this sacred obligation, America has given the Negro people a bad check; a check which has come back marked "insufficient funds." But we refuse to believe that the bank of justice is bankrupt. We refuse to believe that there are insufficient funds in the great vaults of opportunity of this nation. And so we've come to cash this check, a check that will give us upon demand the riches of freedom and the security of justice.

6   We have also come to this hallowed spot to remind America of the fierce urgency of now. This is no time to engage in the luxury of cooling off or to take the tranquilizing drug of gradualism. Now is the time to make real the promises of democracy; now is the time to rise from the dark and desolate valley of segregation to the sunlit path of racial justice; now is the time to lift our nation from the quicksands of racial injustice to the solid rock of brotherhood; now is the time to make justice a reality for all of God's children. It would be fatal for the nation to overlook the urgency of the moment. This sweltering summer of the Negro's legitimate discontent will not pass until there is an invigorating autumn of freedom and equality.

7   Nineteen sixty-three is not an end, but a beginning. And those who hope that the Negro needed to blow off steam and will now be content, will have a rude awakening if the nation returns to business as usual. There will be neither rest nor tranquility in America until the Negro is granted his citizenship rights. The whirlwinds of revolt will continue to shake the foundations of our nation until the bright day of justice emerges.

8   But there is something that I must say to my people, who stand on the worn threshold which leads into the palace of justice. In the process of gaining our rightful place, we must not be guilty of wrongful deeds. Let us not seek to satisfy our thirst for freedom by drinking from the cup of bitterness and hatred. We must forever conduct our struggle on the high plain of dignity and discipline. We must not allow our creative protests to degenerate into physical violence. Again and again we must rise to the majestic heights of meeting physical force with soul force. The marvelous new militancy, which has engulfed the Negro community, must not lead us to a distrust of all white people. For many of our white brothers, as evidenced by their presence here today, have come to realize that their destiny is tied up with our destiny. And they have come to realize that their freedom is inextricably bound to our freedom. We cannot walk alone. And as we walk, we must make the pledge that we shall always march ahead. We cannot turn back.

9   There are those who are asking the devotees of Civil Rights, "When will you be satisfied?" We can never be satisfied as long as the Negro is the victim of the unspeakable horrors of police brutality; we can never be satisfied as long as our bodies, heavy with the fatigue of travel, cannot gain lodging in the motels of the highways and the hotels of the cities; we cannot be satisfied as long as the Negro's basic mobility is from a smaller ghetto to a larger one; we can never be satisfied as long as our children are stripped of their selfhood and robbed of their dignity by signs stating "For White Only"; we cannot be satisfied as long as the Negro in Mississippi cannot vote and a Negro in New York believes he has nothing for which to vote. No! No, we are not satisfied, and we will not be satisfied until "justice rolls down like waters and righteousness like a mighty stream."

10   I am not unmindful that some of you have come here out of great trials and tribulations. Some of you have come fresh from narrow jail cells. Some of you have come from areas where your quest for freedom left you battered by the storms of persecution and staggered by the winds of police brutality. You have been the veterans of creative suffering. Continue to work with the faith that unearned suffering is redemptive. Go back to Mississippi. Go back to Alabama. Go back to South Carolina. Go back to Georgia. Go back to Louisiana. Go back to the slums and ghettos of our Northern cities, knowing that somehow this situation can and will be changed. Let us not wallow in the valley of despair.

11   I say to you today, my friends, so even though we face the difficulties of today and tomorrow, I still have a dream. It is a dream deeply rooted in the American dream. I have a dream that one day this nation will rise up and live out the true meaning of its creed, "We hold these truths to be self-evident, that all men are created equal." I have a dream that one day on the red hills of Georgia, sons of former slaves and the sons of former slave owners will be able to sit down together at the table of brotherhood. I have a dream that one day even the state of Mississippi, a state sweltering with the heat of injustice, sweltering with the heat of oppression, will be transformed into an oasis of freedom and justice. I have a dream that my four little children will one day live in a nation where they will not be judged by the color of their skin, but by the content of their character.

12   I HAVE A DREAM TODAY!

13   I have a dream that one day down in Alabama—with its vicious racists, with its Governor having his lips dripping with the words of interposition and nullification—one day right there in Alabama, little black boys and black girls will be able to join hands with little white boys and white girls as sisters and brothers.

14   I HAVE A DREAM TODAY!

15   I have a dream that one day every valley shall be exalted, every hill and mountain shall be made low. The rough places will be plain and the crooked places will be made straight, "and the glory of the Lord shall be revealed, and all flesh shall see it together."

16   This is our hope. This is the faith that I go back to the South with. With this faith we will be able to hew out of the mountain of despair, a stone of hope. With this faith we will be able to transform the jangling discords of our nation into a beautiful symphony of brotherhood. With this faith we will be able to work together, to pray together, to struggle together, to go to jail together, to stand up for freedom together, knowing that we will be free one day. And this will be the day. This will be the day when all of God's children will be able to sing with new meaning, "My country 'tis of thee, sweet land of liberty, of thee I sing. Land where my father died, land of the pilgrim's pride, from every mountainside, let freedom ring." And if America is to be a great nation, this must become true.

17   So let freedom ring from the prodigious hilltops of New Hampshire; let freedom ring from the mighty mountains of New York; let freedom ring from the heightening Alleghenies of Pennsylvania; let freedom ring from the snow-capped Rockies of Colorado; let freedom ring from the curvaceous slopes of California. But not only that. Let freedom ring from Stone Mountain of Georgia; let freedom ring from Lookout Mountain of Tennessee; let freedom ring from every hill and mole hill of Mississippi. "From every mountainside, let freedom ring."

18   And when this happens, and when we allow freedom to ring, when we let it ring from every village and every hamlet, from every state and every city, we will be able to speed up that day when all of God's children, black men and white men, Jews and Gentiles, Protestants and Catholics, will be able to join hands and sing in the words of the old Negro spiritual: "Free at last. Free at last. Thank God Almighty, we are free at last."

TO THINK ABOUT

1. King's speech borrows heavily from what other form of oratory?
2. Is the cadence of the voice in "I Have a Dream" constant, or does it change? What effect does it have on you, the reader?
3. Dr. King prepared this speech with several audiences in mind. What were they? How can you tell?
4. Read "Right to Life: What Can the White Man Say to the Black Woman?" by Alice Walker (Chapter 52). In the area of race relations, what has changed during the three decades since Martin Luther King, Jr., delivered "I Have a Dream"? What has remained the same?

TO DO

1. Read "I Have a Dream," or portions of it, aloud. Imitate Dr. King's delivery. (If you have never heard a recording of the speech, your reference librarian may be able to help you find one.)
2. Make a list of issues about which you feel strongly. Pick the one that appeals to you the most. Then write a speech defending your point of view. Imitate Martin Luther King's voice if you like. Or go to the library and find another speech in a voice that you feel more comfortable with.

TIP

Inhibition destroys strong writing and strong speaking alike. Don't be timid when you read aloud—or when you set your thoughts down on paper. If it helps, think of yourself as an actor: pour yourself into the character you wish to be. Remember: inhibition amounts to self-censorship.

This does not mean that everything you write in a first draft will survive your own later revisions. But you can't judge the value of something unless you get it out on paper or the screen where you can see it. At least during the first draft: When in doubt, leave it in.

For more on writing without inhibition, see "Write Till You Drop" by Annie Dillard (Chapter 9) and "Obsessions" by Natalie Goldberg (Chapter 16).

25

Reunion

Maxine Hong Kingston

The woman receives an invitation to the twentieth anniversary reunion of her high school class. The woman is, by now, a famous writer. She is also, still, a member of the class of '58. Time stopped on graduation day; in her mind, the class is frozen in position—social as well as physical. The writer struggles to find the proper perspective from which to make a decision. The confident voice of the 38-year-old woman falters from time to time. She seems to be talking to herself. In the end, she finds the answer she has been looking for.

1   I just opened an envelope in the mail to find a mimeograph sheet smelling like a school test and announcing the twentieth-year high school reunion. No Host Cocktail Party. Buffet Dinner. Family Picnic, Dancing. In August. Class of '58. Edison High. Stockton. The lurches in my stomach feel like doubt about the strength to stay grown up.

2   I had not gone to the tenth-year reunion; the friends I really wanted to see, I was seeing. But I've been having dreams about the people in high school, and sit up with an urge to talk to them, find out how they turned out. "Did you grow up?" There are emotions connected with those people that I don't feel for friends I've made since.

3   "When I think of you, I remember the hateful look you gave me on the day we signed yearbooks. That face pops into my mind a few times a year for twenty years. Why did you look at me that way?" I'd like to be able to say that at the No Host Cocktail. And to someone else, "I remember you winking at me across the physics lab."

4   I dreamed that the girl who never talked in all the years of school spoke to me: "Your house has moles living in it." Then my cat said, "I

am a cat and not a car. Quit driving me around." High school is a component of the American subconscious.

5   Another reason I hadn't gone to the tenth was an item in the registration form: "List your publications." (The reunion committee must be the kids who grew up to be personnel officers at universities.) To make a list, it takes more than an article and one poem. Cutthroat competitors in that class. With no snooty questions asked, maybe the people with interesting jail records would come. We were not the class to be jailed for our politics or white-collar crimes but for burglary, armed robbery and crimes of passion. "Reunions are planned by the people who were popular. They want the chance to put us down again," says a friend (Punahou Academy '68), preparing for her tenth.

6   But surely I am not going to show up this year just because I have a "list." And there is more to the questionnaire: "What's the greatest happiness you've had in the last twenty years?" "What do you regret the most?" it asks. I'm going to write across the paper, "These questions are too hard. Can I come anyway?" No, you can't write, "None of your business." It is their business; these are the special people that formed your growing up.

7   I have a friend (Roosevelt High '62) who refused to go to his tenth because he had to check "married," "separated," "divorced" or "single." He could not bear to mark "divorced." Family Picnic.

8   But another divorced friend's reunion (Roosevelt '57) was so much fun that the class decided to have another one the very next weekend—without the spouses, a come-without-the-spouse party. And my brother (Edison '60) and sister-in-law (Edison '62) went to her class reunion, where they had an Old Flames Dance; you asked a Secret Love to dance. Working out the regrets, people went home with other people's spouses. Fifteen divorces and remarriages by summer's end.

9   At my husband Earll's (Bishop O'Dowd '56) reunion, there was an uncomfortableness whether to call the married priests Father or Mister or what.

10   What if you can't explain yourself over the dance music? Twenty years of transcendence blown away at the No Host Cocktail. Cocktails—another skill I haven't learned, like the dude in the old cowboy movies who ordered milk or lemonade or sarsaparilla. They'll have disco dancing. Never been to a disco either. Not cool after all these years.

11   There will be a calling to account. That's why it's hard to go. A judgment by one's real peers. We're going to judge whether The Most Likely to Succeed succeeded.

12   In high school we did not choose our friends. I ended up with certain people, and then wondered why we went together. If she's the pretty

one, then I must be the homely one. (When I asked my sister, Edison '59, she told me, "Well, when I think of the way you look in the halls, I picture you with your slip hanging." Not well groomed.) We were incomplete, and made complementary friendships, like Don Quixote and Sancho Panza. Or more like the Cisco Kid and Pancho. Friendships among equals is a possibility I have found as an adult.

13   No, my motive for going would not be because of my "list." I was writing in high school. Writing did not protect me then, and it won't start protecting me now. I came from a school—no, it's not the school—it's the times; we are of a time when people don't read.

14   There's a race thing too. Suddenly the colored girls would walk up, and my colored girlfriend would talk and move differently. Well, they're athletes, I thought; they go to the same parties. Some years, the only place I ever considered sitting for lunch was the Chinese table. But there were more of us than places at that table. Hurry and get there early, or go late when somebody may have finished and left. Not eat. Who will eat with whom at the Buffet Dinner?

15   I notice that the chairman of the reunion went to Chinese school, too; maybe seeing her name, the Chinese-Americans will come. I will have people to eat with—unless they're mad at me for having written about them. I keep claiming our mutual material. They will have recognized themselves in the writing, and not like me for it. That people don't read is only my own wishful thinking.

16   And Earll says he may have to work in August and may not be able to escort me. Alone at the Dance. Again.

17   One day a popular girl, who had her own car, stamped her foot and shouted to a friend who was walking home with me. "Come here!" she ordered. "We go home with one another." To be seen going home alone was bad. They drove off. "I remember you shouting her away from me," I could say at the reunion, not, I swear, to accuse so much as to get the facts straight. Nobody came out and said that there were groups. I don't even know whether the friendships had a name; they were not called groups or crowds or gangs or cliques or anything. ("Clicks," the kids today say.) "Were there groups?" I could ask at last. "Which one was I in?"

18   My son, who is a freshman (Class of '81), says he can't make friends outside his group. "My old friends feel iced out, and then they ice me out."

19   What a test of character the reunion would be. I'm not worried about looks. I and every woman of my age know that we look physically better at thirty-eight than eighteen. I'll have objective proof of the superiority of older women when I see the women who are eighteen in my dreams.

20   John Gregory Dunne (Portsmouth Priory '50) said to his wife, Joan Didion (McClatchy High '52), "It is your obligation as an American writer to go to your high school reunion." And she went. She said she dreamed about the people for a long time afterward.

21   I have improved: I don't wear slips anymore; I got tired of hanging around with homely people. It would be nice to go to a reunion where we look at one another and know without explanations how much we all grew in twenty years of living. And know that we ended up at thirty-eight the way we did partly because of one another, psyches and memories intertwining, companions in time for a while, lucky to meet again. I wouldn't miss such a get-together for anything.

TO THINK ABOUT

1. Here is a woman weighing a decision: on the one hand, on the other hand. What is the implied role of you, the reader?
2. Consider how this piece might have appeared had Kingston chosen to write it in the form of an internal dialogue such as A. G. Mojtabai's "On Wearing the Chador" (Chapter 36).
3. The memories the narrator chooses to include in this piece are social in nature. She says nothing about classes or teachers; the academic aspect of high school—the aspect which is, after all, the primary reason for high school—is nowhere in evidence. Why do you think this is so?
4. In what ways was the social structure at your high school similar to the one at Kingston's Edison High School? In what ways was it different? If there are differences, what factors might account for them? (Geography, time, demographics?)
5. We are often told that our time in high school represented "the best years of our lives." Do you think Maxine Hong Kingston agrees? Do you?

TO DO

1. Make a list of incidents that you remember from your high school days. Review the list. Mark the incidents that have some significance for you. Write an essay about your high school days. You might focus on one particular incident, or you might write a collage made up of a number of scenes. (For examples of the collage form see "Rolling into the '80s" by Sara Davidson, Chapter 8, "A Mask on the Face of Death," by Richard Selzer, Chapter 40, "Choices" by

Patricia Volk, Chapter 49, and "Reading Philosophy at Night" by
Charles Simic, Chapter 43.)
2. Draw a chart outlining the social structure of your high school. Use
the chart as the basis for an essay.
3. The next time you are ambivalent about going to a social event,
make a list of the pros and cons. Then make an essay out of the list.
And don't be surprised if the act of writing helps you make your decision.

TIP

Often it is the accumulation of small details that tells the story.
The hateful look of the girl who signed Kingston's yearbook, the registration form with its question about publications, the hanging slip, the
Chinese table. We are all repositories of such details. When we write
them, they turn old themes into new and original prose.

26

The Death of a Young Man

Susan Landgraf

Reporters usually have an idea in advance about what they might be writing about on a given day. Many cover specific beats, and even general assignment reporters have some sense of what to expect when they gather information about a fire, an accident, or a robbery. But reporters are human beings like the rest of us, and, like the rest of us, they encounter surprises as they go about their daily routines. When they do, their experience in translating complex events into comprehensible prose under tight deadline pressure enables them to make sense of their own lives as well.

1   I watched a young man die last night.

2   The moon was full while I held his hand and promised him it would be all right.

3   It wasn't. It took forever for him to die—about 90 minutes from the moment of impact with another car to open-heart surgery at Valley General Hospital.

4   Doctors see a lot of this—death. So do the medics who hooked and tied him to tubes and machines. So do the firemen who cut his compact car loose and lifted him onto the stretcher. So do the police who took the report. So does the nurse who stopped and held the young man's head for five, ten, fifteen minutes until help arrived.

5   Reporters, too, see death. When the squawk box bleeps in the office, they run to cover accidents like this one. But usually it is another reporter. I hear him tell about it. I read about it in the paper.

6   But this time I was there immediately following the collision. And I was there, watching him bleed to death. Listening to him gag his last minutes away. Cursing. Praying. Crying inside.

7   Waiting.

8   Loretta Harvey, headed home from her day at the hospital, held the

young man's head. I whispered, Oh, God, keep breathing. A gagging sound. Or like sandpaper on a blackboard.

9   I didn't know where he was by then—conscious, unconscious, alive or mostly dead. Where do you go when your breath is like sandpaper and the blood is running from your eyes, your nose and your mouth down into your lungs along with your teeth and the last few minutes you've got left?

10   Where is someone? I asked. Where are they?

11   It's terrible to stand helpless. His hand was resting on the edge of the car window. I held his hand, and told him, "It's going to be all right." Wherever he was, I didn't want him to be alone. I wanted him to have somebody.

12   "It's going to be all right," I told him again and again, like I did when my children were small and had fallen, scraped their knees, bumped their foreheads.

13   How ridiculous to offer so little. And yet, that's all I had.

14   They spilled from several aid cars—volunteers from Fire District 40 crunching the broken glass and parts of both cars that covered the road. "Going to have to cut him away." The sound of the big scissors drowned out the young man's gagging breaths.

15   A fireman crawled into the car to relieve the nurse. He called for someone to hold his legs to keep him from sliding. I was closest.

16   "Let Farrell through." Medic One was out on another run. But Wilson, Director of Medic One, was on his way home from the store. I felt better as he managed to get into the small car, even smaller following the crash. "Light," he demanded. And there was light.

17   While the scissors cut the car roof away, I continued to hold on to the fireman—because that was all there was I could do—that and hold my breath. Somehow, if I held my breath I could transfer some of my energy. Something. Anything.

18   I choked on my sobs. Medic One came. There were needles and bottles and tape and more light. The stretcher. Now Wilson was thumping on his chest. The young man had run out of seconds—almost.

19   I ran back to my car for the camera. It had to be done. It was something to do. But my stomach flipped and flopped like a fish on the riverbank, a hook still in its mouth. He was so young, this young man.

20   He was put in the aid unit and taken to the hospital. I was first in line in a long line of backed up traffic. At the state patrolman's wave of the hand, I headed home to my family, worried because I was so late.

21   They worried with me while I sobbed about a young man whose name I didn't even know. But I had watched him, listened to him dying—and it was personal now, more personal than a name.

22   The medic told me what I was feeling wasn't unusual. Each time he and the other medics go out on a call it's personal, he said.

23   "We're super aggressive," he related. "We're fighting to win. We huddle together and talk it over. We function as a team. We know what needs to be done."

24   And they do it—whatever they can. Like Wilson. Off duty, he did what he could with what he had while the firemen and bystanders did whatever they could. He had ripped out the window of the car, crawled into space where there wasn't any to work. And he'd kept the young man breathing for a while.

25   But this time it wasn't enough. The doctors cracked his chest wide open for open-heart surgery. They used ten units of donated blood. But the patient died on the operating table, Wilson said.

26   Again I cursed any driver who forgets driving is a matter of life and death. "I'll never drive dumb," my fifteen-year-old son said.

27   But out on the street—in the middle of a scene like last night—there is no right and wrong—only life and death, Wilson said afterwards.

28   The next morning at 5:30 A.M. when I was running, which I do most mornings, the moon was huge in the Western sky. I'd been taking pictures of the moon that night just before the accident. It just wasn't his day, the medic had said.

29   Today was another day. While I'd slept, the earth and the moon had changed faces. A twenty-five-year-old man's family had been notified.

30   For some reason, I thought of circles. I thought about what a friend had said. She said she runs for her grandmother who was murdered in New York last year and for her aunt with arthritis. She runs for them because they can't and she can.

31   It's melodramatic, I know. But I kept looking over my shoulder at the moon this morning and I cried for a young man because he died last night. But I'm still alive.

32   And even though it's such a small gesture—I ran for John Eastlick this morning.

TO THINK ABOUT

1. What is the rhythm of this piece? How does Landgraf achieve it? How does the rhythm affect the impact of the story on you, the reader?
2. What can you infer about the narrator of this piece? Is she someone you'd feel at ease with? Why or why not?
3. This is a piece about death. What else? What is the theme?

4. Why do you think Susan Landgraf withheld the name of the accident victim until the last paragraph? What is the effect of this decision?

TO DO

1. Think of a brief, intense episode in your life. It should be recent, so
that the details are still fresh in your mind. Write an account of the
incident using Susan Landgraf's rhythm. To do this you will need to
write short sentences and short paragraphs. As a rule, use simple,
declarative sentences. Subject first, verb second, and not too much
after that. (It's all right to use longer, more complex sentences occasionally, but the short, simple sentence should be your first option.)

TIP

Write the good stuff first. Note Landgraf's lead: "I watched a young
man die last night." A less experienced, less confident writer might have
been tempted to begin earlier in the chronology, or with background information. Beginners worry that if they use their strongest material first,
they will have nothing left for the ending. Good writers hold nothing
back. They know that if they start strongly, strong material will follow.
(For more on this idea, see Annie Dillard's "Write Till You Drop,"
Chapter 9, and Natalie Goldberg's "Obsessions," Chapter 16.)

27

Achievement Test

Lewis H. Lapham

Every month, in an essay in Harper's Magazine, *which he edits, social critic Lewis Lapham examines some aspect of life and thought in the United States. He is rarely pleased by what he discovers. He makes sweeping, damning judgments, which he supports with an eclectic array of data. He is particularly adept at skewering men and women of power, and their sycophants. He is a breaker of codes; he will tell you what the hollow phrases of his hollow subjects truly mean. His voice is formal and formidable. Here he accuses Woodrow Wilson and George Bush of betraying the Jeffersonian concept of education in America.*

Diogenes struck the father when the son swore.

—Robert Burton

1   No American schoolmaster ever outlined the lesson at hand quite as plainly as did Woodrow Wilson. At the turn of the new century, while he was still president of Princeton University, Wilson presented the Federation of High School Teachers with explicit instructions: "We want one class of persons to have a liberal education, and we want another class of persons, a very much larger class of necessity in every society, to forgo the privilege of a liberal education and fit themselves to perform specific difficult manual tasks."

2   I came across Wilson's remark during the same month that President Bush announced yet another grand design for American education (one of possibly fifty such grand designs that I have heard announced by as many politicians over the past thirty years), and I was struck by both the constant and the variable. The pedagogical objective remains firmly in place, but the privileged classes have lost the courage to say what they mean. They continue to require the services of competent do-

mestic labor (i.e., "decent help"), but they no longer write their own speeches, and their language has gone rotten with bureaucratic euphemism.

3   At a White House press conference on April 18, posed against the familiar backdrop of the American flag, Bush made a show of presenting new plans and initiatives that he described as "revolutionary." "For the sake of the future, of our children, and our nation," Bush said, "we must transform America's schools. The days of the status quo are over."

4   Maybe on an otherwise slow afternoon this summer at Kennebunkport, somebody will explain to Mr. Bush the meaning of the phrase "status quo." It is the ground and condition of his success as a politician, and if somehow it were to be abruptly removed (together with the helicopter, the applause, and the campaign contributions), I suspect he might find it hard to get work in any kind of new social order that placed a high value on disciplined thought or an advanced degree of literacy.

5   The President left the business of explaining the lesson plan to its author, Lamar Alexander, the newly appointed secretary of education and the man best known for his financial sleights of hand. As governor of Tennessee and, later, as president of the University of Tennessee, Alexander proved himself extraordinarily adept at the art of the miraculous windfall. In one series of stock transactions he earned $569,000 without investing so much as a cent; in another deal he and his wife paid $5,000 for stock that proved within four years to be worth $800,000. He worked similar wonders with Whittle Communications, Kentucky Fried Chicken, the *Knoxville Journal*, and various Tennessee banks. As a man obviously blessed with the entrepreneurial spirit of the age, Alexander approached the task of improving the nation's schools as if it were a problem in corporate management.

6   If the nation's intellectual infrastructure had fallen into as alarming a state of disrepair as its material infrastructure (i.e., if its collective mathematical and literary skills had been as poorly maintained as its bridges, ports, prisons, and roads), then what was needed was the stimulus of private enterprise. Operate the schools as if they were a chain of successful motels; impose uniform rules of procedure; cut costs; meet the customer's demands for better service; teach the kitchen staff to speak English; insist that the desk clerks know how to work the imported technology.

7   Alexander's brief addressed the profit-and-loss statements of the national economy, not the intellectual hopes or ambitions of the nation's children. What was wanted was a new generation of myrmidons fit "to perform specific difficult tasks." As long as the economy could make do with semiliterate or unskilled labor, then what difference did it make whether "another class of persons" learned to solve quadratic equations

or read the novels of Henry James? Obviously, it made no difference at all, and so matters might have safely continued well into the twenty-third century if the economy hadn't suddenly found itself at a loss for workers familiar with the signs and digits of the new information order. For the past ten years committees of alarmed businessmen have been complaining about workers who cannot read or write or add or think or subtract. The corporate chairmen then go on to worry about the loss of America's place in the world, about our declining rates of productivity, about our failure to compete on equal terms with the Germans and the Japanese.

8   Attempting to allay these concerns, Alexander proposed a number of specific remedies: grants of public money for students qualified to attend private or parochial schools; standardized achievement tests (in English, math, science, history, and geography); vocational requirements aligned with the requirements of the labor markets; construction of 535 new schools, presumably innovative, funded and designed by benevolent corporations. The federal government, of course, committed relatively little money to its new and revolutionary plan—no more than $690 million, a sum well short of what the Pentagon spent for the fireworks display in Iraq. President Bush and Secretary Alexander offered their proposals more in the spirit of suggestions to the state and municipal authorities that pay most of the costs of American public education. But even if the administration had been willing to back its advice with cash, I'm afraid that the result would be as malformed as one of the secretary's business deals or one of the President's longer sentences. Change the schools into the intellectual equivalent of factories or sweatshops and you turn freedom of mind into an enemy of the state. The unauthorized answer slows down production and threatens to lower the average test score.

9   The difficulty, as Woodrow Wilson well and clearly understood, is political. It is the status quo that must be protected and transformed, not the children or the schools. But how do you teach people to solve the new equations unless you also teach them how to think? And if you teach too many people how to think, then how can you be sure that they won't ask the wrong kind of questions? Why would any politician wish to confront an informed citizenry that could read the federal budget, decipher the news from Washington, and break down the election-year images into their subsets of component lies? Why would the purveyors of American goods and services choose to afflict themselves with a public intelligent enough to see through the scrim of the paid advertisements? The success of the American dream, like the success of MasterCard and the Republican Party, presupposes the eager and uncritical consumption of junk in all its commercial declensions. Teach a man to think for himself and maybe he won't buy the after-shave lotion or believe that the

glorious victory in Kuwait proves the need for a newer and more expensive collection of tanks. So troublesome a man might even bother to vote.

10   Recognizing the possibility of unrest implicit in too thorough a course of study, the schoolmasters of Woodrow Wilson's generation took it upon themselves to rig the curricula in a way that discouraged the habits of skepticism or dissent. They redefined democracy as "primarily a mode of associated living" (as opposed to a dedication to the belief in liberty), and they argued that American schools should cut the cloth of their teaching to what John Dewey called "the circumstances, needs, and opportunities of industrial civilization." They had in mind the training of a contented labor force, prospective members of the national economic team, "socially efficient" workers who understood that what was great about America was the greatness of its gross national product and not the greatness of its character and spirit.

11   The new program displaced the older republican hope of a citizenry schooled to the task of self-government. Jefferson had urged the teaching of political history so that Americans might learn "how to judge for themselves what will secure or endanger their freedom." The managers of the newly emerging nation-state, like Messrs. Alexander and Bush, didn't have much use for citizens, especially citizens likely to see the would-be despot behind the mask of the popular general or the avuncular judge. Jefferson had asked, in effect, how could free men protect their liberties if they never learned that it was the business of most politicians to remove those liberties. The Wilson administration subtracted a good many liberties from the public domain during the First World War, and Wilson's propaganda ministry invented the syllabus of the great books of Western civilization (what we now know as "the canon") as a means of political indoctrination. The course was meant to quiet what a dean at Columbia University called "the destructive element in our society," to produce students who "shall be safe for democracy," and to make of the American troops in France what *History Teachers Magazine* called "thinking bayonets."

12   For the past seventy or eighty years the country's educational authorities have done their best to suppress the habit of critical thought. The objective (in 1991, as in 1905 or 1920) conforms to the requirements of a market geared to blind and insatiable consumption. Because the schools serve an economic system (as opposed to an intellectual ideal), they promote, quite properly, the habits of mind necessary to the preservation of that system. A successful American education bears comparison to the commercial procedure for changing caterpillars into silk instead of moths. Silkworms can be turned to a profit, but moths blow

around in the wind and do nothing to add to the wealth of the corporation or the power of the state.

13   The American people have spent billions of dollars on education over the past forty years, and by now I would have thought that we might have acquired the wit or the courage to say that the condition of the schools accurately reflects our intent. We are a people blessed with a genius for large organizational tasks, and if we were serious in our pious blathering about the schools—if we honestly believed that mind took precedence over money—then our educational system surely would stand as the eighth wonder of the world. But we don't like, and we don't trust, the forces of intellect—not unless they can be tied securely to a commercial profit or a scientific benefit.

14   If many of our public schools resemble penal institutions, and if, despite the achievements of a relatively few gifted or fortunate individuals, the population at large sinks further into the sloughs of illiterate superstition, then I cannot help but think that the result is neither an accident nor a mistake. We make it as difficult as possible for our children to learn anything other than their proper place in the economic order because we fear the power of untrammeled thought. Most of what passes for education in the United States deadens the desire for learning because it fails to awaken the student to the unique value of his or her own mind. If the public schools employ the devices of overcrowded classrooms, recitations by rote, questions shaped to the simple answer of right or wrong, it is because the society regards the realm of thought as a subversive conspiracy likely to cause nothing but trouble. An inept and insolent bureaucracy armed with badly written textbooks instills in the class the attitudes of passivity, compliance, and boredom. The students major in the arts of failure and the science of diminished expectations.

15   Outside the schoolroom we wage the same relentless campaign against free or unauthorized expression, and I think it is probably fair to estimate that the nation annually lays waste to roughly 50 percent of its intellectual capacity. George Orwell once observed that almost everything that goes by the name of pleasure represents a more or less successful attempt to destroy consciousness. The United States now spends upwards of $350 billion a year on liquor, pornography, and drugs, and the Cold War against the American intellect thus constitutes a more profitable business than the old arrangement with the Russians. Subsidized by the state and supported by the peep-show operators of the mass media, the erotic entertainments tether the public mind to the posts of sexual fantasy. Liberty, said Jefferson, has ambitious enemies, and what they cannot gain with restrictive laws and the closing of as many libraries as possible, they accomplish with bread and circuses.

16   The idea of freedom stands in as much need of revision as the geography of the supposedly lost frontier. Within the circles of advanced opinion, it is taken for granted that the new technologies (if only we can train enough people to operate them) will save us all, that man has vanquished nature, that his machines have made nonsense of the seasons and subjugated the tribes of Paleolithic instinct. The illuminati who make these confident announcements then proceed to talk in a lighter and more conversational tone of voice about the corporate cul de sac in which they find themselves penned like so many sheep, about the faithlessness of their husbands or wives, the forgery of their tax returns, the silence of their children. Most people have the same hopes and aspirations—work in which they can find meaning and ways in which they can express their capacity to love. But if we haven't been taught to make the acquaintance of our own minds, how, in this most advanced of nations and most enlightened of times, can we manage to achieve those deceptively modest ends? And if our textbooks teach us that America is nothing more than the sum of its profits, then how do we expect to reinvent our politics, or our history, or our schools?

17   Some years ago in this space, I published a few melancholy notes about the reduced circumstances of our political discourse, and, from a woman in Maryland, I received a stern reminder to the effect that the fault, dear Brutus, was not in our stars. "We do not," she said, "ask nearly enough of ourselves—not of parents, not of children, not of women, not of men, not of our institutions, not of our talents, not of our national or our personal character, not of our Constitution's promise, which we betray." In that one sentence, she said most of what needs to be said about the emptiness of the nation's politics and the shabbiness of the nation's schools.

18   If we could stop thinking of ourselves primarily as consumers, perhaps we could understand the lost frontier as being always and everywhere present—as near at hand as the wish to murder, cheat, steal, lie, and generally conduct oneself in a manner unbecoming in an ape. Suppose that we could learn to recognize it in the death of a child in the next street, in any afternoon's proceedings in any criminal court, in the faces of people stupefied by their fear of poverty or the dark. Think how many of its large and various capacities the United States could put to use if only it knew why it was doing so.

TO THINK ABOUT

1. What is the effect of Lapham's voice on you, the reader? In conversation, would you be comfortable with him? Do the voice and the substance of the essay complement one another?
2. Lapham describes a Wilsonian model of education based on class: a liberal education for the upper class, a utilitarian education for the larger, lower class. Do you believe this is the dominant model in the United States today? Why or why not?
3. Lapham suggests that politicians and other power brokers prefer an ignorant electorate to an educated one. Find evidence in the recent pronouncements of prominent politicians to support or refute this point of view.
4. Lapham quotes an unnamed correspondent as follows: "We do not ask nearly enough of ourselves—not of parents, not of children, not of women, not of men, not of our institutions, not of our talents, not of our national or our personal character, not of our Constitution's promise, which we betray." What is the context of this statement? Think of examples with which to support or refute it.

TO DO

1. Scan the newspapers for an event reflecting on government policy in any major area—the economy, trade, housing, health care, the environment. Then go to the library. Do some research on the subject in question. (You might also want to interview a resident expert on your campus.) Finally, write an essay putting your news event in an historical context.
2. Write an essay evaluating your own education to date. Cite its strengths and weaknesses as specifically as you can. Be sure to include an assessment of your own involvement as well. Have you been active in pursuing educational goals, or has your role been primarily passive? (See "What a Freshman Needs to Know," by Andrew Merton, Chapter 34.)

28

The Sound of Music: Enough Already

Fran Lebowitz

Fran Lebowitz is a professional kvetch. *Give her a parade and she'll rain on it. Give her a social convention and she'll give it back; she has no use for it. Give her the rich, the famous, the trendy—particularly the trendy—and she will expose them for what they are: superficial, misguided, stupid, and beyond the tolerance level of any sane person.*

With Lebowitz, nothing is given. Nothing is safe. Including the reader. The difference between Lebowitz's screeds and conventional polemics is the humor; Lebowitz is intentionally outrageous and, therefore, funny.

1   First off, I want to say that as far as I am concerned, in instances where I have not personally and deliberately sought it out, the only difference between music and Muzak is the spelling. Pablo Casals practicing across the hall with the door open—being trapped in an elevator, the ceiling of which is broadcasting "Parsley, Sage, Rosemary, and Thyme"—it's all the same to me. Harsh words? Perhaps. But then again these are not gentle times we live in. And they are being made no more gentle by this incessant melody that was once real life.

2   There was a time when music knew its place. No longer. Possibly this is not music's fault. It may be that music fell in with a bad crowd and lost its sense of common decency. I am willing to consider this. I am willing even to try and help. I would like to do my bit to set music straight in order that it might shape up and leave the mainstream of society. The first thing that music must understand is that there are two kinds of music—good music and bad music. Good music is music that I want to hear. Bad music is music that I don't want to hear.

3   So that music might more clearly see the error of its ways I offer the following. If you are music and you recognize yourself on this list, you are bad music.

1. Music in Other People's Clock Radios

4   There are times when I find myself spending the night in the home of another. Frequently the other is in a more reasonable line of work than I and must arise at a specific hour. Ofttimes the other, unbeknownst to me, manipulates an appliance in such a way that I am awakened by Stevie Wonder. On such occasions I announce that if I wished to be awakened by Stevie Wonder I would sleep with Stevie Wonder. I do not, however, wish to be awakened by Stevie Wonder and that is why God invented alarm clocks. Sometimes the other realizes that I am right. Sometimes the other does not. And that is why God invented *many* others.

2. Music Residing in the Hold Buttons of Other People's Business Telephones

5   I do not under any circumstances enjoy hold buttons. But I am a woman of reason. I can accept reality. I can face the facts. What I cannot face is the music. Just as there are two kinds of music—good and bad—so there are two kinds of hold buttons—good and bad. Good hold buttons are hold buttons that hold one silently. Bad hold buttons are hold buttons that hold one musically. When I hold I want to hold silently. That is the way it was meant to be, for that is what God was talking about when he said, "Forever hold your peace." He would have added, "and quiet," but he thought you were smarter.

3. Music in the Streets

6   The past few years have seen a steady increase in the number of people playing music in the streets. The past few years have also seen a steady increase in the number of malignant diseases. Are these two facts related? One wonders. But even if they are not—and, as I have pointed out, one cannot be sure—music in the streets has definitely taken its toll. For it is at the very least disorienting. When one is walking down Fifth Avenue, one does not expect to hear a string quartet playing a Strauss waltz. What one expects to hear while walking down Fifth Avenue is traffic. When one does indeed hear a string quartet playing a Strauss waltz while one is walking down Fifth Avenue, one is apt to become confused and imagine that one is not walking down Fifth Avenue

at all but rather that one has somehow wound up in Old Vienna. Should one imagine that one is in Old Vienna one is likely to become quite upset when one realizes that in Old Vienna there is no sale at Charles Jourdan. And that is why when I walk down Fifth Avenue I want to hear traffic.

4. Music in the Movies

7   I'm not talking about musicals. Musicals are movies that warn you by saying, "Lots of music here. Take it or leave it." I'm talking about regular movies that extend no such courtesy but allow unsuspecting people to come to see them and then assault them with a barrage of unasked-for tunes. There are two major offenders in this category: black movies and movies set in the fifties. Both types of movies are afflicted with the same misconception. They don't know that movies are supposed to be movies. They think that movies are supposed to be records with pictures. They have failed to understand that if God had wanted records to have pictures, he would not have invented television.

5. Music in Public Places Such as Restaurants, Supermarkets, Hotel Lobbies, Airports, Etc.

8   When I am in any of the above-mentioned places I am not there to hear music. I am there for whatever reason is appropriate to the respective place. I am no more interested in hearing "Mack the Knife" while waiting for the shuttle to Boston than someone sitting ringside at the Sands Hotel is interested in being forced to choose between sixteen varieties of cottage cheese. If God had meant for everything to happen at once, he would not have invented desk calendars.

Epilogue

9   Some people talk to themselves. Some people sing to themselves. Is one group better than the other? Did not God create all people equal? Yes, God created all people equal. Only to some he gave the ability to make up their own words.

TO THINK ABOUT

1. How would it be to sit down and have a conversation with Fran Lebowitz? What kind of relationship does she establish with you, the reader?

2. Underneath all that bluster, Lebowitz makes a serious point. What is it?
3. Come on, admit it: Lebowitz made you feel guilty about something. Like a lapse in taste. How did she do that? How do you feel now?
4. Do you think she literally believes everything she says? (For example: ". . . the only difference between music and Muzak is the spelling. Pablo Casals practicing across the hall with the door open—being trapped in an elevator, the ceiling of which is broadcasting 'Parsley, Sage, Rosemary and Thyme'—it's all the same to me.") If so, why are you listening to her? If not, why does she write the way she does?

TO DO

1. Make a list of things people are doing out there that are popular and trendy, and that drive you crazy (even though maybe you've done them yourself, just so you wouldn't seem, you know, out of it).
2. Read Fran Lebowitz aloud to yourself, just to get in the mood. Then write about the things and people on your list the way she would.
3. Write a fan letter to Fran Lebowitz, using her voice.

TIP

This kind of writing works best when the writer trashes the social conventions of his or her own circle—not those of another group.

29

The Case for Short Words

Richard Lederer

Richard Lederer is best known as a collector of linguistic bloopers. His Anguished English *and other books are packed with errors in spelling and usage that result in meanings never intended by their creators. Such collections could be amassed only by one who truly loves the language, and Lederer does. He loves English for its range, its complexity—and, at bottom, for its simplicity. Even back when it was still fashionable for English teachers to stress the importance of huge vocabularies filled with important-sounding multisyllabic words, Lederer was telling his students at St. Paul's School in Concord, New Hampshire, that small was better, less was more. Here he practices what he has preached, using the gentle, persistent voice of a memorable teacher.*

1   When you speak and write, there is no law that says you have to use big words. Short words are as good as long ones, and short, old words—like *sun* and *grass* and *home*—are best of all. A lot of small words, more than you might think, can meet your needs with a strength, grace, and charm that large words do not have.

2   Big words can make the way dark for those who hear what you say and read what you write. Small words cast their clear light on big things—night and day, love and hate, war and peace, and life and death. Big words can add fat to your prose. Small words are the ones we seem to have known from the time we were born, like the hearth fire that warms the home.

3   Short words are bright like sparks that glow in the night, prompt like the dawn that greets the day, sharp like the blade of a knife, hot like salt tears that scald the cheek, quick like moths that flit from flame to flame, and terse like the dart and sting of a bee.

4   Here is a sound rule: use small, old words where you can. If a long word says just what you want to say, do not fear to use it. But know that our tongue is rich in crisp, brisk, swift, short words. Make them the

spine and the heart of what you speak and write. Short words are like fast friends. They will not let you down.

5   The title of this chapter and the four paragraphs that you have just read are wrought entirely of words of one syllable. In setting myself this task, I did not feel especially cabined, cribbed, or confined. In fact, the structure helped me to focus on the power of the message I was trying to put across.

6   One study shows that eleven words account for twenty-five percent of all spoken English words, and all eleven are monosyllabic. In order of frequency they are: *I, you, the, a, to, is, it, that, of, and, in, what, he, this, have, do, she, not, on,* and *they.* Other studies indicate that the fifty most common words in written English are each made of a single syllable.

7   For centuries our finest poets and orators have recognized and employed the power of small words to make a straight point between two minds. A great many of our proverbs punch home their points with pithy monosyllables: "Where there's a will, there's a way," "A stitch in time saves nine," "Spare the rod and spoil the child," "A bird in the hand is worth two in the bush."

8   Nobody used the short word more skillfully than William Shakespeare, whose dying King Lear laments:

> And my poor fool is hang'd! No, no, no life!
> Why should a dog, a horse, a rat have life,
> And thou no breath at all?. . .
> Do you see this? Look on on her, look, her lips.
> Look there, look there!

9   Shakespeare's contemporaries made the Bible a centerpiece of short words—"And God said, Let there be light: and there was light. And God saw the light, that it was good." The descendants of such mighty lines live on in the twentieth century. When asked to explain his policy to parliament, Winston Churchill responded with these ringing monosyllables: "I will say: it is to wage war, by sea, land, and air, with all our might and with all the strength that God can give us." In his "Death of the Hired Man" Robert Frost observes that "Home is the place where, when you go there,/They have to take you in." And William H. Johnson uses ten two-letter words to explain his secret of success: "If it is to be,/It is up to me."

10   You don't have to be a great author, statesman, or philosopher to tap the energy and eloquence of small words. Each winter I asked my ninth graders at St. Paul's School to write an essay composed entirely of one-syllable words. My students greeted my request with obligatory moans and groans, but when they returned to class with their essays, most felt that, with the pressure to produce high-sounding polysyllables

relieved, they were able to create some of their most powerful and luminous prose. Here are examples from one of my ninth-grade classes:

> What can you say to a boy who has left home? You can say that he has done wrong, but he does not care. He has left home so that he will not have to deal with what you say. He wants to go as far from you as he can. He will do what he wants to do.
>
> This boy does not want to be forced to go to church, to comb his hair, or to be on time. A good time for this boy does not lie in your reach, for what you have he does not want. He dreams of ripped jeans, shorts with no starch, and old socks.
>
> So now this boy is on a bus to a place he dreams of, a place with no rules. This boy now walks a strange street, his long hair blown back by the wind. He wears no coat or tie, just jeans and an old shirt. He hates your world, and he has left it.

> —*Charles Shaffer*

> For a long time we cruised by the coast and at last came to a wide bay past the curve of a hill, at the end of which lay a small town. Our long boat ride at an end we all stretched and stood up to watch as the boat nosed its way in.
>
> The town climbed up the hill that rose from the shore, a space in front of it left bare for the port. Each house was a clean white with sky blue or grey trim; in front of each one was a small yard, edged by a white stone wall strewn with green vines.
>
> As the town basked in the heat of noon, not a thing stirred in the streets or by the shore. The sun beat down on the sea, the land, and the back of our necks, so that, in spite of the breeze that made the vines sway, we all wished we could hide from the glare in a cool, white house. But, as there was no one to help dock the boat, we had to stand and wait.
>
> At last the head of the crew leaped from the side and strode to a large house on the right. He shoved the door wide, poked his head through the gloom, and roared with a fierce voice. Five or six men came out, and soon the port was loud with the clank of chains and creak of planks as the men caught ropes thrown by the crew, pulled them taut, and tied them to posts. They they set up a rough plank so we could cross from the deck to the shore. We all made for the large house while the crew watched, glad to be rid of us.

> —*Celia Wren*

11   You too can tap into the vitality and vigor of compact expression. Take a suggestion from the highway department. At the boundaries of your speech and prose place a sign that reads "Caution: Small Words at Work."

TO THINK ABOUT

1. The first four paragraphs of this essay are composed entirely of one-syllable words. What effect does this have on the rhythm of the piece? How does the rhythm change after the fourth paragraph?
2. Lederer treats words as living things—". . . like fast friends. They will not let you down." Small words, he says, "are the ones we seem to have known from the time we were born, like the hearth fire that warms the home." What are some of the words that have a special meaning to you? What is the nature of your relationship with them?
3. Lederer stresses a simple, basic vocabulary. He uses little slang, little ornamentation. Compare his linguistic style to your own. Which do you prefer? Why?
4. In many specialized fields—the law, medicine, dozens of academic disciplines—it is fashionable to write in a complex, opaque style that is the opposite of what Lederer advocates. Why do you think this happens? Does it serve a purpose?

TO DO

1. Try the exercise Lederer assigned his students and himself. Write an essay composed entirely of one-syllable words. Or, if you prefer, revise an old essay of yours, using only single-syllable words.
2. Do some freewriting about any subject that appeals to you. Write for 30 minutes. Then read what you have written. Analyze your own prose style, your choice of words. Write a critique of your own writing.

TIP

When you limit yourself to words of one syllable, you eliminate most adverbs, with their *-ly* suffixes, from your writing. This is not a bad thing. Adverbs clutter as often as they clarify. Think, for example, of the word *immediately*. With its five clunky syllables it accomplishes the opposite of its literal meaning. Examine these two sentences:

1. He immediately jumped out of the way.
2. He jumped out of the way.

Which conveys immediacy more effectively?

30

A House and Its Memories
Alan Lupo

When people die it is not the end of them. Often, for the survivors, it is only the beginning or continuation of a sorting-out process: Who were these people? How did they fit into history? How did they shape us?

When a parent dies, the sorting-out process is literal, physical work. Here Boston Globe *columnist Alan Lupo sorts through his parents' belongings after both are gone. He is not in any hurry. His voice is tinged with sadness. Its pace matches the pace of his work.*

1   In bits and pieces, two lives slowly disappear. What was home to my parents since 1957 is now just a piece of real estate, as bit by bit, piece by piece, I remove the physical evidence of two first-generation Americans who lived for eight decades.

2   This was the first and only home Esther and Max ever owned. She was 50 and he was 49 when they bought it, a single-family, five-room house in the center of town, an easy walk to shopping for a woman who never drove.

3   It was not as happy a home as it should have been, but it was theirs and was filled with what they thought was valuable, a term misused if one defines it only by money.

4   Now my wife and I clean it out. We practice a sort of triage. Some things are to be inherited; others to be given away; still others to be thrown into green plastic bags and left for the trash collectors.

5   My family will keep Esther's knitted afghans, the products of long and loving labor. "When I die," she used to joke, "will they remember me for anything? They'll say, 'She made nice afghans.'" She would be pleased to see grandson and granddaughter wrapped up to the neck in those afghans.

6   I collect Max's shirt studs and tie clips. Max had been a classy dresser. If proof be required, it is found in a drawer. There is a picture of

Max as a young salesman at Filene's. A full head of black hair parted in the middle, penetrating hazel eyes, a classy suit and a colorful red pin-striped shirt.

7   What is to be kept? What is to be given away? What is to be thrown out? I wonder who made me God all of a sudden. I never wanted the power to dispose of the remains of the lives of others. I want to keep everything, all the pots and pans, all the dishes and cutlery, all the towels and furniture polish. My wife smiles. She has been through this before; she played God for her own parents.

8   You have to be tough. You have to keep telling yourself that when you throw out a skillet that even the poor could not use, you are not throwing out the memories of your parents or your own past. Memories are more than a collection of items.

9   The house looks a lot better than it has in many years. A new heating unit is humming away in the basement. Rugs have been pulled up. Floors, doors and cabinets have been varnished. Ceilings and walls are freshly painted.

10   The house is becoming aseptic, devoid of the presence of its former occupants and visitors. It becomes a place to be marketed to someone else. New lives will begin here, as the inevitable process of regeneration goes on 34 years after the only people known to this house have left it. It must be that way. So goes the rebirth of neighborhoods.

11   When I drive down another street, the one where I grew up, I always look at the family's old apartment, the one we left 34 years ago. I don't know the names of the occupants or most of their neighbors. Only one person, I believe, is left from the 1940s and '50s.

12   And 34 years from now, who in my parents' last neighborhood will know or care that the couple who lived in this five-room house bridged the history of a nation from its first decade to, in the case of my father, its last? From a deadly influenza epidemic to cures for cancer. From trenches in France to trenches in Kuwait. From horses and wagons to space travel. From 2-cent newspapers to cable television. From parents who spoke in the tongues of Europe to cookie-cutter American kids who all talk, like, you know, the same.

13   In truth, the world of Max and Esther had begun disappearing long before their demise. Gone were the dance halls, social clubs and speakeasies of their youth. Few remained of the department stores and clothing outlets. Long gone was the 25-cent lunch at Kresge's or the trilby (egg and onion sandwich) at Hayes-Bickford. Buildings, streets, whole neighborhoods had changed or even disappeared. Familiar landmarks went the way of old friends and relatives.

14   Once a local television crew came to interview them about the radio scare that Orson Welles had created in 1938 with his realistic

production of "The War of the Worlds," and, often, I would sit and listen to the talk of old days. With its pictures, pots and pans, and paraphernalia from the early 1900s through the 1960s, the house became testimony to history. In history, there is refuge for the aging, an ally in a nation that pays scant attention to either the old or its own history.

15   Now, I finally cancel the phone service. I had delayed doing so by rationalizing that I might need to use the phone. I rarely did. It became an unnecessary expense. There is something definitive about canceling phone service, about knowing that for the first time in 34 years you cannot call that number.

16   In time, when the final decisions are made on possessions, new people will come to rent or buy the house. I hope they will flourish. I hope also that maybe they will wonder, once in a great while, about the people who lived here before them—people who, for all their faults and virtues, were part of a family and a small part of what America once was.

TO THINK ABOUT

1. The narrator speaks mostly about his parents, little about himself. What can you infer about him, his personality, his values, from his voice and from the things he says?
2. In the Introduction to this book there is an excerpt from another piece by Alan Lupo, "The Mysterious Fred Salvucci Strikes Again" (page 5). Compare the voices in the two pieces. How do they differ? Do they bespeak the same values?
3. "I wonder who made me God all of a sudden," writes Lupo. "I never wanted the power to dispose of the remains of the lives of others." Do you think he is, in fact, playing God? Why is he uncomfortable?
4. In the third paragraph, what is *triage*? What is the original context for the word?

TO DO

1. "In truth, the world of Max and Esther had begun disappearing long before their demise," writes the narrator, who offers a list of items from that world that are gone now. What are some of the markers of your world? Your parents'? Your grandparents'? Make lists. How are these worlds different from one another? What do they have in common? Write an essay on this subject.
2. Make a list of your possessions. Include everything you can think of. Now perform triage on your list. If you were forced to move away

permanently, which items would you take with you? Which would you give away? And which would you throw out? Now write an essay about the triage you have just performed. The piece will say much about you, your values, your dreams.

TIP

Sometimes it is a relief to write about a negative personal experience. At other times, though, trying to write about something traumatic simply increases the pain. If you begin a piece about the death of someone close to you, or some other traumatic incident, and you find yourself unable to make progress, back off. You're not ready; the time will come. Meanwhile, write about something that offers less resistance.

31

On Being a Cripple

Nancy Mairs

*Each of us is many things. For example, I am a man,
Caucasian, a heterosexual, a father, a husband, a teacher, a writer,
a Democrat, a Jew, an American, a New Hampshirite. I am also a
baseball fan and a decent cook. Nancy Mairs is a woman, a daughter, a mother, a grandmother, a wife, a teacher, a writer, a Catholic,
a superb cook, a cripple.*

*You are what you are. Mostly, we take what we are for
granted. Nancy Mairs does not. The subject of her writing is usually
herself.*

*What makes her successful is her ability to study herself as
though she were someone, or something, else. She is the scientist
with herself as her subject. Nancy Mairs the narrator dissects Nancy
Mairs the subject patiently, relentlessly, from the inside. There is a
tough, no-nonsense quality to the voice which, however, coexists
with humor and compassion. There is, above all, no hedging. There
is no question that this is a voice of authority.*

1   The other day I was thinking of writing an essay on being a cripple.
I was thinking hard in one of the stalls of the women's room in my office
building, as I was shoving my shirt into my jeans and tugging up my zipper. Preoccupied, I flushed, picked up my book bag, took my cane down
from the hook, and unlatched the door. So many movements unbalanced
me, and as I pulled the door open I fell over backward, landing fully
clothed on the toilet seat with my legs splayed in front of me: the old
beetle-on-its-back routine. Saturday afternoon, the building deserted, I
was free to laugh aloud as I wriggled back to my feet, my voice bouncing
off the yellowish tiles from all directions. Had anyone been there with
me, I'd have been still and faint and hot with chagrin. I decided that it
was high time to write the essay.

2   First, the matter of semantics. I am a cripple. I choose this word to name me. I choose from among several possibilities, the most common of which are "handicapped" and "disabled." I made the choice a number of years ago, without thinking, unaware of my motives for doing so. Even now, I'm not sure what those motives are, but I recognize that they are complex and not entirely flattering. People—crippled or not—wince at the word "cripple," as they do not at "handicapped" or "disabled." Perhaps I want them to wince. I want them to see me as a tough customer, one to whom the fates/gods/viruses have not been kind, but who can face the brutal truth of her existence squarely. As a cripple, I swagger.

3   But, to be fair to myself, a certain amount of honesty underlies my choice. "Cripple" seems to me a clean word, straightforward and precise. It has an honorable history, having made its first appearance in the Lindisfarne Gospel in the tenth century. As a lover of words, I like the accuracy with which it describes my condition: I have lost the full use of my limbs. "Disabled," by contrast, suggests any incapacity, physical or mental. And I certainly don't like "handicapped," which implies that I have deliberately been put at a disadvantage, by whom I can't imagine (my God is not a Handicapper General), in order to equalize chances in the great race of life. These words seem to me to be moving away from my condition, to be widening the gap between word and reality. Most remote is the recently coined euphemism "differently abled," which partakes of the same semantic hopefulness that transformed countries from "undeveloped" to "underdeveloped," then to "less developed," and finally to "developing" nations. People have continued to starve in those countries during the shift. Some realities do not obey the dictates of language.

4   Mine is one of them. Whatever you call me, I remain crippled. But I don't care what you call me, so long as it isn't "differently abled," which strikes me as pure verbal garbage designed, by its ability to describe anyone, to describe no one. I subscribe to George Orwell's thesis that "the slovenliness of our language makes it easier for us to have foolish thoughts." And I refuse to participate in the degeneration of the language to the extent that I deny that I have lost anything in the course of this calamitous disease; I refuse to pretend that the only differences between you and me are the various ordinary ones that distinguish any one person from another. But call me "disabled" or "handicapped" if you like. I have long since grown accustomed to them; and if they are vague, at least they hint at the truth. Moreover, I use them myself. Society is no readier to accept crippledness than to accept death, war, sex, sweat, or wrinkles. I would never refer to another person as a cripple. It is the word I use to name only myself.

5   I haven't always been crippled, a fact for which I am soundly grateful. To be whole of limb is, I know from experience, infinitely more pleasant and useful than to be crippled; and if that knowledge leaves me open to bitterness at my loss, the physical soundness I once enjoyed (though I did not enjoy it half enough) is well worth the occasional stab of regret. Though never any good at sports, I was a normally active child and young adult. I climbed trees, played hopscotch, jumped rope, skated, swam, rode my bicycle, sailed. I despised team sports, spending some of the wretchedest afternoons of my life, sweaty and humiliated, behind a field-hockey stick and under a basketball hoop. I tramped alone for miles along the bridle paths that webbed the woods behind the house I grew up in. I swayed through countless dim hours in the arms of one man or another under the scattered shot of light from mirrored balls, and gyrated through countless more as Tab Hunter and Johnny Mathis gave way to the Rolling Stones, Creedence Clearwater Revival, Cream. I walked down the aisle. I pushed baby carriages, changed tires in the rain, marched for peace.

6   When I was twenty-eight I started to trip and drop things. What at first seemed my natural clumsiness soon became too pronounced to shrug off. I consulted a neurologist, who told me that I had a brain tumor. A battery of tests, increasingly disagreeable, revealed no tumor. About a year and a half later I developed a blurred spot in one eye. I had, at last, the episodes "disseminated in space and time" requisite for a diagnosis: multiple sclerosis. I have never been sorry for the doctor's initial misdiagnosis, however. For almost a week, until the negative results of the test were in, I thought that I was going to die right away. Every day for the past ten years, then, has been a kind of gift. I accept all gifts.

7   Multiple sclerosis is a chronic degenerative disease of the central nervous system, in which the myelin that sheathes the nerves is somehow eaten away and scar tissue forms in its place, interrupting the nerves' signals. During its course, which is unpredictable and uncontrollable, one may lose vision, hearing, speech, the ability to walk, control of bladder and/or bowels, strength in any or all extremities, sensitivity to touch, vibration, and/or pain, potency, coordination of movements—the list of possibilities is lengthy and, yes, horrifying. One may also lose one's sense of humor. That's the easiest to lose and the hardest to survive without.

8   In the past ten years, I have sustained some of these losses. Characteristic of MS are sudden attacks, called exacerbations, followed by remissions, and these I have not had. Instead, my disease has been slowly progressive. My left leg is now so weak that I walk with the aid of a brace and a cane; and for distances I use an Amigo, a variation on the

electric wheelchair that looks rather like an electrified kiddie car. I no longer have much use of my left hand. Now my right side is weakening as well. I still have the blurred spot in my right eye. Overall, though, I've been lucky so far. My world has, of necessity, been circumscribed by my losses, but the terrain left me has been ample enough for me to continue many of the activities that absorb me: writing, teaching, raising children and cats and plants and snakes, reading, speaking publicly about MS and depression, even playing bridge with people patient and honorable enough to let me scatter cards every which way without sneaking a peek.

9   Lest I begin to sound like Pollyanna, however, let me say that I don't like having MS. I hate it. My life holds realities—harsh ones, some of them—that no right-minded human being ought to accept without grumbling. One of them is fatigue. I know of no one with MS who does not complain of bone-weariness; in a disease that presents an astonishing variety of symptoms, fatigue seems to be a common factor. I wake up in the morning feeling the way most people do at the end of a bad day, and I take it from there. As a result, I spend a lot of time *in extremis* and, impatient with limitation, I tend to ignore my fatigue until my body breaks down in some way and forces rest. Then I miss picnics, dinner parties, poetry readings, the brief visits of old friends from out of town. The offspring of a puritanical tradition of exceptional venerability, I cannot view these lapses without shame. My life often seems a series of small failures to do as I ought.

10   I lead, on the whole, an ordinary life, probably rather like the one I would have led had I not had MS. I am lucky that my predilections were already solitary, sedentary, and bookish—unlike the world-famous French cellist I have read about, or the young woman I talked with one long afternoon who wanted only to be a jockey. I had just begun graduate school when I found out something was wrong with me, and I have remained, interminably, a graduate student. Perhaps I would not have if I'd thought I had the stamina to return to a full-time job as a technical editor; but I've enjoyed my studies.

11   In addition to studying, I teach writing courses. I also teach medical students how to give neurological examinations. I pick up freelance editing jobs here and there. I have raised a foster son and sent him into the world, where he has made me two grandbabies, and I am still escorting my daughter and son through adolescence. I go to Mass every Saturday. I am a superb, if messy, cook. I am also an enthusiastic laundress, capable of sorting a hamper full of clothes into five subtly differentiated piles, but a terrible housekeeper. I can do italic writing and, in an emergency, bathe an oil-soaked cat. I play a fiendish game of Scrabble. When I have the time and the money, I like to sit on my front steps with my husband,

drinking Amaretto and smoking a cigar, as we imagine our counterparts in Leningrad and make sure that the sun gets down once more behind the sharp childish scrawl of the Tucson Mountains.

12   This lively plenty has its bleak complement, of course, in all the things I can no longer do. I will never run again, except in dreams, and one day I may have to write that I will never walk again. I like to go camping, but I can't follow George and the children along the trails that wander out of a campsite through the desert or into the mountains. In fact, even on the level I've learned never to check the weather or try to hold a coherent conversation: I need all my attention for my wayward feet. Of late, I have begun to catch myself wondering how people can propel themselves without canes. With only one usable hand, I have to select my clothing with care not so much for style as for ease of ingress and egress, and even so, dressing can be laborious. I can no longer do fine stitchery, pick up babies, play the piano, braid my hair. I am immobilized by acute attacks of depression, which may or may not be physiologically related to MS but are certainly its logical concomitant.

13   These two elements, the plenty and the privation, are never pure, nor are the delight and wretchedness that accompany them. Almost every pickle that I get into as a result of my weakness and clumsiness— and I get into plenty—is funny as well as maddening and sometimes painful. I recall one May afternoon when a friend and I were going out for a drink after finishing up at school. As we were climbing into opposite sides of my car, chatting, I tripped and fell, flat and hard, onto the asphalt parking lot, my abrupt departure interrupting him in mid-sentence. "Where'd you go?" he called as he came around the back of the car to find me hauling myself up by the door frame. "Are you all right?" Yes, I told him, I was fine, just a bit rattly, and we drove off to find a shady patio and some beer. When I got home an hour or so later, my daughter greeted me with "What have you done to yourself?" I looked down. One elbow of my white turtleneck with the green froggies, one knee of my white trousers, one white kneesock were blood-soaked. We peeled off the clothes and inspected the damage, which was nasty enough but not alarming. That part wasn't funny: The abrasions took a long time to heal, and one got a little infected. Even so, when I think of my friend talking earnestly, suddenly, to the hot thin air while I dropped from his view as though through a trap door, I find the image as silly as something from a Marx Brothers movie.

14   I may find it easier than other cripples to amuse myself because I live propped by the acceptance and the assistance and, sometimes, the amusement of those around me. Grocery clerks tear my checks out of my checkbook for me, and sales clerks find chairs to put into dressing rooms when I want to try on clothes. The people I work with make sure I

teach at times when I am least likely to be fatigued, in places I can get to, with the materials I need. My students, with one anonymous exception (in an end-of-the-semester evaluation), have been unperturbed by my disability. Some even like it. One was immensely cheered by the information that I paint my own fingernails; she decided, she told me, that if I could go to such trouble over fine details, she could keep on writing essays. I suppose I became some sort of bright-fingered muse. She wrote good essays, too.

15   The most important struts in the framework of my existence, of course, are my husband and children. Dismayingly few marriages survive the MS test, and why should they? Most twenty-two- and nineteen-year-olds, like George and me, can vow in clear conscience, after a childhood of chicken pox and summer colds, to keep one another in sickness and in health so long as they both shall live. Not many are equipped for catastrophe: the dismay, the depression, the extra work, the boredom that a degenerative disease can insinuate into a relationship. And our society, with its emphasis on fun and its association of fun with physical performance, offers little encouragement for a whole spouse to stay with a crippled partner. Children experience similar stresses when faced with a crippled parent, and they are more helpless, since parents and children can't usually get divorced. They hate, of course, to be different from their peers, and the child whose mother is tacking down the aisle of a school auditorium packed with proud parents like a Cape Cod dinghy in a stiff breeze jolly well stands out in a crowd. Deprived of legal divorce, the child can at least deny the mother's disability, even her existence, forgetting to tell her about recitals and PTA meetings, refusing to accompany her to stores or church or the movies, never inviting friends to the house. Many do.

16   But I've been limping along for ten years now, and so far George and the children are still at my left elbow, holding tight. Anne and Matthew vacuum floors and dust furniture and haul trash and rake up dog droppings and button my cuffs and bake lasagna and Toll House cookies with just enough grumbling so I know that they don't have brain fever. And far from hiding me, they're forever dragging me by racks of fancy clothes or through teeming school corridors, or welcoming gaggles of friends while I'm wandering through the house in Anne's filmy pink babydoll pajamas. George generally calls before he brings someone home, but he does just as many dumb thankless chores as the children. And they all yell at me, laugh at some of my jokes, write me funny letters when we're apart—in short, treat me as an ordinary human being for whom they have some use. I think they like me. Unless they're faking. . . .

17   Faking. There's the rub. Tugging at the fringes of my consciousness always is the terror that people are kind to me only because I'm a cripple.

My mother almost shattered me once, with that instinct mothers have—blind, I think, in this case, but unerring nonetheless—for striking blows along the fault-lines of their children's hearts, by telling me, in an attack on my selfishness, "We all have to make allowances for you, of course, because of the way you are." From the distance of a couple of years, I have to admit that I haven't any idea just what she meant, and I'm not sure that she knew either. She was awfully angry. But at the time, as the words thudded home, I felt my worst fear, suddenly realized. I could bear being called selfish: I am. But I couldn't bear the corroboration that those around me were doing in fact what I'd always suspected them of doing, professing fondness while silently putting up with me because of the way I am. A cripple. I've been a little cracked ever since.

18   Along with this fear that people are secretly accepting shoddy goods comes a relentless pressure to please—to prove myself worth the burdens I impose, I guess, or to build a substantial account of goodwill against which I may write drafts in times of need. Part of the pressure arises from social expectations. In our society, anyone who deviates from the norm had better find some way to compensate. Like fat people, who are expected to be jolly, cripples must bear their lot meekly and cheerfully. A grumpy cripple isn't playing by the rules. And much of the pressure is self-generated. Early on I vowed that, if I had to have MS, by God I was going to do it well. This is a class act, ladies and gentlemen. No tears, no recriminations, no faint-heartedness.

19   One way and another, then, I wind up feeling like Tiny Tim, peering over the edge of the table at the Christmas goose, waving my crutch, piping down God's blessing on us all. Only sometimes I don't want to play Tiny Tim. I'd rather be Caliban, a most scurvy monster. Fortunately, at home no one much cares whether I'm a good cripple or a bad cripple as long as I make vichyssoise with fair regularity. One evening several years ago, Anne was reading at the dining-room table while I cooked dinner. As I opened a can of tomatoes, the can slipped in my left hand and juice spattered me and the counter with bloody spots. Fatigued and infuriated, I bellowed, "I'm so sick of being crippled!" Anne glanced at me over the top of her book. "There now," she said, "do you feel better?" "Yes," I said, "yes, I do." She went back to her reading. I felt better. That's about all the attention my scurviness ever gets.

20   Because I hate being crippled, I sometimes hate myself for being a cripple. Over the years I have come to expect—even accept—attacks of violent self-loathing. Luckily, in general our society no longer connects deformity and disease directly with evil (though a charismatic once told me that I have MS because a devil is in me) and so I'm allowed to move largely at will, even among small children. But I'm not sure that this revision of attitude has been particularly helpful. Physical imperfection, even freed of moral disapprobation, still defies and violates the ideal, es-

pecially for women, whose confinement in their bodies as objects of desire is far from over. Each age, of course, has its ideal, and I doubt that ours is any better or worse than any other. Today's ideal woman, who lives on the glossy pages of dozens of magazines, seems to be between the ages of eighteen and twenty-five; her hair has body, her teeth flash white, her breath smells minty, her underarms are dry; she has a career but is still a fabulous cook, especially of meals that take less than twenty minutes to prepare; she does not ordinarily appear to have a husband or children; she is trim and deeply tanned; she jogs, swims, plays tennis, rides a bicycle, sails, but does not bowl; she travels widely, even to out-of-the-way places like Finland and Samoa, always in the company of the ideal man, who possesses a nearly identical set of characteristics. There are a few exceptions. Though usually white and often blonde, she may be black, Hispanic, Asian, or Native American, so long as she is unusually sleek. She may be old, provided she is selling a laxative or is Lauren Bacall. If she is selling a detergent, she may be married and have a flock of strikingly messy children. But she is never a cripple.

21   Like many women I know, I have always had an uneasy relationship with my body. I was not a popular child, largely, I think now, because I was peculiar: intelligent, intense, moody, shy, given to unexpected actions and inexplicable notions and emotions. But as I entered adolescence, I believed myself unpopular because I was homely: my breasts too flat, my mouth too wide, my hips too narrow, my clothing never quite right in fit or style. I was not, in fact, particularly ugly, old photographs inform me, though I was well off the ideal; but I carried this sense of self-alienation with me into adulthood, where it regenerated in response to the depredations of MS. Even with my brace I walk with a limp so pronounced that, seeing myself on the videotape of a television program on the disabled, I couldn't believe that anything but an inch-worm could make progress humping along like that. My shoulders droop and my pelvis thrusts forward as I try to balance myself upright, throwing my frame into a bony S. As a result of contractures, one shoulder is higher than the other and I carry one arm bent in front of me, the fingers curled into a claw. My left arm and leg have wasted into pipe-stems, and I try always to keep them covered. When I think about how my body must look to others, especially to men, to whom I have been trained to display myself, I feel ludicrous, even loathsome.

22   At my age, however, I don't spend much time thinking about my appearance. The burning egocentricity of adolescence, which assures one that all the world is looking all the time, has passed, thank God, and I'm generally too caught up in what I'm doing to step back, as I used to, and watch myself as though upon a stage. I'm also too old to believe in the accuracy of self-image. I know that I'm not a hideous crone, that in fact, when I'm rested, well dressed, and well made up, I look fine. The

self-loathing I feel is neither physically nor intellectually substantial. What I hate is not me but a disease.

23   I am not a disease.

24   And a disease is not—at least not singlehandedly—going to determine who I am, though at first it seemed to be going to. Adjusting to a chronic incurable illness, I have moved through a process similar to that outlined by Elisabeth Kübler-Ross in *On Death and Dying.* The major difference—and it is far more significant than most people recognize—is that I can't be sure of the outcome, as the terminally ill cancer patient can. Research studies indicate that, with proper medical care, I may achieve a "normal" life span. And in our society, with its vision of death as the ultimate evil, worse even than decrepitude, the response to such news is, "Oh well, at least you're not going to *die.*" Are there worse things than dying? I think that there may be.

25   I think of two women I know, both with MS, both enough older than I to have served me as models. One took to her bed several years ago and has been there ever since. Although she can sit in a high-backed wheel-chair, because she is incontinent she refuses to go out at all, even though incontinence pants, which are readily available at any pharmacy, could protect her from embarrassment. Instead, she stays at home and insists that her husband, a small quiet man, a retired civil servant, stay there with her except for a quick weekly foray to the supermarket. The other woman, whose illness was diagnosed when she was eighteen, a nursing student engaged to a young doctor, finished her training, married her doctor, accompanied him to Germany when he was in the service, bore three sons and a daughter, now grown and gone. When she can, she travels with her husband; she plays bridge, embroiders, swims regularly; she works, like me, as a symptomatic-patient instructor of medical students in neurology. Guess which woman I hope to be.

26   At the beginning, I thought about having MS almost incessantly. And because of the unpredictable course of the disease, my thoughts were always terrified. Each night I'd get into bed wondering whether I'd get out again the next morning, whether I'd be able to see, to speak, to hold a pen between my fingers. Knowing that the day might come when I'd be physically incapable of killing myself, I thought perhaps I ought to do so right away, while I still had the strength. Gradually I came to understand that the Nancy who might one day lie inert under a bedsheet, arms and legs paralyzed, unable to feed or bathe herself, unable to reach out for a gun, a bottle of pills, was not the Nancy I was at present, and that I could not presume to make decisions for that future Nancy, who might well not want in the least to die. Now the only provision I've made for the future Nancy is that when the time comes—and it is likely

to come in the form of pneumonia, friend to the weak and the old—I am not to be treated with machines and medications. If she is unable to communicate by then, I hope she will be satisfied with these terms.

27   Thinking all the time about having MS grew tiresome and intrusive, especially in the large and tragic mode in which I was accustomed to considering my plight. Months and even years went by without catastrophe (at least without one related to MS), and really I was awfully busy, what with George and children and snakes and students and poems, and I hadn't the time, let alone the inclination, to devote myself to being a disease. Too, the richer my life became, the funnier it seemed, as though there were some connection between largesse and laughter, and so my tragic stance began to waver until, even with the aid of a brace and a cane, I couldn't hold it for very long at a time.

28   After several years I was satisfied with my adjustment. I had suffered my grief and fury and terror, I thought, but now I was at ease with my lot. Then one summer day I set out with George and the children across the desert for a vacation in California. Part way to Yuma I became aware that my right leg felt funny. "I think I've had an exacerbation," I told George. "What shall we do?" he asked. "I think we'd better get the hell to California," I said, "because I don't know whether I'll ever make it again." So we went on to San Diego and then to Orange, up the Pacific Coast Highway to Santa Cruz, across to Yosemite, down to Sequoia and Joshua Tree, and so back over the desert to home. It was a fine two-week trip, filled with friends and fair weather, and I wouldn't have missed it for the world, though I did in fact make it back to California two years later. Nor would there have been any point in missing it, since in MS, once the symptoms have appeared, the neurological damage has been done, and there's no way to predict or prevent that damage.

29   The incident spoiled my self-satisfaction, however. It renewed my grief and fury and terror, and I learned that one never finishes adjusting to MS. I don't know now why I thought one would. One does not, after all, finish adjusting to life, and MS is simply a fact of my life—not my favorite fact, of course—but as ordinary as my nose and my tropical fish and my yellow Mazda station wagon. It may at any time get worse, but no amount of worry or anticipation can prepare me for a new loss. My life is a lesson in losses. I learn one at a time.

30   And I had best be patient in the learning, since I'll have to do it like it or not. As any rock fan knows, you can't always get what you want. Particularly when you have MS. You can't, for example, get cured. In recent years researchers and the organizations that fund research have started to pay MS some attention even though it isn't fatal; perhaps they have begun to see that life is something other than a quantitative

phenomenon, that one may be very much alive for a very long time in a life that isn't worth living. The researchers have made some progress toward understanding the mechanism of the disease: It may well be an autoimmune reaction triggered by a slow-acting virus. But they are nowhere near its prevention, control, or cure. And most of us want to be cured. Some, unable to accept incurability, grasp at one treatment after another, no matter how bizarre: megavitamin therapy, gluten-free diet, injections of cobra venom, hypothermal suits, lymphocytopharesis, hyperbaric chambers. Many treatments are probably harmless enough, but none are curative.

31   The absence of a cure often makes MS patients bitter toward their doctors. Doctors are, after all, the priests of modern society, the new shamans, whose business is to heal, and many an MS patient roves from one to another, searching for the "good" doctor who will make him well. Doctors too think of themselves as healers, and for this reason many have trouble dealing with MS patients, whose disease in its intransigence defeats their aims and mocks their skills. Too few doctors, it is true, treat their patients as whole human beings, but the reverse is also true. I have always tried to be gentle with my doctors, who often have more at stake in terms of ego than I do. I may be frustrated, maddened, depressed by the incurability of my disease, but I am not diminished by it, and they are. When I push myself up from my seat in the waiting room and stumble toward them, I incarnate the limitation of their powers. The least I can do is refuse to press on their tenderest spots.

32   This gentleness is part of the reason that I'm not sorry to be a cripple. I didn't have it before. Perhaps I'd have developed it anyway—how could I know such a thing?—and I wish I had more of it, but I'm glad of what I have. It has opened and enriched my life enormously, this sense that my frailty and need must be mirrored in others, that in searching for and shaping a stable core in a life wrenched by change and loss, change and loss, I must recognize the same process, under individual conditions, in the lives around me. I do not deprecate such knowledge, however I've come by it.

33   All the same, if a cure were found, would I take it? In a minute. I may be a cripple, but I'm only occasionally a loony and never a saint. Anyway, in my brand of theology God doesn't give bonus points for a limp. I'd take a cure; I just don't need one. A friend who also has MS startled me once by asking, "Do you ever say to yourself, 'Why me, Lord?'" "No, Michael, I don't," I told him, "because whenever I try, the only response I can think of is 'Why not?'" If I could make a cosmic deal, who would I put in my place? What in my life would I give up in exchange for sound limbs and a thrilling rush of energy? No one. Nothing. I might as well do the job myself. Now that I'm getting the hang of it.

TO THINK ABOUT

1. Why does Mairs identify herself as "crippled," rather than "handicapped" or "disabled"? Why does she use the word "crippled" only when describing herself, never others?
2. Are you comfortable with a narrator as direct and honest as Nancy Mairs? Would you be comfortable speaking with her? Why or why not?
3. What euphemisms are you in the habit of using? Why? Are there times when euphemisms are justified? At what point does a euphemism become a lie?
4. Mairs rejected suicide because she decided she was incapable of imagining what her future self would want her to do. Compare her reasoning to Cynthia Vann's in "A Death in the Family" (Chapter 47). When you are making a decision, do you take into consideration what some future version of yourself might desire?

TO DO

1. Make a list of all the things you are—all the labels that make up parts of your identity. Examine the list. Mark the items with which you feel the strongest affinity. Then choose from that smaller list the item about which you are the most curious: what does it *mean* to be a man, a woman, a son, a daughter, a brother, a sister, a lover, a diabetic, a Baptist, a dancer, an athlete, a rape victim, a scholar?
2. Go to the library. Do some research on the facet of your identity that you have chosen to write about.
3. Then write an essay on your chosen subject. The essay should consist primarily of your own experiences, supplemented by some of your research material.

TIP

We have been brought up to be polite. We know we should not impose ourselves on others. If we go on too long about our beliefs, our hopes, our failures, our love lives, our political beliefs, our disappointments, we are rude, boorish, dull.

And so when we sit down to write about ourselves we are inhibited by years of conditioning. But if we are to write well about ourselves we must suspend these unwritten rules. Let it all out. Get it down. Look at it.

But won't it be as dull on paper as it is in conversation?

No—not unless readers are shown the unedited first draft.

Conversation is almost always a first draft. Good writing almost never is.

32

On Not Liking Sex
Nancy Mairs

We like tasks that are easily defined, recipes that are easily followed. We hope our essays will be strong, definitive statements, free of ambivalence and loose ends. Such essays exist, like closed chapters in our lives; there are many in this book. (See, for example, "High Heels" by Caryl Rivers, Chapter 39; "Uncommon Decency," by Harry Stein, Chapter 46; and even "On Being a Cripple," by Nancy Mairs, Chapter 31.) But some subjects resist precision and neat endings; these subjects—because of, not despite, their complex and elusive natures—draw us to them.

Nancy Mairs once wrote a brief, conclusive essay titled "On Not Liking Sex." She put it away. A few years later, she took it out and read it. She didn't like it. So she surrounded it with another essay, not as brief, pretty, or easy, but more insightful and rewarding.

1   "The other day, sitting in a tweed chair with my knees crossed, drinking a cup of coffee and smoking a cigarette, I looked straight at my therapist and said, 'I don't like sex.' I have known this man for years now. I have told him that I don't like my husband, my children, my parents, my students, my life. I may even have said at some time, 'I don't like sex very much.' But the difference between not liking sex very much and not liking sex is vast, vaster even than the Catholic Church's gulf between salvation and damnation, because there's no limbo, no purgatory. An irony here: For in another age (perhaps in this age within the bosom of the Holy Mother Church) I would be the woman whose price is above rubies, pure and virtuous, purity and virtue having always attached themselves, at least for women, to the matter of sex. As it is, I am, in my metaphor, one of the damned. My therapist has a homelier metaphor. I have, he says, what our society considers 'the worst wart.' In 1981 in the United States of America one cannot fail to like sex. It's not normal. It's not nice."

2   This paragraph opened a brief essay I wrote a couple of years ago entitled "On Not Liking Sex." The essay, which I have preserved here in quotation marks, was a brittle, glittery piece, a kind of spun confection of the verbal play I'd like to engage in at cocktail parties but can muster only at a solitary desk with a legal-size yellow pad in front of me. It was, in fact, as you can see if you read it straight through, cocktail party chatter. And yet it was true, insofar as any truth can be translated into words. That is, it said some things, and suggested others, about me and the times I live in which were accurate enough as far as they went.

3   But they certainly didn't go very far. Hardly to the end of the block. Certainly not across the street. This essay is an almost perfect example of a phenomenon I've only recently become aware of, though clearly at a deeper level I've understood its workings for a very long time, a kind of pretense at serious writing which I use to keep busy and out of trouble: the kind of trouble you get when you run smack into an idea so significant and powerful that the impact jars you to the bone. It's a way of staying out of the traffic. It is not babble, and it is not easy. On the contrary, it requires painstakingly chosen diction, deliberately controlled syntax, and seamless organization. A rough spot is a trouble spot, a split, a crack, out of which something dreadful (probably black, probably with a grin) may leap and squash you flat.

4   If this essay was an exercise in making careful statements that would ensure that I never said what I really had to say, then what did I have to say? I don't know. If I'd known then, I couldn't have written such a piece in the first place. And the only progress I've made since then is to have gained a little courage in the face of things that leap out of cracks in the pavement. If I look at the essay again closely, if I listen for the resonances among the words with the not-yet-words, perhaps I can discover some portion of the significance—for the woman just turned forty in the 1980s in the United States of America—of not liking sex.

5   The title and the first paragraph, by using words as though, like algebraic notation, they had fixed meanings in the context of a given problem, claim to have signified an attitude they have in fact obscured. Even if *on* and *not* may be allowed a certain fixity as they function here, *liking* and *sex* may not. *Sex*, in its most general sense, is simply the way one is: male or female just as black or brown, blue- or hazel-eyed, long-or stubby-fingered, able or not to curl one's tongue into a tube. The genes take care of it. One may dislike one's sex, apparently, just as my daughter dislikes her nose, which is round and tends toward rosy under the sun; some people, thanks to the technological genius of modern medicine, even change theirs. But I like my sex. I suffer from penis envy, of course, to the extent that freedom and privilege have attached themselves to this fleshy sign; I've never wished for the actual appendage,

however, except on long car trips through sparsely populated areas. In fact, looked at this way, *not liking sex* doesn't make sense to me at all, any more than do *having sex, wanting sex, demanding sex, refusing sex.* Such phrases clarify the specialized use of the word as shorthand for sexual activity, particularly sexual intercourse.

6   So I don't like sexual activity. But *like* can mean both to take pleasure in, enjoy, and to wish to have, want; and wanting something seems to me quite a different matter from enjoying it. The former is volitional, a reaching out for experience, whereas the latter is a response to an experience (whether sought for or not) already in progress. In these terms I can and often do enjoy sex. But I do not necessarily want to engage in sexual activity even though I may enjoy doing so.

7   "The human psyche being the squirmy creature that it is, I have trouble pinning down my objections to sex. I do not seem to object to the act itself which, if I can bring myself to commit it, I like very well. I object to the idea. My objections are undoubtedly, in part, Puritanical. Not for nothing did John Howland, Stephen Hopkins, Thomas Rogers, and Elder William Brewster bring on the Mayflower the seed that would one day bloom in me. If it feels good, it's bad. Sex feels good. My objections may also be aesthetic: It's a sweaty, slimy business. Certainly they are mythic, Eros and Thanatos colliding in the orgasm to explode the frail self back into the atoms of the universe. Love is Death."

8   The human psyche squirms indeed, especially when it is striving to distance itself from its desires by creating platonic distinctions between things in themselves and the ideas of things. I don't object to the idea of sex. In fact, I don't feel any particular response one way or the other to the idea of sex. Sex for me as for most, I should think, is not ideational but sensual, and it is this distinction that gives me trouble, a distinction that resembles that between wanting and enjoying. I don't object to the *idea* of sex: I object to the *sense* of sex. An act is a sign. Directly apprehended, it has always at least one meaning and usually a multiplicity of meanings. These I must sort out—their implications, their resonances— in order to understand how I, with a singularly human perversity, can not want what I enjoy.

9   Puritanism, aesthetics, and myth all play a part in this response, no doubt, though the reference to the Mayflower is misleading (the Pilgrims were not Puritans, though many of their descendants were), and as far as I know, the Puritans did not prohibit the sex act—no matter what it felt like—so long as it was confined to the marriage bed. The kind of puritanism that has dogged me is more diffuse than that of my foremothers, perhaps the inevitable legacy of their hard-scrabble existence in tiny

communities clinging to the flinty, bitter-wintered New England coast, no longer a religion but still a code of conduct, close-mouthed, grudging of joy, quick to judge and reject. We conducted ourselves at all levels with restraint. Our disapproval of Catholics was not particularly theological; rather, we thought them primitive, childishly taken with display, with their candles and crosses and croziers, play-acting at religion. We painted our houses white with black or green shutters, grey with blue shutters, sometimes soft yellow or dark brown, and we shuddered at the pink and turquoise and lime green on the little capes and ranches that belonged, we assumed, to the Italians. When we met, we greeted one another with a nod, perhaps a small smile, a few words, a firm handshake, even a kiss on the cheek, depending on the degree of our intimacy, but we did not fall into each other's arms with loud smackings, everybody jabbering at once. As a child I was given to fits of weeping and outbursts of delight which to this day my mother refers to with a sigh as "Nancy's dramatics"; I do not, of course, have them now.

10   Here is the real aesthetics of the matter: the refinement of decoration and gesture to a state so etiolated that voices pierce, perfumes smother, colors clash and scream and shout. I still dislike wearing red and certain shades of pink and orange. The entire sensory world impinges—presses, pinches, pummels—unless one keeps a distance. Touch comes, eventually, to burn. Sex isn't bad so much because it feels good as because it's poor form—the kind of rowdy, riotous behavior one squelches in children as they become young ladies (honest to God, I was never permitted to refer to female human beings as women but only as ladies) and gentlemen. Sex is indecorous.

12   As for the sweat and slime, the basis for this objection strikes me as more medical than aesthetic. After all, one can get a good deal grubbier on a hike up a small mountain, which is just good clean fun. But the body itself is not clean. It is, according to pathologists like my ancestor Rudolf Virchow, a veritable pesthouse. I grew up knowing that my breath was pestilent ("cover your mouth when you sneeze"), that my mouth was pestilent ("don't kiss me—you've got a cold"). And then along came men, themselves crawling with germs, who breathed on me, who wanted to put their mouths on mine and make me sick. Rudolf may have done wonders for German public health, but he sure put a kink in my private sex life. Oddly enough, this phobia of germs did not include my genitalia, perhaps because they lay untouched and unpondered until long after it had been formed. Nowadays, with the threat of venereal disease widely publicized, I don't suppose one can be so insouciant. The germs lurk at every orifice, and sex is simply contrary to good sanitary practices.

13   Poor sanitary practices may give you a cold or a stomach flu or her-pes, but they are not, in Tucson in 1983, likely to do you in. The equa-tion of sex with death is of another order altogether, though not the less dreadful for not being literal. As late as the Renaissance *to die* was used as we use *to come* to signify orgasm; and although we have abandoned the explicit connection, we have not lost the construct that underlies it. Orgasm shares, briefly, the characteristics we imagine death to have, the annihilation (or at least the transmogrification) of consciousness, the ex-tinction of the *I* that forms and controls being. The loss of my hard-won identity, even for an instant, risks forfeiture of self: not perhaps the death that ends in the coffin but certainly the death that ends in the cell: I am afraid of going away and never coming back.

14   "But most strongly, my objections are what I reluctantly term 'po-litical.' My reluctance stems from the sense that 'political' in this con-text implies the kind of radical lesbianism that suggests that medical technology is sufficiently advanced to permit the elimination of the male entirely. I learned, in one of the most poignant affairs of my life, that I am not lesbian. Nor am I even a good feminist, since I seldom think abstractly and tend to run principles together like the paints on a sloppy artist's palette, the results being colorful but hardly coherent. No, when I say 'political,' I mean something purely personal governing the nature of the relationship between me and a given man. In this sense, sex is a political act. In it, I lose power, through submission or, in one in-stance, through force. In either case, my integrity is violated; I become possessed."

15   Here's the heart of the matter—politics—and I've dashed it off and done it up with ribbons of lesbianism and feminism so that the plain package hardly shows. True, I'm not lesbian, but thanks to the funda-mental heterosexual bias of our culture no one would be likely to as-sume that I was. And I am, in fact, a perfectly good if unsystematic femi-nist. Who in my audience, I wonder, was I worried about when I made that self-deprecatory moue, as if to say, "Don't expect too much of me; I'm just a nonradical heterosexual little woman, a bit daffy perhaps, but harmless"? And what the hell (now that I've got the ribbons off) is in the box that made me wrap it up so tight?

16   Politics. Power. Submission. Force. Violation. Possession. Sex is not merely a political act; it is an act of war. And no act is ever "purely per-sonal." It is a nexus that accretes out of earlier and other acts older than memory, older than dreams: the exchange of women, along with goods, gestures, and words, in the creation of allies; the ascription to women of

all that lurks terrible in the darkened brain; the protection and penetration of the maidenhead in rituals for ensuring paternity and perpetuating lineage; the conscription of women's sons for the destruction of human beings, of women's daughters for their reproduction; enforcement of silence; theft of subjectivity; immurement; death. If I think that what I do, in or out of bed, originates in me, I am a much madder woman than I believe myself to be. I am no original but simply a locus of language in a space and time that permits one—in politics as in sex—to fuck or get fucked. Aggression is the germ in all the words.

17   From such an angle, sex is always rape, and indeed I tangle the two words at the level just below articulation. Perhaps I do so because my first sexual intercourse was a rape. At least it occurred in the safety of my own bed by someone I knew intimately, so that although I was furious, I was never in fear for my life. We were both nineteen, had been high-school sweethearts grown apart, and he had come to spend a weekend at the Farm, where I was working as a mother's helper for the summer. We spent the evening deep in conversation, I remember, and after I went to bed, he came into my room, jumped on top of me, deflowered me, and went away again. I don't believe we ever exchanged a word or an embrace. I felt some pain, and in the morning I found blood on my thighs and on the sheets, which I had secretly to wash, so I know that all of this really happened, but I never permitted myself the least feeling about it, not as much as I might have given a nightmare. I *knew* that I was furious, but I *felt* nothing. I don't know what response he expected, but he got none at all. He left the next day, without my ever having spoken to him, and we never met again.

18   Nor do I know what effect he intended his act to have. I'm sure that he was marking me, for we grew up at the tail end of the time when virginity had real significance, and in defloration he claimed me in only a slightly more subtle manner than incising his initials into some hidden area of my flesh. He knew that I was in love with another man, that I planned to be married within a year, and for a long time I believed that he was trying, through some sort of magical thinking, to force me to marry him instead. We really did believe that a woman belonged to the man who first "had" her. But now I think that he wasn't marking me for himself so much as spoiling me for George. Whatever its true interpretation, his act makes clear my absence from the transaction. The business was between him and George, the item of exchange one tarnished coin.

19   To sense myself such a cipher robs me of power. In sex, as in many other instances, I feel powerless. Part of this feeling arises from the fact that, as new symptoms of multiple sclerosis appear and worsen, my power literally drains away. But to what extent is multiple sclerosis merely the physical inscription of my way of being in the world? In sex,

as in the rest of my life, I am acted upon. I am the object, not the agent. I live in the passive voice. The phallus penetrates me; I do not surround, engulf, incorporate the phallus. No wonder Caleb raped me. Rape was his only grammatical option.

20   Thus, I see that in a queer and cruel way I raped him by forcing him to rape me. I always made myself the object of his desire. How many times, I remember now, we came to the brink of intercourse, and always at the last I turned him away, pretending that I couldn't overcome my moral scruples. What I really couldn't overcome was a barrier so ludicrous that I don't expect you to believe it: my underpants. I couldn't figure out how to get rid of them. The women in films and romantic novels, where I'd gotten my impressions of the mechanics of intercourse, didn't struggle with underpants. Did I think they just melted away? After all, I took my underpants off every day as matter-of-factly as I kicked them under the bed to drive my mother wild with despair over my inability to keep some man a decent house. Why then could I not just take them off an extra time? The gesture seemed too overt, too clumsy and pedestrian for the occasion. I couldn't bear to look a fool. So I lay in bondage to the concept of woman as image, not agent, kept a virgin till I was nineteen by Carter Lollipop Pants, red ones and navy ones, their combed cotton grim as iron through my crotch. But for Caleb, who knew nothing of my quandary, I was withholding a treasure that must have seemed of great worth, since I guarded it so jealously. I think I can understand his fury when I threatened to give it to someone else.

21   Ah, but I'm so old now. I can't blame myself for having been a fool, or him for having believed me a pearl of great price instead of a human being, for whatever she was worth. We were both too young to give tongue to the grammar of our intercourse. All I can do now is use the leverage of my understanding to pry open the box I have stripped and look at the contents squarely. In sex, that political act, I lose power because I have still not learned what it might be and how to claim it. "For this reason, I have preferred casual lovers to a permanent, long-term partner. They have fewer expectations, thus minimizing possession and obligation. Less is at stake. With them, I can concentrate on the act itself without worrying about its implications. They will be gone long before they learn enough about me to threaten my privacy or come to consider sexual access a right or even a privilege. But even lovers, the romantic ones at least, are risky. They can be more interested in being in love than in bed. My latest lover pitched me out on the grounds that he wasn't in love with me (don't ask me why he took me in—life is complicated enough as it is); and with the irony that won't work in fiction but does splendidly in life, I had fallen in love with him, only the second time that I have done so and the only time that doing so was a mistake. The

experience was so nearly disastrous that I learned precipitously the lesson that had long been floating just outside the periphery of my vision: Celibacy is power."

22   An agoraphobe, a depressive, I have long since learned that avoidance is the most comfortable way to cope with situations that make me uneasy, and God knows sex makes me uneasy. In the playfulness of the opening of a sexual relationship, the issue of power is eclipsed by curiosity, exhilaration, voluptuousness. I find my delight in the process chronicled in my journal: "I sit beside Richard. It is terribly hot—I can feel the steam from both our bodies. We play the touching game—arms touch, knees brush, shoulders press together—at first by 'accident,' testing for response, then deliberately. I love this game, as often as I've played it and as silly as it is; it has a kind of rhythm and elegance when played properly, with good humor, without haste. Richard is very good at it. When, at one point, we have looked at one another for a long moment, he smiles a little and I say, 'What?' He starts to say something, then breaks off: 'You know.' I laugh and say, 'I've been wondering what would happen if I leaned over and kissed you.' It is a dumb idea—I don't know most of the people there very well, but Richard does, and they all know that I'm married. 'I think we'd better wait to do that on our own,' he replies. 'Soon.' 'Yes,' I say, 'yes, soon.' If I hadn't driven my own car, it could have been right then. Wasn't. The kiss is yet to come."

23   But in truth I do not like sex, even in brief affairs. In the rush of excitement I think I do, but afterwards I am always embarrassed by it. If I could stay balanced in the delicious vertigo of flirtation, I might not feel ashamed, but I can't. I always want to tumble dizzily into bed. And after I've been there, even once, my privacy has been not merely threatened but ruptured. My privacy I carry around me as a bubble of space. Quite literally. I hate to be touched. I hate to be known. If the bubble is pricked, I may disintegrate, leaking out vaporously and vanishing on the wind. The man who has even once seen me up close, naked and transported, knows more about me than I can bear for him to know. For this reason, I have not, in fact, preferred casual lovers to a permanent, long-term partner; if I had, I wouldn't still be married after twenty years. I have taken a casual lover every now and then in the hope that I can reduce sex to pure, unfreighted fun; but the baggage always catches up with me.

24   One of the cases, of course, carries love. Lovers and husbands alike are risky to a woman who cannot bear to be loved any more than to be touched. I can feel love creep around me, pat me with soft fingers, and I stiffen and struggle for breath. By contrast, I quite readily fall in love and have loved, in some way, all but one of the men I've slept with. So what

all the bobbing and weaving about my "latest lover" might mean I'm not sure. I hadn't, at the time I wrote the essay, got over him, and my immediate judgment now is that one oughtn't to try to write the truth while in the kind of turmoil that at that time was threatening my sanity and therefore my life. But on second thought I see that here are simply two truths. I wrote the truth when I said that I'd fallen in love with only two lovers in my life, though I can't think now who I had in mind: I write the truth when I say that I've fallen in love with all but one. Quod scripsi, scripsi. Anyway, I must have learned some lesson from the bitterness the last one brought me, for I have not taken another.

25   All the same, celibacy is not power. Celibacy is celibacy: the withholding of oneself from sexual union. When it is actively chosen as a means of redirecting one's attention, as it is by some religious, it may both reflect and confer personal power. But when it is clutched at as a means of disengaging oneself from the tentacles of human conflict, it is simply one more technique for avoiding distress. As I stay at home to avoid agoraphobic attacks. I stay out of bed to avoid claustrophobic ones. I am celibate not for the love of God but for the fear of love.

26   "Avoiding sex altogether is not difficult. You must simply rent a tiny apartment, large enough only for yourself and possibly a very small black cat, and let no one into it. If you want friends, meet them at their houses, if they'll have you, at bars and restaurants, at art galleries, poetry readings, concerts. But don't take them home with you. Keep your space inviolate. During attacks of loneliness and desire, smoke cigarettes. Drink Amaretto. Throw the I Ching. Write essays. Letting someone into your space is tantamount to letting him between your legs, and more dangerous, since you risk his touching the inner workings of your life, not merely your body. Ask him if he wouldn't rather drive into the country for a picnic."

27   This advice is sound. I have tested all of it. Then I swallowed a handful of Elavil one Hallowe'en and almost succeeded in avoiding sex altogether.

28   "All this I have learned. What I haven't learned is what to do with the grief and guilt that not liking sex inevitably arouses. The grief is so protean and private that I will not attempt to articulate it. But the guilt is a decidedly public matter, since it could not exist—not in its present form anyway—in the absence of post-Freudian social pressure to regard sex as the primary source not of joy (I doubt that contemporary society knows much about joy) but of satisfaction. If I don't like sex, I am abnormal, repressed, pathetic, sick—the labels vary but the significance is con-

sistent—I do not belong in the ranks of healthy human beings, health requiring as one of its terms sexual activity and fulfillment."

29   By separating out grief from the complex of responses I feel to not wanting sex, and by tying it off as a "private" matter, I hoped perhaps that, like a vestigial finger or toe, it would drop away. But the dissociation is not authentic, because in fact all my responses are private insofar as the construct they form is my peculiar *I*, and all are public insofar as that *I* is a linguistic product spoken by a patriarchal culture that insists that my God-created function is to rejoice, through my person, the heart of a man. Moreover, failure to do so results not in guilt, as I have stated it, but in shame, which is a truly protean (and, say some feminists, distinctively feminine) emotion, pervasive and inexpiable. About guilt one can do something: Like a wound in the flesh, with proper cleansing it will heal, the scar, however twisted and lumpy, proof against infection. Shame, like the vaginal wound always open to invasion, is an inoperable state. My tongue has given me these distinctions. With it I must acknowledge my shame.

30   Shamelessness, like shame, is not a masculine condition. That is, there is no *shameless man* as there is a *shameless woman* or, as my grandmother used to say, a *shameless hussy*. A man without shame is in general assumed simply to have done nothing he need feel guilty about. A woman without shame is a strumpet, a trollop, a whore, a witch. The connotations have been, immemorially, sexual. Here is the thirteenth-century author of the *Ancrene Riwle*, a priest instructing three anchoresses in the correct manner of confession: "A woman will say, 'I have been foolish' or 'I had a lover,' whereas she should confess, 'I am a stud mare, a stinking whore.'" And somewhat later, in the *Malleus Maleficarum*, a warning to Inquisitors: "All witchcraft comes from carnal Lust which is in Women insatiable." My sexuality has been the single most powerful disruptive force mankind has ever perceived, and its repression has been the work of centuries.

31   Now, suddenly, the message has changed. Now, after ages of covering my face and my genitals—St. Paul's veil over my hair, my breasts bound, my waist girded in whalebone, my face masked with kohl and rouge, my length swathed in white cambric pierced by a lace-edged buttonhole through which to guide the erect penis to my hidden treasure—I am supposed to strip to the skin and spread my legs and strive for multiple orgasm.

32   Knowing what The Fathers have given me to know of the dangers of female sexuality, how could I dare?

33   "If I got this message from one person at a time, I might be able to deal with it with rationality, distance, even amusement. But I get it im-

personally, from all sides, in a barrage so relentless that the wonder is that I survive my guilt, let alone cope with it. I get the message from the bookshelves, where I find not only *The Joy of Sex* but also *More Joy of Sex*, written by a man whose very name promises physical contentment. (I have read some of these books. They contain many instructions on how to do it well. I know how to do it well. I just don't know whether I want to do it at all.) The message comes with my jeans, which I may buy no longer merely for durability and comfort but for the ache they will create in some man's crotch. It foams in my toothpaste, my bath soap, even my dish detergent. It follows me through the aisles of the supermarket and the drugstore. It ridicules my breastless body, my greying hair."

34   Or has the message really changed? The body swaddled has become the body naked but it is, all the same, the female body, artifice of desire, still inscribed after stripping with the marks of straps cut into the shoulders, underwires into the breasts, zipper into the belly, squeezed and shaved and deodorized until it is shapely and sanitary enough to arouse no dread of its subjective possibilities. The mechanics of its eroticism have been altered so that, instead of receiving male desire as a patient vessel, it is supposed to validate male performance by resonating when it is played upon. Nonetheless, it remains a thing, alien, "other," as Simone de Beauvoir has pointed out, to the man who dreams of it—and also to the woman who wears it, sculpturing it to the specifications of the male-dominated advertising, publishing, fashion, and cosmetic industries.

35   An object does not know its own value. Even a sentient being, made into an object, will feel uncertain of her worth except as it is measured by the standards of the agora, the market place, which will reflect whatever male fantasies about women are current. Thanks to astonishing technological advances in the broadcasting of these standards, almost everyone in the world knows what they are and can weigh his object or her self against them, no matter how bizarre the means for their attainment may be. Somewhere I read that it takes the concerted pushing and pulling of three people to get a high-fashion model zipped into her jeans and propped into position for photographing. We all see the photographs, though not the three laborers behind them, and believe that the ideal woman looks like that. Thus a standard has been fixed, and most of us, lacking the appropriate sturdy personnel, won't meet it.

36   Through such manipulation I have learned to despise my body. I have, perhaps, more reason than most for doing so, since my body is not merely aging but also crippled. On the fair market, its value is slipping daily as the musculature twists and atrophies, the digestive system grinds spasmodically, the vision blurs, the gait lurches and stumbles. But long before I knew I had multiple sclerosis, I hadn't much use for it. Nor have I had much use for the man who desires it. He lacks taste, it seems

to me: the kind of man who prefers formica to teak, Melmac to Limoges, canned clam chowder to bouillabaisse. Who wants to have sex with a man who can't do better than you?

37   "Were I living in the Middle Ages, my difficulty could be quickly solved. I would become an anchoress, calling from my cell, 'And all shall be well, and all manner of thing shall be well.' God would love me. My fellow creatures would venerate me. But the wheel has turned and tipped me into a time when God has been dead for a century and my fellow creatures are likely to find me more pitiable than venerable. I shall no doubt be lonelier than any anchoress.

38   Nonetheless, my bed will stay narrow."

39   I love closure. Especially in any kind of writing. I like to tie off the tale with some statement that sounds as though nothing further can be said. Never mind the Princess's hysterical weeping on the morning after her wedding night, her later infidelities, the first son's cleft palate, the Prince's untimely death during an ill-advised raid on a neighboring kingdom, the old King's driveling madness: They lived happily ever after, or, if the tale is a modern one like mine, unhappily ever after. But their development ceased. I love closure enough to pretend that quick resolution lies along the length of a cell (in which I might prostrate myself praying not "All shall be well" but "I am a stud mare, a stinking whore"), enough to believe that virtue lies easy in a narrow bed. True, at the time I wrote the essay I was sleeping alone in a narrow bed, but it's widened again now to queen size, with George in one half, or sometimes two thirds, and often Vanessa Bell and Lionel Tigress too.

40   My sexuality is too complicated a text to be truncated neatly at any point. What has woven it together until now, I see, to prevent it from being a mere tangle of random terror and revulsion, has been my coherent inverse equation of autonomy with physical violation. Such a connection is predicated upon the denial of my own subjectivity in sexual experience. Afraid of being reduced by another to an object, I have persisted in seeing myself as such. Why did I lie, limp as a doll, while Caleb butted at me? Why didn't I writhe, scratch, bite? Why didn't I at least give him a thorough tongue-lashing the next morning before he left my life forever? Over and over I have demanded that I be raped and have then despised both the rapist and myself.

41   I understand now some of the teachings that helped me compose such a tale of invasion, illness, self-immolation. And I will not close it off with an *ever after*, happy or unhappy. Tomorrow the Princess gets out of bed again: She washes her hair, drinks her coffee, scribbles some pages, tells a joke to her son, bakes a spinach quiche. And the day after. And the

day after that. All the while she is telling herself a story. In it, she is aging now, and she drags one foot behind her when she walks. These are changes she can scrutinize in her mirror. They tell her that the true texts are the ones that do not end but revolve and reflect and spin out new constellations of meaning day after day, page after page, joke after joke, quiche after quiche. She has been learning much about vision and revision. She has been learning much about forgiveness. In this story, she is the writer of essays. She has a black typewriter and several reams of paper. One day, she thinks, she could find herself writing an essay called "On Liking Sex." There's that to consider.

TO THINK ABOUT

1. "On Not Liking Sex" is an essay within an essay. What is the primary advantage of this form?
2. Mairs describes the syntax, diction, and seamless organization of her earlier essay as a means of avoiding "a rough spot . . . a trouble spot, a split, a crack, out of which something dreadful (probably black, probably with a grin) may leap and squash you flat." What does she mean? Have you attempted to avoid such trouble spots in your own writing?
3. Before she reveals the central insight of the piece, Mairs analyzes her aversion to sex through several filters. What are they?
4. Mairs writes: "Poor sanitary practices may give you a cold or a stomach flu or herpes, but they are not, in Tucson in 1983, likely to do you in." How might she have revised this sentence in the mid-1990s?

TO DO

1. Fill in the blank: On Not Liking ____. Make a list of words that would fit in this spot. Write the list quickly, including all words that come into your head, even those that surprise you. Then fill in the blank with the word that intrigues you the most. Write the essay to fit the title.
2. Dig out a piece of your own writing, preferably at least a year old. An essay is fine, but a short story or a poem will serve equally well. Read it. Think about the circumstances under which you wrote it, and about what has changed since that time. Then write an essay about that piece of writing, and about the person who wrote it.

TIP

It is possible to think of "On Not Liking Sex" as a layered essay, each layer representing a level of awareness. At the bottom level, the least aware, is Nancy Mairs as the *subject* of the earlier essay. Next is Mairs, the *narrator* of that essay. Third is Mairs, the narrator of the later essay. (At this level, the narrator in the early essay becomes a subject as well.) Finally, it is possible to think of Nancy Mairs the writer, who, after all, chose the narrative voice she would use for the later essay.

After you have written a first draft, write an evaluation of it. What is the theme? What are the strengths and weaknesses? Are there passages in which you did not say precisely what you meant to say?

When you evaluate your own essay critically, you add a layer of awareness: *This* is what I meant to say. Often the revision process will include incorporating material that is part of that evaluation.

33

It Hurts to Be in Love

Andrew Merton

During the 1970s I wrote frequently for Boston Magazine. *Late in 1973 the magazine's editor asked several of us regular contributors to write about love for the February 1975 issue, which was to be a Valentine special. I was not in the habit of writing about love. I was in the habit of writing about politics. Writing about love turned out to be tricky, because there is a lot about love that is painful and embarrassing, and any attempt to gloss over this fact results in writing filled with greeting-card clichés.*

I chose to focus on a period of my love life that had ended nearly a decade earlier. This meant that I could comment on it honestly from a safe distance. I chose the persona of an inept, love-sick schlemiel, a fellow who knew exactly what he wanted; knew, also, that it was hopelessly out of reach, and reached it anyway—only to discover that it was not really what he wanted. And I chose the stilted voice of someone who thinks he is much more of an authority than he really is, someone who is grammatically correct to the point of eschewing contractions, even when contractions are appropriate. (Kurt Vonnegut, Max Shulman, and the novelist Mark Harris are masters of this sort of voice.)

1   I am a kind and romantic person. My friends, those I have not crossed, will say that about me. I do not like violence, especially when it is being carried out upon my body. Even before I was not a virgin anymore, I had a large and frequent problem, which was how to conduct romance without the violence which always seemed to follow. In the eleventh grade, for example, I finally got a girl to show me her breasts.

2   I am going to pause here to say that the reason that boys in their early teens become fascinated with the breasts of girls in their early teens is that boys in their early teens are short. When a teen-age boy looks straight ahead at a teen-age girl he is looking straight at her breasts, for she is generally taller than he is. In order to look at her face, the boy

must tilt his head up, or at least raise his eyes in what amounts to a *significant glance,* and this takes more courage than most well-bred boys have, or had in my era, which was the late fifties. I never had this problem, however, I was always able to see beyond the breasts, as it were, to the *person* behind them, and especially the person's legs, for I was a short, skinny kid who was too shy even to hold my head level when looking at a girl. So I spent a lot of time staring at the floor and whatever was near it, which was legs.

3   But I *was* curious about breasts and one late fall day in 1959 in my room on the second floor of my parents' one-and-one-half story ranch house on Long Island I started unbuttoning the blouse of my friend Linda Ferguson and she did not stop me. At this moment I felt the way Noah must have felt when the clouds started lifting on the morning of the forty-first day. I knew there was *something* behind there, and now I was finally going to find out what. Now, here is where the violence part comes in: I had thought that my parents would not be coming home for a while, but they came home nine seconds after Linda Ferguson had allowed me to place my right hand on her left breast. I knew that my parents would become violent if they found out about Linda's breast, or even about Linda.

4   Fortunately my bedroom had a dormer window that opened out onto the roof, and I climbed out the window and tugged Linda out after me. We slunk across the roof to a low place just above my mother's flower garden, dropped to the ground, and separated. Linda walked home and I came into the house through the front door, greeting my parents with a cheerful hello. I said I had been out for a walk. My father wondered why I had not worn shoes since it was forty degrees outside, but I said I had to do my homework and did not have time to chat. The next time I saw Linda Ferguson, she declared that she liked me better as just a friend, and though I argued that I could be a friend and touch her breast at the same time, I could not persuade her. It was at least a year before I got to see another breast, in which interim those nine seconds with Linda took on holy dimensions.

5   To eliminate this continuing threat of parental violence, I went to college in northern New England. On the application form, under "State your reasons for choosing our college rather than some other college," I did not state that at three hundred miles the curvature of the earth would prevent my parents from getting a direct view of what I was doing, but if the admissions people had read between the lines they could have figured out that all I really wanted was a place to make out in privacy.

6   This did not work out, however, for a couple of reasons, the first of which was that college administrations in the early 1960s felt that it was

their duty to prevent sex. The word "sublimate" was very big then. These administrators thought that by preventing sex on campus they would force the students to sublimate their sexual energies, directing them instead to the pursuit of electrical engineering or Shakespeare. While this may have been true in some cases, it mostly made college students very horny. Anyway, part of the administration's thinking was based on the assumption that sex takes place only between 9 p.m. and 7 a.m., so co-eds living in dormitories had to be in by nine o'clock every week night. Boys were not allowed in girls' rooms. At all. Unless the boy was the brother of a co-ed and he was helping her move in, in which case some other co-ed would walk ten feet in front of him yelling, "Man on the floor! Man on the floor!" And neither were co-eds allowed in the men's dormitories. I knew one couple who had a standing date (but only in a manner of speaking) between eight and nine every night. He picked her up at her dormitory, they raced out to a wooded spot half a mile away, made love, and raced back to the dormitory before the nine o'clock curfew. Once he did not pick her up until eight-twenty, but they headed for the woods anyway. They decided not to come back, and the university sent the police looking for her (the university was not worried about *him*), and she was suspended from school for a year, for her own good, naturally. So even if a person had a girl friend all to himself, scheduling was a big problem.

7   But I did not have a girl friend all to myself, for I soon realized that most of the girls worth having were already had. Usually by all-state halfbacks with names like "Moose" or "Killer" or "Thug." So, oblivious to the risks involved, I started chasing these women. At this point I had filled out to a mature and virile 145 pounds. My friends warned me that the odds on my surviving freshman year were not good, and they formed a pool among themselves, the proceeds of which would go to the individual who came closest to guessing the exact hour at which I would be rendered incorporate. I had many friends, only one of whom did not take part in the betting, and this was a girl. Her name was Jenny, and she came from a little town north of the White Mountains, from a family which ran a general store. She was the first in her family to go to college. I do not remember where I met her. In the dinner line, probably. She was not sexy, so I was able to talk to her without getting a nervous stomach. I told Jenny about my adventures with girls who had large boy friends, because I could not tell my other friends without them snickering.

8   Despite them, or perhaps to spite them, I survived that first year, becoming a sex object in the process. This bothered me, for in my dealings with women I have always taken into consideration the whole person, and not just those things which qualify somebody for the centerfold

of a magazine. And here I suddenly found myself being treated as nothing more than a piece of meat. Very unnerving. In high school, when I was horny and short, I would have enjoyed being treated as a piece of meat. In college, it was something I could not avoid once I had grown to my proper height and joined a rock 'n' roll band. Certain women were unable to resist medium-height bass guitar players who scream a lot. Once we played a gig at a Dartmouth College fraternity which was known as the jock house because most of the campus athletes were members. This was not a refined party. By midnight there was a sticky film of beer all over the floor, and I and my fellow musicians took to standing on wooden chairs to avoid being electrocuted by our equipment.

9   Just as we launched into "Roll Over, Beethoven," a dark and passionate small woman grabbed me by my belt buckle and pulled me off the chair. She got a death grip around my neck and pushed her face against mine, kissing me in a surgical manner. In order to push her away I would have had to stop playing, which would have upset Weasel, our lead singer. (The band was called Weasel and the Wharf Rats.) I had no choice; I had to kiss her back. Following perhaps thirty seconds of this, she pulled her face away from mine and said over her shoulder to a large and hulking linebacker type: "He kisses better than you, you bum, and what are you going to do about it?" I grinned a sickly grin, hoping the hulk would take all this in the playful spirit in which it was no doubt intended, but he did not. He reached over the small woman and grabbed my shoulders, and started shaking me back and forth. I attempted to continue to play bass riffs to "Roll Over, Beethoven," but the woman was now squashed against my steel strings, so the result was more than a trifle muffled. My fellow musicians, I noticed, were watching this event with awe and fascination. "We were wondering," one of the Wharf Rats told me later, "how we would get home in the event he threw you off a cliff, since you had the car keys." We musicians stick together under all circumstances except adversity. Fortunately several of the hulk's learned colleagues perceived that unless I lived, they would have to listen to bassless rock 'n' roll for the next two hours, so they dragged him away. To this day, whenever I hear "Roll Over, Beethoven" I get a special feeling in the pit of my stomach.

10   During November of my sophomore year, I fell in love with Maureen Cappuccino, a fiery maiden of Irish-Italian extraction who wore around her neck the high school ring of a former all-state defensive lineman named Claw, attending a vocational institution a mere ten miles from our campus. Maureen often had trouble deciding whether to kiss me (she had grown fond of me, perhaps because of my suicidal devotion) or berate me with tears and fists for complicating her life. I was a psychology major at the time most sick kids are. You figure, hell, if you can

be a psychologist and help people maybe you are not as sick as they are. Today it is even worse: any psychopath can take a six-week course and become a counselor . . . Anyway, I wrote a song to Maureen Cappuccino, the chorus of which went like this:

> You're my number one neurosis,
> You're my favorite fixation,
> You're the center of
> My phenomenal field,
> And furthermore, by unanimous decision of
> My id, my ego, superego, and libido,
> You have just been chosen
> Miss Traumatic Experience, 1964!

11   ASCAP and BMI both turned it down. It was, after all, written in November; so by the time anybody got around to recording it, 1964 would be over and the thing would be dated. I sang the song to Maureen, though, and I think she liked it. She gave me a large hickey.

12   But she could not decide between me and Claw, and during this time I grew wan and thin. Maureen, naturally, was the only woman I would ever love. Were I to lose her to Claw, I would devote my life to hobbies like jumping off tall buildings or baiting lions. I kept a graph, and on this graph I charted each day what I felt my prospects were at that moment, on a scale of minus nine to plus one. I was not very optimistic.

13   Maureen Cappuccino was smart about many things, but she had trouble keeping track of the days of the week—something vital to my health, since, as she often warned me, "If Claw ever found out about you he would kill you, since he is more limited than you and I in dealing with adverse circumstances." And then she would discover that today was Tuesday. She had thought it was Monday and safe, but she had a date with Claw on Tuesday and maybe I should leave because that was Claw's car pulling up now . . . At least three times, Claw walked in the dormitory's main entrance as I walked out, and each time, I *knew* he knew, and I knew the flower of my youth was about to be trampled, but it did not happen. My friend Jenny told me that I was living on borrowed time, and although she laughed when she said it I think she thought it was true.

14   This situation continued for three months, during which my grade point average at school dropped to 1.1 of a possible 4.0. Finally, Maureen decided that enough was enough. "I love Claw," she said to me dramatically, "but I now realize that life is more than talk of blitzes, red dogs, and whether Haystacks Calhoun is a better wrestler than Killer Kowalski. I will tell Claw this, and henceforth you may visit me any time, free from fear of maiming and dismemberment." Claw was coming

to see her that very night, she said. She would call me as soon as he left, and we would live happily ever after.

15   She called. Claw understood, she said. "Claw said he knows he is not an intellectual like me," she said. Yes, I said. "Claw said he wished us happiness but will kill you if he sees us together because he will not be able to help himself, being a poor boy from the country," she said. "But this will not happen because there is no reason for me to see him again." "I will be right over," said I, and was.

16   It was a cold night in February. It would have been nice to stay in Maureen's dormitory room and have a beer and otherwise celebrate properly, but as I have explained, this was illegal, which probably saved my life on this particular night, though it was a stupid rule anyway. Maureen and I would be forced to have our celebration in my Volkswagen bug. But as we were leaving her dormitory, a large and melancholy creature, bundled up against the winter cold, entered. I recognized him immediately by his bulk: it was Claw. He did not notice me right away, which gave me an opportunity to run, but I found that I did not have control of my legs. I grasped a nearby object for support and reflected on the many things in life I had missed—the age of twenty-five, for example, would have been a fun experience, I thought. I watched Maureen and Claw from what seemed to be a great distance. Claw had come back for his high school ring. "I will send it to you," said Maureen, edging him toward the door. "Why don't you just give it to me," said Claw. "Because," said Maureen, not knowing what to say. "Because exams are coming and I must go to the library to study." "But you have no books," Claw pointed out. "They are already at the library," said Maureen. "I left them there. I will send you the ring." She almost had him out, but then he looked around suddenly and saw me. "Is this the creep?" he said. He sounded as though he knew the answer to this question. "I will kill him." He took a deep breath and his shoulders doubled in width. "No," said Maureen. "Do not kill him, for he is not the creep. He is just some guy who is going to help me with my geography course, with which I am having trouble." I tried to nod, but could not.

17   I do not think that Claw believed Maureen. I do not know why he did not rend me. It is possible that a phenomenon which had never happened to Claw before was happening now: the phenomenon of doubt, bothering him just enough to short-circuit the direct lines from his brain to his fists. Or it is possible that somewhere inside his defensive lineman's heart there emerged a tiny spark of tenderness that prevented him from turning Maureen into a widow before she was even married. In any case, Claw glared at me for a while longer; then he looked at the floor for a while, and then he turned and walked out into the cold and windy night. At which time I felt pain. This was not because I felt sorry for Claw. This was because the object which I had grabbed in order to steady

myself turned out to be a hot water pipe which was at that very moment inflicting second degree burns upon my hand. Win a little, lose a little.

18   Maureen and I got married after that, but it did not work out. We tried to keep it going, but this effort became mechanical. Excitement was missing. I told my friend Jenny about this, and she said, "I know what is missing that was there before," and I said "What?" and she said, "Claw." Maureen and I split up the same week we both graduated from college.

19   I spent a lot of time talking with Jenny after that. As I have said, she was not sexy. Some people thought she was not healthy because she looked thin enough to have anorexia nervosa, but she did not have an anorexia nervosa personality. And she ate well enough. She was just thin. She did not have a boy friend.

20   I did not think of myself as her boy friend, either. I just kept calling her up and telling her how miserable I was now that things with Maureen had not worked out. And following several hours of this I would say, "And how are you," and she would tell me she was fine. Toward the end of one of these phone calls I noticed that it was time to eat, and I said, "Why don't we go out and get some dinner," and we did. We ate at an Italian place and I talked about doom, because it was 1967 and I was about to be drafted. I saw that Jenny's eyes, which seemed too large for her face, were a deep rich liquid brown. Jenny said she had gone out with a fellow for a couple of years, but that he had enlisted in the Air Force and she had not heard form him since. "I am sorry to hear that," I said, and I was, for I did not consider Jenny a lover, but a friend. I took her home, and went home myself, feeling better.

21   A few months later I stayed the night at my friend Jenny's place. There was this understanding: that we would not ever get married or be anything but close friends.

22   There were no linebackers to worry about. There was no feeling that I had won anything. There was a feeling that if Jenny ever needed anything, I would help, and vice versa. There was affection.

23   Later on I got into a couple of situations with women who had other men who might have done violent things to me, had they known. I think I did this out of habit. But these situations did not last very long because I would tell my friend Jenny about them, and she would laugh and say, "You are at it again" and "When are you going to grow up?" and I would think about that.

24   And I started realizing I had other friends who were women.

25   I started going to dinner with some of them. Sometimes I would spend the night with them, and sometimes not. Eventually, one of these friends became more than a friend, and I am with her now.

26   The most difficult thing about this transition from friend to more-than-friend was telling my other friends that I would be seeing less of them, literally. The most reassuring thing was that I was willing to do it.

TO THINK ABOUT

1. The subject of "It Hurts to Be in Love" is young love in the 1950s and 1960s. In the mid-1990s, what has changed? What has remained the same?
2. What can you infer from this piece about the young Merton's sense of what it means to be a man? How does he modify this concept?
3. Read Nora Ephron's "A Few Words About Breasts" (Chapter 11). How does the adolescent Ephron's concept of what it means to be a woman compare to the adolescent Merton's concept of what it means to be a man?
4. When Jenny explains that the lack of excitement in the relationship between Merton and Maureen is due to the absence of Claw, what does she mean?

TO DO

1. Make a list of people you love or have loved. Include not only lovers in the sexual sense but parents, siblings, other relatives, friends. Choose one person from the list to write about.
2. Write the piece primarily as a series of scenes, anecdotes, bits of dialogue, which trace the evolution of the relationship. Focus on turning points in the relationship, the moments of discovery and insight. Avoid the temptation to romanticize love—to write only of its sublime aspects while leaving out the ridiculous.

TIP

When writing about your own love life, it is wise to choose an episode that is completed. It is nearly impossible to achieve the necessary distance when writing about an affair you are currently negotiating; it's like writing about a storm at sea while you're still out there bailing water.

34

What a Freshman Needs to Know

Andrew Merton

I have taught at the University of New Hampshire for over twenty years. I know that the question in students' minds when they first enter my classroom is: What does he want? *Or, perhaps:* What do I have to do to do well in this class? *For over twenty years I have tried to answer the question for them. And at the beginning of the 1989–1990 school year I put my answer in writing.*

The form I chose was an imagined dialogue between myself and a hypothetical new student. The student turned out to be intelligent, slightly skeptical, eager to learn. The voice I chose for myself was . . . well, I'll let you be the judge.

1   This is it: your first day of college. High school is a distant memory. Here you sit, in your first class, wondering what to expect.

2   The following exchange probably will not take place in that first class. But it should.

3   **Student:** What's the most important thing for me to remember if I am to succeed in college?

Teacher: Learn to use the active voice.

Student (disgusted): I didn't mean the most important grammatical point. I meant . . .

Teacher: I understood what you meant. I repeat: the most important thing for you to remember if you are to succeed in college is to use the active voice. Can you give me examples of the active and passive voice?

Student: Sure. Active: Tom hit Joe. Passive: Joe was hit by Tom.

Teacher: Excellent.

Student: But what difference does it make which one I use? They both mean the same thing.

Teacher: For one thing, the active voice is more efficient: you're using three words to convey information which requires five words in the passive voice. What happens when you reduce the passive version to three words?

Student: Joe was hit. You lose the person responsible for the action.

Teacher: Right. And that's something you can get away with only in the passive voice. In the active voice, you must assign responsibility.

Student: OK. I see your point. The active voice makes more sense grammatically. But what does that have to do with . . .

Teacher: Let me give you another example. Passive: I was prevented from coming to class. I was detained for 45 minutes. For this reason my assignment was handed in late. Active: I drove 75 miles per hour in a 35-mile-per-hour zone. A state trooper arrested me for speeding. He detained me for 45 minutes. I missed class and failed to hand in my assignment on time. I won't let it happen again.

4   By consistently writing in the active voice you force yourself to take responsibility for what you write. You become a more authoritative writer. You discover that you have something to say. You begin to feel a sense of pride in your work. Students who develop the habit of writing in the active voice also learn to think in the active voice.

Student: What if something does come up that prevents me from coming to class or handing in an assignment on time?

Teacher: My reaction will depend on who you are and how you're doing.

Student: You mean you don't treat all students alike?

Teacher: I do at the outset. But students quickly demonstrate to me that they are separate individuals. Their behavior and performance in my class determines how I treat them.

5   Let's say that on the Friday of the eighth week of the course you tell me that your mother is ill, you have to go home, and it is possible you won't be back for Tuesday's class. And in fact this happens. Let's also say you've been doing well in the course and you haven't missed any previous classes or conferences. I am likely to be sympathetic.

6   But let's say your work has not been particularly good, and that your work habits have been erratic. At various times you have told me that your papers were late, or of poor quality, because 1) your boyfriend or girlfriend was in town: 2) your car broke down: 3) your roommate kept you up all night: 4) the coach kept you late at practice: 5) you had to study for an exam for another class. And then you miss a class, and later tell me that your mother was ill. In this case I am likely to express my heartfelt sympathy for your mother as I throw you out of the class.

Student: Even if my mother's illness is legitimate?

Teacher: Yes. You have used up your margin of error. Your tenuous position is not something that has happened to you. It is something that you have made happen. Active voice.

Student: That again.

Teacher: Students who think in the active voice are on their way to becoming effective and self-assured adults.

Student: What are students who write and think in the passive voice?

Teacher: Victims.

Student: That's kind of strong, isn't it?

Teacher: No. As a matter of fact, it is chronically weak. Passive people think things are always happening to them: they do not control their own destinies.

Student: Why would anyone want to think that way?

Teacher: To avoid responsibility. Someone who flunks an exam and reacts passively—"I was given the wrong material to study"—is bound to repeat the mistake. But a student who uses the active voice—"I got the assignment wrong: next time I'll keep asking questions until it is clear in my mind"—has learned from his error, and is not likely to repeat it.

Student: I never realized grammar was so important.

TO THINK ABOUT

1. Compare this piece to "Choices" by Patricia Volk (Chapter 49). What are the similarities? The differences?
2. The contrast between the active voice and the passive voice serves as the analogy framing the piece. Think of other components of grammar that might be useful as analogies in other situations.
3. If you were given an opportunity to question this teacher, what would you ask?

TO DO

1. Write a companion piece to "What a Freshman Needs to Know." Call it "What a Teacher Needs to Know." Use the same format, but this time have the teacher asking most of the questions and the student providing the answers.
2. Make a list of all the teachers you can remember. Then pick the one who, for whatever reason, strikes you as a promising subject for an essay. This need not be the best or worst teacher you ever had, but it should be someone who—intentionally or unintentionally—provided you with a new insight or direction. Write a piece about the teacher, using description and anecdotes as much as possible.

TIP

When you write dialogue, you can't tell in advance what your characters will say. In your conversation between a teacher and a student, the student may not say precisely what you thought he or she would—even if that student is supposed to be you. That's okay. Keep writing. Let the dialogue run its course: you are likely to learn some things you didn't know you knew. If you were unable to make a point you wished to make, well, that's what revision is for.

35

Obāchan*
Gail Y. Miyasaki

We are shaped by our ancestors. Who they were is part of who we are. In America, where nearly all of our ancestors came from somewhere else, this is sometimes easy to forget. Here Gail Miyasaki, a third-generation Japanese-American born in Hawaii, remembers her grandmother, when both were younger. It is a fond memory, even though the grandmother has her blind spots. The voice is calm, nostalgic, tinged with longing.

1   Her hands are now rough and gnarled from working in the cane-fields. But they are still quick and lively as she sews the "futon" cover. And she would sit like that for hours Japanese-style with legs under her, on the floor steadily sewing.

2   She came to Hawaii as a "picture bride." In one of her rare self-reflecting moments, she told me in her broken English-Japanese that her mother had told her that the streets of Honolulu in Hawaii were paved with gold coins, and so encouraged her to go to Hawaii to marry a strange man she had never seen. Shaking her head slowly in amazement, she smiled as she recalled her shocked reaction on seeing "Ojitchan's" (grandfather's) ill-kept room with only lauhula mats as bedding. She grew silent after that, and her eyes had a faraway look.

3   She took her place, along with the other picture brides from Japan, beside her husband on the plantation's canefields along the Hamakua coast on the island of Hawaii. The Hawaiian sun had tanned her deep brown. But the sun had been cruel too. It helped age her. Deep wrinkles lined her face and made her skin look tough, dry, and leathery. Her bright eyes peered out from narrow slits, as if she were constantly squinting into the sun. Her brown arms, though, were strong and firm, like those of

---

*Grandmother.

a much younger woman, and so different from the soft, white, and plump-dangling arms of so many old teachers I had had. And those arms of hers were always moving—scrubbing clothes on a wooden washboard with neat even strokes, cutting vegetables with the big knife I was never supposed to touch, or pulling the minute weeds of her garden.

4   I remember her best in her working days, coming home from the canefields at "pauhana"* time. She wore a pair of faded blue jeans and an equally faded navy-blue and white checked work shirt. A Japanese towel was wrapped carefully around her head, and a large straw "papale" or hat covered that. Her sickle and other tools, and her "bento-bako" or lunch-box, were carried in a khaki bag she had made on her back.

5   I would be sitting, waiting for her, on the back steps of her planta-tion-owned home, with my elbows on my knees. Upon seeing me, she would smile and say, "Tadaima" (I come home). And I would smile and say in return, "Okaeri" (Welcome home). Somehow I always felt as if she waited for that. Then I would watch her in silent fascination as she scraped the thick red dirt off her heavy black rubber boots. Once, when no one was around, I had put those boots on, and deliberately flopped around in a mud puddle, just so I could scrape off the mud on the back steps too.

6   Having retired from the plantation, she now wore only dresses. She called them "makule-men doresu," Hawaiian for old person's dress. They were always gray or navy-blue with buttons down the front and a belt at the waistline. Her hair, which once must have been long and black like mine, was now streaked with gray and cut short and perma-nent-waved.

7   The only time she wore a kimono was for the "Bon"† dance. She looked so much older in a kimono and almost foreign. It seemed as if she were going somewhere, all dressed up. I often felt very far away from her when we all walked together to the Bon dance, even if I too was wearing a kimono. She seemed almost a stranger to me, with her bent figure and her short pigeon-toed steps. She appeared so distantly Japanese. All of a sudden, I would notice her age; there seemed something so old in being Japanese.

8   She once surprised me by sending a beautiful "yūkata" or summer kimono for me to wear to represent the Japanese in our school's annual May Day festival. My mother had taken pictures of me that day to send to her. I have often wondered, whenever I look at that kimono, whether she had ever worn it when she was a young girl. I have wondered too what she was thinking when she looked at those pictures of me.

---

*Drudgery, tedious work.
†The Lantern Festival, the Buddhist's All Soul's Day.

9   My mother was the oldest daughter and the second child of the six children Obāchan bore, two boys and four girls. One of her daughters, given the name of Mary by one of her school teachers, had been disowned by her for marrying a "haole" or Caucasian. Mary was different from the others, my mother once told me, much more rebellious and independent. She had refused to attend Honokaa and Hilo High Schools on the Big Island of Hawaii, but chose instead to go to Honolulu to attend McKinley High School. She smoked cigarettes and drove a car, shocking her sisters with such unheard of behavior. And then, after graduation, instead of returning home, Mary took a job in Honolulu. Then she met a haole sailor. Mary wrote home, telling of her love for this man. She was met with harsh admonishings from her mother.

10   "You go with haole, you no come home!" was her mother's ultimatum.

11   Then Mary wrote back, saying that the sailor had gone home to America, and would send her money to join him, and get married. Mary said she was going to go.

12   "Soon he leave you alone. He no care," she told her independent daughter. Her other daughters, hearing her say this, turned against her, accusing her of narrow-minded, prejudiced thinking. She could not understand the words that her children had learned in the American schools; all she knew was what she felt. She must have been so terribly alone then.

13   So Mary left, leaving a silent, unwavering old woman behind. Who could tell if her old heart was broken? It certainly was enough of a shock that Honolulu did not have gold-paved streets. Then, as now, the emotionless face bore no sign of the grief she must have felt.

14   But the haole man did not leave Mary. They got married and had three children. Mary often sends pictures of them to her. Watching her study the picture of Mary's daughter, her other daughters know she sees the likeness to Mary. The years and the pictures have softened the emotionless face. She was wrong about this man. She was wrong. But how can she tell herself so, when in her heart, she only feels what is right?

15   "I was one of the first to condemn her for her treatment of Mary," my mother told me. "I was one of the first to question how she could be so prejudiced and narrow-minded." My mother looked at me sadly and turned away.

16   "But now, being a mother myself, and being a Japanese mother above all, I *know* how she must have felt. I just don't know how to say I'm sorry for those things I said to her."

17   Whenever I see an old Oriental woman bent with age and walking with short steps, whenever I hear a child being talked to in broken English-Japanese, I think of her. She is my grandmother. I call her "Obāchan."

TO THINK ABOUT

1. What is the narrator's attitude toward her grandmother? What is the relationship she establishes with you, the reader? What is the persona she adopts?
2. At one point Miyasaki says her grandmother "appeared so distantly Japanese." What does this mean?
3. The grandmother, herself a "picture bride," objected when her daughter Mary married a *haole*, a Caucasian. How does the narrator treat this situation? Do you know of any similar taboos in your own family? What are they? Do you understand their origins?
4. What image or passage from "Obāchan" do you remember most vividly? (Don't look at the text.) Why?

TO DO

1. Make a list of your older relatives. From that list choose the person who best exemplifies an aspect of your heritage you would like to explore: ethnic, religious, cultural, political, or some combination thereof. Then write a profile of him or her, using "Obāchan" as a model.

TIP

The most effective way to write about long periods of time is to write about moments. "Obāchan" covers many years, from the writer's childhood to the present. A beginning writer might be tempted to say something general about every single year. Miyasaki understands it is not the years that matter, but certain images, episodes, incidents, moments that stay in the reader's mind.

36

On Wearing the Chador

A. G. Mojtabai

We all talk to ourselves. Not only that, we talk back.
Sometimes the subjects of these inner conversations are inconse-
quential: Do I wear the blue shirt or the yellow one? Do I order the
steak or the veggie stir fry? But often we split ourselves in two in or-
der to explore both sides of important issues before—or after—mak-
ing a decision. My roommate has an alcohol problem; do I do anything about it? I'm not crazy about the person I'm going out with
now; do I end the relationship? *Nearly always in these conversa-*
tions, the two inner voices are distinctly different from one another.
In this essay, the writer enters into a dialogue with herself to dis-
cuss her earlier decision to wear the chador, the traditional veil,
while living in Iran.

1   Question: *You are guilty, you know.*

2   A: Undoubtedly. What is it this time?

3   Q: *Of compromise, conciliation, yes, I'd even say of collaboration*
with the oppressor.

4   A: Which particular oppressor? Would you mind—I mean, what exactly did I do?

5   Q: *When you lived in Iran—and that was long before the present*
regime—you put on the veil.

6   A: I did.

7   Q: *Not just once, either. You can't tell me you put it on just to see*
how it felt.

8   A: I put it on as often as required. I was a foreigner trying to fit in.
You know? When I went into a Catholic church, I covered my head. So
it's the same sort of thing. In Iran, when the situation called for it, I put
on the chador. I thought of it as nothing more than one of those little
concessions to circumstance that social life exacts from each of us now
and then. It was nothing more than having a sense of occasion. I put on
the chador for funerals, as did all the women in the family (whether

228

young or old, old-fashioned or Westernized). When visiting a mosque or shrine that was not open to tourists, I put on the chador.

9   Q: *Funerals I can understand, but for anything else you could have chosen not to.*

10   A: I *could* have, I could have stayed away. But the chador was my passport to what otherwise I would not have been privileged to see. And it isn't that oppressive as garments go. It's more like a body-length kerchief than anything else I can name. It is a bit inconvenient, though, I must admit. The problem is in its lack of fastenings. So the ends are either bitten together and held with the teeth (cure for an idle tongue), or clutched together (keeping one hand out of mischief). It was holding or biting the thing closed, while managing to walk or talk, that was a nuisance.

11   Q: *All diversionary. The problem—the question before us—is your putting on the veil, not once but repeatedly. I'd like to suggest a certain amount of self-deception, bad faith, play-acting.*

12   A: There was some of that. Play-acting, I mean.

13   Q: *That's right, admit to the lesser charge.*

14   A: Well, let's at least look at the play-acting part. Sure, it's there. It's part of the reason that men in drag take to the chador. And prostitutes. Although, with prostitutes, it's also for self-protection. But coquettish women also use the chador to great effect. Beautiful eyes, but so-so nose? Banish the nose and expose the eyes; let the rest be inferred from the eyes.

15   In Pakistan, where women are often completely veiled, wearing either little gauzy curtains over the face, or a cover of heavy, coarse fabric with only a crocheted grillwork for the eyes to peep through, I was struck by the fact that hands and feet were elaborately ornamented, even bejeweled, and intricately painted with henna. And, given these conditions, how provocative the slightest exposure becomes! Where the erotic is denied release, *everything* becomes suffused with erotic feeling. And the prohibition gives it all an extra poignancy. Only think what the sight of a woman's ankle once meant, and then think of nudist camps.

16   Q: *You seem to be straying again. The point at issue is the veil and you. You and the veil. You put on the chador. I would go further—you enjoyed it. Hmmm? Just a little bit?*

17   A: Well—I have to confess to a little of that. It was something of a masquerade. I was no one, I was anyone I wanted to be, I was a native—I belonged. And then, you have to remember, unlike so many women *condemned* to the chador, I could take it off when I chose. For me, it was always something of a costume. For my mother-in-law, it was something very different, something closely bound up with her sense of self. It was more than the fact that she was a devout Muslim. The chador seemed to

be a sort of second skin for her. She even wore the chador in the house, toga-fashion, although it is never required in the privacy of family quarters.

18   During the reign of Riza Shah Pahlevi, father of the recently deposed Shah, there was an effort to modernize Iran as Kemal Ataturk had modernized Turkey, and there was an active campaign to eliminate the chador. Gendarmes were stationed in the bazaar to spray acid on the chadors of the women passing through. The drive was not a success; women, especially poor women, refused to change. My mother-in-law simply changed to a floor-length dress and scarf, at once complying with the letter of the new directive and dissenting from its spirit. The point, after all, had been modernization.

19   For poor women, who have few clothes, the chador is a great equalizer, a sort of uniform; it matters little what you are wearing underneath. But you were asking?

20   Q: *You enjoyed it.*

21   A: A little, yes, in spite of every scruple. I didn't enjoy it in the heat, when every added layer was a burden. I didn't enjoy it in the wind, or stepping into places where foreigners entered at peril, when I had to hold on for dear life. But when the covering held secure, and I gazed out, safe in my anonymity, that was something. I felt—somehow beyond reproach, invulnerable, snug, enclosed. I felt curiously *free*. Dead to the world, I was all alive.

22   It was a little like that old dream of invisibility. You know—wishing for moments when you can see without being seen? Doesn't everyone have that fantasy at one time or another? It's partly a dream of superiority, looking out, judging everyone you see, while remaining beyond judgment yourself. But it's also, in large part, motivated by genuine curiosity. And it's a writer's dream, isn't it, to become a nothing, a transparency, a clear lens—no longer a murky, distorting medium? The less intrusive you are, the more the people around you can be themselves.

23   But, of course, I could put off the veil largely when I chose; I was not doomed to invisibility—I mustn't forget that. And, in Pakistan, I did not put on the *burqa*, ever—I never covered my face. But, then, Pakistan wasn't a real test for me; I wasn't a native-by-adoption there, and was not expected to conform to local custom.

24   Q: *You have some qualms about covering the face?*

25   A: Yes. There, I think, I'd draw the line. And the custom of blackening the faces of women in news photographs, recommended by the Saudi Arabian Government in its tightening of Islamic law—that chills me through and through. Blacking out the face—canceling out—the sense that a woman's presence in the outside world can only be a disruptive force, *that* I find frightening.

26   Q: *Yet you put on the chador?*

27   A: Yes, but you see, the matter wasn't simple.
28   Q: *It never is.*
29   A: One small concession, as I said.
30   Q: *Which leads to yet another, and another.*

TO THINK ABOUT

1. What is the persona of the voice asking the questions? What is the persona of the answering voice? What is the relationship between the two?
2. These two voices articulate competing themes. What are they? Does one theme emerge triumphant over the other?
3. The answering voice says that although she wore the chador, she would draw the line at covering her face. Why might this be considered merely a rationalization for behavior she knows, at bottom, was against her principles?
4. Compare this essay to Alice Walker's "Right to Life: What Can the Black Man Say to the White Woman?" (Chapter 52). Each essay is a dialogue. How do they differ from one another?

TO DO

1. Mojtabai says wearing the chador effectively rendered her invisible in Iran, allowing her to observe without being observed. Make a list of the places you would go if you had this power. This may lead you to an essay.
2. Make a list of difficult decisions you have made recently, or must make in the near future. Eliminate the inconsequential ones. From the remaining items, choose the one intriguing you the most. Then split yourself in two. Write a dialogue with yourself exploring the issue.

TIP

You are likely to have more success writing about a past decision than one you are facing now. There are two reasons for this. First, in dealing with a past episode you have concrete data with which to work, and second, you have probably achieved enough distance from that episode to provide you with a reasonable perspective from which to write. (Like most of the tips in this book, this is not a rule. It is a suggestion. It *is* possible to write a fine piece on a decision you have only just made, or even about one you have not yet made. See, for example, "Reunion" by Maxine Hong Kingston, Chapter 25.)

37

Three Days and a Question

Grace Paley

Grace Paley is one of the premier short story writers in America. What happens in her stories is what happens in other short stories: people love, hate, cheat, repent, die, live. What separates Paley's stories from the rest are her ear and her voice. She has a keen ear for voices, for dialogue. And her own voice is a mother's voice, plain and simple yet steeped in nuance, a voice brimming with compassion and love and sadness and sorrow that the world is not a better, fairer place.

"Three Days and a Question" is nonfiction, three vignettes held together, primarily, by the author's voice. It is not a hurried voice. It is, above all, a conversational voice. Probably you have places to rush off to, but wait, sit a minute. This is worth hearing.

1   On the first day I joined a demonstration opposing the arrest in Israel of members of Yesh Gvul, Israeli soldiers who had refused to serve in the occupied territories. Yesh Gvul means: *There is a Limit.*

2   TV cameras and an anchorwoman arrived and *New York Times* stringers with their narrow journalism notebooks. What do you think? the anchorwoman asked. What do *you* think, she asked a woman passerby—a woman about my age.

3   Anti-Semites, the woman said quietly.

4   The anchorwoman said, But they're Jewish.

5   Anti-Semites, the woman said, a little louder.

6   What? One of our demonstrators stepped up to her. Are you crazy? How can you . . . Listen what we're saying.

7   Rotten anti-Semites—all of you.

8   What? What What the man shouted. How you dare to say that—all of us Jews. Me, he said. He pulled up his shirtsleeve. Me? You call me? You look. He held out his arm. Look at this.

9   I'm not looking, she screamed.

232

10   You look at my number, what they did to me. My arm . . . you have no right.

11   Anti-Semite, she said between her teeth. Israel hater.

12   No, no he said, you fool. My arm—you're afraid to look . . . my arm . . . my arm.

13   On the second day Vera and I listen at PEN to Eta Krisaeva read her stories that are not permitted publication in her own country. Czechoslovakia. Then we walk home in the New York walking night, about twenty blocks—shops and lights, other walkers talking past us. Late-night homeless men and women asleep in dark storefront doorways on cardboard pallets under coats and newspapers. Scraps of blanket. Near home on Sixth Avenue a young man, a boy, passes—a boy the age a younger son could be—head down, bundles in his arms, on his back.

14   Wait, he says, turning to stop us. Please, please wait. I just got out of Bellevue. I was sick. They gave me something. I don't know . . . I need to sleep somewhere. The Y, maybe.

15   That's way uptown.

16   Yes, he says. He looks at us. Carefully he says, AIDS. He looks away. Oh. Separately, Vera and I think: A boy—only a boy. Mothers after all, our common trade for more than thirty years.

17   Then he says, I put out my hand. We think he means to tell us he tried to beg. I put out my hand. No one will help me. No one. Because they can see. Look at my arm. He pulls his coatsleeve back. Lesions, he says. Have you ever seen lesions? That's what people see.

18   No. No, we see a broad fair forehead, a pale countenance, fear. I just have to sleep, he says.

19   We shift in our pockets. We give him what we find—about eight dollars. We tell him, Son, they'll help you on 13th Street at the Center. Yes, I know about that place. I know about them all. He hoists the bundle of his things to his back to prepare for walking. Thank you, ladies. Goodbye.

20   On the third day I'm in a taxi. I'm leaving the city for a while and need to get to the airport. We talk—the driver and I. He's a black man, dark. He's not young. He has a French accent. Where are you from? Haiti, he answers. Ah, your country is in bad trouble. Very bad. You know that, Miss.

21   Well, yes. Sometimes it's in the paper.

22   They thieves there. You know that? Very rich, very poor. You believe me? Killing—it's nothing to them, killing. Hunger. Starving people. Everything bad. And you don't let us come. Starving. They send us back.

23   We're at a red light. He turns to look at me. Why they do that? He

doesn't wait for me to say, Well . . . because . . . He says, Why hard.

24   The light changes. We move slowly up traffic-jammed Third Avenue. Silence. Then, Why? Why they let the Nicaragua people come? Why they let Vietnamese come? One time American people want to kill them people. Put bomb in their children. Break their head. Now they say, Yes Yes, come come come. Not us. Why?

25   Your New York is beautiful country. I love it. So beautiful, this New York. But why, tell me, he says, stopping the cab, switching the meter off. Why, he says, turning to me again, rolling his short shirtsleeve back, raising his arm to the passenger divider, punching and pulling the bare skin of his upper arm, tell me—this skin, this black skin—why? Why you hate this skin so much?

26   Question: Those gestures, those arms, the three consecutive days throw a formal net over the barest unchanged accidental facts. How? Why? They become—probably—in this city one story told.

TO THINK ABOUT

1. What is the persona this narrator establishes? What is the relationship she establishes with you, the reader?
2. In the first vignette a Jewish woman attacks Jewish peace demonstrators, including a concentration camp survivor, as anti-Semites. What is the rationale behind this attack? Can you think of parallel situations in recent American history?
3. In each vignette someone displays an arm. What do these three arms, and their owners, have in common?
4. This is a first-person piece. The narrator is part of each vignette. What is her role?

TO DO

1. Make a list of types of people who are discriminated against. Consider regional and local groups as well as national and international ones. What do these groups have in common? What are some distinctions among them? Do you belong to one of them? There's an essay here.
2. Write about people less fortunate than yourself. They are not difficult to find, and their stories need telling. All around you people are battling alcohol, drugs, disease, poverty, discrimination. They are in your dorm, your family. They are downtown. Look at them. Look at

their arms, their bodies, their faces. Listen to them, talk to them. Think in terms of scenes, of dialogue. Write down what you see, what you hear. If you show the details, then what you felt—your compassion, your sorrow, your anger, your humanity—will come through. You won't have to explain.

TIP

We tend to spend most of our time with people who are very much like us: same age, same level of education, same economic status, same interests, similar backgrounds, similar values. This is natural. We are more comfortable with people with whom we share a world view. But it severely limits what we can write about with any sort of authority.

It is crucial for writers to speak with people of other classes, other races, other views, on a regular basis. Otherwise, our view of the world is limited to stereotypes, and our own convictions grow stale and weak.

38

Clown
Anna Quindlen

Anna Quindlen consistently combines political, cultural, and personal issues to produce original, insightful observations. Here she defends her young son's attachment to a calico doll named Clown. In the process, she skewers adults who object to "comfort objects" of this sort.

She begins with a voice that is not her own. It is a voice borrowed from A. A. Milne's Winnie-The-Pooh. *And we grownups are lured into the story. Then she switches to a voice that is more naturally hers, but a trace of Milne remains.*

1   This is a story about Clown.

2   ("A whole story about Clown?" asked his owner, age 4, sounding just like Christopher Robin in the Winnie-the-Pooh books.

3   ("That's right," I said, trying my best to sound like the narrator.

4   ("Why?"

5   ("Because he's so important," I said.

6   ("He has a hole in his head," said his owner.

7   ("I know," I replied.)

8   Actually, this is a story about the great-grandson of Clown. The original was given to me at a baby shower five years ago. He was made of little red calico puffs strung together, with a fabric face and a felt clown hat. A year later I saw his double in a toy store and had the presence of mind to snap him up. I did the same the next year, and the next, so that as each Clown fell prey to the inevitable dissolution of the fabric, remnant to remnant, thread to thread, I could whisk in a new one to take his place. Clown the phoenix, risen from disintegration one morning on a pillow, again intact and shiny new.

. . .

9   Now we are down to Clown IV—The Last Generation. Believe me, he looks it. Most of Clown's face is gone, and all of his hat has disap-

peared. His legs are tangled, and while his red parts are still red, his white parts are now gray. (You have to sneak Clown into the washer while his owner is at school for the morning. Even then, he will come home, hold Clown to his face, sniff suspiciously and then say, "Did you wash Clown?")

10   The periodic resurrections were necessary because Clown had become what the books call a comfort object. Along with his calloused little sucking thumb, my son needed Clown to go to sleep at night, or to relax if he was particularly unnerved or upset. Clown the Valium. Clown is never permitted to leave the house, except to go away for the weekends. One weekend I drove 90 miles to the country and discovered that Clown was still lying on the floor in the city kitchen, his soiled calico limbs akimbo, his felt hat amid the dust balls. My son cried and cried. Worse still, my husband arrived and looked as though he'd discovered me in a clinch with the oil deliveryman. "You forgot Clown?" he said, while his son clung to his leg and snuffled disconsolately.

11   We take Clown very seriously, as we do anything that has become of enduring importance to our kids. The surprise to me is not that I have come to put this Godforsaken hunk of red rag high up on my priority list. The surprise is the hostility that other adults manifest toward Clown, or to the younger child's purple plush dinosaur, Max, or ragged blankets, tattered teddy bears, all the other things children use to help themselves feel in control of a scary and uncontrollable world.

12   Lots of adults seem offended by children's comfort objects, perhaps because they are reminded of how much comfort they need. Most of them are immediately offended by the thumb, a prejudice that I find tough to take because I sucked my thumb for a long, long time. (No, my teeth do not stick out.) Both of my sons have had their thumbs pulled from their mouths by people who had seemed reasonably nice up until that moment. Oddly enough, neither of them gets discombobulated by this; they seem to put it in the same category as adults who insist on tucking in your shirt even though they know that 15 minutes later it will be out again. They just wait a minute and then put their thumbs back in their mouths.

13   But Clown's owner does not like it when someone ridicules Clown. He knows very well that Clown is a connection to an earlier life, a simpler and more primitive life, a baby life. "When I am 6, I will not sleep with my Clown anymore," he says occasionally, as though he has been asked, which he hasn't. But Clown is a friend, too, and he doesn't allow you to mock his friends, which is another of the pivotal differences between children and adults.

14   It is interesting to watch a big person make fun of the thing that, in some way, soothes a smaller one. Makes you wonder who really is the grown-up here.

15   Adults have their own comfort objects. They usually don't call them that, because grown-ups don't like anything that makes them seem publicly vulnerable, as Edmund Muskie, for example, could tell you. To adults, they're just habits. There are cigarettes, of course, as a substitute for thumb sucking, and alcohol and obsessions with money, with food and with sex. Clown may be grungy, but he seems pretty benign next to some of those counterparts.

. . .

16   Sometimes his owner will engage in self-hypnosis with the aid of Clown and his thumb, and he will suddenly dredge up some memory of the time when he was really quite small, and I realize that this pathetic old thing unlocks a closet into a time he felt was easier. It's kind of comical, really: the idea of his ruminating about those days when he sat in a Sassy seat and couldn't even walk and had no brother and didn't go to school and the world was slow and easy. Sometimes I expect him to launch into the story about how he walked five miles through the snow to school.

17   Adults are dumb if they don't realize that even the very young have their good old days, even if their good old days were last week. Truth is, the way lots of adults have treated Clown—and son of Clown, and grandson of Clown, and now great-grandson of Clown—has often convinced me that they *are* dumb. Or jealous. Clown's owner is still of an age, and an inclination, to wear his needs on his sleeve. And as all of us nominal grown-ups know, that will never, never do.

TO THINK ABOUT

1. Why does Quindlen begin with the voice of A. A. Milne? What is the effect of this voice on you, the reader?
2. Contrast the borrowed Milne voice with Quindlen's natural voice. What sort of persona can you infer from this voice? How comfortable would you feel talking with this narrator?
3. What is your attitude about children's comfort objects such as blankets, dolls, and thumbs? What is your attitude toward adult comforts such as money, drugs, food, and sex? Quindlen draws a parallel between the two types. Why?
4. In 1972, when Senator Edmund Muskie of Maine was running for president, a newspaper editorial attacking his wife caused him to burst into tears in public. The episode is widely believed to have cost him votes. Would the result be the same in the 1990s? Why or why not?

TO DO

1. Spend an afternoon in the attic of your parents' home. Bring a notebook with you. See if you can find treasures from your own good (or not-so-good) old days. Write about then. Write about now. Free-associate; write about whatever comes into your head.
2. Make a list of inanimate objects that have meant something to you at different times during your life. Write an essay about one or more of them.
3. Borrow a voice from one of your favorite children's books. Use it to make a point about the silly behavior of grownups.

TIP

An essay about an object usually is not so much about the object as it is about the person who is attached to the object. Thus, the essay should include enough about the circumstances of the writer's life to put the object in its proper context.

39

High Heels
Caryl Rivers

Caryl Rivers, author of novels, nonfiction books, and hundreds of newspaper and magazine articles, has made a good living as a writer by not taking herself too seriously. But this does not mean she takes her material lightly, or that she writes about inconsequential matters.

In "High Heels," Rivers traces the evolution of her attitude about high-heeled shoes. She uses the wisecracking voice of a stand-up comic; there are moments, pauses at the ends of sentences that cry out for a snare drum. Most of the gags are aimed at the narrator herself. Readers may begin by laughing along; by the end, they may be reexamining their own attitudes about fashion and about themselves.

1   The fashion flash is out; spike heels are back. Terrific.

2   Next it's going to be the rack and thumbscrews. Spike heels are strictly for masochists; you'll love three-inch stilettos if you're the kind of person who thinks a fun afternoon is sitting around having somebody rub ground glass into your cheekbone.

3   I saw my first pair of spike heels when I was a sophomore in high school, at one of those back-to-school fashion shows sponsored by a department store. A model tottered along the runway wearing a pair of black patent leather spikes that narrowed at the bottom to the width of a ball point pen. I was hooked. I had to have a pair.

4   The reason for my fascination had more to do with my particular pair of feet than with fashion in general. I was one of those people who grew like a German Shepherd puppy—my feet grew first. I caught up with them, eventually, but the growth lag left me with a permanent sense that my feet wore name tags—the Monitor and the Merrimac. One of my favorite children's tales was one called (honest to God) Fairy Foot, which was about a prince with normal-sized feet who lived in a land

called Stumpingham, where everybody else had feet the size of rowboats. Fairy Foot suffered much discrimination and, not being smart enough to dream up Affirmative Action, he just sulked a lot. I identified with Fairy Foot, a projection of wish fulfillment, no doubt. Like the black folks who used to use hair straightener and skin bleach, I could not afford the psychic cost of identifying with my own kind—the big-footed Stumping-hamians.

5   The wonderful thing about the spike heel was that it changed the entire structure of the foot. No longer would the foot just lie there, stretched out, its entire length exposed to public gaze. It would tilt into the air like a high-rise building, and while the foot would not shrink in size, it would certainly appear to do so. Suddenly all the flat ballerina-style shoes in my closet looked obscene, ugly barges designed more for the conveyance of sludge than for the enhancement of feet. Whenever I ventured into a shoestore, after admiring a cute little size-five flat shoe in the window, I was always aghast at the sheer magnitude of the size ten that the salesman brought out. How could a mere five sizes make so much difference in the esthetics of a shoe?

6   My greed to own a pair of spike heels was untempered by practical considerations, like whether or not I could learn to walk in them. I had barely managed the style that used to be called "Cuban" heels. (Why they had this particular nickname I don't know, except that they were so squat and comfortable that Fidel could have worn them on the dead run carrying a Thompson submachine gun in the Sierra Maestra.) I saved up my sheckels for a pair of white, linen spikes, and after a half-hour of practice, I was almost permanently crippled. If I had been a horse, they would have shot me. But I worked at it, and after considerable time I could move around with the same ease as one of those Chinese women with hobbled feet. So what if I looked arthritic? My feet looked, if not ex-actly small, different; more like the Washington Monument than the Pentagon.

7   The problem was, however, that three-inch spikes put me over the six-foot mark. I had been tall before. Now I was the Wilt Chamberlain of high school girls. I gazed desperately about for anybody tall. If a tall ax murderer had asked me to the prom, I would have said yes like a shot.

8   As it was, I had a lot of thrilling conversations on dates about free throws and the zone defense. I had a wardrobe of spikes for tall fellows and a neat row of ballerinas for short fellows. A cold chill would run down my spine at the thought, "What if I fell in love with somebody short?" Would I wear my ballerinas and look him in the eye or clamber aboard my spikes and stare out over the top of his head?

9   In college, I hung around with a group of girls who averaged five-ten in height. In our spike heels we were a formidable group, outlined, like

the Horsemen of Notre Dame, against a gray-blue October sky. We ruined more vinyl floors than I care to remember.

10   I got to the point where I could move well on my spikes by putting most of the weight on my toes and moving at a half-trot. I was working as a reporter in Washington then, and there were times when my feet just gave out. I was not an uncommon sight in the halls of Congress, walking from a hearing room bare-footed, shoes in my hand. My worst moment came in the Rose Garden at the White House, where I was covering President Johnson, who was receiving a delegation of farmers who were presenting him with a bagful of soybean seeds. (As a glamour beat, the White House is highly overrated, but that's another story.) It had rained the night before, and to my dismay, my heels sunk to a depth of three inches in deep loam. When I tried to move, nothing happened. It took a UPI reporter and a Secret Service man to haul me out. But for them, I might have withered and died on the spot, and White House tour guides could have pointed me out as the first person to die of Terminal Spike Heels.

11   Spike heels went out of fashion, finally, and my toes uncurled. I now rely on sneakers, boots, wedgies, and—when the occasion demands—shoes with heels that one can stand upon without being in constant danger of falling sideways. I no longer look like a foot fetishist's mad fantasy or a character in the Stomp'em, Tromp'em variety of porno flick. I have come to terms with my feet and I no longer worry about their size. After all, Jackie O sports a pair of size tens, and the paparazzi do not turn away in disgust. So what if my lower extremities are large and rather flat? They run fast, and when I treat them properly, they never cause me pain. Theirs is an inner beauty, and I have a new respect for them. I have made them a vow: I will never, never, never again torture them by cramming them into a pair of spike heels. They are, and shall remain, Free Feet.

TO THINK ABOUT

1. When does the writer begin to establish a persona? How?
2. What effect does the brief first paragraph have on you, the reader?
3. What is the theme of "High Heels"? (Remember, a theme is not simply a topic. A theme is a statement, a message.)
4. What are the advantages of this kind of presentation over a more formal, academic approach? What are the disadvantages?

TO DO

1. Read the first two paragraphs of "High Heels" aloud (privately, if you are shy, but it's more fun with other people around), imitating what you imagine to be Rivers's style of speaking.
2. Think of an object or convention you once admired but now find foolish. Write a page about it *using Caryl Rivers's voice.* Then keep writing. If you sense the voice changing, don't worry. That's your own, natural voice emerging.

TIP

The object or convention you select should be something you feel strongly about. This feeling need not be as simple as love or hate. Indeed, it may be a complex mixture of many emotions: nostalgia, regret, anger, joy, incredulity. It is not necessary for you to sort these feelings out before you begin writing. What is important is that you feel *something.* Remember, one of your goals is to make your readers feel something about your subject. If the writer feels nothing, the reader hasn't got a chance.

40

A Mask on the Face of Death

Richard Selzer

Richard Selzer is a surgeon who writes compellingly about the nonmedical aspects of disease. In 1988 he visited Haiti, where sexual mores and social conditions had combined to produce an AIDS epidemic. Selzer shows various facets of Haitian society in a series of scenes, presented chronologically. For the most part he does little explaining, preferring to show, rather than tell. He is both observer and participant, a reporter who becomes a character in his own story.

Throughout most of the piece Selzer the narrator maintains a distance from his material, even when he describes a tension-filled exchange between Selzer the character and the director of a hospital that refuses to treat people with AIDS. But at the end the carefully maintained distance vanishes, and the narrator gives full vent to his own emotions.

1   It is ten o'clock at night as we drive up to the Copacabana, a dilapidated brothel on the rue Dessalines in the red-light district of Port-au-Prince. My guide is a young Haitian, Jean-Bernard. Ten years before, J-B tells me, at the age of fourteen, "like every good Haitian boy" he had been brought here by his older cousins for his *rite de passage*. From the car to the entrance, we are accosted by a half dozen men and women for sex. We enter, go down a long hall that breaks upon a cavernous room with a stone floor. The cubicles of the prostitutes, I am told, are in an attached wing of the building. Save for a red-purple glow from small lights on the walls, the place is unlit. Dark shapes float by, each with a blindingly white stripe of teeth. Latin music is blaring. We take seats at the table farthest from the door. Just outside, there is the rhythmic lapping of the Caribbean Sea. About twenty men are seated at the tables or lean

against the walls. Brightly dressed women, singly or in twos or threes, stroll about, now and then exchanging banter with the men. It is as though we have been deposited in act two of Bizet's *Carmen.* If this place isn't Lillas Pastia's tavern, what is it?

2   Within minutes, three light-skinned young women arrive at our table. They are very beautiful and young and lively. Let them be Carmen, Mercedes and Frasquita.

3   "I want the old one," says Frasquita, ruffling my hair. The women laugh uproariously.

4   "Don't bother looking any further," says Mercedes. "We are the prettiest ones."

5   "We only want to talk," I tell her.

6   "Aaah, aaah," she crows. "*Massissi.* You are *massissi.*" It is the contemptuous Creole term for homosexual. If we want only to talk, we must be gay. Mercedes and Carmen are slender, each weighing one hundred pounds or less. Frasquita is tall and hefty. They are dressed for work: red taffeta, purple chiffon and black sequins. Among them a thousand gold bracelets and earrings multiply every speck of light. Their bare shoulders are like animated lamps gleaming in the shadowy room. Since there is as yet no business, the women agree to sit with us. J-B orders beer and cigarettes. We pay each woman $10.

7   "Where are you from?" I begin.

8   "We are Dominican."

9   "Do you miss your country?"

10   "Oh, yes, we do." Six eyes go muzzy with longing. "Our country is the most beautiful in the world. No country is like the Dominican. And it doesn't stink like this one."

11   "Then why don't you work there? Why come to Haiti?"

12   "Santo Domingo has too many whores. All beautiful, like us. All light-skinned. The Haitian men like to sleep with light women."

13   "Why is that?"

14   "Because always, the whites have all the power and the money. The black men can imagine they do, too, when they have us in bed."

15   Eleven o'clock. I looked around the room that is still sparsely peopled with men.

16   "It isn't getting any busier," I say. Frasquita glances over her shoulder. Her eyes drill the darkness.

17   "It is still early," she says.

18   "Could it be that the men are afraid of getting sick?" Frasquita is offended.

19   "Sick! They do not get sick from us. We are healthy, strong. Every week we go for a checkup. Besides, we know how to tell if we are getting sick."

20   "I mean sick with AIDS." The word sets off a hurricane of taffeta, chiffon and gold jewelry. They are all gesticulation and fury. It is Carmen who speaks.

21   "AIDS!" Her lips curl about the syllable. "There is no such thing. It is a false disease invented by the American government to take advantage of the poor countries. The American President hates poor people, so now he makes up AIDS to take away the little we have." The others nod vehemently.

22   "*Mira, mon cher.* Look, my dear," Carmen continues. "One day the police came here. Believe me, they are worse than the *tonton macoutes* with their submachine guns. They rounded up one hundred and five of us and they took our blood. That was a year ago. None of us have died, you see? We are all still here. *Mira,* we sleep with all the men and we are not sick."

23   "But aren't there some of you who have lost weight and have diarrhea?"

24   "One or two, maybe. But they don't eat. That is why they are weak."

25   "Only the men die," says Mercedes. "They stop eating, so they die. It is hard to kill a woman."

26   "Do you eat well?"

27   "Oh, yes, don't worry, we do. We eat like poor people, but we eat." There is a sudden scream from Frasquita. She points to a large rat that has emerged from beneath our table.

28   "My God!" she exclaims. "It is big like a pig." They burst into laughter. For a moment the women fall silent. There is only the restlessness of their many bracelets. I give them each another $10.

29   "Are many of the men here bisexual?"

30   "Too many. They do it for money. Afterward, they come to us." Carmen lights a cigarette and looks down at the small lace handkerchief she has been folding and unfolding with immense precision on the table. All at once she turns it over as though it were the ace of spades.

31   "*Mira, blanc* . . . look, white man," she says in a voice suddenly full of foreboding. Her skin too seems to darken to coincide with the tone of her voice.

32   "*Mira,* soon many Dominican women will die in Haiti!"

33   "Die of what?"

34   She shrugs. "It is what they do to us."

35   "Carmen," I say, "if you knew that you had AIDS, that your blood was bad, would you still sleep with men?" Abruptly, she throws back her head and laughs. It is the same laughter with which Frasquita had greeted the rat at our feet. She stands and the others follow.

36   "*Méchant!* You wicked man," she says. Then, with terrible solemnity, "You don't know anything."

37   "But you are killing the Haitian men," I say.

38   "As for that," she says, "everyone is killing everyone else." All at once, I want to know everything about these three—their childhood, their dreams, what they do in the afternoon, what they eat for lunch.

39   "Don't leave," I say. "Stay a little more." Again, I reach for my wallet. But they are gone, taking all the light in the room with them— Mercedes and Carmen to sit at another table where three men have been waiting. Frasquita is strolling about the room. Now and then, as if captured by the music, she breaks into a few dance steps, snapping her fingers, singing to herself.

40   Midnight. And the Copacabana is filling up. Now it is like any other seedy nightclub where men and women go hunting. We get up to leave. In the center a couple are dancing a *méringue.* He is the most graceful dancer I have ever watched; she, the most voluptuous. Together they seem to be riding the back of the music as it gallops to a precisely sexual beat. Closer up, I see that the man is short of breath, sweating. All at once, he collapses into a chair. The woman bends over him, coaxing, teasing, but he is through. A young man with a long polished stick blocks my way.

41   "I come with you?" he asks. "Very good time. You say yes? Ten dollars? Five?"

42   I have been invited by Dr. Jean William Pape to attend the AIDS clinic of which he is the director. Nothing from the outside of the low whitewashed structure would suggest it as a medical facility. Inside, it is divided into many small cubicles and a labyrinth of corridors. At nine A.M. the hallways are already full of emaciated silent men and women, some sitting on the few benches, the rest leaning against the walls. The only sounds are subdued moans of discomfort interspersed with coughs. How they eat us with their eyes as we pass.

43   The room where Pape and I work is perhaps ten feet by ten. It contains a desk, two chairs and a narrow wooden table that is covered with a sheet that will not be changed during the day. The patients are called in one at a time, asked how they feel and whether there is any change in their symptoms, then examined on the table. If the patient is new to the clinic, he or she is questioned about sexual activities.

44   A twenty-seven-year-old man whose given name is Miracle enters. He is wobbly, panting, like a groggy boxer who has let down his arms and is waiting for the last punch. He is neatly dressed and wears, despite the heat, a heavy woolen cap. When he removes it, I see that his hair is thin,

dull reddish and straight. It is one of the signs of AIDS in Haiti, Pape tells me. The man's skin is covered with a dry itchy rash. Throughout the interview and examination he scratches himself slowly, absentmindedly. The rash is called prurigo. It is another symptom of AIDS in Haiti. This man has had diarrhea for six months. The laboratory reports that the diarrhea is due to an organism called cryptosporidium, for which there is no treatment. The telltale rattling of the tuberculous moisture in his chest is audible without a stethoscope. He is like a leaky cistern that bubbles and froths. And, clearly, exhausted.

45   "Where do you live?" I ask.

46   "Kenscoff." A village in the hills above Port-au-Prince.

47   "How did you come here today?"

48   "I came on the *tap-tap.*" It is the name given to the small buses that swarm the city, each one extravagantly decorated with religious slogans, icons, flowers, animals, all painted in psychedelic colors. I have never seen a *tap-tap* that was not covered with passengers as well, riding outside and hanging on. The vehicles are little masterpieces of contagion, if not of AIDS then of the multitude of germs which Haitian flesh is heir to. Miracle is given a prescription for a supply of Sera, which is something like Gatorade, and told to return in a month.

49   "*Mangé kou bêf,*" says the doctor in farewell. "Eat like an ox." What can he mean? The man has no food or money to buy any. Even had he food, he has not the appetite to eat or the ability to retain it. To each departing patient the doctor will say the same words—"*Mangé kou bêf.*" I see that it is his way of offering a hopeful goodbye.

50   "Will he live until his next appointment?" I ask.

51   "No." Miracle leaves to catch the *tap-tap* for Kenscoff.

52   Next is a woman of twenty-six who enters holding her right hand to her forehead in a kind of permanent salute. In fact, she is shielding her eye from view. This is her third visit to the clinic. I see that she is still quite well nourished.

53   "Now, you'll see something beautiful, tremendous," the doctor says. Once seated upon the table, she is told to lower her hand. When she does, I see that her right eye and its eyelid are replaced by a huge fungating ulcerated tumor, a side product of her AIDS. As she turns her head, the cluster of lymph glands in her neck to which the tumor has spread is thrown into relief. Two years ago she received a blood transfusion at a time when the country's main blood bank was grossly contaminated with AIDS. It has since been closed down. The only blood available in Haiti is a small supply procured from the Red Cross.

54   "Can you give me medicine?" the woman wails.

55   "No."

56   "Can you cut it away?"

57   "No."

58   "Is there radiation therapy?" I ask.

59   "No."

60   "Chemotherapy?" The doctor looks at me in what some might call weary amusement. I see that there is nothing to do. She has come here because there is nowhere else to go.

61   "What will she do?"

62   "Tomorrow or the next day or the day after that she will climb up into the mountains to seek relief from the *houngan*, the voodoo priest, just as her slave ancestors did two hundred years ago."

63   Then comes a frail man in his thirties, with a strangely spiritualized face, like a child's. Pus runs from one ear onto his cheek, where it has dried and caked. He has trouble remembering, he tells us. In fact, he seems confused. It is from toxoplasmosis of the brain, an effect of his AIDS. This man is bisexual. Two years ago he engaged in oral sex with foreign men for money. As I palpate the swollen glands of his neck, a mosquito flies between our faces. I swat at it, miss. Just before coming to Haiti I had read that the AIDS virus had been isolated from a certain mosquito. The doctor senses my thought.

64   "Not to worry," he says. "So far as we know there has never been a case transmitted by insects."

65   "Yes," I say. "I see."

66   And so it goes until the last, the thirty-sixth AIDS patient has been seen. At the end of the day I am invited to wash my hands before leaving. I go down a long hall to a sink. I turn on the faucets but there is no water.

67   "But what about *you*?" I ask the doctor. "You are at great personal risk here—the tuberculosis, the other infections, no water to wash. . . " He shrugs, smiles faintly and lifts his hands palm upward.

68   We are driving up a serpiginous steep road into the barren mountains above Port-au-Prince. Even in the bright sunshine the countryside has the bloodless color of exhaustion and indifference. Our destination is the Baptist Mission Hospital, where many cases of AIDS have been reported. Along the road there are slow straggles of schoolchildren in blue uniforms who stretch out their hands as we pass and call out, "Give me something." Already a crowd of outpatients has gathered at the entrance to the mission compound. A tour of the premises reveals that in contrast to the aridity outside the gates, this is an enclave of productivity, lush with fruit trees and poinsettia.

69   The hospital is clean and smells of creosote. Of the forty beds, less than a third are occupied. In one male ward of twelve beds, there are two

patients. The chief physician tells us that last year he saw ten cases of AIDS each week. Lately the number has decreased to four or five.

70   "Why is that?" we want to know.

71   "Because we do not admit them to the hospital, so they have learned not to come here."

72   "Why don't you admit them?"

73   "Because we would have nothing but AIDS here then. So we send them away."

74   "But I see that you have very few patients in bed."

75   "That is also true."

76   "Where do the AIDS patients go?"

77   "Some go to the clinic in Port-au-Prince or the general hospital in the city. Others go home to die or to the voodoo priest."

78   "Do the people with AIDS know what they have before they come here?"

79   "Oh, yes, they know very well, and they know there is nothing to be done for them."

80   Outside, the crowd of people is dispersing toward the gate. The clinic has been canceled for the day. No one knows why. We are conducted to the office of the reigning American pastor. He is a tall, handsome Midwesterner with an ecclesiastical smile.

81   "It is voodoo that is the devil here." He warms to his subject. "It is a demonic religion, a cancer on Haiti. Voodoo is worse than AIDS. And it is one of the reasons for the epidemic. Did you know that in order for a man to become a *houngans* he must perform anal sodomy on another man? No, of course you didn't. And it doesn't stop there. The *houngans* tell the men that in order to appease the spirits they too must do the same thing. So you have ritualized homosexuality. That's what is spreading the AIDS." The pastor tells us of a nun who witnessed two acts of sodomy in a provincial hospital where she came upon a man sexually assaulting a houseboy and another man mounting a male patient in his bed.

82   "Fornication," he says. "It is Sodom and Gomorrah all over again, so what can you expect from these people?" Outside his office we are shown a cage of terrified, cowering monkeys to whom he coos affectionately. It is clear that he loves them. At the car, we shake hands.

83   "By the way," the pastor says, "what is your religion? Perhaps I am a kinsman?"

84   "While I am in Haiti," I tell him, "it will be voodoo or it will be nothing at all."

85   Abruptly, the smile breaks. It is as though a crack had suddenly appeared in the face of an idol.

86   From the mission we go to the general hospital. In the heart of Port-au-Prince, it is the exact antithesis of the immaculate facility we have

just left—filthy, crowded, hectic and staffed entirely by young interns and residents. Though it is associated with a medical school, I do not see any members of the faculty. We are shown around by Jocelyne, a young intern in a scrub suit. Each bed in three large wards is occupied. On the floor about the beds, hunkered in the posture of the innocent poor, are family members of the patients. In the corridor that constitutes the emergency room, someone lies on a stretcher receiving an intravenous infusion. She is hardly more than a cadaver.

87   "Where are the doctors in charge?" I ask Jocelyne. She looks at me questioningly.

88   "We are in charge."

89   "I mean your teachers, the faculty."

90   "They do not come here."

91   "What is wrong with that woman?"

92   "She has had diarrhea for three months. Now she is dehydrated." I ask the woman to open her mouth. Her throat is covered with the white plaques of thrush, a fungus infection associated with AIDS.

93   "How many AIDS patients do you see here?"

94   "Three or four a day. We send them home. Sometimes the families abandon them, then we must admit them to the hospital. Every day, then, a relative comes to see if the patient has died. They want to take the body. That is important to them. But they know very well that AIDS is contagious and they are afraid to keep them at home. Even so, once or twice a week the truck comes to take away the bodies. Many are children. They are buried in mass graves."

95   "Where do the wealthy patients go?"

96   "There is a private hospital called Canapé Vert. Or else they go to Miami. Most of them, rich and poor, do not go to the hospital. Most are never diagnosed."

97   "How do you know these people have AIDS?"

98   "We don't know sometimes. The blood test is inaccurate. There are many false positives and false negatives. Fifteen percent of those with the disease have negative blood tests. We go by their infections—tuberculosis, diarrhea, fungi, herpes, skin rashes. It is not hard to tell."

99   "Do they know what they have?"

100   "Yes. They understand at once and they are prepared to die."

101   "Do the patients know how AIDS is transmitted?"

102   "They know, but they do not like to talk about it. It is taboo. Their memories do not seem to reach back to the true origins of their disaster. It is understandable, is it not?"

103   "Whatever you write, don't hurt us any more than we have already been hurt." It is a young Haitian journalist with whom I am drinking a rum punch. He means that any further linkage of AIDS and Haiti in the

media would complete the economic destruction of the country. The damage was done early in the epidemic when the Centers for Disease Control in Atlanta added Haitians to the three other high-risk groups— hemophiliacs, intravenous drug users and homosexual and bisexual men. In fact, Haitians are no more susceptible to AIDS than anyone else. Although the CDC removed Haitians from special scrutiny in 1985, the lucrative tourism on which so much of the country's economy was based was crippled. Along with tourism went much of the foreign business investment. Worst of all was the injury to the national pride. Suddenly Haiti was indicted as the source of AIDS in the western hemisphere.

104   What caused the misunderstanding was the discovery of a large number of Haitian men living in Miami with AIDS antibodies in their blood. They denied absolutely they were homosexuals. But the CDC investigators did not know that homosexuality is the strongest taboo in Haiti and that no man would ever admit to it. Bisexuality, however, is not uncommon. Many married men and heterosexually oriented males will occasionally seek out other men for sex. Further, many, if not most, Haitian men visit female prostitutes from time to time. It is not difficult to see that once the virus was set loose in Haiti, the spread would be swift through both genders.

105   Exactly how the virus of AIDS arrived is not known. Could it have been brought home by the Cuban soldiers stationed in Angola and thence to Haiti, about fifty miles away? Could it have been passed on by the thousands of Haitians living in exile in Zaire, who later returned home or immigrated to the United States? Could it have come from the American and Canadian homosexual tourists, and, yes, even some U.S. diplomats who have traveled to the island to have sex with impoverished Haitian men all too willing to sell themselves to feed their families? Throughout the international gay community Haiti was known as a good place to go for sex.

106   On a private tip from an official at the Ministry of Tourism, J-B and I drive to a town some fifty miles from Port-au-Prince. The hotel is owned by two Frenchmen who are out of the country, one of the staff tells us. He is a man of about thirty and clearly he is desperately ill. Tottering, short of breath, he shows us about the empty hotel. The furnishings are opulent and extreme—tiger skins on the wall, a live leopard in the garden, a bedroom containing a giant bathtub with gold faucets. Is it the heat of the day or the heat of my imagination that makes these walls echo with the painful cries of pederasty?

107   The hotel where we are staying is in Pétionville, the fashionable suburb of Port-au-Prince. It is the height of the season but there are no tourists, only a dozen or so French and American businessmen. The swimming pool is used once or twice a day by a single person.

Otherwise, the water remains undisturbed until dusk, when the fruit bats come down to drink in midswoop. The hotel keeper is an American. He is eager to set me straight on Haiti.

108   "What did and should attract foreign investment is a combination of reliable weather, an honest and friendly populace, low wages and multilingual managers."

109   "What spoiled it?"

110   "Political instability and a bad American press about AIDS." He pauses, then adds: "To which I hope you won't be contributing."

111   "What about just telling the truth?" I suggest.

112   "Look," he says, "there is no more danger of catching AIDS in Haiti than in New York or Santo Domingo. It is not where you are but what you do that counts." Agreeing, I ask if he had any idea that much of the tourism in Haiti during the past few decades was based on sex.

113   "No idea whatsoever. It was only recently that we discovered that that was the case."

114   "How is it that you hoteliers, restaurant owners and the Ministry of Tourism did not know what *tout* Haiti knew?"

115   "Look. All I know is that this is a middle-class, family-oriented hotel. We don't allow guests to bring women, or for that matter men, into their rooms. If they did, we'd ask them to leave immediately."

116   At five A.M. the next day the telephone rings in my room. A Creole-accented male voice.

117   "Is the lady still with you, sir?"

118   "There is no lady here."

119   "In your room, sir, the lady I allowed to go up with a package?"

120   "There is no lady here, I tell you."

121   At seven A.M. I stop at the front desk. The clerk is a young man.

122   "Was it you who called my room at five o'clock?"

123   "Sorry," he says with a smile. "It was a mistake, sir. I meant to ring the room next door to yours." Still smiling, he holds up his shushing finger.

124   Next to Dr. Pape, director of the AIDS clinic, Bernard Liautaud, a dermatologist, is the most knowledgeable Haitian physician on the subject of the epidemic. Together, the two men have published a dozen articles on AIDS in international medical journals. In our meeting they present me with statistics:

- There are more than one thousand documented cases of AIDS in Haiti, and as many as one hundred thousand carriers of the virus.
- Eighty-seven percent of AIDS is now transmitted heterosexually. While it is true that the virus was introduced via the bisexual community, that route has decreased to 10 percent or less.

- Sixty percent of the wives or husbands of AIDS patients tested positive for the antibody.
- Fifty percent of the prostitutes tested in the Port-au-Prince area are infected.
- Eighty percent of the men with AIDS have had contact with prostitutes.
- The projected number of active cases in four years is ten thousand. (Since my last visit, the Haitian Medical Association broke its silence on the epidemic by warning that one million of the country's six million people could be carriers by 1992.)

125   The two doctors have more to tell. "The crossing over of the plague from the homosexual to the heterosexual community will follow in the United States within two years. This, despite the hesitation to say so by those who fear to sow panic among your population. In Haiti, because bisexuality is more common, there was an early crossover into the general population. The trend, inevitably, is the same in the two countries."

126   "What is there to do, then?"

127   "Only education, just as in America. But here the Haitians reject the use of condoms. Only the men who are too sick to have sex are celibate."

128   "What is to be the end of it?"

129   "When enough heterosexuals of the middle and upper classes die, perhaps there will be the panic necessary for the people to change their sexual lifestyles."

130   This evening I leave Haiti. For two weeks I have fastened myself to this lovely fragile land like an ear pressed to the ground. It is a country to break a traveler's heart. It occurs to me that I have not seen a single jogger. Such a public expenditure of energy while everywhere else strength is ebbing—it would be obscene. In my final hours, I go to the Cathédral of Sainte Trinité, the inner walls of which are covered with murals by Haiti's most renowned artists. Here are all the familiar Bible stories depicted in naïveté and piety, and all in such an exuberance of color as to tax the capacity of the retina to receive it, as though all the vitality of Haiti had been turned to paint and brushed upon these walls. How to explain its efflorescence at a time when all else is lassitude and inertia? Perhaps one day the plague will be rendered in poetry, music, painting, but not now. Not now.

TO THINK ABOUT

1. Selzer begins his essay with an account of his interview with three prostitutes in a Port-au-Prince brothel. He makes no moral judgments. What is the purpose of this strategy?
2. Although Selzer is not in any imminent danger as he tours Haiti, there is dramatic tension throughout the piece. What are the sources of this tension.
3. Near the end of the essay Selzer presents us with a series of statistics illustrating the pervasive nature of the AIDS epidemic in Haiti. What effect do these statistics have on you, the reader, coming, as they do, *after* a collection of anecdotal material? Would the statistics have had the same impact earlier in the piece?
4. What is Selzer's theme? Does he ever state it explicitly?

TO DO

1. Free-write for fifteen minutes on the subject of AIDS. Write as fast as you can. Then read what you have written. Perhaps you have the raw material for an essay.
2. Write an essay based on a series of on-location interviews you conduct. For example, you could do a piece on the social scene on your campus by visiting various hangouts during the course of a weekend, interviewing whoever is there. You might also talk with non-students—faculty, counselors, police, the dean of students—about the quality of student life outside the classroom. Does the official version match the reality you have seen? In any case, write it up, allowing the scenes themselves to convey your message.

TIP

The trick to this sort of interviewing is not simply to ask your subjects about the issue in question—*What do you think of the social life here at the university?*—but to ask them about *themselves*—their families, their values, their aspirations, their heroes, the important people and moments in their lives. This way you will be able to give their thoughts on social life some meaning by putting them in context.

41

The Specimen Collectors
Richard Selzer

Behold the surgeon, Richard Selzer. Before his retirement, he routinely cut into living flesh, sliced away at diseased tissue, and (who knows—perhaps regretfully!) sewed up the wound. Behold the surgeon as writer, exploring the psyches and the souls of surgeons and their patients in a series of magnificent essays (see, especially, the collections Mortal Lessons *and* Confessions of a Knife, *from which this essay is drawn.) Never was there a lung too cancer-ridden, a tumor too pustular for him to describe in horrific detail. And yet, a person has his limits. Here Dr. Selzer describes, with evident dread, a species of medical practitioner who inspires fear and loathing among all but its own kind: the pathologist. Selzer's voice is straight out of a nightmare. The cadence, the locution, will resonate horribly with something already lodged stubbornly in your brain.*

Selzer is kidding. Of course.

1   There is a little-known race of men about which I feel it my duty to warn the general public. They are called pathologists. These men present to the world as their high purpose the diagnosis of disease based on the laboratory examination of either all (*O terrore!*) or some portion of the body, their materials having been excavated in their morgues or snipped off for them by only slightly less scurrilous surgeons. Such is the livelihood of pathologists. But what of their passion? And dark it is, rapacious. For these are the dreadful Specimen Collectors of Medicine. Cynical, jaded men who scorn your workaday carrion, and pant only after corporeal exotica much as the gourmet who despises porridge but would sell his father's name for a ragout of cuckoo tongue. So unscrupulous they, that not even the liver of Saint Sebastian would be outside their traffic, but the Dear Piece must be snatched from its reliquary to turn up a year later in Bratislava, say, dried and pinned to a cork board on the wall of some godless Czech pathologist. Beneath it, doubtless, some shameless

legend: "Liver of saint with stellate laceration, anterior surface, right lobe. Unusually good condition." A casual lunch with two pathologists is likely to reveal that one owns a piece of an early Christian, the other the rear footpad of a lion.

2   Behold the specimen collector at work. The great stone morgue is alive with activity. It is a very Baghdad bazaar. Beneath the fluorescent lights, on a dozen slabs, lies the "catch" in various stages of evisceration and dismemberment. Each corpse wears upon its great toe a label bearing its name. A "twisty" is used to secure it there. It is said that the mere act of dying seems to confer upon all of us the appearance of beatitude, as though each one has been freshly taken down from the Cross. In the morgue, this is not believable.

3   Step aside! A gurney rattles in, bringing a newcomer. Now another gurney evacuates a graduate toward the hearse gaping at the end of a ramp. Interns, residents, dieners and licensed embalmers, each wearing a long gray lab coat, tug, haul, and slice, all the while calling out to each other in hearty voice. Their brains seem but feebly illuminated, like those of men who pass sentence or carry out execution. What clatter of cutlery! What rivers of multicolored water! One knows at once that here, at least, the world's work is being done.

4   Above each of the slabs, there is a hanging scale such as is used in delicatessen stores. Now and then, a kidney will flop up on the scale, then bounce itself to stillness. "Right kidney . . . 200 grams," a voice calls out. Somewhere this is recorded. The kidney is retrieved from the scale; cubes and slices of it are taken and arranged on trays. From these pieces, microscopic slides will be made.

5   In the morgue, then, a great tussling herd, heads and rumps rising, falling. And everywhere a clanging, a jostling, a shouting. Into this clamor slouches the dread pathologist. He wears the grayest lab coat of all. He sidles along the awful avenues between the slabs, deaf to the greetings of the others. His neck is wry; his mouth hangs open, the lips moist, the tongue lolling between. How quickly he scuttles! It is no wonder. Word has reached him that one of the bodies, a woman, harbors in her left ovary a dermoid cyst containing three perfectly formed teeth, two molars and a canine. He will, he *must* have it, and hastens toward his prize as glinty as a streetwalker stepping up to a sailor. In a moment he is at her, rummaging; his shoulders hunch; his elbows are furious. Now and then, he turns his head to shoot a glance behind him, the way a pigeon will do, standing guard over a potato chip. Minutes later, he straightens. Something round and pink is in his hand. It is not a peach.

6   No, gentle reader, pathology is not the most delicate of the medical arts. I have known a pathologist who, armed with a tree trunk and a couple of paving stones, could pass for Cyclops. This same man has been

observed playing "soldier" with a collection of lithopedions that he keeps in a cigar box in a locked drawer. These "stone babies" are the calcified result of pregnancies which, by one route or another, have found their way into the free peritoneal cavity. In that he causes no symptoms, the innocent little lithopedion is discovered by purest chance. Surgeons in search of other, more dangerous game, will come upon him in the environs of some organ beneath which, slumbrous, he has lain for many years, and from which den he never thought to leave. He, whose gentle fate was to have kept everlasting watch among the bones and the dust of his mother, is now untimely pluck'd and delivered into the world as statuary. His sleepless permanence now disturbed, he shall like Ozymandias, King of Kings, crumble into sand.

7   The best place to see a pathologist is in the basement of a medical school. There, where the walls sweat and trickle, where whispers echo through uncarpeted tunnels, and where great pipes course along the ceiling carrying God-knows-what effluent from the premises. Among these dews and damps, he nethers, shouldering from tank to slab and back again, his eyes hooded, and always in hand a bottle or tray the contents of which are best left unspecified. Where he passes, a chill gathers; you catch the rank whiff of formaldehyde. Should such a man smile at you, be on guard. His grin may be no impulse toward congeniality but a crafty device to lay hold of some part of you upon which his acquisitive eye has fastened.

8   Just as pets are said to take on some of the physical features of their masters, so does the pathologist each year grow more whey-faced and thin, so does he fall into long silences, so does he become more reminiscent of the material with which he works. Of what does such a man dream? In the unsoiled regions of sleep do beautiful women come to him, smiling? Do they feed him cold grapes in bannered pavilions? Or is it some ulcered stomach that he sees just beyond his grasp, toward which a hated rival races? I have often suspected that some hideous and secret covenant lay behind this fanatical accumulation of human flesh. These grim suspicions are not easily proven, since the perpetrators are a canny tribe, all of whom have closed their mouths on the pill of silence. As soon ask a horse why he eats fodder.

9   Enter the subterranean study of a pathologist, and you are in the cave of Grendel. From the ceiling, suspended by wires, hang lungs, the delicate arborizations of which are filled with red, white, and blue rubber; red for the arteries, blue for the veins, and the bronchial tree done in white, all conspiring to the illusion of a garden of patriotic blooms. As the door clicks gassily shut behind you, the lungs are set in motion by the breeze. You look about. At first there is no sign of life. All is silent,

still. Suddenly, you hear a cough! Terrified, you stare at the swinging lungs. Could it be! Now something scurries! A segment of the offal strewn upon the floor stirs, lifts, and arranges itself into the shape of a human being. You blink, and there he hunkers, sorting bones, one of which suggests a recent severe gnawing. The very idea of all those bones! From God-knows-how-many unrelated corpses pitted and brought to conclave by no last wish of their living owners, but by the unslakable thirst of the specimen collector. Gone, any hoped-for corporeal integrity; gone, eternal solitude. A man ought to have the comfort of knowing that he will either lie alone in splendor, or next to his most congenial companion. But higgledy-piggledy your skull, my pelvis? No offense, but, well, I'd prefer not to. Our said parts having achieved no such propinquity in life, I see no reason why they should be thrust together clackety-clack in death. In the office of the pathologist, except for the organs of the great and near great, all of the specimens are anonymous. It seems a soulless thing to cut out the best part of a man, and fail to label it: Liver of Henry Huckaby, b. 1914, d. 1977. It is little enough to do. Perhaps a droll or goodnatured epitaph would do. Something like:

10   Saving This Piece, May the Rest Rest in Peace.

11   If for no other reason than to preserve the integrity of your remains from pathologists, immediate cremation would seem the only possible choice of a decorous man. In the words of Thomas Browne,

> To be gnaw'd out of our graves, to have our sculs made drinking bowls, and our bones turned into pipes to delight and sport our Enemies, are Tragicall abominations, escaped in burning Burials.

12   I am firmly of the belief that pathologists are born and not made. I have observed even first-year interns hurrying from the morgue to their lockers with some bit of finger, the odd kneecap. It is a thought that saddens the heart. If these things be done in the green tree, what shall be done in the dry? And pathologists go it alone. They have forgone the banter and slap of fellowship, preferring their private, more recondite joys. Perhaps I should be kinder. Perhaps they are the victims of the slow toxin of formaldehyde that produces a chemical madness; perhaps they have heard too long the nightingale of Death caroling in their drafty halls, and have become enchanted at the sound, ever after to be ruled by a wild taste. Is the pathologist then so different from the poet, the composer or painter who strives to solidify into art his secret delight? For each man, his own poetry; although some, written in runic rhyme, is indecipherable by the rest of us. It is quite to be expected that the specimen collector would issue it in his will that he be buried with full Pathological Honors—in Lung and Monstrosity—Thus, up to his neck in

pickled treasure, he would disdain the death that for others holds out such fear.

13   The truth is that pathology is less an occupation concerned with diagnosis, than a preoccupation with the oddments and endments of the flesh. So famished are its practitioners for specimens that, in time, they become themselves a confusion of hungers. Hence their reprehensible penchant for comparing the manifestations of disease to items of food. As in "cheesy pus," "coffee-ground vomitus," "nutmeg liver," "currant jelly stool," and the *peau d'orange* breast of cancer. In this, they have the precedent of Petronius who likened the perianal warts of his boy-lovers unto an "orchard of figs." Let a pathologist read aloud his reports, and every decent gorge rises. Tumors are the size of grapes, walnuts, plums, eggs, lemons, oranges, grapefruit, and melons. Pumpkin and watermelon being invoked only for the rare ovarian cyst. And while it is not, strictly speaking, one of the edibilia, toothpaste is the favorite simile for the stools passed in obstructive jaundice. Toothpaste and stool! A sophomoric misalliance indeed.

14   It is in the nature of pathologists that they are easily provoked to rage and violence. I have known one so fastidious as to require three bites in the eating of a single cherry. This same man could bare-handle a brain out of its skull in something under three minutes from first incision to the reefing up. Another, who was rendered dyspneic by a minuet, would hew at a cow, root and branch, to wrest from it a tiny trophy of pituitary. And I recall one pathologist on the faculty of the medical school that I attended. His prize possession was a cyclops, a one-eyed full-term monstrosity that sported a tubular proboscis. The thing swam in a great sealed jar of formaldehyde on his desk. Rumor had it that Professor Fenstermacher sang German lullabies to it in the dead of night. One day, the cyclops, jar and all, was missing from his desk. To this day I shudder at the image of him stalking the aisles of the laboratory where we students shrank over our microscopes. In his hand, a huge femur which he waved about like a cudgel.

15   "Tsyklops," he strangled, "he iss gone. Somevun hass taken my Tsyklops. Vich vun off you hass taken my Tsyklops from me?" He would surely have laid out any number of us with his femur had not a gifted ventriloquist in our midst called out:

16   "Schwartzkopf!"

17   At the sound of the name of his most hated rival, Fenstermacher froze, his eyes silver slits of murder.

18   "Jawohl! Schwartzkopf!" he nickered, and, brandishing the bone like a troll, he lurched from the room. Later, a substitute was called in to teach the class for the duration of his sentence.

19   Such specimen collectors are medical mutineers who see flesh as art deco rather than as the spirit thickened. Now what is the time-honored method of dealing with mutineers? Why, they are brought before a tribunal of officers and peers, convicted, and shot through the heart by their shipmates. For these latter know well that a mutinous mind is a weevil in a sack of flour. It must be extracted for the greater good of society.

20   So would I exhort all honest internists, pediatricians, and family practitioners to drive the swine of pathology from the temple of Aesculapius, and herd them into some apt enclosure where they can be picked off with a minimum of mess.

TO THINK ABOUT

1. What sort of narrative voice does Selzer use in "The Specimen Collectors"? Compare it with the voice in "A Mask on the Face of Death" (Chapter 40). Which voice do you think is more natural to Selzer?
2. Selzer writes: "Such specimen collectors are medical mutineers who see flesh as art deco rather than as the spirit thickened." What does this imply about the attitude of other medical types—surgeons included? Does Selzer make this implication seriously or in jest?
3. Selzer concludes that pathologists should be taken out and shot. What is the strategic value of ending the essay this way?
4. What is your reaction to Selzer's cavalier treatment of dead and dismembered bodies? Are you offended? Amused? Both? Why do you react the way you do?

TO DO

1. Think of a movie or television actor who might make a fitting narrator for Selzer's tale. Then read the first paragraph aloud, imitating that actor.
2. Make a list of subjects you *least* want to write about. Examine the list. Find the subject you are *most* uncomfortable with, the one you wish to stay away from, no matter what. Free-write on this subject for twenty minutes. (Don't worry—you don't have to show it to anybody.) Then read what you have written. See if you have the makings of an essay.

TIP

Sometimes it is good strategy to exaggerate for effect. Let us say you want to write about a subject that is creepy, crawly, or otherwise likely to make readers uncomfortable, but you don't know how to begin. Try exaggerating the creepiness and the crawliness. Selzer knew his audience was likely to be squeamish about pathologists and their work; rather than try to deny the ghoulish aspects of pathology, he blows them up to outlandish proportions. Readers are forced to laugh at their own preconceived notions.

42

Talking AIDS to Death
Randy Shilts

The late Randy Shilts was a reporter with the San Francisco Chronicle *when a mysterious, deadly disease began killing homosexual men in that city. He chronicled the spread of AIDS as it became an epidemic. And he chronicled battles on two fronts: the scientific battle, in which researchers raced to conquer the disease, and the political battle, in which AIDS activists battled a conservative national administration that had other priorities. Eventually he wrote a book,* And the Band Played On, *in which he charged that politics was obstructing the war against AIDS.*

He expected the book to result in national outrage and quick government action. In this essay he discusses what happened. It was not what he had anticipated.

His voice has a prickly quality to it, an edge; here is an angry narrator who gets angrier as he goes along. But he conveys other emotions as well. And in the end, anger gives way to something else.

1   *I'm talking to my friend Kit Herman when I notice a barely perceptible spot on the left side of his face. Slowly, it grows up his cheekbone, down to his chin, and forward to his mouth. He talks on cheerfully, as if nothing is wrong, and I'm amazed that I'm able to smile and chat on, too, as if nothing were there. His eyes become sunken; his hair turns gray; his ear is turning purple now, swelling into a carcinomatous cauliflower, and still we talk on. He's dying in front of me. He'll be dead soon if nothing is done.*

2   Dead soon if nothing is done.

3   "Excuse me, Mr. Shilts, I asked if you are absolutely sure, if you can categorically state that you definitely cannot get AIDS from a mosquito."

4   I forget the early-morning nightmare and shift into my canned response. All my responses are canned now. I'm an AIDS talk-show jukebox.

Press the button, any button on the AIDS question list, and I have my canned answer ready. Is this Chicago or Detroit?

5   "Of course you can get AIDS from a mosquito," I begin.

6   Here I paused for dramatic effect. In that brief moment, I can almost hear the caller murmur, "I *knew* it."

7   "If you have unprotected anal intercourse with an infected mosquito, you'll get AIDS," I continue. "Anything short of that and you won't."

8   The talk-show host likes the answer. All the talk-show hosts like my answers because they're short, punchy, and to the point. Not like those boring doctors with long recitations of scientific studies so overwritten with maybes and qualifiers that they frighten more than they reassure an AIDS-hysteric public. I give good interview, talk-show producers agree. It's amazing, they say, how I always stay so cool and never lose my temper.

9   "Mr. Shilts, has there ever been a case of anyone getting AIDS from a gay waiter?"

10   "In San Francisco, I don't think they allow heterosexuals to be waiters. This fact proves absolutely that if you could get AIDS from a gay waiter, all northern California would be dead by now."

11   I gave that same answer once on a Bay Area talk show, and my caller, by the sound of her a little old lady, quickly rejoined, "What if that gay waiter took my salad back into the kitchen and ejaculated into my salad dressing? Couldn't I get AIDS then?"

12   I didn't have a pat answer for that one, and I still wonder at what this elderly caller thought went on in the kitchens of San Francisco restaurants. Fortunately, this morning's phone-in—in Chicago, it turned out—is not as imaginative.

13   "You know, your question reminds me of a joke we had in California a couple of years back," I told the caller. "How many heterosexual waiters in San Francisco does it take to screw in a light bulb? The answer is both of them."

14   The host laughs, the caller is silent. Next comes the obligatory question about whether AIDS can be spread through coughing.

15   I had written a book to change the world, and here I was on talk shows throughout America, answering questions about mosquitoes and gay waiters.

16   This wasn't exactly what I had envisioned when I began writing *And the Band Played On.* I had hoped to effect some fundamental changes. I really believed I could alter the performance of the institutions that had allowed AIDS to sweep through America unchecked.

17   AIDS had spread, my book attested, because politicians, particularly those in charge of federal-level response, had viewed the disease as a

political issue, not an issue of public health—they deprived researchers of anything near the resources that were needed to fight it. AIDS had spread because government health officials consistently lied to the American people about the need for more funds, being more concerned with satisfying their political bosses and protecting their own jobs than with telling the truth and protecting the public health. And AIDS had spread because indolent news organizations shunned their responsibility to provide tough, adversarial reportage, instead basing stories largely on the Official Truth of government press releases. The response to AIDS was never even remotely commensurate with the scope of the problem.

18   I figured the federal government, finally exposed, would stumble over itself to accelerate the pace of AIDS research and put AIDS prevention programs on an emergency footing. Once publicly embarrassed by the revelations of its years of shameful neglect, the media would launch serious investigative reporting on the epidemic. Health officials would step forward and finally lay bare the truth about how official disregard had cost this country hundreds of thousands of lives. And it would never happen again.

19   I was stunned by the "success" of my book. I quickly acquired all the trappings of bestsellerdom: *60 Minutes* coverage of my "startling" revelations, a Book-of-the-Month Club contract, a miniseries deal with NBC, translation into six languages, book tours on three continents, featured roles in movie-star-studded AIDS fund raisers, regular appearances on network news shows, and hefty fees on the college lecture circuit. A central figure in my book became one of *People* magazine's "25 Most Intriguing People of 1987," even though he had been dead for nearly four years, and the *Los Angeles Herald Examiner* pronounced me one of the "in" authors of 1988. The mayor of San Francisco even proclaimed my birthday last year "Randy Shilts Day."

20   And one warm summer day as I was sunning at a gay resort in the redwoods north of San Francisco, a well-toned, perfectly tanned young man slid into a chaise next to me and offered the ultimate testimony to my fifteen minutes of fame. His dark eyelashes rising and falling shyly, he whispered, "When I saw you on *Good Morning America* a couple weeks ago, I wondered what it would be like to go to bed with you."

21   "You're the world's first AIDS celebrity," enthused a friend at the World Health Organization, after hearing one of WHO's most eminent AIDS authorities say he would grant me an interview on one condition— that I autograph his copy of my book. "It must be great," he said.

22   It's not so great.

23   The bitter irony is, my role as an AIDS celebrity just gives me a more elevated promontory from which to watch the world make the same mistakes in the handling of the AIDS epidemic that I had hoped my

work would help to change. When I return from network tapings and celebrity glad-handing, I come back to my home in San Francisco's gay community and see friends dying. The lesions spread from their cheeks to cover their faces, their hair falls out, they die slowly, horribly, and sometimes suddenly, before anybody has a chance to know they're sick. They die in my arms and in my dreams, and nothing at all has changed.

24   Never before have I succeeded so well; never before have I failed so miserably.

25   I gave my first speech on the college lecture circuit at the University of California at Los Angeles in January 1988. I told the audience that there were 50,000 diagnosed AIDS cases in the United States as of that week and that within a few months there would be more people suffering from this deadly disease in the United States than there were Americans killed during the Vietnam War. There were audible gasps. During the question-and-answer session, several students explained that they had heard that the number of AIDS cases in America was leveling off.

26   In the next speech, at the University of Tennessee, I decided to correct such misapprehension by adding the federal government's projections—the 270,000 expected to be dead or dying from AIDS in 1991, when the disease would kill more people than any single form of cancer, more than car accidents. When I spoke at St. Cloud State University in Minnesota three months later, I noted that the number of American AIDS cases had that week surpassed the Vietnam benchmark. The reaction was more a troubled murmur than a gasp.

27   By the time I spoke at New York City's New School for Social Research in June and there were 65,000 AIDS cases nationally, the numbers were changing so fast that the constant editing made my notes difficult to read. By then as many as 1,000 Americans a week were learning that they, too, had AIDS, or on the average, about one every fourteen minutes. There were new government projections to report, too: by 1993, some 450,000 Americans would be diagnosed with AIDS. In that year, one American will be diagnosed with the disease every thirty-six seconds. Again, I heard the gasps.

28   For my talk at a hospital administrators' conference in Washington in August, I started using little yellow stick-ons to update the numbers on my outline. That made it easier to read; there were now 72,000 AIDS cases. Probably this month, or next, I'll tell another college audience that the nation's AIDS case load has topped 100,000, and there will be gasps again.

29   The gasps always amaze me. Why are they surprised? In epidemics, people get sick and die. That's what epidemics do to people and that's why epidemics are bad.

30   When Kit Herman was diagnosed with AIDS on May 13, 1986, his doctor leaned over his hospital bed, took his hand, and assured him, "Don't worry, you're in time for AZT." The drug worked so well that all Kit's friends let themselves think he might make it. And we were bolstered by the National Institutes of Health's assurance that AZT was only the first generation of AIDS drugs, and that the hundreds of millions of federal dollars going into AIDS treatment research meant there would soon be a second and third generation of treatments to sustain life beyond AZT's effectiveness. Surely nothing was more important, considering the federal government's own estimates that between 1 and 1.5 million Americans were infected with the Human Immunodeficiency Virus (HIV), and virtually all would die within the next decade if nothing was done. The new drugs, the NIH assured everyone, were "in the pipeline," and government scientists were working as fast as they possibly could.

31   Despite my nagging, not one of dozens of public-affairs-show producers chose to look seriously into the development of those long-sought second and third generations of AIDS drugs. In fact, clinical trials of AIDS drugs were hopelessly stalled in the morass of bureaucracy at the NIH, but this story tip never seemed to cut it with producers. Clinical trials were not sexy. Clinical trials were boring.

32   I made my third *Nightline* appearance in January 1988 because new estimates had been released revealing that one in sixty-one babies born in New York City carried antibodies to the AIDS virus. And the link between those babies and the disease was intravenous drug use by one or both parents. Suddenly, junkies had become the group most likely to catch and spread AIDS through the heterosexual community. Free needles to junkies—now there was a sizzling television topic. I told the show's producers I'd talk about that, but that I was much more interested in the issue of AIDS treatments—which seemed most relevant to the night's program, since Ted Koppel's other guest was Dr. Anthony Fauci, associate NIH director for AIDS, and the Reagan administration's most visible AIDS official.

33   After fifteen minutes of talk on the ins and outs and pros and cons of free needles for intravenous drug users, I raised the subject of the pressing need for AIDS treatments. Koppel asked Fauci what was happening. The doctor launched into a discussion of treatments "in the pipeline" and how government scientists were working as fast as they possibly could.

34   I'd heard the same words from NIH officials for three years: drugs were in the pipeline. Maybe it was true, but when were they going to come out of their goddamn pipeline? Before I could formulate a polite retort to Fauci's stall, however, the segment was over, Ted was thanking us, and the red light on the camera had blipped off. Everyone seemed sat-

isfied that the government was doing everything it possibly could to develop AIDS treatments.

35   Three months later, I was reading a week-old *New York Times* in Kit's room in the AIDS ward at San Francisco General Hospital. It was April, nearly two years after my friend's AIDS diagnosis. AZT had given him two years of nearly perfect health, but now its effect was wearing off, and Kit had suffered his first major AIDS-related infection since his original bout with pneumonia—cryptococcal meningitis. The meningitis could be treated, we all knew, but the discovery of this insidious brain infection meant more diseases were likely to follow. And the long-promised second and third generations of AIDS drugs were still nowhere on the horizon.

36   While perusing the worn copy of the *Times*, I saw a story about Dr. Fauci's testimony at a congressional hearing. After making Fauci swear an oath to tell the truth, a subcommittee headed by Congressman Ted Weiss of New York City asked why it was taking so long to get new AIDS treatments into testing at a time when Congress was putting hundreds of millions of dollars into NIH budgets for just such purposes. At first Fauci talked about unavoidable delays. He claimed government scientists were working as fast as they could. Pressed harder, he finally admitted that the problem stemmed "almost exclusively" from the lack of staffing in his agency. Congress had allocated funds, it was true, but the Reagan administration had gotten around spending the money by stingily refusing to let Fauci hire anybody. Fauci had requested 127 positions to speed the development of AIDS treatments; the administration had granted him eleven. And for a year, he had not told anyone. For a year, this spokesman for the public health answered reporters that AIDS drugs were in the pipeline and that government scientists had all the money they needed. It seemed that only when faced with the penalty of perjury would one of the administration's top AIDS officials tell the truth. That was the real story, I thought, but for some reason nobody else had picked up on it.

37   At the international AIDS conference in Stockholm two months later, the other reporters in "the AIDS pack" congratulated me on my success and asked what I was working on now. I admitted that I was too busy promoting the British and German release of my book to do much writing myself, and next month I had the Australian tour. But if I *were* reporting, I added with a vaguely conspiratorial tone, *I'd* look at the *scandal* in the NIH. Nobody had picked up that *New York Times* story from a few months ago about staffing shortages on AIDS clinical trials. The lives of 1.5 million HIV-infected Americans hung in the balance, and the only way you could get a straight answer out of an administration AIDS official was to put him under oath and make him face the

charge of perjury. Where I went to journalism school, *that* was a news story.

38   One reporter responded to my tip with the question "But who's going to play *you* in the miniseries?"

39   A few minutes later, when Dr. Fauci came into the press room, the world's leading AIDS journalists got back to the serious business of transcribing his remarks. Nobody asked him if he was actually telling the truth, or whether they should put him under oath to ensure a candid response to questions about when we'd get AIDS treatments. Most of the subsequent news accounts of Dr. Fauci's comments faithfully reported that many AIDS treatments were in the pipeline. Government scientists, he said once more, were doing all they possibly could.

40   The producer assured my publisher that Morton Downey, Jr., would be "serious" about AIDS. "He's not going to play games on this issue," the producer said, adding solemnly, "His brother has AIDS. He understands the need for compassion." The abundance of Mr. Downey's compassion was implicit in the night's call-in poll question: "Should all people with AIDS be quarantined?"

41   Downey's first question to me was, "You *are* a homosexual, aren't you?"

42   He wasn't ready for my canned answer: "Why do you ask? Do you want a date or something?"

43   The show shifted into an earnest discussion of quarantine. In his television studio, Clearasil-addled high school students from suburban New Jersey held up MORTON DOWNEY FAN CLUB signs and cheered aggressively when the truculent, chain-smoking host appeared to favor a kind of homespun AIDS Auschwitz. The youths shouted down any audience member who stepped forward to defend the rights of AIDS sufferers, their howls growing particularly vitriolic if the speakers were gay. These kids were the ilk from which Hitler drew his Nazi youth. In the first commercial break, the other guest, an AIDS activist, and I told Downey we would walk off the show if he didn't tone down his gay-baiting rhetoric. Smiling amiably, Downey took a long drag on his cigarette and assured us, "Don't worry, I have a fallback position."

44   That comment provided one of the most lucid moments in my year as an AIDS celebrity. Downey's "fallback position," it was clear, was the opposite of what he was promoting on the air. Of course, he didn't *really* believe that people with AIDS, people like his brother, should all be locked up. This was merely a deliciously provocative posture to exploit the working-class resentments of people who needed someone to hate. AIDS sufferers and gays would do for this week. Next week, if viewership dropped and Downey needed a new whipping boy, maybe he'd move on to Arabs, maybe Jews. It didn't seem to matter much to him, since he

didn't believe what he was saying anyway. For Morton Downey, Jr., talking about AIDS was not an act of conscience; it was a ratings ploy. He knew it, he let his guests know it, his producers certainly knew it, and his television station knew it. The only people left out of the joke were his audience.

45   The organizers of the Desert AIDS Project had enlisted actor Kirk Douglas and CBS morning anchor Kathleen Sullivan to be honorary co-chairs of the Palm Springs fund raiser. The main events would include a celebrity tennis match pitting Douglas against Mayor Sonny Bono, and a $1,500-a-head dinner at which I would receive a Lucite plaque for my contributions to the fight against AIDS. The next morning I would fly to L.A. to speak at still another event, this one with Shirley MacLaine, Valerie Harper, and Susan Dey of *L.A. Law.*

46   The desert night was exquisite. There were 130 dinner guests, the personification of elegance and confidence, who gathered on a magnificent patio of chocolate-brown Arizona flagstone at the home of one of Palm Spring's most celebrated interior designers. A lot of people had come simply to see what was regarded as one of the most sumptuous dwellings in this sumptuous town.

47   When I was called to accept my reward, I began with the same lineup of jokes I use on talk shows and on the college lecture circuit. They work every time.

48   I told the crowd about how you get AIDS from a mosquito.

49   Kirk Douglas laughed; everybody laughed.

50   Next, I did the how-many-gay-waiters joke.

51   Kirk Douglas laughed; everybody laughed.

52   Then I mentioned the woman who asked whether she could get AIDS from a waiter ejaculating in her salad dressing.

53   That one always has my college audiences rolling in the aisles, so I paused for the expected hilarity.

54   But in the utter stillness of the desert night air, all that could be heard was the sound of Kirk Douglas's steel jaw dropping to the magnificent patio of chocolate-brown Arizona flagstone. The rest was silence.

55   "You've got to remember that most of these people came because they're my clients," the host confided later. "You said that, and all I could think was how I'd have to go back to stitching slipcovers when this was done."

56   It turned out that there was more to my lead-balloon remark than a misjudged audience. Local AIDS organizers told me that a year earlier, a rumor that one of Palm Springs's most popular restaurants was owned by a homosexual, and that most of its waiters were gay, had terrified the elite community. Patronage at the eatery quickly plummeted, and it had nearly gone out of business. Fears that I dismissed as laughable were the

genuine concerns of my audience, I realized. My San Francisco joke was a Palm Springs fable.

57   As I watched the busboys clear the tables later that night, I made a mental note not to tell that joke before dinner again. Never had I seen so many uneaten salads, so much wasted iceberg lettuce.

58   A friend had just tested antibody positive, and I was doing my best to cheer him up as we ambled down the sidewalk toward a Castro Street restaurant a few blocks from where I live in San Francisco. It seems most of my conversations now have to do with who has tested positive or lucked out and turned up negative, or who is too afraid to be tested. We had parked our car near Coming Home, the local hospice for AIDS patients and others suffering from terminal illnesses, and as we stepped around a nondescript, powder-blue van that blocked our path, two men in white uniforms emerged from the hospice's side door. They carried a stretcher, and on the stretcher was a corpse, neatly wrapped in a royal-blue blanket and secured with navy-blue straps. My friend and I stopped walking. The men quickly guided the stretcher into the back of the van, climbed in the front doors, and drove away. We continued our walk but didn't say anything.

59   I wondered if the corpse was someone I had known. I'd find out Thursday when the weekly gay paper came out. Every week there are at least two pages filled with obituaries of the previous week's departed. Each week, when I turn to those pages, I hold my breath, wondering whose picture I'll see. It's the only way to keep track, what with so many people dying.

60   Sometimes I wonder if an aberrant mother or two going to mass at the Most Holy Redeemer Church across the street from Coming Home Hospice has ever warned a child, "That's where you'll end up if you don't obey God's law." Or whether some youngster, feeling that first awareness of a different sexuality, has looked at the doorway of this modern charnel house with an awesome, gnawing dread of annihilation.

61   "Is the limousine here? Where are the dancers?"

62   The room fell silent. Blake Rothaus had sounded coherent until that moment, but he was near death now and his brain was going. We were gathered around his bed in a small frame house on a dusty street in Oklahoma City. The twenty-four-year-old was frail and connected to life through a web of clear plastic tubing. He stared up at us and seemed to recognize from our looks that he had lapsed into dementia. A friend broke the uncomfortable silence.

63   "Of course, we all brought our dancing shoes," he said. "Nice fashionable pumps at that. I wouldn't go out without them."

64   Everyone laughed and Blake Rothaus was lucid again.

65   Blake had gone to high school in a San Francisco suburb. When he was a sophomore, he told us, he and his best friend sometimes skipped school, sneaking to the city to spend their afternoons in the gay neighborhood around Castro Street.

66   It's a common sight, suburban teenagers playing hooky on Castro Street. I could easily imagine him standing on a corner not far from my house. But back in 1982, when he was eighteen, I was already writing about a mysterious, unnamed disease that had claimed 330 victims in the United States.

67   Blake moved back to Oklahoma City with his family after he graduated from high school. When he fell ill with AIDS, he didn't mope. Instead, he started pestering Oklahoma health officials with demands to educate people about this disease and to provide services for the sick. The state health department didn't recoil. At the age of twenty-two, Blake Rothaus had become the one-man nucleus for Oklahoma's first AIDS patient services. He was the hero of the Sooner State's AIDS movement and something of a local legend.

68   Though the state had reported only 250 AIDS cases, Oklahoma City had a well-coordinated network of religious leaders, social workers, health-care providers, gay-rights advocates, state legislators, and businessmen, all committed to providing a sane and humane response to this frightening new disease.

69   "I think it's the old Dust Bowl mentality," suggested one AIDS organizer. "When the hard times come, people pull together."

70   My past year's travels to twenty-nine states and talks with literally thousands of people have convinced me of one thing about this country and AIDS: most Americans want to do the right thing about this epidemic. Some might worry about mosquitoes and a few may be suspicious of their salad dressing. But beyond these fears is a reservoir of compassion and concern that goes vastly underreported by a media that needs conflict and heartlessness to fashion a good news hook.

71   In Kalamazoo, Michigan, when I visited my stepmother, I was buttonholed by a dozen middle-aged women who wondered anxiously whether we were any closer to a vaccine or a long-term treatment. One mentioned a hemophiliac nephew. Another had a gay brother in Chicago. A third went to a gay hairdresser who, she quickly added, was one of the finest people you'd ever meet. When I returned to my conservative hometown of Aurora, Illinois, nestled among endless fields of corn and soy, the local health department told me they receive more calls than they know what to do with from women's groups, parishes, and community organizations that want to do something to help. In New

Orleans, the archconservative, pro-nuke, anti-gay bishop had taken up the founding of an AIDS hospice as a personal mission because, he said, when people are sick, you've got to help them out.

72   Scientists, reporters, and politicians privately tell me that of course *they* want to do more about AIDS, but they have to think about the Morton Downeys of the world, who argue that too much research or too much news space or too much official sympathy is being meted out to a bunch of miscreants. They do as much as they can, they insist; more would rile the resentments of the masses. So the institutions fumble along, convinced they must pander to the lowest common denominator, while the women and men of America's heartland pull me aside to fret about a dying cousin or co-worker and to plead, "When will there be a cure? When will this be over?"

73   "I think I'll make it through this time," Kit said to me, "but I don't have it in me to go through it again."

74   We were in room 3 in San Francisco General Hospital's ward 5A, the AIDS ward. The poplar trees outside Kit's window were losing their leaves, and the first winter's chill was settling over the city. I was preparing to leave for my fourth and, I hoped, final media tour, this time for release of the book in paperback and on audiocassette; Kit was preparing to die.

75   The seizures had started a week earlier, indicating he was suffering either from toxoplasmosis, caused by a gluttonous protozoa that sets up housekeeping in the brain; or perhaps it was a relapse of cryptococcal meningitis; or, another specialist guessed, it could be one of those other nasty brain infections that nobody had seen much of until the past year. Now that AIDS patients were living longer, they fell victim to even more exotic infections than in the early days. But the seizures were only part of it. Kit had slowly been losing the sight in his left eye to a herpes infection. And the Kaposi's sarcoma lesions that had scarred his face were beginning to coat the inside of his lungs. When Kit mentioned he'd like to live until Christmas, the doctors said he might want to consider having an early celebration this year, because he wasn't going to be alive in December.

76   "I can't take another infection," Kit said.

77   "What does that mean?"

78   "Morphine," Kit answered, adding mischievously, "lots of it."

79   We talked briefly about the mechanics of suicide. We both knew people who'd made a mess of it, and people who had done it right. It was hardly the first time the subject had come up in conversation for either of us. Gay men facing AIDS now exchange formulas for suicide as casually as housewives swap recipes for chocolate-chip cookies.

80   Kit was released from the hospital a few days later. He had decided to take his life on a Tuesday morning. I had to give my first round of interviews in Los Angeles that day, so I stopped on the way to the airport to say goodbye on Monday. All day Tuesday, while I gave my perfectly formed sound bites in a round of network radio appearances, I wondered: Is this the moment he's slipping out of consciousness and into that perfect darkness? When I called that night, it turned out he'd delayed his suicide until Thursday to talk to a few more relatives. I had to give a speech in Portland that day, so on the way to the airport I stopped again. He showed me the amber-brown bottle with the bubble-gum-pink morphine syrup, and we said another goodbye.

81   The next morning, Kit drank his morphine and fell into a deep sleep. That afternoon, he awoke and drowsily asked what time it was. When told it was five hours later, he murmured, "That's amazing. I should have been dead hours ago."

82   And then he went back to sleep.

83   That night, Kit woke up again.

84   "You know what they say about near-death experiences?" he asked. "Going toward the light?"

85   Shaking his head, he sighed. "No light. Nothing."

86   His suicide attempt a failure, Kit decided the timing of his death would now be up to God. I kept up on the bizarre sequence of events by phone and called as soon as I got back to San Francisco. I was going to tell Kit that his theme song should be "Never Can Say Goodbye," but then the person on the other end of the phone told me that Kit had lapsed into a coma.

87   The next morning, he died.

88   Kit's death was like everything about AIDS—anticlimactic. By the time he actually did die, I was almost beyond feeling.

89   The next day, I flew to Boston for the start of the paperback tour, my heart torn between rage and sorrow. All week, as I was chauffeured to my appearances on *Good Morning America, Larry King Live,* and various CNN shows, I kept thinking, It's all going to break. I'm going to be on a TV show with some officious government health spokesman lying to protect his job, and I'm going to start shouting, "You lying son of a bitch. Don't you know there are people, real people, people I love out there dying?" Or I'll be on a call-in show and another mother will phone about her thirty-seven-year-old son who just died and it will hit me all at once, and I'll start weeping.

90   But day after day as the tour went on, no matter how many official lies I heard and how many grieving mothers I talked to, the crack-up never occurred. All my answers came out rationally in tight little sound bites about institutional barriers to AIDS treatments and projections about 1993 case loads.

91   By the last day of the tour, when a limousine picked me up at my Beverly Hills hotel for my last round of satellite TV interviews, I knew I had to stop. In a few weeks I'd return to being national correspondent for the *Chronicle,* and it was time to get off the AIDS celebrity circuit, end the interviews and decline the invitations to the star-studded fund raisers, and get back to work as a newspaper reporter. That afternoon, there was just one last radio interview to a call-in show in the San Fernando Valley, and then it would be over.

92   The first caller asked why his tax money should go toward funding an AIDS cure when people got the disease through their own misdeeds.

93   I used my standard jukebox answer about how most cancer cases are linked to people's behavior but that nobody ever suggested we stop trying to find a cure for cancer.

94   A second caller phoned to ask why her tax money should go to finding an AIDS cure when these people clearly deserved what they got.

95   I calmly put a new spin on the same answer, saying in America you usually don't sentence people to die for having a different lifestyle from yours.

96   Then a third caller phoned in to say that he didn't care if all those queers and junkies died, as did a fourth and fifth and sixth caller. By then I was shouting, "You stupid bigot. You just want to kill off everybody you don't like. You goddamn Nazi."

97   The talk-show host sat in stunned silence. She'd heard I was so *reasonable.* My anger baited the audience further, and the seventh and eighth callers began talking about "you guys," as if only a faggot like myself could give a shit about whether AIDS patients all dropped dead tomorrow.

98   In their voices, I heard the reporters asking polite questions of NIH officials. Of course, they had to be polite to the government doctors; dying queers weren't anything to lose your temper over. I heard the dissembling NIH researchers go home to their wives at night, complain about the lack of personnel, and shrug; this was just how it was going to have to be for a while. They'd excuse their inaction by telling themselves that if they went public and lost their jobs, worse people would replace them. It was best to go along. But how would they feel if *their* friends, *their* daughters, were dying of this disease? Would they be silent—or would they shout? Maybe they'll forgive me for suspecting they believed that ultimately a bunch of fags weren't worth losing a job over. And when I got home, I was going to have to watch my friends get shoved into powder-blue vans, and it wasn't going to change.

99   The history of the AIDS epidemic, of yesterday and of today, was echoing in the voices of those callers. And I was screaming at them, and the show host just sat there stunned, and I realized I had rendered myself utterly and completely inarticulate.

100   I stopped, took a deep breath, and returned to compound-complex sentences about the American tradition of compassion and the overriding need to overcome institutional barriers to AIDS treatments.

101   When I got home to San Francisco that night, I looked over some notes I had taken from a conversation I'd had with Kit during his last stay in the hospital. I was carping about how frustrated I was at the prospect of returning to my reporting job. If an internationally acclaimed best seller hadn't done shit to change the world, what good would mere newspaper stories do?

102   "The limits of information," Kit said. "There's been a lot written on it."

103   "Oh," I said.

104   Kit closed his eyes briefly and faded into sleep while plastic tubes fed him a cornucopia of antibiotics. After five minutes, he stirred, looked up, and added, as if we had never stopped talking, "But you don't really have a choice. You've got to keep on doing it. What else are you going to do?"

TO THINK ABOUT

1. How does Shilts's opening segment about his talk-show appearance affect you? How does it make you feel about the narrator?
2. Imagine a conversation between Randy Shilts and Richard Selzer ("A Mask on the Face of Death," Chapter 40) on the subject of AIDS. Now imagine yourself joining the conversation. Your perspective is different from theirs. What is it? In what sort of voice would you express it?
3. How does Shilts characterize most media coverage of the AIDS epidemic? Do you agree?
4. Shilts says government officials should resign to protest the lack of support for AIDS research. They don't, he says, because they rationalize that their leaving would only make things worse. Do you think officials in this position should resign? Why or why not?
5. From time to time Shilts returns to the story of his friend Kit Herman, dying of AIDS. Why?

TO DO

1. Free-write about AIDS for 30 minutes. Write as fast as you can. Then do some research. Spend a day in the library, then interview friends and experts. If you know someone who has AIDS, or is HIV-

positive, interview that person. Now combine your research with your original piece of free-writing to form an essay.
2. List difficult moral choices you have had to make. Choose one and write about it. Did you make the right choice? Why or why not?

TIP

To be effective, it is not necessary to be nice. It *is* necessary, however, (1) not to aim your anger directly at your reader, and (2) to enlist your reader in your cause. This is not difficult when your reader has a stake in what you say. Shilts presumes that his readers have a stake in the eradication of AIDS; join me, he implies, in fighting these idiots who are blocking the way. For another example of this approach, read Kurt Vonnegut's "The First Amendment" (Chapter 50).

43

Reading Philosophy at Night

Charles Simic

Pulitzer Prize–winning poet Charles Simic grew up in Yugoslavia under the Nazi occupation of World War II. This was a world in which children strove to carry on the rituals of childhood— learning, playing, imagining—amidst the larger, life-and-death games of the adults. There were mixed emotions. The American bombers are coming. That's good! But they may bomb us by mistake. That's not so good.

In this piece Simic traces the evolution of his love of philosophy in various contexts, including his childhood before and just after the war. The result is just the opposite of what one might expect from a philosophical treatise. It is neither dry nor analytical. It is, rather, a tragicomic adventure with liberal dashes of magic and poetry thrown in. The pace of the narrative voice varies from calm and reasoned (in the beginning) to near-manic (toward the end); the sensibility is that of a sly magician who, underneath the glitz, still hopes against hope that he will one day pull the world out of his hat.

It is night again around me; I feel as though there had been lightning—for a brief span of time I was entirely in my element and in my light.

—*Nietzsche*

The mind loves the unknown. It loves images whose meaning is unknown, since the meaning of the mind itself is unknown.

—*Magritte*

1   I wore Buster Keaton's expression of exaggerated calm. I could have been sitting on the edge of a cliff with my back to the abyss trying to look normal.

2   Now I read philosophy in the morning. When I was younger and lived in the city it was always at night. "That's how you ruined your eyes," my mother keeps saying. I sat and read late into the night. The

quieter it got, the more clearheaded I became—or so it seemed to me. In a sparsely furnished room above an Italian grocery, I would be struggling with some intricate philosophical argument that promised a magnificent insight at its conclusion. I could sense it with my whole being. I couldn't put the book away, and it was getting really late. I had to be at work in the morning. Even had I tried to sleep, my head would have been full of Kant or Hegel. So, I wouldn't sleep. At some point I'd make that decision. I'd be sitting there with the open book, my face reflected dimly in the dark windowpane, the great city all around me grown quiet. I was watching myself watch myself. A very strange experience.

3   The first time it happened I was twenty. It was six o'clock in the morning. It was winter. It was dark and very cold. I was in Chicago riding the el to work seated between two heavily bundled-up old women. The train was overheated, but each time the door opened at one of the elevated platforms, a blast of cold air would send shivers through us. The lights, too, kept flickering. As the train changed tracks, the lights would go out for a moment and I would stop reading the history of philosophy I had borrowed from the library the previous day. "Why is there something rather than nothing?" the book asked, quoting Parmenides. It was as if my eyes were opened. I could not stop looking at my fellow passengers. How incredible, I thought, all of us being here, existing.

4   Philosophy is like a homecoming. I have a recurring dream about the street where I was born. It is always night. I'm walking past vaguely familiar buildings trying to find our house, but somehow it is not there. I retrace my steps on that short block of only a few buildings, all of which are there except the one I want. The effort leaves me exhausted and saddened.

5   In another version of this same dream, I catch a glimpse of our house. There it is, at last, but for some reason I'm unable to get any closer to it. No lights are on. I look for our window, but it is even darker there on the third floor. The entire building seems abandoned. "It can't be," I tell myself in horror.

6   Once in one of these dreams, many years ago, I saw someone at our window, hunched over as if watching the street intently. That's how my grandmother would wait late into the night for us to come home, except that this was a stranger. Even without being able to make out his face, I was sure of that.

7   Most of the time, however, there's no one in sight during the dream. The facades of buildings still retain their pockmarks and other signs of the war. The streetlights are out and there's no moon in the sky, so it's not clear to me how I am able to see all this in complete darkness. The street I am walking on is long, empty, and seemingly without end.

8   Whoever reads philosophy reads himself as much as he reads the philosopher. I am in dialogue with certain decisive events in my life as much as I am with the ideas on the page. Meaning is the matter of my existence. My effort to understand is a perpetual circling around a few obsessive images.

9   Like everyone else, I have my hunches. All my experiences make a kind of untaught ontology, which precedes all my readings. What I am trying to conceptualize with the help of the philosopher is that which I have already intuited.

10   That's one way of looking at it.

> The Meditation of yesterday filled my mind with so many doubts that it is no longer in my power to forget them. And yet, I do not see in what manner I can resolve them; and, just as if I had all of a sudden fallen into very deep water, I am so disconcerted that I can neither make certain of setting my feet on the bottom, nor can I swim and so support myself on the surface. I shall nevertheless make an effort and follow anew the same path as that on which I yesterday entered, i.e., I shall proceed by setting aside all that in which the least doubt could be supposed to exist, just as if I had discovered that it was absolutely false; and I shall ever follow in this road until I have met with something which is certain, or at least, if I can do nothing else, until I have learned for certain that there's nothing in the world that is certain. Archimedes, in order that he might draw the terrestrial globe out of its place, and transport it elsewhere, demanded only that one point should be fixed and immovable; in the same way I shall have the right to conceive high hopes if I am happy enough to discover one thing only which is certain and indubitable.

11   I love this passage of Descartes; his beginning again, his not wanting to be fooled. It describes the ambition of philosophy in all its nobility and desperation. I prefer this doubting Descartes to the later one, famous in his certainties. The poetry of indeterminacy still casts its spell. Of course, he's greedy for the absolute, but so is everybody else. Or are they?

12   There's an Eastern European folk song that tells of a girl who kept tossing an apple higher and higher until she tossed it as high as the clouds. To her surprise the apple didn't come down. One of the clouds got it. She waited with arms outstretched, but the apple stayed up there. All she could do was plead with the cloud to return her apple, but that's another story. I like the first part when the impossible still reigns.

13   I remember lying in a ditch and staring at some pebbles while German bombers were flying over our heads. That was long ago. I don't remember the face of my mother nor the faces of the people who were there with us, but I still see those perfectly ordinary pebbles.

14   "It is not 'how' things are in the world that is mystical, but that it exists," says Wittgenstein. I felt precisely that. Time had stopped. I was watching myself watching the pebbles and trembling with fear. Then time moved on and the experience was over.

15   The pebbles stayed in their otherness, stayed forever in my memory. Can language do justice to such moments of heightened consciousness? Speech is always less. When it comes to conveying what it means to be truly conscious, one approximates, one fails miserably.

16   Wittgenstein puts it this way: "What finds its reflection in language, language cannot represent. What expresses 'itself' in language, we cannot express by means of language." This has been my experience many times. Words are impoverishments, splendid poverties.

17   I knew someone who once tried to persuade me otherwise. He considered himself a logical positivist. These are people who remind you, for example, that you can speak of a pencil's dimension, location, appearance, and state of motion or rest but not of its intelligence and love of music. The moment I hear that, the poet in me rebels and I want to write a poem about an intelligent pencil in love with music. In other words, what these people regard as nonsense, I suspect to be full of imaginative possibilities.

18   There's a wonderful story told about Wittgenstein and his Cambridge colleague, the Italian economist Piero Sraffa. Apparently they often discussed philosophy. "One day," as Justus Hartnack has it, "when Wittgenstein was defending his view that a proposition has the same logical form as the fact it depicts, Sraffa made a gesture used by Neapolitans to express contempt and asked Wittgenstein what the logical form of that was? According to Wittgenstein's own recollection, it was this question which made him realize that his belief that a fact could have a logical form was untenable."

19   As for my "logical" friend, we argued all night. "What cannot be said, cannot be thought," he claimed. And then—after I blurted out something about silence being the language of consciousness—"You're silent because you have nothing to say!" In any case, it got to the point where we were calling each other "you dumb shit." We were drinking large quantities of red wine, misunderstanding each other totally, and only stopped bickering when his disheveled wife came to the bedroom door and told us to shut up.

20   Then I told him a story.

21   One day in Yugoslavia, just after the war, we made a class trip to the town War Museum. At the entrance we found a battered German

tank, which delighted us. Inside the museum one could look at a few rifles, hand grenades, and uniforms, but not much else. Most of the space was taken up by photographs. These we were urged to examine. One saw people who had been hanged and people about to be hanged. The executioners stood around smoking. There were piles of corpses everywhere. Some were naked. Men and women with their genitals showing. That made some kid laugh.

22   Then we saw a man having his throat cut. The killer sat on the man's chest with a knife in his hand. He seemed pleased to be photographed. The victim's eyes I don't remember. A few men stood around gawking. There were clouds in the sky.

23   There were always clouds, blades of grass, tree stumps, bushes, and rocks no one was paying any attention to. In one photograph the earth was covered with snow. A miserable, teeth-chattering January morning and someone making someone else's life even more miserable. Or the rain would be falling. A small, hard rain that would wash the blood off the hands immediately, that would make one of the killers catch a bad cold. I imagined him sitting that same night with feet in a bucket of hot water and sipping tea.

24   That occurred to me later. Now that we had seen all there was to see, we were made to sit on the lawn outside the museum and eat our lunch. It was poor fare. Most of us had plum jam spread on slices of bread. A few had lard sprinkled with paprika. One kid had nothing but bread and scallions. I guess that's all they had at his home that day. Everybody thought it was funny. Someone snatched his thick slice of black bread and threw it up in the air. It got caught in a tree. The poor kid tried to get it down by throwing stones at it. He kept missing. Then he tried climbing the tree. He kept sliding back. Even our teacher who came to see what the commotion was all about thought it was hilarious.

25   As for the grass, there was plenty of it, each blade distinct and carefully sharpened, as it were. There were also clouds in the sky and many large flies of the kind one encounters in slaughterhouses, which kept pestering us and interrupting our laughter.

26   And here's what went through my head just last night as I lay awake thinking of my friend's argument:

27   *The story you told him had nothing to do with what you were talking about.*

28   *The story had everything to do with what we were talking about.*

29   *I can think of a hundred objections after all these years.*

30   *Only idiots want something neat, something categorical—and I never talk unless I know!*

31   *Aha! You're mixing poetry and philosophy. Wittgenstein wouldn't give you the time of day!*

32   *"Everything looks very busy to me," says Jasper Johns, and that's my problem, too.*

33   *I remember a strange cat, exceedingly emaciated, that scratched on my door the day I was scratching my head over Hegel's Phenomenology of the Spirit.*

34   *Who said, "Whatever can be brought must be fictitious"?*

35   *You got me there! How about a bagel Hegel?*

36   *Still and all . . . And above all! Let's not forget "above all."*

37   *Here's what Nietzsche said to the ceiling: "The rank of the philosopher is determined by the rank of his laughter." But he couldn't really laugh. No matter how hard Friedrich tried, he couldn't really laugh.*

38   *I know because I'm a connoisseur of paradox. All the good-looking oxymorons are in love with me and come to visit me in my bed at night.*

39   *Have a tomato Plato!*

40   Wallace Stevens has several beautiful poems about solitary readers. "The House Was Quiet and the World Was Calm" is one. It speaks of a "truth in a calm world." It happens! The world and the mind growing so calm that truth becomes visible.

41   It must be late at night "where shines the light that lets be the things that are"—the light of insomnia. The solitude of the reader of philosophy and the solitude of the philosopher drawing together. The impression that one is thinking and anticipating another man's subtlest turns of thought and beginning to truly understand.

42   Understanding depends on the relationship of what we are to what we have been: the being of the moment. Consciousness stirring up our conscience, our history. Consciousness as the light of clarity and history as the dark night of the soul.

43   The pleasures of philosophy are the pleasures of reduction—the epiphanies of hinting in a few words at complex matters. Both poetry and philosophy, for instance, are concerned with Being. What is a lyric poem, one might say, but the recreation of the experience of Being. In both cases, that need to get it down to its essentials, to say the unsayable and let the truth of Being shine through.

44   History, on the other hand, is antireductive. Nothing tidy about it. Chaos! Bedlam! Hopeless tangle! My own history and the history of this century like a child and his blind mother on the street. She mumbles, talks to herself, sings and wails as she leads the way across some busy intersection.

45   You'd think the sole meaning of history is to stand truth happily upon its head!

46   Poor poetry. Like imperturbable Buster Keaton alone with the woman he loves on an ocean liner set adrift on the stormy sea. Or an

even better example: Again drifting over an endless ocean, he comes across a billboard, actually a target for battleship practice. Keaton climbs it, takes out his fishing rod and bait, and fishes peacefully. That's what great poetry is. A superb serenity in the face of chaos. Wise enough to play the fool.

47   And always the contradictions: I have Don Quixote and his windmills in my head and Sancho Panza and his mule kicking in my heart.

48   That's just some figure of speech. Who could live without them? Do they tell the truth? Do they conceal it? I really don't know. That's why I keep going back to philosophy. I want to learn how to think clearly about these matters.

49   It is morning. It is night. The book is open. The text is difficult, the text is momentarily opaque. My mind is wandering. My mind is struggling to grasp the always elusive, the always hinting—whatever it is.

50   *It, it,* I keep calling it. An infinity of "it" without a single antecedent—like a cosmic static in my ear.

51   Just then, about to give up, I find the following on a page of Heidegger: "No thinker has ever entered into another thinker's solitude. Yet it is only from its solitude that all thinking, in a hidden mode, speaks to the thinking that comes after or that went before."

52   For a moment it all comes together: poetry, philosophy, history. I see—in the sense of being able to picture and feel—the human weight of another's solitude. So many of them seated with a book. Day breaking. Thought becoming image. Image becoming thought.

TO THINK ABOUT

1. Simic's essay is neither linear nor chronological. It is a collage of scenes and images from various periods of his life. Find an internal logic, a progression, in the way these chunks of writing are organized.
2. What is the point of the narrator's story about his visit to the War Museum? What is the effect of this story on you?
3. The section about "what went through my head just last night as I lay awake thinking" (beginning with paragraph #26) has a different rhythm from the rest of the essay. Why?

TO DO

Write an essay in the form of a collage. Begin with the scene, the reflection, the bit of dialogue, the image you most wish to write.
Then, knowing that no scene, no reflection, no bit of dialogue, no
image exists in isolation, jot down other bits that are somehow connected to it.

It may not have occurred to you until now that a connection
exists. You may not know just what the connection is. That's all
right. Trust your intuition. If it is on the mark, the connection will
work.

TIP

Think of the blank line between sections of your collage in the
same way you think of periods at the ends of sentences and indentations
at the beginnings of paragraphs. The vertical space is a tool that indicates
to your reader that a major shift is taking place.

Notice, also, that there is often no written transition from one
chunk of a collage to the next. The transition is intuitive. If the writer's
intuition is on the mark, the reader should be able to follow.

44

The Big A

Harry Stein

Harry Stein excels at writing about tough choices. Is a certain amount of groveling necessary to get ahead in this world? Are racial jokes ever acceptable—even when told by the race in question? Is turning the other cheek always advisable? Is there any harm in gossip? Is a little crime—say, on the level of stealing office stationery—ever excusable? Does the end ever justify the means? He has tackled them all. And, in the end, he always answers his own question, although often he is not happy with his own answer.

Here he tackles adultery. Is it ever okay? His attitude, and his voice, changes subtly throughout the essay. But his determination to find an answer for a difficult question does not waver.

1 A bunch of us guys were sitting around one night, like refugees from a Löwenbräu commercial, talking about—what else?—women. We liked 'em, liked 'em a whole lot. Couldn't get enough of 'em, in fact. But then one of the guys got a kind of twisted look on his face, and he said that a few weeks earlier he'd had a chance to start something with someone very special, but he hadn't done it. So we all asked why. And he shrugged his shoulders and looked a little sheepish. "She was living with some guy. I just couldn't get used to the idea of her going home to him still smelling of me."

2 Honest to God, that's an actual verbatim quote. And maybe we weren't so much like the guys in the Löwenbräu ads after all, because, dumb as it sounded, no one laughed when he said it. I think we all more or less understood how the guy felt. Romantic comedies notwithstanding, these situations almost always end up more melodrama than bedroom farce, with someone's ego lying on the carpet; only genuine Löwenbräu guys saunter cavalierly into messes like that.

3 Just recently, at dinner at the home of a friend, I found myself sit-

ting across from a strikingly intelligent woman who had dark hair, luminous green eyes, and the most unmistakably flirtatious manner this side of Scarlett O'Hara.

4   "Where do you live?" I asked at the end of the evening. "I'll call you."

5   She smiled. "That'd be nice. I should tell you, though, I'm married." A beat. "But it doesn't bother me, if it doesn't bother you."

6   "Uhhh. . . ."

7   The cliché, as I'd been raised on it, had never worked like *that.* Think back on any episode of "Love, American Style"; the scenario almost never changed: The man was the bounder, his wife or girlfriend the victim, and the other woman some manner of shrew, though once in a while, when played with great angst, she might pass for victim number two.

8   And for years the cliché was a not inaccurate reflection of real life. During one period of her life, a friend I'll call Barbara, now in her late thirties, was involved with so many married men that she took to referring to herself as "the adultery specialist."

9   "Every single adulterous relationship," she insists now, "was exactly the same. Even the dialogue never changed: 'I wish I'd met you (fill in the blank) years ago,' and, of course, 'I never knew it could be like this.' The wife would always commit suicide if he left her and she always hated sex, but she was someone I'd like a lot if I ever met her."

10   Now, often as not, it is the husband or boyfriend who gets screwed, figuratively, as the literal antics proceed apace. This societal adjustment has not been an easy thing for some men to accept. "Jesus Christ," a fellow of my acquaintance recently complained upon learning that his wife had turned the tables on him, "where is Hester Prynne now that we need her?"

11   But the sad and quite obvious truth is that smarmy is smarmy, no matter who's at which end of the stick, and a great many women are finding out what great numbers of men have always known: It ain't much fun being the scoundrel. A book editor I know, a married woman fresh from one of those affairs featuring hotel one-nighters and restaurants where everyone manages to face the wall, emerged from the experience sounding like Fred MacMurray in *The Apartment.*

12   "The sneaking-around part wasn't too bad," she says. "What I couldn't stand was the guilt about my family. Do you know that I actually missed my son's birthday? And meanwhile I was leading this poor guy on, letting him believe that I might leave my husband."

13   And yet it continues, this avalanche of infidelity, this tidal wave of two-timing, outstripping the birth rate and the death rate, outstripping any rate you can think of, with the possible exception of Texaco's

third-quarter earnings. Driven by despair or desperation or loneliness or horniness, we just cannot stop.

14   There are, of course, a lot of people who maintain that infidelity can be therapeutic; they use such terms as "safety valve," and "realism," and "irrepressible physical needs."

15   "It's damn easy to be self-righteous about it," as one guy I know puts it, "when you're not trapped in a deadend marriage." And, let's face it, some of what these people say seems to make a lot of sense. The French have gone so far as to devise an entire system of social relationships based on satisfying irrepressible physical needs without anyone ever having to be late for dinner.

16   But it is, I think, no coincidence that the French are as emotionally blocked as any people on the planet; that even in their most intimate relationships—spouse to spouse, parent to child—certain basic feelings and needs are rarely expressed. In France this is known as reserve; elsewhere it is called being screwed up. The bottom line, quite simply, is that it is impossible for people to compartmentalize their lives, to keep a single aspect of their existence under lock and key yet be blissfully open about the rest. Human beings don't function that way.

17   And yet, it seems so routinely to work out badly even when everyone plays it completely straight. "Sometimes," Katharine Hepburn was recently quoted as saying, "I wonder if men and women really suit each other. Perhaps they should live next door and just visit now and then." And she had Spencer Tracy!

18   We try variation after variation: marriage contracts, separate vacations, living together for years on end without marriage, and still, so often, there is the slow unraveling. "Let's see other people," one partner finally suggests—code for the fact that someone wants out—and the relationship limps along its melancholy way.

19   How, I wonder, did it work out so nicely for my grandparents? Hardly past childhood when they met, thoroughly unwordly, desperately poor, fixed up by a *matchmaker,* for God's sake, and they made it through sixty-odd years together, Papa and Mama. When my grandmother died, my grandfather, eighty-six and barely able to walk, still a socialist and exclusively a Yiddish speaker, came to live with us for a while. I am still haunted by the wail that came in the very early hours of the morning through the thin wall that separated our bedrooms: "Mama, Mama. . . "

20   It is, of course, those kinds of precedents that shine through the generations in almost every family, that keep us all believing in the happily ever after.

21   "Why," asked the most promiscuous woman I know, when I had told her about my grandparents, "can't people settle down with someone that way and be happy? That's all I want."

22   Why indeed. Well, for one thing, my grandfather didn't sit around in his yarmulke and prayer shawl lusting after Bo Derek. And, strongwilled as she was, the only career goal my grandmother ever had was to become the mother of a rabbi. A world without expectations, a world with clearly labeled slots, is hard to get lost in. They had each other, those two, and they knew how to be satisfied.

23   What is less obvious is that my grandparents might still have opted to be just as discontented as the rest of us. Indeed, my other grandfather, just a bit more Americanized, a bit more fluent in English, *was* something of a philanderer. I have in my possession a letter written in the mid-Forties from my father to my mother describing an attempt to reconcile her parents after one of their periodic splits:

> Ma told me she'd consider going back to him for a down payment of $500 to refurnish the apartment (which personally I consider steep even at wartime price levels) plus a guarantee of no more running around. Of course, she changed her mind in the next breath. Anyway, ten minutes after this conversation, Pop phoned with an offer of $1,000 plus a month's vacation, just the two of them (with Yiddish vaudeville entertainment), and she's so bewildered she says all right. So after a bit of hemming on the phone, he says he'll come right over, and does. So for a while things are all right. I keep the ball rolling, talking about this and that and events of the day; then I go to bed. They remained on more or less businesslike terms, and I could hear a lot of whispering about let's get down to business and how's about furnishing the apartment, and she gets a down payment of $50, I think, and he sleeps over only two rooms away, which for them is like having an orgy. . . .

24   I discovered that note two weeks after emerging from a long relationship—one that had been marked by a little adultery and a lot of acrimony—and if the note wasn't quite comforting, at least it put things in perspective. Even in relatively simpler times, one's world was obviously of one's own making.

25   When it comes to infidelity, we have seven millennia of human history to draw upon, and the evidence appears conclusive: Duplicity, no matter how it's dressed up, generally makes most everyone involved feel rotten. The alternative—nurturing trust and trying not to let it wither—is, God knows, nothing like a sure thing either, and it's a hell of a lot more work, but what choice do we have?

TO THINK ABOUT

1. Stein offers two possible answers to his question about adultery: (a) it's acceptable, even though a lot of guilt and pain will result; or (b) it's unacceptable, although fidelity involves a lot of frustration and hard work. List other possible answers to the question.
2. In his lead paragraph Stein says of women: "We liked 'em, liked 'em a whole lot. Couldn't get enough of 'em, in fact." Stein is not in the habit of using the slang *'em* as a substitute for *them*. Why does he do it here? What is its effect?
3. Stein says the nature of adultery has changed recently, with women now taking the initiative as often as men. How do you feel about this? Why? Do you think this move toward adulterous equality has any bearing on Stein's conclusion that adultery is unacceptable?

TO DO

1. Read "Infidelity" by Barbara Lazear Ascher (Chapter 3). Compare her approach to Stein's. Write an essay explaining why the approach of one of these writers is preferable to the other. You might want to do some further reading and bring in other approaches to the subject.
2. Stein implies that adultery was less likely to happen during simpler times, when options were limited and roles were clearer and less flexible. Find out whether he was right. Do some library research. Interview people in their forties, sixties, eighties. Write about what you find.
3. Consider a dilemma you are facing, or have faced, that appears to have no satisfactory solution. Write an essay in which you weigh the consequences of each option and, ultimately, choose a course of action.

TIP

Remember that the verb *to essay* means to explore. We explore, we essay into the unknown, into gray areas in which good and evil, right and wrong, the best choice and the worst, are neither starkly defined nor pure.

45

On Becoming Mr. Ethics
Harry Stein

Harry Stein had specialized in light, humorous pieces before an editor at Esquire *asked him if he would be interested in writing a monthly column on ethics. After hesitating briefly, Stein accepted. And after he had been writing the column for a few months he found that something unexpected was happening to him: His own behavior was changing. He discovered that thinking about ethics, and writing about ethics, forced him to become an ethical person, to weigh his actions for their ethical implications much more carefully than he had ever done before.*

In the piece that follows, Stein goes into detail about how the act of writing changed him.

Stein uses a deceptively simple story-telling style that enables him to weave scenes, dialogue, background information, and the observations of other people into a seamless narrative. The voice is often wry, sometimes self-righteous, sometimes remorseful, always ready to second-guess itself.

1   In mid-1980, nine months into the life of the "Ethics" column I was writing on a monthly basis for *Esquire* magazine, I decided that it was time to pull back and examine the enterprise at hand. Now, nine months is not an extraordinarily long time as columns go—Drew Pearson's ran for thirty-seven years, and Art Buchwald will probably be turning out his on his deathbed—but given its unusual nature, and its unexpected impact on my own life, I felt such an exercise was called for.

2   An ethics column had, within the inner sanctums of *Esquire*, been a long time in gestation. I am told that the notion had first raised its hoary head several editors and two ownerships before, and had subsequently been passed on from regime to regime like some kind of ancient curse. I first learned of the idea shortly after the most recent management change in 1979. The incoming editor in chief appeared an earnest young man, but when the notion of an ethics column was pulled out of a

broom closet and dusted off in his office, he reportedly snapped his fingers and lit up like a pinball machine. "Hey," he said, "I had damn near the same idea myself."

3   Five minutes later, the editor who had dragged the idea from the broom closet to the editor in chief suggested that I was the man for the job. This was a nice thing for the editor, who is my friend, to have done, but it was also unfathomable. Who was I to be handing down ethical judgments? I was, as my friend well knew, a congenital exaggerator and an occasional liar. I had never even taken an ethics course in college, opting instead to sign up for Sociology 52, Social Problems (T, Th, S at 8:00 A.M.), to fulfill my social sciences requirement.

4   When he proposed me for the job, my friend the editor did not mention any of this. "He's a basically thoughtful guy" is what he told the editor in chief, "and I promise you the column won't be boring. A subject like this, in the wrong hands, could be *really* boring."

5   "Thanks," I told him afterward, "but as it happens I have no idea how to make an ethics column interesting."

6   "Listen, just make it funny. Make a serious point every month, but stick in some laughs too."

7   Humor I could do. A humor column I had done. But still . . . funny ethics?

8   "Why not? We could even give you a pseudonym—Shecky Spinoza."

9   And that is pretty much how I approached it—not as a lark, exactly, but not as the weightiest proposition in the world either. The truth is, I'd have preferred to be given a humor column minus the serious point. But if this was the one they'd handed me, I was damn well going to make the best of it.

10   It did not take long to find out just how sticky a situation I had blithely strolled into.

11   As the subject for my initial column, I chose kissing ass. This was a practice that I had always deemed loathsome, had railed against at a hundred dinner parties. But, now, obliged to set down 1,400 words putting the matter forever to rest, it suddenly looked to be all gray areas. In this society, don't people *have* to do it at least a little? Finally, whom does kissing up to people really hurt? Why *not* play the game?

12   So after completing a grim-faced, tough-as-nails first draft of the column, I sat down and rewrote it, equivocating. The final version had it both ways, taking the position that anyone who sucks up to superiors is a crud and that anyone who doesn't is something of a jackass.

13   Pretty nearly the same thing happened with the next effort and the one after that. The first draft would be dripping with righteous rage; then

I'd get to thinking about it and soften it a little and, to be fair, a little more; then I'd go through it one more time to add the kidding around.

14   But, in fact, even as I strained over those early pieces, something else was going on.

15   During the height of Watergate, Jeb Magruder announced that the reason he found himself in such sorry circumstances was that somewhere along the line he had misplaced his "ethical compass." This inspired much mirth at the time—one columnist, I remember, called upon his readers to be on the lookout for Jeb's ethical compass—but there was something to what Magruder was saying, and it was applicable to a great many of us.

16   The fact is, very few people in this society make a habit of thinking in ethical terms; indeed, in many quarters, speaking about right and wrong is taken as prima facie evidence of softness—and "soft" is the one adjective that no American of stature or ambition needs to have associated with his name. That is the kind of thinking that has become general in this country, and Watergate was an almost inevitable consequence.

17   Nor were the values that motivated Nixon and his cronies so terribly different from the ones that drive millions of us in our professional and even our personal lives; looking out for number one invariably means that others get stepped on.

18   Yet, astonishingly, the notion that such behavior might be destructive is rarely raised, let alone seriously considered. Seemingly, we have reached the point where we are hardly aware of the possibility.

19   Well, suddenly, through no fault of my own but simply as a result of having to get out the appropriate number of words every month, there I was, obliged to look at the world with new—ethical—eyes. And it was a revelation. Questions that six months before would have seemed trivial or routine or utterly remote suddenly took on moral implications. Do I let the guy behind the cash register in the bookstore know that he has just mistakenly given the customer ahead of me a twenty-dollar bill instead of a five? Am I supportive of the friend who's cheating on his wife? Is there an appropriate individual response to a President who, with chilling cynicism, dangerously manipulates events to his political advantage? All at once there seemed a right and a wrong to everything—and an obligation to act on that knowledge.

20   Like some born-again humanist, I found myself bearing public witness to my new-found faith—occasionally to the mortification of my companions. Around Christmas-time, I made a point of looking into the affiliations of all sidewalk Santas who crossed my path, discovering that those who claimed to be collecting for Cambodian relief were actually undercover Hare Krishnas. I took it upon myself to expose them

single-handedly (though their faith permits them to solicit under what appear to be false pretenses, it forbids them to lie in response to direct questions about their beliefs). When calls to the news media and various governmental agencies initially proved fruitless, I took to standing beside them on street corners and subway platforms, sneering at them and warning people away.

21   A short while later, I launched a campaign against three-card monte hustlers, those sidewalk entrepreneurs, at the time pervasive in New York City, who invite passersby to relinquish their money in a rigged game. Though at first I imitated the tactics I'd successfully employed earlier, I became considerably more discreet when, one afternoon, one of the entrepreneurs retreated from the scene, visited a nearby construction site, and returned with a brick.

22   The entrepreneur did, of course, have a kind of point. Self-righteousness is a particularly loathsome trait—for years I myself had loathed individuals as disparate as Billy Graham and William Kunstler for flaunting theirs—and others could hardly be blamed for taking offense at mine. Indeed, that part of me that remained lucid found itself frequently twitching in embarrassment at some of the things it heard the rest of me saying.

23   But as Feodor D., that canny old fox, told us back in tenth grade, an obsession is an obsession, and eventually, unapologetically, this one found its way into the column. Looking again, I discovered that even the murkiest of grays resolved on closer examination into either black or white. Certainly there were times when adultery might appear a reasonable option—as in the case of the woman I spoke to who detested her husband, absolutely loathed the son of a bitch, but had two children and no marketable skills—but it is still a fundamentally rotten thing to do, it is still behavior that debases. Suddenly, abruptly, that was as obvious as an ad for Bon Jour jeans. It is simply that in a society in which moral and ethical laissez-faire (otherwise known as "Hey, if it works for you . . . ") has been elevated to a national credo, it had become terribly easy to lose track of the obvious.

24   Inevitably, too, all of this had an impact on my personal life. When I was in the midst of grappling with the adultery question for the column, I sought the counsel of a woman I knew well and hoped to know better.

25   "Being unfaithful? I think it's unforgivable," she said, with impressive certainty. Then she paused. "Wait a minute, does this apply to you and me?"

26   "I don't know," I said. "Does it?"

27   "Well . . . I'm still seeing that other guy, you know."

28   "I haven't exactly been celibate myself."

29   But very quickly, we decided that it should apply to us. And it does. We are married now, with a child.

30   "You remind me," kidded a friend recently, "of Thomas More. Once he became Lord Chancellor of England, this guy, who was supposed to accede to the king's every wish, suddenly became an utter fanatic on behalf of the issues." He laughed. "Talk about taking a job seriously."

31   There is—I refer you to Sir Thomas's neck—such a thing as taking one's job *too* seriously, and that was a charge that others pressed on me with mounting frequency. Several people whom I'd known for years greeted my new attitude with derision or anger. "How dare you?" raged one, a fellow who'd been cited under an alias as a negative example in one essay. "The gall, the utter presumption, of your making these kinds of moral judgments!" Another friend, spotting a light piece I'd written in *Playboy,* called me long-distance expressing relief that I had not yet completely lost my sense of humor. One chum began referring to me, with more sarcasm than bonhomie, as Mr. Ethics.

32   These were observations to which I was acutely sensitive, but I came to realize too that in some ways, filling the column every month was simply a no-win proposition. Bertrand Russell himself might often have looked like a goody-two-shoes if he had tried to work out these issues neatly. Moreover, I sensed more than a little defensiveness in the excessively hostile reactions. It is not news that compromises come as easily to many as sleep after a trying day; it was now clear that a lot of those people do not like to be reminded of that fact. I was no longer surprised to run across friends who treaded gingerly on conversational terrain where once we frolicked.

33   But there were also considerable compensations. The mail in response to the column—and there was a great deal—revealed the vastness of the reservoir of hope and conscience that stil exists in this land. There was the letter from the jocular fellow recounting in fascinating detail his bungled first—and last—experience as a shoplifter; and the one from the young mother wondering how to keep her child untainted by racism; and my favorite of all, the short note on elegant stationery from the woman in Ojai, California, whose husband, a once prominent literary agent, had been blacklisted and who never thought she'd live to see the day when ideals and idealism made the pages of a national magazine.

34   I never got such mail when I wrote my humor column.

35   But there was another kind of response to the column that was even more intriguing. "There are," as a woman I hardly know put it a few weeks ago, by way of self-definition, "a lot of closet ethical people. It's hard to speak up for something merely because it's right—you're always afraid of looking silly. Well, it's nice to have a bit of reinforcement."

36   This notion that one has to overcome peer pressure or simple em
barrassment in order ot act properly arose with surprising fre
quency. It is, of course, a melancholy thought: My God, are we re
ally *that* far gone?

37   But then I stop and consider my own case. It was, after all, only a
matter of months since I'd gotten over the embarrassment myself.

TO THINK ABOUT

1. In the third paragraph of the piece Stein says, "I was, as my friend
   well knew, a congenital exaggerator and an occasional liar." Given
   the context of this statement, what sort of expectations does it establish in the reader's mind?
2. Stein traces his evolution as an ethical thinker and actor through
   several stages. What are they? How does his persona change with
   each one? How do you feel about him at each stage?
   Stein cites several of his own ethical dilemmas, as well as those
   of his acquaintances and of several public figures. Do these examples bring to mind similar dilemmas that you have experienced? If so,
   why?
3. Are you one of those "closet ethical people" cited by one of Stein's
   sources in the third-to-last paragraph? If so, why?

TO DO

1. Write about your own attitude toward ethical behavior. Is it dis-
   paraging? Self-righteous? Ambivalent? Use specific examples to illustrate your point.
2. If the specific examples you choose fail to illustrate your original
   point, maybe you should reexamine your point. That's okay. In fact,
   it's good.
3. Write about a situation in which your behavior did not meet your
   own standards for ethical behavior. Why did you fail to act as you
   thought you should have? Was peer pressure a contributing factor?

TIP

Most good writing involves making value judgments, either implicitly or explicitly. Do not shy away from them. As readers, we seek judgments from writers; writers who avoid making judgments for fear of of-
fending readers wind up with no readers.

46

Uncommon Decency
Harry Stein

In the early 1980s Harry Stein wrote an ethics column for Esquire *magazine. The issues he tackled ranged from greed to vengeance, racial slurs to gossip. The pieces worked because of the personal manner in which Stein approached his subjects. Rather than examine them from a scholarly distance, Stein used experiences from his own life as his raw material. The persona in print was that of a man who recognized his own faults, and did his best to live an ethically admirable life in a world that often seemed not to care one way or the other.*

1   It was one of those days that mercifully seem to come to New York just once each spring, a day of rain so heavy that it obscured vision and rushed over gutters onto sidewalks already strewn with umbrellas destroyed by the wind.

2   I was late, and more than a little annoyed; there was no shelter at the Seventy-sixth Street and Lexington Avenue bus stop, where I waited, and my umbrella, too, was threatening to collapse.

3   Finally the bus arrived. I handed the driver my transfer, wiped the water from my glasses, and began to move toward the rear.

4   "Hey, buddy," came the shout.

5   I continued walking.

6   "Hey, *you*, get back here!"

7   I noticed a few pairs of eyes staring my way. "Are you talking to me?" I asked.

8   "Who does it look like I'm talking to?" The driver motioned me back. "That'll be seventy-five cents. This transfer is valid only if you catch the bus at Seventy-ninth Street." Technically he was, of course, correct; such a regulation certainly exists in a book somewhere.

9   "But I get on here all the time," I protested.

10   "I don't give a damn what you do. Seventy-five cents or get off the bus."

11   So I gave him his money—and a good deal more than that in abuse. "You know," I said, taking a seat behind him, "it's people like you who give this city such a lousy reputation. What's the difference if I get on here—especially on a day like this?"

12   There was no response. Indeed, with the wall of plastic between us, I was not even sure he'd heard. "You son of a bitch," I muttered.

13   He had heard. A moment later a huge hand was on my shoulder. "One more word from you and I'm throwing you off. I don't have to take that from no one."

14   For the rest of the ride I reserved my comments for the elderly gentleman beside me. I said that I hoped I had ruined the driver's day.

15   He smiled benignly. "That's not a very nice sentiment," he said.

16   "Why shouldn't I feel that way? He's ruined mine."

17   And, indeed, it was hours before that sense of irritation and dismay left me, days before I was able to talk about the encounter without wishing I were massive enough to have *dared* the guy to throw me off his bus. And it was weeks before it occurred to me that maybe I'd acted almost as badly as he had.

18   Mine was not a particularly strict upbringing—my parents did a lot of cajoling—but in our house certain rules of behavior were never in question. It was assumed that one was always solicitous of people's feelings and ready to offer comfort, and contemptuous of those who cavalierly slighted others. "Always," went my mother's admonition (which to a four-year-old did not sound like a cliché), "put yourself in the other person's shoes."

19   In retrospect, I see that this was, as much as anything else, a matter of politics. My parents, children of immigrants, raised in relative poverty, were of the fervent conviction that the world was divided between people who cared about others and people who did not, between the generous-spirited and the petty, between us and them. Thus it was that in their teens they became radicals, marching on behalf of the Scottsboro Boys; that in their twenties they campaigned for FDR; that in their thirties, after the coming of Jackie Robinson, they became fervent Brooklyn Dodgers fans. Thus it was, too, that in her sixties my mother spotted from her bedroom window a local newspaper vendor being hustled away by the police for having an improper license. Though extremely ill, she dashed out of bed to help him, then spent the next two days phoning city agencies on his behalf.

20   I now realize that it is naive to estimate the contents of people's hearts on the basis of their political affiliations—though seeing any gathering of Reagan Zealots always gives me renewed pause—but the princi-

ple remains valid: if one is to lay any claim to character, he must live his convictions daily, reflexively, in a hundred tiny ways. "I stopped seeing a man because he was rude to waiters," reported a woman of my acquaintance, and I understood perfectly. Someone without respect for waiters or salesclerks or business subordinates is unquestionably going to be found wanting on all the big issues. Indeed, when Jimmy Carter was in office, one woman I know actually turned against him because she had heard somewhere that Rosalynn had a habit of hiding stale crackers in corners to gauge the efficacy of maids. "I worked as a maid in a hotel one summer," she said. "I know all about the indecency of people like that."

21   On the face of it, showing consistent consideration for others should not seem a terribly difficult proposition. It truly doesn't require much more energy to be thoughtful than to be thoughtless, to be a small presence for good instead of just another schlump on the street.

22   But somehow it seems that fewer and fewer of us are able to manage it. Indeed, we seem to behave worse toward one another today than we ever have before. There was a time, well within memory, when certain elementary rules of human intercourse were enforced in this society by popular assent, when not to abide by them was to be regarded as a lout or worse: Just a generation or so ago, virtually no citizen over the age of sixty would ever have been obliged to stand on a crowded bus or subway. Today the public conveyances are full of elderly standees while kids and teenagers and legions of young men and women in designer jeans sit staring blankly ahead. We have, quite simply, become a society where lack of consideration is the norm, where it is entirely legitimate to give a damn only about oneself.

23   What is particularly curious about all of this is that there is a good deal more warmth in the air now than ever before. Every time we dial Information, some operator tells us to have a good day; "Have a Coke and a smile," recommends one electronic voice; "Reach out, reach out and touch someone," advises another. It is almost as if the reduction to ad copy of expressions of human need has rendered us less capable of actually responding to others. Incessantly bombarded by platitudes, we simply don't listen so well anymore or see so clearly or, finally, feel so deeply.

24   It is, to be sure, a grim picture, and there is little reason to believe it will soon change. So we are left with our consciences, each of us having to choose whether we will, in fact, reach out and touch someone or simply continue to look the other way.

25   Those who choose right can do an inestimable amount of good— can, indeed, set even cynical strangers to speculating on the possibilities of the human heart.

26   At dusk on the Friday of Labor Day weekend, 1973, ten miles short of Indianapolis, the old Chevy in which my girlfriend and I had driven from the East Coast to the West and nearly back again finally gave out. Almost out of money, we limped into a gas station off the highway. The owner-mechanic's diagnosis came in five minutes: our drive shaft was shot; we needed a new one.

27   My face fell. "How much will that cost?" I asked.

28   He studied us—disheveled twenty-four-year-olds with a pair of anti-Nixon bumper stickers on our useless vehicle—for a moment. "Wait here," he said. And then, to his assistant, "Eddie, I'll be back in a while."

29   Although according to Eddie the place was due to close for the weekend in an hour, the owner was gone for three hours, until after 10:00 P.M., and when he returned it was with a drive shaft for our Chevy. A *used* drive shaft, found, we eventually understood, after a search of every junkyard and auto graveyard in town.

30   "How much do we owe you?" I asked finally. Then, quickly, I added, "We only have thirty-five dollars; we'll send you the rest."

31   He furrowed his brow. "Well, let's see," he said. "It'll cost you another fifteen bucks for gas to get to New York, and you'll need a motel room tonight, and you've gotta eat. . . . Let's say seven dollars."

32   "Seven dollars? That's ridiculous."

33   "Nope, seven dollars it is."

34   After I'd stopped resisting and paid him his money, he clapped a hand on my shoulder and smiled a smile I'll remember years after the bitterness of the run-in with the bus driver has left me. "Have a good weekend," he said.

TO THINK ABOUT

1. What is your initial reaction to the narrator's encounter with the bus driver? How do your feelings change as the opening scene unfolds? Why?
2. How is the essay organized? Note Stein's use of scenes and dialogue.
3. What kind of person is the narrator? What kind of conversation might you expect to have with him?
4. Is there anything in this essay you disagree with? (If so, pay attention. You may have the germ of another essay.)

TO DO

1. Make a list of potential ethical dilemmas which you face frequently. You may be surprised to discover how many value-laden choices you face every week.

2. Make another list—this one of situations in which you behaved in a manner you now regret.
3. From these lists, pick the item that intrigues you the most, and write about it.

TIP

___

When you look at your list you will see some items you feel comfortable writing about, and others that make you uncomfortable. You will be drawn toward the comfortable ones, but remember, good writers take risks. Often the uncomfortable items will trigger more compelling writing than the comfortable ones will.

47

A Death in the Family

Cynthia Vann

When an old person dies we mourn, but at least we have the consolation that he or she lived a long life. When a young person dies we rage at the injustice of it. When a young person commits suicide, we grope, usually in vain, for an adequate response.

Cynthia Vann is a free-lance writer from Bangor, Maine. Here she writes about the tendency of certain members of her family to attempt suicide. Her voice is abrupt, intense, sometimes compassionate, sometimes harsh, always determined. The result is a resounding affirmation of life.

1   My cousin Elise drank some liquid drain cleaner. My mother was on the phone telling me about it. It burns. Scar tissue develops quickly. There were certain imperatives: tracheotomies and breathing tubes. My mother talked, but I couldn't listen because it hurt so much and, anyway, I already knew what was going on. The doctors were doing what they could.

2   My relatives were clinging together in the hallway and those that weren't there were on their way. Uncle Theo was flying in from his parish some thousand miles off. Other priests, who weren't relatives, would arrive and offer kind words and cups of coffee. A tired-looking doctor would say that Elise might or might not live.

3   There would be a pair of police detectives, hesitant and embarrassed, who would be very relieved to find that the family didn't need to be told that attempted suicide is a crime. And before the night was over, there would be a mass in the hospital chapel; but everyone would be too despairing to pay attention and the older people in the family would absent-mindedly mumble Latin phrases they thought they'd forgotten. I would show up and mumble with them.

4   I already knew what was going on because we'd played that scene before. I was thinking of Elise. I pictured her trembling, looking very much the boy-girl, rummaging in the cabinet for an appropriately lethal weapon to use on herself. There were words on the bottle. Caution. Caustic. She held it awkwardly, rested it on the edge of the counter, poured a large or a small amount into the cup.

5   The family was in the other room, just across the mint-green wall that Elise herself had painted only months before. They weren't paying attention. Noises, the shuffle of boxes and bottles, mean nothing in a house full of people. Liquid drain cleaner doesn't sound any different from milk or orange juice. What if one of them had walked in . . . would Elise have carried her drink to the basement, waited for a gloomier day? Maybe she'd have abandoned the plot against herself.

6   The last time I saw Elise was at the funeral of Pamela. Elise's older sister, Pamela, walked into the ice of the beautiful lake and kept walking until she found a weak spot. Had she not mailed her mother a note outlining her plan, we wouldn't have found her till the spring thaw.

7   Elise and I sat in an upstairs room. We could see the lake and the marks left by the men who'd come with the axes to free Pam's body. Elise sat curled on the bed with an old Hudson Bay blanket rolled up to her chin. The red of the blanket drew the color from her pale skin and she looked too much like the possible ghosts of all her sisters and her mother and my mother. She said, "You know something? I'm a homosexual."

8   I told her I'd guessed it years ago. She said she hadn't known that long. I said she should have asked, I'd have told her. We laughed. She asked if I minded. I said no and she smiled. Pamela knew and said it didn't make any difference at all. Pamela was right. Elise went on to tell me she sometimes blamed the older girls in the family for the things that troubled her. She said, "And you're the oldest." She asked if I knew why Pam killed herself. I didn't know, still don't.

9   Two years before that, Sarah tried to kill herself. She wasn't one for display, simply made a potion and slept her way into a coma that lasted six days. She wasn't half-hearted, merely inept in that she allowed herself to be found. Our family needs its own chapel in the hospital.

10   Pain and confusion and guilt creep in. I sometimes have nightmares. We grew up together, were the young wave of a large clan, diverged to go our own ways and now come crashing back together to mourn. Families aren't supposed to shrink in number, don't implode. Ours does. My mother and my aunt divide the dead ones' jewelry among the survivors. It is lovely jewelry; it once belonged to our grandmother and her sisters. I don't want any more of it.

11   I am too young to inherit the possessions of my contemporaries. Or

worse, to inherit the things of little girls, years younger than myself. I see them flailing. Elise falls to the floor, taking dishes that shatter and cut into her. Pamela, dear Pam, that water must have been so cold. I wake up in the night; yet I keep the black pearl necklace and the cameo and the rest of it.

12   My aunt and uncle suffer. The fragility of others is a secret we share. We wonder if we've done it wrong. And, I admit, there is just the lightest touch of anger. I remember another event.

13   My brother and I stood at the attic window and watched a blizzard take hold. We were going to be snowed in. Our mother had called and said she would stay in the city. We were going to throw a party for the younger kids. We intended to enjoy the storm.

14   A neighboring farmer called and said he thought he could see our mother's car down the road from his house. He'd gone in his attic to survey the storm; otherwise he'd never have seen it. It was nearly drifted over and he thought we should hurry before she was suffocated. His heart was weak and he couldn't help us. Act quickly, he said.

15   I went back to the attic window with a pair of binoculars and watched. My brother walked in snow up to his knees and after a time he vanished from sight. Half an hour, almost an hour passed, and finally, slowly, they emerged. Johnny was dragging her. He was walking backwards and he had his arms wrapped around her and was pulling her through the snow. He is almost six-and-a-half feet tall and the snow was nearly to his waste. I thought he'd found her dead, suffocated in the car. Or maybe she'd tried to walk, had fallen and was frozen. He stopped.

16   I could see his back heaving and it looked as though he might collapse. She moved! Was alive! She tried to stand, but she dropped over. He pulled her over his shoulder, staggering sideways from the effort, and almost fell. He turned around and began fighting toward the house. The wind changed directions, he bent his head against the bite and kept moving.

17   When I ran out to greet them, I was blinded by the wind and fell off the porch into snow that was so deep I couldn't get back to the house. I'll never forget the sight of them. Their skin was as red as the red of their coats and what I'd thought was a scarf was really my mother's hair come loose, white with clinging sleet and making circles in the wind. I saw my brother's hands, without gloves, paste-colored and smeared with frozen blood.

18   Behind me in the doorway the little kids laughed when I fell, but then one of them sensed something and they all started to scream. I struggled and turned and there was Elise, seven or eight years old, on her knees, holding the railing and extending one hand to me. I yelled at her

but she paid no attention. My brother saw us and bellowed in alarm and Elise crawled back in the doorway.

19   Hours later—our mother wrapped in blankets and peacefully sleeping, the little kids in bed for the night—my brother and I sat drinking cocoa with too much brandy in it. He was using a hair dryer to warm his hands and even now, 18 years later, they still bother him. I said something about how lucky we were and he said luck had nothing to do with it, if he hadn't been home then I'd have done it. I am too short to have made it through that snow and never could have saved her; but we didn't talk about that.

20   My cousins committed crimes having nothing to do with the law. I don't know why. We are a blood-related family and on the surface appear so similar. There may not be an answer; I've discovered that many questions have no answers. But that snowstorm afternoon means something to me. My brother wanted our mother to live. He wanted it to a degree that is roughly equal to how much I want to live, every day. And in fact, when I go, they'll have to tear me off this planet.

TO THINK ABOUT

1. Who is this piece primarily about? What does the narrator's voice reveal about her personality and her values?
2. What is the narrator's attitude toward Elise, Pamela, and Sarah? What is yours?
3. In some states attempted suicide is a crime. Should it be? Why or why not?

TO DO

1. Read "'So long 4 ever'" by Elissa Ely (Chapter 10), a piece in which a psychiatrist writes about her dealings with a suicidal girl. Compare the narrative voices of Ely and Cynthia Vann. Imagine a conversation between the two writers. Now add your own voice to the mix.
2. Free-write for fifteen minutes on the subject of suicide. Write as fast as you can; do not allow your hand to stop moving. Then examine what you have written. It is likely that you have the germ of an essay.

TIP

_____

When we write about people who have died we have a tendency to idealize, to sanitize, to avoid the negative and exaggerate the positive. This is natural. We have been taught not to speak ill of the dead. Unfortunately this leads to bad writing—to overly sentimental one-dimensional portraits that lack credibility.

Write about the dead the same way you write about the living: rely primarily on anecdotes, scenes, dialogue. The more you show, the less you have to tell.

48

Drugs

Gore Vidal

Gore Vidal, master of the historical novel (Julian, Burr, Lincoln, Empire, Hollywood), breaker of literary taboos (Myra Breckinridge, his novel about a man-woman who has undergone a sex change operation, caused a minor scandal when it was published in 1968), professional gadfly (hundreds of essays critiquing the status quo), and distant cousin of former U.S. Senator Albert Gore and his son, Vice-President Al Gore, has no use for legislated morality. He would do away with laws limiting speech, sexual behavior, abortion, and other matters of personal choice, including the choice to end one's own life. Here he argues that the legalization of all drugs would do more to alleviate the drug problem in the United States than all the wars against drugs ever waged. His voice is strong, resolute, unapologetic, even scornful.

1   It is possible to stop most drug addiction in the United States within a very short time. Simply make all drugs availabe and sell them at cost. Label each drug with a precise description of what effect—good and bad—the drug will have on the taker. This will require heroic honesty. Don't say that marijuana is addictive or dangerous when it is neither, as millions of people know—unlike "speed," which kills most unpleasantly, or heroin, which is addictive and difficult to kick.

2   For the record, I have tried—once—almost every drug and liked none, disproving the popular Fu Manchu theory that a single whiff of opium will enslave the mind. Nevertheless many drugs are bad for certain people to take and they should be told why in a sensible way.

3   Along with exhortation and warning, it might be good for our citizens to recall (or learn for the first time) that the United States was the creation of men who believed that each man has the right to do what he wants with his own life as long as he does not interfere with his neigh-

bor's pursuit of happiness (that his neighbor's's idea of happiness is persecuting others does confuse matters a bit).

4   This is a startling notion to the current generation of Americans. They reflect a system of public education which has made the Bill of Rights, literally, unacceptable to a majority of high school graduates (see the annual Purdue reports) who now form the "silent majority"—a phrase which that underestimated wit Richard Nixon took from Homer who used it to describe the dead.

5   Now one can hear the warning rumble begin: if everyone is allowed to take drugs everyone will and the GNP will decrease, the Commies will stop us from making everyone free, and we shall end up a race of Zombies, passively murmuring "groovie" to one another. Alarming thought. Yet it seems most unlikely that any reasonably sane person will become a drug addict if he knows in advance what addiction is going to be like.

6   Is everyone reasonably sane? No. Some people will always become drug addicts just as some people will always become alcoholics, and it is just too bad. Every man, however, has the power (and should have the legal right) to kill himself if he chooses. But since most men don't, they won't be mainliners either. Nevertheless, forbidding people things they like or think they might enjoy only makes them want those things all the more. This psychological insight is, for some mysterious reason, perennially denied our governors.

7   It is a lucky thing for the American moralist that our country has always existed in a kind of time-vacuum: we have no public memory of anything that happened before last Tuesday. No one in Washington today recalls what happened during the years alcohol was forbidden to the people by a Congress that thought it had a divine mission to stamp out Demon Rum—launching, in the process, the greatest crime wave in the country's history, causing thousands of deaths from bad alcohol, and creating a general (and persisting) contempt among the citizenry for the laws of the United States.

8   The same thing is happening today. But the government has learned nothing from past attempts at prohibition, not to mention repression.

9   Last year when the supply of Mexican marijuana was slightly curtailed by the Feds, the pushers got the kids hooked on heroin and deaths increased dramatically, particularly in New York. Whose fault? Evil men like the Mafiosi? Permissive Dr. Spock? Wild-eyed Dr. Leary? No.

10   The Government of the United States was responsible for those deaths. The bureaucratic machine has a vested interest in playing cops and robbers. Both the Bureau of Narcotics and the Mafia want strong laws against the sale and use of drugs because if drugs are sold at cost there would be no money in it for anyone.

11   If there was no money in it for the Mafia, there would be no friendly playground pushers, and addicts would not commit crimes to pay for the next fix. Finally, if there was no money in it, the Bureau of Narcotics would wither away, something they are not about to do without a struggle.

12   Will anything sensible be done? Of course not. The American people are as devoted to the idea of sin and its punishment as they are to making money—and fighting drugs is nearly as big a business as pushing them. Since the combination of sin and money is irresistible (particularly to the professional politician), the situation will only grow worse.

TO THINK ABOUT

1. What sort of persona does Vidal the narrator adopt for this piece? Is it effective? What is the nature of the relationship he establishes with his reader?
2. In the second paragraph Vidal acknowledges that he has "tried— once—almost every drug and liked none. . . ." What effect does this admission have on his credibility?
3. Vidal draws a parallel between the government's war on drugs and the Prohibition era. Read about Prohibition and decide whether or not Vidal's comparison is valid.
4. "Drugs" was published more than twenty years ago. How might changing conditions have affected Vidal's argument?
5. Vidal writes: "It is a lucky thing for the American moralist that our country has always existed in a kind of time-vacuum; we have no public memory of anything that happened before last Tuesday." To test this observation, consider: What are the most talked-about issues in the news today? What were they six months ago? A year ago? Five years ago?

TO DO

1. Make a list of public policies you think are harmful or unjust. Pick the one that outrages you the most. Go to the library and read about the history and implementation of that policy. You might also want to interview someone on campus or in the community who has expertise on this subject.
2. Then write an essay in which you argue for the discontinuation of that policy.

TIP

The most effective argument is one that points out the flaws in the opposing position. Thus, before you begin writing an argument it might be useful to make a list of the major arguments of the opposition. Then, as you write, check off each argument as you counter it.

49

Choices

Patricia Volk

A good writer takes risks. When a good writer writes about herself, she holds nothing back, nothing that is germane to her subject. She does this knowing that she exposes herself to second-guessing, even ridicule. She hopes for empathy, for understanding. She knows that whether or not she gets it is not important.

Here is a brief essay about choices, about how we make them and how we avoid them. It seems simple, a series of anecdotes, scenes, bits of dialogue. And yet it is layered, complex. In the beginning the voice seems sure of itself. But there is an underlying sense of doubt—a voice questioning its own assertions. Toward the end, there is a shift in tone.

In essence, the narrator carries on several conversations at once: with the characters in the essay, with herself, and with us. The voice, filled with irony and doubt, seems to ask us to respond.

1   Life is simpler when you think you have no choices. There are no big decisions, no risk of self-recrimination, no anguish over making a mistake. How can you be responsible for making a mistake when you have no choice?

2   After graduating with a bachelor's degree in fine arts, I had to get a job. Nobody made a living just painting.

3   After each child was born I had to go back to work. Somebody had to work.

4   Stuck in a job a long time ago I had to stay because job security is important when you've got two kids, a husband in school and a housekeeper you have to have because you have to work.

5   Now, on my way downtown in the morning, sometimes I get rides

with Harold. We grew up together and when he sees me walking to work Harold picks me up. He chose to head up a multimillion-dollar corporation even though he'd rather be sculpting. He tells me he feels good only when he sculpts. We commiserate in his limo and discuss our aging brain cells. How much prime time do we have left? How do we want to spend it? Do we have a choice? Our states of mind are so similar I'm not sure we should talk to each other. When I tell him I understand how desperate he is I worry I am egging him on, but to what? What I want for myself?

6   I lay out his future in front of him.

· · ·

7   "I don't have a choice, Harold," I tell him. "But look at you. You sell your co-op and you sell your business, and still you have millions. *Millions.*"

8   His jaw hangs open like a glove compartment. I decide this is encouraging.

9   "Then you move out of the city and live in your weekend place in Cornwall Bridge." I am warming to Harold's rosy future. "You send the kids to the Housatonic Valley Regional High School and the Y summer program. You live below your means on the 10 percent interest on the millions."

10   "Ten percent of millions, Harold," I say. "Can you sculpt on it?"

11   He holds his head in his hands.

12   "My 5-year-old just got into Columbia Prep," he says. "I have no choice."

13   Then there's Rita. Rita's son is in my daughter's class. We see each other at school meetings, and sometimes afterward we go for coffee. Once she invited me up to her apartment. We sat there in the dining room, me facing the Vlaminck, she the Laurencin. She began telling me about her relationship with her husband. She told me more than I wanted to know. She told me she embezzled from him. Rita has it worked out with the liquor store that when she orders a case of wine for $3.99 a bottle, they bill her husband $8.99 and give her the difference, cash. She gloats, telling me this while she plays with the Royal Imari espresso cups her husband gave her for their anniversary.

14   "Rita," I ask her, "if you need money, why don't you work?"

15   "My degree is in English lit," she says. "What in the world could I do?"

16   Rick and I are in the kitchen, cooking side by side. The easy intimacy comes over us that happens when you're busy together but can't look at each other.

17   "I used to not love my job," I tell him. "Then I started not liking it. Then I started hating it. Then I started loathing it. Now, I *despise* it."

18   "I think despise comes before loathe, don't you?"

            . . .

19   So I tell him my Six-Month Plan. "When I have a bad day at work," I tell him, "I turn to six months from that day in my calendar and write the words, *'Quit If Still Hate.'* But six months later, when I reach that page I'm always so surprised. I'm always loving the job again."

20   "Ambivalence is a form of neurosis," he says poking at the chicken. "You always act like you have no choice."

21   "What about when I got out of school and wanted to paint?"

22   "You didn't have to get a job," he says. "You could have lived in Chinatown and waited tables. You chose a real job so you could live in a doorman building."

23   "I wouldn't have felt safe in Chinatown 20 years ago," I tell him, folding in whipped cream.

24   "That was a choice," he says.

25   "Well what about the kids? When you were in school? I had to go back to work then—didn't I?"

26   "We could have gotten a loan. We could have postponed the children."

27   "What about *now?*"

28   While drenched in the shower, you discover the shampoo bottle is empty. Do you use bath gel? When the lamb chops you ordered pink come well-done, do you assume it's fate? Are you living in a SOOTY 1 BR, low flr, no amenities, airshaft vu, $2540 mo. apartment?

29   Convincing yourself you have no choice propels you. It pulls you forward as if your car is caught in the suck of a speeding truck.

            . . .

30   Consider Woody Allen. In a recent interview, he expressed a desire to spend his time writing instead of making movies. But, he said, how can he give up making movies when everybody makes it so nice for him? He has complete control over his movies, a rare thing. How could he give that up? He has no choice.

31   And consider Emily Bauer. She is the heroine of "This Far and No More," the true story of a 40-year-old woman who is stricken with a devastating and incurable disease. She slips quickly into the hell of a useless body, a respirator, feeding tubes. Unable to speak, unable to move anything except her eyelids, she blinks a message to her husband. She wants to die. Her eyelids ask him to help her die. The only choice she can still make is made. He helps her.

32   Eyelids. They call to mind the nictitating membrane. It is the third eyelid, a protective organ found on various animals. In the alligator it is thick, dense, blinding. When the alligator's third eyelid covers his eye,

the alligator can no longer see. Like people who believe they have no choice, he cannot see by the same mechanism that protects him.

TO THINK ABOUT

1. Volk begins: "Life is simpler when you think you have no choices." This may appear to be the theme of the essay; it is, in fact, half the theme. What is the other half?
2. The choices Volk cites range from the nearly inconsequential ("Do you use bath gel?") to the profound ("The only choice she can still make is made"). Why?
3. What is the effect of the simile that ends the essay?
4. The narrator implies that she is annoyed with Harold and Rita for failing to acknowledge the choices available to them. How does she feel about the choices she has made in her own life?
5. What kind of voice does this narrator use? Would you feel comfortable in conversation with her? Why or why not?

TO DO

1. Make a list of important choices you have made. At the time you made them, did you view them as choices?
2. Make another list, this one consisting of matters in which you feel you have no choice. Then analyze the items on the list. Did these obligations come about as a result of previous choices? Do you still have choices? What would be the consequences if you now chose differently?
3. An underlying concern in "Choices" is the pull we all feel between obligation and conformity, on the one hand, and personal fulfillment, on the other. Write an essay about this dichotomy. Use anecdotes, scenes, and dialogue as your primary material. Keep generalizations to a minimum.

TIP

Beginning writers sometimes write essays full of questions: *Why do I live the way I do? Believe what I believe? Make the choices I make? Why is there injustice, hunger, bigotry, war?* It's fine to ask questions, as Patricia Volk does at the beginning of "Choices." But it is important to try to answer them, even if the answers are not definitive. (Think of your own reading habits. Do you read to find questions? Or answers?)

This does not mean you must come up with a complete solution for every problem you write about. It does mean you must make progress; by the end of the essay, you (and your reader) should be closer to the answer than you were at the beginning.

50

The First Amendment

Kurt Vonnegut

*As a U.S. infantryman in World War II, Kurt Vonnegut wit-
nessed the firebombing of the city of Dresden, Germany. The event
became the springboard for* Slaughterhouse-Five, *the novel that remains Vonnegut's masterpiece. When, from time to time, ad hoc
parents' groups persuade school officials to ban certain books from
high school libraries and classrooms,* Slaughterhouse-Five *usually
makes the list.*

In the following excerpt from his memoir Palm Sunday,
*Vonnegut reflects on book-burners, and on the Bill of Rights, which
protects free speech. These passages include three different literary
forms: a letter from Vonnegut to a school board member in Drake,
North Dakota, where* Slaughterhouse-Five *was burned; an op-ed
piece in* The New York Times; *and a speech Vonnegut delivered at a
civil liberties fundraiser on Long Island. Vonnegut's voice—abrupt,
self-effacing, angry, funny—is the unifying factor.*

1   I am a member of what I believe to be the last recognizable generation of full-time, life-time American novelists. We appear to be standing
more or less in a row. It was the Great Depression which made us similarly edgy and watchful. It was World War II which lined us up so nicely,
whether we were men or women, whether we were ever in uniform or
not. It was an era of romantic anarchy in publishing which gave us
money and mentors, willy-nilly, when we were young—while we
learned our craft. Words printed on pages were still the principal form of
long-distance communication and stored information in America when
we were young.

2   No more.

3   Nor are there many publishers and editors and agents left who are
eager to find some way to get money and other forms of encouragement
to young writers who write as clumsily as members of my literary generation did when we started out. The wild and wonderful and expensive

guess was made back then that we might acquire some wisdom and learn how to write halfway decently by and by. Writers were needed that much back then.

4   It was an amusing and instructive time for writers—for hundreds of them.

5   Television wrecked the short-story branch of the industry, and now accountants and business school graduates dominate book publishing. They feel that money spent on someone's first novel is good money down a rat hole. They are right. It almost always is.

6   So, as I say, I think I belong to America's last generation of novelists. Novelists will come one by one from now on, not in seeming families, and will perhaps write only one or two novels, and let it go at that. Many will have inherited or married money.

7   The most influential of my bunch, in my opinion, is still J. D. Salinger, although he has been silent for years. The most promising was perhaps Edward Lewis Wallant, who died so young. And it is my thinking about the death of James Jones two years ago, who was not all that young, who was almost exactly my age, which accounts for the autumnal mood of this book. There have been other reminders of my own mortality, to be sure, but the death of Jones is central—perhaps because I see his widow Gloria so often and because he, too, was a self-educated midwesterner, and because he, too, in a major adventure for all of us, which was the Second World War, had been an enlisted man. And let it here be noted that the best-known members of my literary generation, if they wrote about war, almost unanimously despised officers and made heroes of sketchily educated, aggressively unaristocratic enlisted men.

8   James Jones told me one time that his publisher and Ernest Hemingway's, Charles Scribner's Sons, had once hoped to get Jones and Hemingway together—so that they could enjoy each other's company as old warriors.

9   Jones declined, by his own account, because he did not regard Hemingway as a fellow soldier. He said Hemingway in wartime was free to come and go from the fighting as he pleased, and to take time off for a fine meal or woman or whatever. Real soldiers, according to Jones, damn well had to stay where they were told, or go where they were told, and eat swill, and take the worst the enemy had to throw at them day after day, week after week.

10   It may be that the most striking thing about members of my literary generation in retrospect will be that we were allowed to say absolutely anything without fear of punishment. Our American heirs may find it incredible, as most foreigners do right now, that a nation would

want to enforce as a law something which sounds more like a dream, which reads as follows:

> Congress shall make no law respecting an establishment of religion, or prohibiting the free exercise thereof, or abridging the freedom of the press, or the right of the people peaceably to assemble, and to petition the Government for a redress of grievances.

11   How could a nation with such a law raise its children in an atmosphere of decency? It couldn't—it can't. So the law will surely be repealed soon for the sake of children.

12   And even now my books, along with books by Bernard Malamud and James Dickey and Joseph Heller and many other first-rate patriots, are regularly thrown out of public-school libraries by school board members, who commonly say that they have not actually read the books, but that they have it on good authority that the books are bad for children.

13   My novel *Slaughterhouse-Five* was actually burned in a furnace by a school janitor in Drake, North Dakota, on instructions from the school committee there, and the school board made public statements about the unwholesomeness of the book. Even by the standards of Queen Victoria, the only offensive line in the entire novel is this: "Get out of the road, you dumb motherfucker." This is spoken by an American antitank gunner to an unarmed American chaplain's assistant during the Battle of the Bulge in Europe in December 1944, the largest single defeat of American arms (the Confederacy excluded) in history. The chaplain's assistant had attracted enemy fire.

14   So on November 16, 1973, I wrote as follows to Charles McCarthy of Drake, North Dakota:

> Dear Mr. McCarthy:
>
> I am writing to you in your capacity as chairman of the Drake School Board. I am among those American writers whose books have been destroyed in the now famous furnace of your school.
>
> Certain members of your community have suggested that my work is evil. This is extraordinarily insulting to me. The news from Drake indicates to me that books and writers are very unreal to you people. I am writing this letter to let you know how real I am.
>
> I want you to know, too, that my publisher and I have done absolutely nothing to exploit the disgusting news from Drake. We are not clapping each other on the back, crowing about all the books we will sell because of the news. We have declined to go on television, have written no fiery letters to editorial pages, have granted no lengthy interviews. We are angered and sickened and saddened. And no copies of this letter have been sent to anybody else. You now hold the only copy in your hands. It is a strictly private letter from me to the people of Drake, who have done so much to damage my reputation in the eyes of their children and then in the eyes of the world. Do

you have the courage and ordinary decency to show this letter to the people, or will it, too, be consigned to the fires of your furnace?

I gather from what I read in the papers and hear on television that you imagine me, and some other writers, too, as being sort of rat-like people who enjoy making money from poisoning the minds of young people. I am in fact a large, strong person, fifty-one years old, who did a lot of farm work as a boy, who is good with tools. I have raised six children, three my own and three adopted. They have all turned out well. Two of them are farmers. I am a combat infantry veteran from World War II, and hold a Purple Heart. I have earned whatever I own by hard work. I have never been arrested or sued for anything. I am so much trusted with young people and by young people that I have served on the faculties of the University of Iowa, Harvard, and the City College of New York. Every year I receive at least a dozen invitations to be commencement speaker at colleges and high schools. My books are probably more widely used in schools than those of any other living American fiction writer.

If you were to bother to read my books, to behave as educated persons would, you would learn that they are not sexy, and do not argue in favor of wildness of any kind. They beg that people be kinder and more responsible than they often are. It is true that some of the characters speak coarsely. That is because people speak coarsely in real life. Especially soldiers and hardworking men speak coarsely, and even our most sheltered children know that. And we all know, too, that those words really don't damage children much. They didn't damage us when we were young. It was evil deeds and lying that hurt us.

After I have said all this, I am sure you are still ready to respond, in effect, "Yes, yes—but it still remains our right and our responsibility to decide what books our children are going to be made to read in our community." This is surely so. But it is also true that if you exercise that right and fulfill that responsibility in an ignorant, harsh, un-American manner, then people are entitled to call you bad citizens and fools. Even your own children are entitled to call you that.

I read in the newspaper that your community is mystified by the outcry from all over the country about what you have done. Well, you have discovered that Drake is a part of American civilization, and your fellow Americans can't stand it that you have behaved in such an uncivilized way. Perhaps you will learn from this that books are sacred to free men for very good reasons, and that wars have been fought against nations which hate books and burn them. If you are an American, you must allow all ideas to circulate freely in your community, not merely your own.

If you and your board are now determined to show that you in fact have wisdom and maturity when you exercise your powers over the education of your young, then you should acknowledge that it was a rotten lesson you taught young people in a free society when you denounced and then burned books—books you hadn't even read. You should also resolve to expose your children to all sorts of opinions and information, in order that they will be better equipped to make decisions and to survive.

Again: you have insulted me, and I am a good citizen, and I am very real.

14   That was seven years ago. There has so far been no reply. At this very moment, as I write in New York City, *Slaughter-house-Five* has been banned from school libraries not fifty miles from here. A legal battle begun several years ago rages on. The school board in question has found lawyers eager to attack the First Amendment tooth and nail. There is never a shortage anywhere of lawyers eager to attack the First Amendment, as though it were nothing more than a clause in a lease from a crooked slumlord.

15   At the start of that particular litigation, on March 24th of 1976, I wrote a comment for the Op-Ed page of the Long Island edition of *The New York Times*. It went like this:

A school board has denounced some books again—out in Levittown this time. One of the books was mine. I hear about un-American nonsense like this twice a year or so. One time out in North Dakota, the books were actually burned in a furnace. I had a laugh. It was such an ignorant, dumb, superstitious thing to do.

It was so cowardly, too—to make a great show of attacking artifacts. It was like St. George attacking bedspreads and cuckoo clocks.

Yes, and St. Georges like that seem to get elected or appointed to school committees all the time. They are actually proud of their illiteracy. They imagine that they are somehow celebrating the bicentennial when they boast, as some did in Levittown, that they hadn't actually read the books they banned.

Such lunks are often the backbone of volunteer fire departments and the United States Infantry and cake sales and so on, and they have been thanked often enough for that. But they have no business supervising the educations of children in a free society. They are just too bloody stupid.

Here is how I propose to end book-banning in this country once and for all: Every candidate for school committee should be hooked up to a lie-detector and asked this question: "Have you read a book from start to finish since high school? Or did you even read a book from start to finish in high school?"

If the truthful answer is "no," then the candidate should be told politely that he cannot get on the school committee and blow off his big bazoo about how books make children crazy.

Whenever ideas are squashed in this country, literate lovers of the American experiment write careful and intricate explanations of why all ideas must be allowed to live. It is time for them to realize that they are attempting to explain America at its bravest and most optimistic to orangutans.

From now on, I intend to limit my discourse with dimwitted Savonarolas to this advice: "Have somebody read the First Amendment to the United States Constitution out loud to you, you God damned fool!"

Well—the American Civil Liberties Union or somebody like that will come to the scene of trouble, as they always do. They will explain what is in the Constitution, and to whom it applies.

They will win.

And there will be millions who are bewildered and heartbroken by the legal victory, who think some things should never be said—especially about religion.

They are in the wrong place at the wrong time.

Hi ho.

16   Why is it so ordinary for American citizens to show such scorn for the First Amendment? I discussed that some at a fund raiser for the American Civil Liberties Union at Sands Point, New York, out on Long Island, on September 16, 1979. The house where I spoke, incidentally, was said to be the model for Gatsby's house in F. Scott Fitzgerald's *The Great Gatsby*. I saw no reason to doubt the claim.

17   I said this in such a setting:

"I will not speak directly to the ejection of my book *Slaughterhouse-Five* from the school libraries of Island Trees. I have a vested interest. I wrote the book, after all, so why wouldn't I argue that it is less repulsive than the school board says?

"I will speak of Thomas Aquinas instead. I will tell you my dim memories of what he said about the hierarchy of laws on this planet, which was flat at the time. The highest law, he said, was divine law, God's law. Beneath that was natural law, which I suppose would include thunderstorms, and our right to shield our children from poisonous ideas, and so on.

"And the lowest law was human law.

"Let me clarify this scheme by comparing its parts to playing cards. Enemies of the Bill of Rights do the same sort of thing all the time, so why shouldn't we? Divine law, then, is an ace. Natural law is a king. The Bill of Rights is a lousy queen.

"The Thomist hierarchy of laws is so far from being ridiculous that I have never met anybody who did not believe in it right down to the marrow of his or her bones. Everybody knows that there are laws with more grandeur than those which are printed in our statute books. The big trouble is that there is so little agreement as to how those grander laws are worded. Theologians can give us hints of the wording, but it takes a dictator to set them down just right—to dot the *i*'s and cross the *t*'s. A man who had been a mere corporal in the army did that for Germany and then for all of Europe, you may remember, not long ago. There was nothing he did not know about divine and natural law. He had fistfuls of aces and kings to play.

"Meanwhile, over on this side of the Atlantic, we were not playing with a full deck, as they say. Because of our Constitution, the highest card anybody had to play was a lousy queen, contemptible human law. That remains true today. I myself celebrate that incompleteness, since it has obviously been so good for us. I support the American Civil Liberties Union because it goes to court to insist that our government officials be guided by nothing grander than human law. Every time the circulation of this idea or that one is discouraged by an official in this country, that official is scorning the Constitution, and urging all of us to participate in far grander systems, again: divine or natural law.

"Cannot we, as libertarians, hunger for at least a little natural law? Can't we learn from nature at least, without being burdened by another person's idea of God?

"Certainly. Granola never harmed anybody, nor the birds and bees—not to mention milk. God is unknowable, but nature is explaining herself all the time. What has she told us so far? That blacks are obviously inferior to whites, for one thing, and intended for menial work on white man's terms. This clear lesson from nature, we should remind ourselves from time to time, allowed Thomas Jefferson to own slaves. Imagine that.

"What troubles me most about my lovely country is that its children are seldom taught that American freedom will vanish, if, when they grow up, and in the exercise of their duties as citizens, they insist that our courts and policemen and prisons be guided by divine or natural law.

"Most teachers and parents and guardians do not teach this vital lesson because they themselves never learned it, or because they dare not. Why dare they not? People can get into a lot of trouble in this country, and often have to be defended by the American Civil Liberties Union, for laying the groundwork for the lesson, which is this: That no one really understands nature or God. It is my willingness to lay this groundwork, and not sex or violence, which has got my poor book in such trouble in Island Trees—and in Drake, North Dakota, where the book was burned, and in many other communities too numerous to mention.

"I have not said that our government is anti-nature and anti-God. I have said that it is non-nature and non-God, for very good reasons that could curl your hair.

"Well—all good things must come to an end, they say. So American freedom will come to an end, too, sooner or later. How will it end? As all freedoms end: by the surrender of our destinies to the highest laws.

"To return to my foolish analogy of playing cards: kings and aces will be played. Nobody else will have anything higher than a queen.

"There will be a struggle between those holding kings and aces. The struggle will not end, not that the rest of us will care much by then, until somebody plays the ace of spades. Nothing beats the ace of spades.

"I thank you for your attention."

TO THINK ABOUT

1. Vonnegut writes: "How could a nation with such a law [the First Amendment] raise its children in an atmosphere of decency? It couldn't—it can't. So the law will surely be repealed soon for the sake of the children." What is his tone? His underlying message?
2. Think about Vonnegut's manners. His characterization of book-banners as "just too bloody stupid," and their acts as "ignorant, dumb, superstitious" certainly is not polite. Why do you suppose he used the tone he did?
3. Vonnegut proposes that only people who have read at least one book since high school should be allowed to run for school board. Is he serious? What do you think of this idea?
4. Vonnegut uses a card metaphor to characterize God's law, natural law, and man's law. Does the metaphor work? What is the significance of the ace of spades?
5. Is Vonnegut a cynic or a skeptic? What's the difference?

TO DO

1. Read aloud Vonnegut's speech to the civil liberties group. Deliver the speech in the tone of voice you think Vonnegut might have used. Does the recitation change or expand your sense of the speech?
2. Read *Slaughterhouse-Five*. Write about its effect on you.
3. Read the Constitution, including the Bill of Rights and the other amendments. Find one which directly affects your life. Write about it in specific terms.

TIP

You are about to write something, but you hold back. You are inhibited. Here, perhaps, is why: even though you know that what you are about to write is valid, you also know that it is outrageous. That is, people just don't *say* what you are about to say, even though it is true.

Stop censoring yourself. There are enough teachers and editors and classmates and other readers out there to evaluate your work for you and tell you what's wrong with it. *Your* job is to be true to your ideas—and to present them as fully, as specifically as possible.

This is not to say that everything you write is going to work. It *is* to say that unless you get it out of your head and onto a sheet of paper, you'll never know.

51

Introduction to *Palm Sunday*
Kurt Vonnegut

We writers know two things about what we write: (1) It's terrific, and (2) it stinks. That is to say, when it comes to our own material we are manic-depressive. We set impossibly high standards for ourselves. We write something. We like it. But we know in our hearts that it does not meet our standards. (Nothing ever will.) We don't like it anymore.

And so when we must write something about our own writing—evaluating it, summarizing it, critiquing it—we have a difficult time.

When Kurt Vonnegut put together a collection of his own writings in Palm Sunday, *he was faced with the task of writing an introduction to his own essays, reviews, and speeches.*

Vonnegut is not a shy writer. He often takes on organized religion, government, even the human species itself. (In the novel Galapagos *he imagines that humans evolve into seal-like creatures with limited, seal-like brains—a vast improvement over the current situation.) And, it turns out, he is not shy about criticizing his own work. Because it is magnificent. (Or is it?)*

Vonnegut delivers hyperbolic material in deadpan fashion. The contrast keeps the reader off balance. Each sentence is loaded. Eventually, the thing goes off.

1   This is a very great book by an American genius. I have worked so hard on this masterpiece for the past six years. I have groaned and banged my head on radiators. I have walked through every hotel lobby in New York, thinking about this book and weeping, and driving my fist into the guts of grandfather clocks.

2   It is a marvelous new literary form. This book combines the tidal power of a major novel with the bone-rattling immediacy of front-line journalism—which is old stuff now, God knows, God knows. But I have

also intertwined the flashy enthusiasms of musical theater, the lethal left jab of the short story, the sachet of personal letters, the oompah of American history, and oratory in the bow-wow style.

3   This book is so broad and deep that it reminds me of my brother Bernard's early experiments with radio. He built a transmitter of his own invention, and he hooked it up to a telegraph key, and he turned it on. He called up our cousin Richard, about two miles away, and he told Richard to listen to his radio, to tune it back and forth across the band, to see if he could pick up my brother's signals anywhere. They were both about fifteen.

4   My brother tapped out an easily recognizable message, sending it again and again and again. It was "SOS." This was in Indianapolis, the world's largest city not on a navigable waterway.

5   Cousin Richard telephoned back. He was thrilled. He said that Bernard's signals were loud and clear simply everywhere on the radio band, drowning out music or news or drama, or whatever the commercial stations were putting out at the time.

6   This is certainly that kind of masterpiece, and a new name should be created for such an all-frequencies assault on the sensibilities. I propose the name *blivit*. This is a word which during my adolescence was defined by peers as "two pounds of shit in a one-pound bag."

7   I would not mind if books simpler than this one, but combining fiction and fact, were also called blivits. This would encourage *The New York Times Book Review* to establish a third category for best sellers, one long needed, in my opinion. If there were a separate list for blivits, then authors of blivits could stop stepping in the faces of mere novelists and historians and so on.

8   Until that happy day, however, I insist, as only a great author can, that this book be ranked in both the fiction and nonfiction competitions. As for the Pulitzer prizes: this book should be eligible for a mega-grand slam, sweeping fiction, drama, history, biography, and journalism. We will wait and see.

9   This book is not only a blivit but a collage. It began with my wish to collect in one volume most of the reviews and speeches and essays I had written since the publication of a similar collection, *Wampeters, Foma & Granfalloons,* in 1974. But as I arranged those fragments in this order and then that one, I saw that they formed a sort of autobiography, especially if I felt free to include some pieces not written by me. To give life to such a golem, however, I would have to write much new connective tissue. This I have done.

10   The reader should expect me to chat about this and that, and then to include a speech or a letter or a song or whatever, and then to chat some more.

11   I do not really consider this to be a masterpiece. I find it clumsy. I find it raw. It has some value, I think, as a confrontation between an American novelist and his own stubborn simplicity. I was dumb in school. Whatever the nature of that dumbness, it is with me still.

12   I have dedicated this book to the de St. Andrés. I am a de St. Andrés, since that was the maiden name of a maternal great-grandmother of mine. My mother believed that this meant that she was descended from nobles of some kind.

13   This was an innocent belief, and so should not be mocked or scorned. Or so I say. My books so far have argued that most human behavior, no matter how ghastly or ludicrous or glorious or whatever, is innocent. And here seems as good a place as any to include a statement made to me by Marsha Mason, the superb actress who once did me the honor of starring in a play of mine. She, too, is from the Middle West, from St. Louis.

14   "You know what the trouble is with New York?" she asked me.

15   "No," I said.

16   "Nobody here," she said, "believes that there is such a thing as innocence."

TO THINK ABOUT

1. The writer devises a new literary form he calls a blivit. What is the purpose of this invention?
2. Toward the end of the piece Vonnegut's tone changes. How?
3. In the process of lampooning his own material, Vonnegut skewers at least two conventions of the literary world. What are they?
4. Toward the end of his piece, Vonnegut writes "I was dumb in school. Whatever the nature of that dumbness, it is with me still." Still later he argues that "most human behavior, no matter how ghastly or ludicrous or glorious or whatever, is innocent." Is there a relationship between Vonnegut's concepts of dumbness and innocence? What are their opposites?

TO DO

1. Write an evaluation of your own writing the way Kurt Vonnegut might. Choose a piece you like a lot. Then choose something you

don't like. Then compare the two evaluations. Which of *them* works better as a piece of writing?
2. List the times in your life when you lost some of your innocence. Pick the one that is most compelling to you. Write an essay about it.

TIP

Do not evaluate a piece of your own writing that is hot off the printer. Wait one or two days at least. The time away will allow you to gain the perspective you need for looking at the piece objectively. (If the piece has particularly strong emotional overtones for you, one or two days may not be enough.)

52

Right to Life: What Can the White Man Say to the Black Woman?

Alice Walker

The lines between fiction and poetry, between fiction and nonfiction, and between nonfiction and poetry sometimes blur, disappear. Alice Walker is best known for her novels (The Color Purple, The Temple of My Familiar), but she began her writing career as a poet. This piece is a poem. But it could have been published as prose, as an essay. The lines are long. There are paragraphs. There are elements of drama as well. This is a dialogue in which one voice repeats a question, with variations, like a Greek chorus, while the other answers. The result of this point–counterpoint exchange is rhythmic, musical, hypnotic. Whatever the genre, it is a fine piece of writing.

1   *What is of use in these words I offer in memory and recognition of our common mother. And to my daughter.*

2   *What can the white man say to the black woman?*

3   For four hundred years he ruled over the black woman's womb.

4   Let us be clear. In the barracoons and along the slave shipping coasts of Africa, for more than twenty generations, it was he who dashed our babies' brains out against the rocks.

5   *What can the white man say to the black woman?*

6   For four hundred years he determined which black woman's children would live or die.

7   Let it be remembered. It was he who placed our children on the auction block in cities all across the eastern half of what is now the United States, and listened to and watched them beg for their mothers' arms, before being sold to the highest bidder and dragged away.

8   *What can the white man say to the black woman?*

9   We remember that Fannie Lou Hamer, a poor sharecropper on a Mississippi plantation, was one of twenty-one children; and that on plantations across the South black women often had twelve, fifteen, twenty children. Like their enslaved mothers and grandmothers before them, these black women were sacrificed to the profit the white man could make from harnessing their bodies and their children's bodies to the cotton gin.

10   *What can the white man say to the black woman?*

11   We see him lined up on Saturday nights, century after century, to make the black mother, who must sell her body to feed her children, go down on her knees to him.

12   Let us take note:

13   He has not cared for a single one of the dark children in his midst, over hundreds of years.

14   Where are the children of the Cherokee, my great grandmother's people?

15   Gone.

16   Where are the children of the Blackfoot?

17   Gone.

18   Where are the children of the Lakota?

19   Gone.

20   Of the Cheyenne?

21   Of the Chippewa?

22   Of the Iroquois?

23   Of the Sioux?

24   Of the Mandinka?

25   Of the Ibo?

26   Of the Ashanti?

27   Where are the children of the "Slave Coast" and Wounded Knee?

28   We do not forget the forced sterilization and forced starvations on the reservations, here as in South Africa. Nor do we forget the smallpox-infested blankets Indian children were given by the Great White Fathers of the United States government.

29   *What has the white man to say to the black woman?*

30   When we have children you do everything in your power to make them feel unwanted from the moment they are born. You send them to fight and kill other dark mothers' children around the world. You shove them onto public highways into the path of oncoming cars. You shove their heads through plate glass windows. You string them up and you string them out.

31   *What has the white man to say to the black woman?*

32   From the beginning, you have treated all dark children with absolute hatred.

33   Thirty million African children died on the way to the Americas, where nothing awaited them but endless toil and the crack of a bullwhip. They died of a lack of food, of lack of movement in the holds of ships. Of lack of friends and relatives. They died of depression, bewilderment and fear.

34   *What has the white man to say to the black woman?*

35   Let us look around us: Let us look at the world the white man has made for the black woman and her children.

36   It is a world in which the black woman is still forced to provide cheap labor, in the form of children, for the factories and on the assembly lines of the white man.

37   It is a world into which the white man dumps every foul, person-annulling drug he smuggles into creation.

38   It is a world where many of our babies die at birth, or later of malnutrition, and where many more grow up to live lives of such misery they are forced to choose death by their own hands.

39   *What has the white man to say to the black woman, and to all women and children everywhere?*

40   Let us consider the depletion of the ozone; let us consider homelessness and the nuclear peril; let us consider the destruction of the rain forests—in the name of the almighty hamburger. Let us consider the poisoned apples and the poisoned water and the poisoned air and the poisoned earth.

41   And that all of our children, because of the white man's assault on the planet, have a possibility of death by cancer in their almost immediate future.

42   *What has the white, male lawgiver to say to any of us? To those of us who love life too much to willingly bring more children into a world saturated with death?*

43   Abortion, for many women, is more than an experience of suffering beyond anything most men will ever know; it is an act of mercy, and an act of self-defense.

44   To make abortion illegal again is to sentence millions of women and children to miserable lives and even more miserable deaths.

45   Given his history, in relation to us, I think the white man should be ashamed to attempt to speak for the unborn children of the black woman. To force us to have children for him to ridicule, drug and turn into killers and homeless wanderers is a testament to his hypocrisy.

46   *What can the white man say to the black woman?*

47   Only one thing that the black woman might hear.

48   Yes, indeed, the white man can say, Your children have a right to life. Therefore I will call back from the dead those 30 million who were tossed overboard during the centuries of the slave trade. And the other millions who died in my cotton fields and hanging from my trees.

49   I will recall all those who died of broken hearts and broken spirits, under the insult of segregation.

50   I will raise up all the mothers who died exhausted after birthing twenty-one children to work sunup to sundown on my plantation. I will restore to full health all those who perished for lack of food, shelter, sunlight, and love; and from my inability to see them as human beings.

51   But I will go even further.

52   I will tell you, black woman, that I wish to be forgiven the sins I commit daily against you and your children. For I know that until I treat your children with love, I can never be trusted by my own. Nor can I respect myself.

53   And I will free your children from insultingly high infant mortality rates, short life spans, horrible housing, lack of food, rampant ill health. I will liberate them from the ghetto. I will open wide the doors of all the schools and hospitals and businesses of society to your children. I will look at your children and see not a threat but a joy.

54   I will remove myself as an obstacle in the path that your children, against all odds, are making toward the light. I will not assassinate them for dreaming dreams and offering new visions of how to live. I will cease trying to lead your children, for I can see I have never understood where I was going. I will agree to sit quietly for a century or so, and meditate on this.

55   This is what the white man can say to the black woman.

56   *We are listening.*

TO THINK ABOUT

1. Why do you think Walker chose the dialogue format for this piece?
2. What is your role as reader? What is the writer implicitly asking of you?
3. How does Walker's poem apply to relationships between blacks and whites in the United States today?
4. Historically, some white men have always fought alongside blacks to eliminate the injustices specified in the poem. Yet Walker makes no attempt to differentiate among white men. Is this fair? Why or why not?

TO DO

1. Read Alice Walker's novel *The Color Purple*. Compare the narrative voice to the voice in the piece you have just read.
2. Place yourself in a historical context. List your race, sex, religion, nationality, ethnic, and geographical backgrounds. Assume a persona appropriate for one or more of these elements. Write a dialogue in the manner of "Right to Life: What Can the White Man Say to the Black Woman?"

TIP

Writers do not work in a vacuum. Even the most accomplished professionals show their work-in-progress to discerning readers. (Usually this means someone other than your close friends, who can be counted on to tell you your stuff is terrific, whether it is or not.) Take advantage of the diversity around you. Show your writing to people who *don't* share your background and, perhaps, your views. It is not necessary to make every change suggested by these people. It *is* helpful to know and understand their reactions to your work.

53

Save the Whales, Screw the Shrimp

Joy Williams

It is relatively easy for a writer to engage her readers when writer and reader share the same point of view. It is easy to write a piece about evil dictators or industrial polluters, a piece that readers will read all the way through, and show their friends, and everybody will feel the same sense of affirmation and righteous indignation.

It is much more difficult to write an engaging piece in which the object of the writer's wrath is her own readers.

This is what Joy Williams set out to do in "Save the Whales, Screw the Shrimp." The essay was published in Esquire, *a magazine read by people who consider themselves sensitive to environmental issues, but who generally have above-average incomes, some of which they spend on products harmful to the environment.*

I have met the enemy, says Joy Williams, and he and she are you. *But her voice wavers from time to time, and you* are *allowed to speak.*

1   I don't want to talk about *me*, of course, but it seems as though far too much attention has been lavished on *you* lately—that your greed and vanities and quest for self-fulfillment have been catered to far too much. You just want and want and want. You haven't had a mandala dream since the eighties began. To have a mandala dream you'd have to instinctively know that it was an attempt at self-healing on the part of Nature, and you don't believe in Nature anymore. It's too isolated from you. You've abstracted it. It's so messy and damaged and sad. Your eyes glaze as you travel life's highway past all the crushed animals and the Big Gulp cups. You don't even take pleasure in looking at nature photographs these days. Oh, they can be just as pretty, as always, but don't they make you feel increasingly . . . anxious? Filled with more trepidation than

peace? So what's the point? You see the picture of the baby condor or the panda munching on a bamboo shoot, and your heart just sinks, doesn't it? A picture of a poor old sea turtle with barnacles on her back, all ancient and exhausted, depositing her five gallons of doomed eggs in the sand hardly fills you with joy, because you realize, quite rightly, that just outside the frame falls the shadow of the condo. What's cropped from the shot of ocean waves crashing on a pristine shore is the plastics plant, and just beyond the dunes lies a parking lot. Hidden from immediate view in the butterfly-bright meadow, in the dusky thicket, in the oak and holly wood, are the surveyors' stakes, for someone wants to build a mall exactly there—some gas stations and supermarkets, some pizza and video shops, a health club, maybe a bulimia treatment center. Those lovely pictures of leopards and herons and wild rivers, well, you just know they're going to be accompanied by a text that will serve only to bring you down. You don't want to think about it! It's all so uncool. And you don't want to feel guilty either. Guilt is uncool. Regret maybe you'll consider. *Maybe.* Regret is a possibility, but don't push me, you say. Nature photographs have become something of a problem, along with almost everything else. Even though they leave the bad stuff out—maybe because you *know* they're leaving all the bad stuff out—such pictures are making you increasingly aware that you're a little too late for Nature. Do you feel that? Twenty years too late, maybe only ten? Not *way* too late, just a little too late? Well, it appears that you are. And since you are, you've decided you're just not going to attend this particular party.

2   Pascal said that it is easier to endure death without thinking about it than to endure the thought of death without dying. This is how you manage to dance the strange dance with that grim partner, nuclear annihilation. When the U.S. Army notified Winston Churchill that the first atom bomb had been detonated in New Mexico, it chose the code phrase BABIES SATISFACTORILY BORN. So you entered the age of irony, and the strange double life you've been leading with the world ever since. Joyce Carol Oates suggests that the reason writers—*real* writers, one assumes—don't write about Nature is that it lacks a sense of humor and registers no irony. It just doesn't seem to be of the times—these slick, sleek, knowing, objective, indulgent times. And the word *Environment.* Such a bloodless word. A flat-footed word with a shrunken heart. A word increasingly disengaged from its association with the natural world. Urban planners, industrialists, economists, and developers use it. It's a lost word, really. A cold word, mechanistic, suited strangely to the coldness generally felt toward Nature. It's their word now. You don't mind giving it up. As for *Environmentalist*, that's one that can really bring on the yawns, for you've tamed and tidied it, neutered it quite nicely. An

environmentalist must be calm, rational, reasonable, and willing to compromise, otherwise you won't listen to him. Still, his beliefs are *opinions* only, for this is the age of radical subjectivism. Not long ago, Barry Commoner spoke to the Environmental Protection Agency. He scolded them. They loved it. The way they protect the environment these days is apparently to find an "acceptable level of harm from a pollutant and then issue rules allowing industry to pollute to that level." Commoner suggested that this was inappropriate. An EPA employee suggested that any other approach would place limits on economic growth and implied that Commoner was advocating this. Limits on economic growth! Commoner vigorously denied this. Oh, it was a healthy exchange of ideas, healthier certainly than our air and water. We needed that little spanking, the EPA felt. It was refreshing. The agency has recently lumbered into action in its campaign to ban dinoseb. You seem to have liked your dinoseb. It's been a popular weed killer, even though it has been directly linked with birth defects. You must hate weeds a lot. Although the EPA appears successful in banning the poison, it will still have to pay the disposal costs and compensate the manufacturers for the market value of the chemicals they still have in stock.

3   That's ironic, you say, but farmers will suffer losses, too, oh dreadful financial losses, if herbicide and pesticide use is restricted.

4   Farmers grow way too much stuff anyway. They grow surplus crops with subsidized water created by turning rivers great and small into a plumbing system of dams and canals. Rivers have become *systems*. Wetlands are increasingly being referred to as *filtering systems*—things deigned *useful* because of their ability to absorb urban run-off, oil from roads, et cetera.

5   We know that. We've known that for years about farmers. We know a lot these days. We're very well informed. If farmers aren't allowed to make a profit by growing surplus crops, they'll have to sell their land to developers, who'll turn all that *arable land* into office parks. Arable land isn't Nature anyway, and besides, we like those office parks and shopping plazas, with their monster supermarkets open twenty-four hours a day with aisle after aisle after aisle of *products*. It's fun. Products are fun.

6   Farmers like their poisons, but ranchers like them even more. There are well-funded predominantly federal and cooperative programs like the Agriculture Department's Animal Damage Control Unit that poison, shoot, and trap several thousand animals each year. This unit loves to kill things. It was created to kill things—bobcats, foxes, black bears, mountain lions, rabbits, badgers, countless birds—all to make this great land safe for the string bean and the corn, the sheep and the cow, even though you're not consuming as much cow these days. A burger

now and then, but burgers are hardly cows at all, you feel. They're not all *our* cows in any case, for some burger matter is imported. There's a bit of Central American burger matter in your bun. Which is contributing to the conversion of tropical rain forest into cow pasture. Even so, you're getting away from meat these days. You're eschewing cow. It's seafood you love, shrimp most of all. And when you love something, it had better watch out, because you have a tendency to love it to death. Shrimp, shrimp, shrimp. It's more common on menus than chicken. In the wilds of Ohio, far, far from watery shores, four out of the six entrées on a menu will be shrimp, for some modest sum. Everywhere, it's all the shrimp you can eat or all you *care* to eat, for sometimes you just don't feel like eating all you *can*. You are intensively *harvesting* shrimp. Soon there won't be any left and then you can stop. It takes that, often, to make you stop. Shrimpers shrimp, of course. That's their *business*. They put out these big nets and in these nets, for each pound of shrimp, they catch more than ten times that amount of fish, turtles, and dolphins. These, quite the worse for wear, they dump back in. There is an object called TED (Turtle Excluder Device), which would save thousands of turtles and some dolphins from dying in the nets, but the shrimpers are loath to use TEDs, as they say it would cut the size of their shrimp catch.

7   We've heard about TED, you say.

8   They want you, all of you, to have all the shrimp you can eat and more. At Kiawah Island, off the coast of South Carolina, visitors go out on Jeep "safaris" through the part of the island that hasn't been developed yet. ("Wherever you see trees," the guide says, "really, that's a lot.") The safari comprises six Jeeps, and these days they go out at least four times a day, with more trips promised soon. The tourists drive their own Jeeps and the guide talks to them by radio. Kiawah has nice beaches, and the guide talks about turtles. When he mentions the shrimpers' role in the decline of the turtle, the shrimpers, who share the same frequency, scream at him. Shrimpers and most commercial fishermen (many of them working with drift and gill nets anywhere from six to thirty miles long) think of themselves as an *endangered species*. A recent newspaper headline said, "Shrimpers Spared Anti-Turtle Devices." Even so, with the continuing wanton depletion of shrimp beds, they will undoubtedly have to find some other means of employment soon. They might, for instance, become part of that vast throng laboring in the *tourist industry*.

9   Tourism has become an industry as destructive as any other. You are no longer benign in your traveling somewhere to look at the scenery. You never thought there was much gain in just looking anyway, you've always preferred to *use* the scenery in some manner. In your desire to get away from what you've got, you've caused there to be no place to get

away *to.* You're just all bumpered up out there. Sewage and dumps have become prime indicators of America's lifestyle. In resort towns in New England and the Adirondacks, measuring the flow into the sewage plant serves as a business barometer. Tourism is a growth industry. You believe in growth. *Controlled* growth, of course. Controlled exponential growth is what you'd really like to see. You certainly don't want to put a moratorium or a cap on anything. That's illegal, isn't it? Retro you're not. You don't want to go back or anything. Forward. Maybe ask directions later. Growth is *desirable* as well as being *inevitable.* Growth is the one thing you seem to be powerless before, so you try to be realistic about it. Growth is—it's weird—it's like cancer or something.

10   Recently you, as tourist, have discovered your national parks and are quickly *overburdening* them. Spare land and it belongs to you! It's exotic land too, not looking like all the stuff around it that looks like everything else. You want to take advantage of this land, of course, and use it in every way you can. Thus the managers—or *stewards,* as they like to be called—have developed *wise* and *multiple-use* plans, keeping in mind exploiters' interests (for they have their needs, too) as well as the desires of the backpackers. Thus mining, timbering, and ranching activities take place in the national forests, where the Forest Service maintains a system of logging roads eight times larger than the interstate highway system. The national parks are more of a public playground and are becoming increasingly Europeanized in their look and management. Lots of concessions and motels. You deserve a clean bed and a hot meal when you go into the wilderness. At least your stewards think that you do. You keep your stewards busy. Not only must they cater to your multiple and conflicting desires, they have to manage your wildlife *resources.* They have managed wildfowl to such an extent that the reasoning has become, If it weren't for hunters, ducks would disappear. Duck stamps and licensing fees support the whole rickety duck-management system. Yes! If it weren't for the people who killed them, wild ducks wouldn't exist! Managers are managing all wild creatures, not just those that fly. They track and tape and tag and band. They relocate, restock, and reintroduce. They cull and control. It's hard to keep it all straight. Protect or poison? Extirpate or just mostly eliminate? Sometimes even the stewards get mixed up.

11   This is the time of machines and models, hands-on management and master plans. Don't you ever wonder as you pass that billboard advertising another MASTER-PLANNED COMMUNITY just what master they are actually talking about? Not the Big Master, certainly. Something brought to you by one of the tiny masters, of which there are many. But you like these tiny masters and have even come to expect and require them. In

Florida they've just started a ten-thousand-acre city in the Everglades. It's a *megaproject*, one of the largest ever in the state. Yes, they must have thought you wanted it. No, what you thought of as the Everglades, the Park, is only a little bitty part of the Everglades. Developers have been gnawing at this irreplaceable, strange land for years. It's like they just *hate* this ancient sea of grass. Maybe you could ask them about this sometime. Roy Rogers is the senior vice president of strategic planning, and the old cowboy says that every tree and bush and inch of sidewalk in the project has been planned. Nevertheless, because the whole thing will take twenty-five years to complete, the plan is going to be constantly changed. You can understand this. The important thing is that there be a blueprint. You trust a blueprint. The tiny masters know what you like. You like *a secure landscape* and *access to services.* You like grass—that is, lawns. The ultimate lawn is the golf course, which you've been told has "some ecological value." You believe this! Not that it really matters, you just like to play golf. These golf courses require a lot of watering. So much that the more inspired of the masters have taken to watering them with effluent, *treated* effluent, but yours, from all the condos and villas built around the stocked artificial lakes you fancy.

12   I really don't want to think about sewage, you say, but it sounds like progress.

13   It is true that the masters are struggling with the problems of your incessant flushing. Cuisine is also one of their concerns. Advances in sorbets—sorbet intermezzos—in their clubs and fine restaurants. They know what you want. You want A HAVEN FROM THE ORDINARY WORLD. If you're A NATURE LOVER in the West you want to live in a $200,000 home in A WILD ANIMAL HABITAT. If you're eastern and consider yourself more hip, you want to live in new towns—brand-new reconstructed-from-scratch towns—in a house of NINETEENTH-CENTURY DESIGN. But in these new towns the masters are building, getting around can be confusing. There is an abundance of curves and an infrequency of through streets. It's the new wilderness without any trees. You can get lost, even with all the "mental bread crumbs" the masters scatter about as visual landmarks—the windmill, the water views, the various groupings of landscape "material." You *are* lost, you know. But you trust a Realtor will show you the way. There are many more Realtors than tiny masters, and many of them have to make do with less than a loaf—that is, trying to sell stuff that's already been built in an environment already "enhanced" rather than something being planned—but they're everywhere, willing to show you the path. If Dante returned to Hell today, he'd probably be escorted down by a Realtor, talking all the while about how it was just another level of Paradise.

14   *When have you last watched a sunset? Do you remember where you were? With whom? At Loews Ventana Canyon Resort, the Grand Foyer will provide you with that opportunity through lighting which is computerized to diminish with the approaching sunset!*

15   The tiny masters are willing to arrange Nature for you. They will compose it into a picture that you can look at at your leisure, when you're not doing work or something like that. Nature becomes scenery, a prop. At some golf courses in the Southwest, the saguaro cacti are reported to be repaired with green paste when balls blast into their skin. The saguaro can attempt to heal themselves by growing over the balls, but this takes time, and the effect can be somewhat . . . baroque. It's better to get out the pastepot. Nature has become simply a visual form of entertainment, and it had better look snappy.

16   Listen, you say, we've been at Ventana Canyon. It's in the desert, right? It's very, very nice, a world-class resort. A totally self-contained environment with everything that a person could possibly want, on more than a thousand acres in the middle of zip. It sprawls but nestles, like. And they've maintained the integrity of as much of the desert ecosystem as possible. Give them credit for that. *Great* restaurant, too. We had baby bay scallops there. Coming into the lobby there are these two big hand-carved coyotes, mutely howling. And that's the way we like them, *mute*. God, why do those things howl like that?

17   Wildlife is a personal matter, you think. The attitude is up to you. You can prefer to see it dead or not dead. You might want to let it mosey about its business or blow it away. Wild things exist only if you have the graciousness to allow them to. Just outside Tucson, Arizona, there is a brand-new structure modeled after a French foreign legion outpost. It's the *International Wildlife Museum*, and it's full of dead animals. Three hundred species are there, at least a third of them—the rarest ones—killed and collected by one C. J. McElroy, who enjoyed doing it and now shares what's left with you. The museum claims to be educational because you can watch a taxidermist at work or touch a lion's tooth. You can get real close to these dead animals, closer than you can in a zoo. Some of you prefer zoos, however, which are becoming bigger, better, and bioclimatic. New-age zoo designers want the animals to *flow right out into your space.* In Dallas there will soon be a Wilds of Africa exhibit; in San Diego there's a simulated rain forest, where you can thread your way "down the side of a lush canyon, the air filled with a fine mist from 300 high-pressure nozzles"; in New Orleans you've constructed a swamp, the real swamp not far away on the verge of disappearing.

Animals in these places are abstractions—wandering relics of their true selves, but that doesn't matter. Animal behavior in a zoo is nothing like natural behavior, but that doesn't really matter, either. Zoos are pretty, contained, and accessible. These new habitats can contain one hundred different species—not more than one or two of each thing, of course—on seven acres, three, one. You don't want to see *too much* of anything, certainly. An *example* will suffice. Sort of like a biological Crabtree & Evelyn basket selected with *you* in mind. You like things reduced, simplified. It's easier to take it all in, park it in your mind. You like things inside better than outside anyway. You are increasingly looking at and living in proxy environments created by substitution and simulation. *Resource economists* are a wee branch in the tree of tiny masters, and one, Martin Krieger, wrote, "Artificial prairies and wildernesses have been created, and there is no reason to believe that these artificial environments need be unsatisfactory for those who experience them. . . . We will have to realize that the way in which we experience nature is conditioned by our society—which more and more is seen to be receptive to responsible intervention."

18   Nature has become a world of appearances, a mere source of materials. You've been editing it for quite some time; now you're in the process of deleting it. Earth is beginning to look like not much more than a launching pad. Back near Tucson, on the opposite side of the mountain from the dead-animal habitat, you're building Biosphere II (as compared with or opposed to Biosphere I, more commonly known as Earth)—a $2\frac{1}{2}$-acre terrarium, an artificial ecosystem that will include a rain forest, a desert, a thirty-five-foot ocean, and several thousand species of life (lots of microbes), including eight human beings, who will cultivate a bit of farmland. You think it would be nice to colonize other worlds after you've made it necessary to leave this one.

19   Hey, that's pretty good, you say, all that stuff packed into just $2\frac{1}{2}$ acres. That's only about three times bigger than my entire *house*.

20   It's small all right, but still not small enough to be, apparently, useful. For the purposes of NASA, say, it would have to be smaller, oh much smaller, and energy-efficient too. Fiddle, fiddle, fiddle. You support fiddling, as well as meddling. This is how you learn. Though it's quite apparent the environment has been grossly polluted and the natural world abused and defiled, you seem to prefer to continue pondering effects rather than preventing causes. You want proof, you insist on proof. A Dr. Lave from Carnegie-Mellon—and he's an expert, an economist, and an environmental *expert*—says that scientists will have to prove to you that you will suffer if you don't become less of a "throw-away society." *If you really want me to give up my car or my air conditioner, you'd better prove to me first that the earth would otherwise be uninhabitable,* Dr.

Lave says. *Me* is *you,* I presume, whereas *you* refers to them. You as in
me—that is, *me, me, me*—certainly strike a hard bargain. Uninhabitable
the world has to get before you rein in your requirements. You're a consumer after all, *the* consumer upon whom so much attention is lavished,
the ultimate user of a commodity that has become, these days, everything. To try to appease your appetite for proof, for example, scientists
have been leasing for experimentation forty-six pristine lakes in Canada.

21   They don't want to *keep* them, they just want to *borrow* them.

22   They've been intentionally contaminating many of the lakes with a
variety of pollutants dribbled into the propeller wash of research boats.
It's *one of the boldest experiments in lake ecology ever conducted.*
They've turned these remote lakes into huge *real-world test tubes.*
They've been doing this since 1976! And what they've found so far in
these *preliminary* studies is that pollutants are really destructive. The
lakes get gross. Life in them ceases. It took about eight years to make
this happen in one of them, everything carefully measured and controlled all the while. Now the scientists are slowly reversing the process.
But it will take hundreds of years for the lakes to recover. They think.

23   Remember when you used to like rain, the sound of it, the feel of it,
the way it made the plants and trees all glisten. We needed that rain, you
would say. It looked pretty too, you thought, particularly in the movies.
Now it rains and you go, Oh-oh. A nice walloping rain these days means
overtaxing our sewage treatment plants. It means *untreated waste discharged directly into our waterways.* It means . . .

24   Okay. Okay.

25   *Acid rain!* And we all know what this is. Or most of us do. People
of power in government and industry still don't seem to know what it is.
Whatever it is, they say, they don't want to curb it, but they're willing to
study it some more. Economists call air and water pollution "externali-
ties" anyway. Oh, acid rain. You do get so sick of hearing about it. The
words have already become a white-noise kind of thing. But you think in
terms of *mitigating* it maybe. As for *the greenhouse effect,* you think in
terms of *countering* that. One way that's been discussed recently is the
planting of new forests, not for the sake of the forests alone, oh my heavens, no. Not for the sake of majesty and mystery or of Thumper and
Bambi, are you kidding me, but because, as every schoolchild knows,
trees absorb carbon dioxide. They just soak it up and store it. They just
love it. So this is the plan: you plant millions of acres of trees, and you
can go on doing pretty much whatever you're doing—driving around, using staggering amounts of energy, keeping those power plants fired to the
max. Isn't Nature remarkable? So willing to serve? You wouldn't think it
had anything more to offer, but it seems it does. Of course these

"forests" wouldn't exactly be forests. They would be more like trees. *Managed* trees. The Forest Service, which now manages our forests by cutting them down, might be called upon to evolve in their thinking and allow these trees to grow. They would probably be patented trees after a time. Fast-growing, uniform, genetically-created-to-be-toxin-eating *machines*. They would be *new-age* trees, because the problem with planting the old-fashioned variety to *combat* the greenhouse effect, which is caused by pollution, is that they're already dying from it. All along the crest of the Appalachians from Maine to Georgia, forests struggle to survive in a toxic soup of poisons. They can't *help* us if we've killed them, now can they?

26   All right, you say, wow, lighten up will you? Relax. Tell about yourself.

27   Well, I say, I live in Florida . . .

28   Oh my God, you say. Florida! Florida is a joke! How do you expect us to take you seriously if you still live there! Florida is crazy, it's pink concrete. It's paved, it's over. And a little girl just got eaten by an alligator down there. It came out of some swamp next to a subdivision and just carried her off. That set your Endangered Species Act back fifty years, you can bet.

29   I . . .

30   Listen, we don't want to hear any more about Florida. We don't want to hear about Phoenix or Hilton Head or California's Central Valley. If our wetlands—our *vanishing* wetlands—are mentioned one more time, we'll scream. And the talk about condors and grizzlies and wolves is becoming too de trop. We had just managed to get whales out of our minds when those three showed up under the ice in Alaska. They even had *names.* Bone is the dead one, right? It's almost the twenty-first century! Those last condors are *pathetic.* Can't we just get this over with?

31   Aristotle said that all living beings are ensouled and striving to participate in eternity.

32   Oh, I just bet he said that, you say. That doesn't sound like Aristotle. He was a humanist. We're all humanists here. This is the age of humanism. And it has been for a long time.

33   You are driving with a stranger in the car, and it is the stranger behind the wheel. In the back seat are your pals for many years now—DO WHAT YOU LIKE and his swilling sidekick, WHY NOT. A deer, or some emblematic animal, something from that myriad natural world you've come from that you now treat with such indifference and scorn—steps from the dimming woods and tentatively upon the highway. The

stranger does not decelerate or brake, not yet, maybe not at all. The feeling is that whatever it is *will get out of the way.* Oh, it's a fine car you've got, a fine machine, and oddly you don't mind the stranger driving it, because in a way, everything has gotten too complicated, way, way out of your control. You've given the wheel to the masters, the managers, the comptrollers. Something is wrong, *maybe,* you feel a little sick, *actually,* but the car is luxurious and fast and you're *moving,* which is the most important thing by far.

34   Why make a fuss when you're so comfortable? Don't make a fuss, make a baby. Go out and get something to eat, build something. Make *another* baby. Babies are cute. Babies show you have faith in the future. Although faith is perhaps too strong a word. They're everywhere these days, in all the crowds and traffic jams, there are the babies too. You don't seem to associate them with the problems of population increase. They're just babies! And you've come to believe in them again. They're a lot more tangible than the afterlife, which, of course, you haven't believed in in ages. At least not for yourself. The afterlife now belongs to plastics and poisons. Yes, plastics and poisons will have a far more extensive afterlife than you, that's known. A disposable diaper, for example, which is all plastic and wood pulp—you like them for all those babies, so easy to use and toss—will take around four centuries to degrade. Almost all plastics do, centuries and centuries. In the sea, many marine animals die from ingesting or being entangled in discarded plastic. In the dumps, plastic squats on more than 25 percent of dump space. But your heart is disposed toward plastic. Someone, no doubt the plastics industry, told you it was convenient. This same industry is now looking into recycling in an attempt to get the critics of their nefarious, multifarious products off their backs. That should make you feel better, because *recycling* has become an honorable word, no longer merely the hobby of Volvo owners. The fact is that people in plastics are born obscurants. Recycling (practically impossible) won't solve the plastic glut, only reduction of production will, and the plastics industry isn't looking into that, you can be sure. Waste is not just the stuff you throw away, of course, it's the stuff you use to excess. With the exception of *hazardous waste,* which you do worry about from time to time, it's even thought you have a declining sense of emergency about the problem. Builders are building bigger houses because you want bigger. You're trading up. Utility companies are beginning to worry about your constantly rising consumption. Utility companies! You haven't entered a new age at all but one of upscale nihilism, deluxe nihilism.

35   In the summer, particularly in *the industrial Northeast,* you did get a little excited. The filth cut into your fun time. Dead stuff floating around. Sludge and bloody vials. Hygienic devices—appearing not quite so hygienic out of context—all coming in on the tide. The air smelled funny, too. You tolerate a great deal, but the summer of '88 was truly creepy. It was even thought for a moment that the environment would become a political issue. But it didn't. You didn't want it to be, preferring instead to continue in your politics of subsidizing and advancing avarice. The issues were the same as always—jobs, defense, the economy, maintaining and improving the standard of living in this greedy, selfish, expansionistic, industrialized society.

36   You're getting a little shrill here, you say.

37   You're pretty well off. You expect to be better off soon. You do. What does this mean? More software, more scampi, more square footage? You have created an ecological crisis. The earth is infinitely variable and alive, and you are killing it. It seems safer this way. But you are not safe. You want to find wholeness and happiness in a land increasingly damaged and betrayed, and you never will. More than material matters. You must change your ways.

38   What is this? *Sinners in the Hands of an Angry God?*

39   The ecological crisis cannot be resolved by politics. It cannot be solved by science or technology. It is a crisis caused by culture and character, and a deep change in personal consciousness is needed. Your fundamental attitudes toward the earth have become twisted. You have made only brutal contact with Nature, you cannot comprehend its grace. You must change. Have few desires and simple pleasures. Honor nonhuman life. Control yourself, become more authentic. Live lightly upon the earth and treat it with respect. Redefine the word *progress* and dismiss the managers and masters. Grow inwardly and with knowledge become truly wiser. Make connections. Think differently, behave differently. For this is essentially a moral issue we face and moral decisions must be made.

40   A *moral issue!* Okay, this discussion is now toast. A *moral* issue . . . And who's this *we* now? Who are *you* is what I'd like to know. You're not me, anyway. I admit, someone's to blame and something should be done. But I've got to go. It's getting late. That's dusk out there. That is dusk, isn't it? It certainly doesn't look like any dawn I've ever seen. Well, take care.

TO THINK ABOUT

1. What sort of persona has Williams adopted for this piece? Are you comfortable with this narrator? Is that important?

2. Williams italicizes certain words: *environment, environmentalist, systems, products, endangered species, resources, secure landscape.* What is the significance of these words in the piece? Why does the writer highlight them?
3. Toward the end of the piece Williams gives her readers (as she imagines them) a voice; in fact, she engages in conversation with *you:*
    All right, you say, *wow, lighten up, will you! Relax. Tell me about yourself.*
    Well, I say, *I live in Florida . . .*
    Oh my God, you say. *Florida! Florida is a joke!*
    What is the effect of this strategy?
4. Do you consider yourself an environmentalist? Whether or not you do, how do you define the term?

TO DO

1. For a 24-hour period, keep a journal of everything you do that affects the environment, positively or negatively. Include everything. If you take a shower, turn on a light, eat a fast-food meal, drive a car, recycle a bottle or a newspaper, write it down. (You may want to do some research: How many gallons of water did you use in that ten-minute shower? What's really in those exhaust fumes from your car?)
2. Then write a piece about your effect on the environment. You may want to experiment with the technique used by Joy Williams. Develop the characters of *you* and *I* as you go along.

TIP

Fiction writers know they cannot completely control their characters; the best writing often happens when a character in a novel or short story does something the writer never expected. The same is often true in essays of this kind. In your first draft especially, allow the relationship between your *you* and your *I* to develop naturally. Their conversation will take unexpected turns, and you will make discoveries.

54

New England Voices
Thomas Williams

Writers are conditioned by the environments—physical and cultural—in which they live. A writer from the Pacific Northwest sees the world differently from a writer from Chicago or Dallas or Atlanta. Conversely, two writers from the same region—no matter how different they may be in terms of temperament and background—are likely to share a certain sensibility as a result of their shared surroundings.

During his lifetime Thomas Williams published many novels and dozens of short stories. Much of his work was set in the fictional town of Leah, New Hampshire; nearly everything he wrote dealt with New England and New Englanders. And every word he wrote was suffused with a New England voice, a New England sensibility.

What is a New England voice? In 1985 Williams himself was asked to define it in an introduction to a book of short stories by New England writers. Later he revised that introduction; the result, which follows, appeared in The New York Times Book Review *on January 19, 1986.*

1   A while ago I was asked to write the introduction to a book of short stories by contemporary New England writers and to consider the question of regional writing. My first thought was that all serious writing, from anywhere, so far transcends the regional that the question didn't warrant discussion. I hardly ever think whether fiction from New England is different from Middle Western fiction or Southwestern fiction or whatever fiction. Real writers—the writers who write serious rather than formula fiction—use the images at their fingertips, whatever they are, to give us experience and after that, we hope, some truth.

2   Thirty years ago Henry Steele Commager, in his essay "The Nature of American Nationalism," said that American love of country has always been "a curiously general affair, almost an abstract one. Few

346

Americans have [a] passionate attachment to a particular soil, a particular country or region." He went on to say, "We have a regional literature, but it is rather a tribute to the passing of genuine regionalism that an expression of it."

3   We can all spot the sentimental or patronizing local colorist, but is an expression of genuine regionalism regionalism at all? Does the serious writer ever feel regional? And I have to add that in the last 30 years I've seen the very speech of my own state, New Hampshire, change gradually toward something like Middle Western standard, as though the last generation learned as much of its tongue from Captain Kangaroo and Johnny Carson as it did from its parents and grandparents.

4   Having said that, as if to declare a basic critical stance. I have to admit that there is more to say. Like several of the writers in the volume I introduced, called "New Fiction from New England." I came to New England from somewhere else, and I remember very well my Currier-and-Ives expectations and the shock of a different reality. I was a child and therefore as much a prisoner as if Mohawks, those legendary raiders, had come down from the north and taken me away from an essentially egalitarian and democratic childhood to what seemed to me a place of dark social, religious and historical demarcations and taboos.

5   Until I was 10 I lived on farms and in small towns in the Middle West, then in New York City where I attended the Little Red School House, a private school with leftish liberal inclinations, multiracial when that was quite progressive, in which the teachers and students regarded themselves as friends. When I came to the town I've come to call in my fiction Leah, N.H., then a mill town surrounded by wooded hills, declining farms and exposed granite. I found that in the Leah schools the relationship between faculty and students more resembled that of guards and prisoners of war.

6   I hadn't chosen Leah, but it was where I spent my adolescence—that time of steaming reality when we cast away our toys and fantasies and demanded touch and real risk. I learned about Leah in the way of wounds and small victories, but always with a certain perspective that immunized me forever against nostalgia, the disease that confuses youthful sanguinity with a time and a place. And perhaps against resentment, too, though Leah was the first place I'd lived in that I consciously disliked. When I was old enough I joined the Army, glad to get away. After the murky and dangerous social and familial currents of Leah, the Army with its uniforms, all insignia in plain sight, was a relief.

7   And yet I came back after the war and I'm still here trying to figure this place out. New England is different; for instance, it is an American trait *not* to be as sensitive, socially and culturally, as New England is. Yankees are terrified of being snubbed or, worse, patronized. Sincerity is

not merely appreciated, it is demanded. In a famous example given, I think, by the man of letters and transplanted Westerner Bernard DeVoto, the lost tourist leans from his car window and says, with the gruffness, possibly of embarrassment. "I want to get to St. Johnsbury!" After a pause, one of the men sitting on the store steps says mildly, "We've no objection."

8   Which means in this case that the "moral" transcends what could be called common human decency; quite often the Yankee style is an incentive to cruelty. Of course, a possible reason for all this nervousness is that human relationships are considered more valuable here than elsewhere. I still feel a general resistance to the "Have a nice day!" sort of vapidity, to its glib summary of existence. There is less of that sort of thing here than elsewhere.

9   But here's a slightly more subtle case, this from Robert Bryan and Marshall Dodge's collection of Maine vignettes called "Bert and I." It goes something like this:

10   "Why're you so het up, Tom?"

11   "Oh, I had to shoot my dog."

12   "Was he mad?"

13   "Guess he weren't so damn pleased."

14   The question is how one interprets this exchange. Do you think Tom misunderstands the question, or is ignorant of the fact that "mad" means rabid? It's funny enough that way. But consider the possibility that Tom deliberately misunderstands the question. In considering what his answer will be, he rejects the comforting ordinary for a dark humor that will do better justice to his real emotion. The question, "Was he mad?" is perhaps not insincere, but it is standard, and Tom rejects the standard. He makes the exchange something of a confrontation, with its own dramatic tension (the questioner has been somewhat put down), and the dog, for whom he really grieves, has been made a twinge more real, a force of personality. Again, it's a little cruel—but harder, better.

15   I see the above examples as a tendency, a prickliness, a moral nudge of some kind, but especially as an attitude toward language. The stories in "New Fiction from New England" are by writers who aren't very well known—at least not yet. Some are represented by their first published stories. Names I will be looking for in the future are Rebecca Rule, Daniel Asa Rose, Sharon Stark (her rural Pennsylvania subject matter not at all out of place here), William Evans, Garrett Bauman, Carrie Sherman and Ian Macmillan. Better known are Barry Targan, Peter Meinke, Howard Mosher, Ernest Hebert and Kim Yong Ik.

. . .

16   In a way we are all from New England, all of us who write the American language. Grandmother's house, the Old Homestead, is in

some psychic way here for all of us. I think of Carol Kennicott, the heroine of Sinclair Lewis's "Main Street," who yearned for the village, the white church, the neatness and, she thought, the culture of New England. One of the reasons—or the main reason—for the huge commercial success of "Peyton Place" was that its author, Grace Metalious, seemed to tear veils of sanctimony from a place that we had somehow idealized, and we were pleased, in a puerile fashion, by her crude energy. And I wonder how much the mass appeal of Stephen King's "plain style," as he perceptively calls it, has to do with its New Englandish demonology.

17   We are all haunted, even if at third or fourth hand, by the Puritans, who have to be admired for their adherence to sobriety, egalitarianism and a sense of justice even as they were being driven mad by the torments of Calvinism. And these is also in all of us the logic of the 18th century and those grand doubters who invented our country, as well as the transcendentalism, or romanticism, of the 19th, each in one way or another convincing still. Hawthorne, Melville, Emerson, Thoreau, R. H. Dana, Emily Dickinson, Sarah Orne Jewett, Henry Adams, E. A. Robinson, Frost—an incomplete list, but each voice is as alive to me as that of any contemporary. I'm always surprised by the sanity, the even temper, the humor and the coolness of the literary voices of New England. Some may be Puritan voices wrestling with problems I have myself rejected, but they are very near to my own inner voice. To me religion is such an anathema I suspect that it must have formed my standards in the first place. "Men are not essentially good" may be the deepest and most ineradicable message of that past. Therefore without sentimentality admire the rare good act. Trust no one but be worthy of trust—if you can. Calvinism has more lives than a cat.

18   I see in all this, and in the New England that sustains and abrades me every day, an injunction to use language very carefully, to resist the ordinary consistencies of diction and thought, those automatic responses that obliterate what is darker—the real reason for all these words. In my own case I've always felt that nothing I say will affect the world very much at all, so why not at least be honest? Prepare to abandon all theory, especially literary theory. Emerson wrote in his journal: "It is not in the power of God to make a communication of his will to a Calvinist. For to every inward revelation he holds up his silly book, and quotes chapter and verse." For "Calvinist" read in our day any mind in thrall to dogma. A real Yankee would rather be called "handy in the woods."

19   So is there a "school" of New England writers now? For instance, how would you compare Carolyn Chute's novel, "The Beans of Egypt, Maine" with Donald Hall's "String Too Short to Be Saved"? The two writers, I happen to know, admire each other's work, and is this undogmatic admiration the real connection, after all? Though their styles are

very different, both live here and deal with this place. Each in fact might be the old Yankee who is always watching to see what kind of a damn fool the other is. Caring a lot, in other words. Or, to go back a while, how might one compare Jack Kerouac (the mills of Lowell, Mass., the French-Americans) with the Thornton Wilder of "Our Town"? There is too much to New England, too many parts and places, visitors and natives.

20   But where is New England nowadays, anyway? It is a general belief held by all New Englanders that anything to the south of them is tainted. As for me, I sometimes think that New England is north of a line running east-west through Concord, N.H., just above the birthplace of Mary Baker Eddy, the founder of Christian Science. To the north of that line the condominium owners are mostly seasonal, not year-round residents—at least not in overwhelming numbers. Of course you'll find a few Yankees at town meetings farther south—they sit in a back corner of the high school auditorium in their tacky dresses and green chino work clothes, and there is a common bitter, ironic expression on their faces as the newcomers pass laws concerning the shooting of deer and the removal of the 1956 Ford Fairlane that's been in the yard minding its own business longer than them people have lived here, for God sakes. But New England has been in decline, in one way or another, since the end of the Civil War, and there is a grand tradition of disappointment, even a perverse joy in it, I sometimes think. Perverse enjoyment has always caused a sensitivity to language.

. . .

21   Who New England writers are is something new to think about. If I name those who quickly come to mind, I'm certain to leave out even more obvious ones. But I think of John Irving, perhaps seen on his way to Vienna but carrying with him his baggage of Yankee cynicism and sentiment; John Updike in Tarbox; the late John Cheever and his Wapshots (more than in Shady Hill among the metropolitan commuters); Andre Dubus dealing harsh sympathy to his booze and God-haunted Massachusetts blue-collars; Russell Banks, after his long infatuation with postmoderns, finding his real voice in a trailer park in his native New Hampshire; Ernest Hebert documenting the creeping asphalt; Ruth Doan MacDougal's high school teachers on the edge and over the edge; and Maxine Kumin, May Sarton, Richard Yates, Sydney Lea, John Sayles, Ann Beattie (in her Vermont mode), Paul Theroux, David Plante, Richard Eberhart, Galway Kinnell, Joyce Maynard—and new writers (at least new to me) like Merie Drown, Mary Peterson, Rebecca Rule—these voices all seem so individual in their preoccupations that I can't call them a "school." All I can say is that each seems affected by this dark place

where, for instance, Tom took it upon himself to put his own dog out of its misery.

22   I suppose it is Robert Frost whose actual words reverberate most in my own mind, and in whose cold knowledge I would search for a common "New England" sensibility. There is the deadly, beautiful landscape in "Out, Out," where the young boy's hand has been taken by the buzz saw, and the Poet says with seemingly final chilliness, "So." Or the husband in "Home Burial," who tries to be sympathetic to his grieving wife but by his nature cannot, and finally says, "I'll follow and bring you back by force. I *will!*" And there is the witch of Coos, who kept the knucklebones of her murdered lover in her button box. Mary, the wife in "The Death of the Hired Man," says of home, "I should have called it / Something you somehow haven't to deserve." But those of us who have married this place suspect that our careful words prove the opposite.

TO THINK ABOUT

1. Does Williams's description of the New England voice fairly describe his own voice in this essay?
2. Williams cites a joke about a mad dog as a fine example of the New England voice: funny, dark, cryptic, "a little cruel, but harder, better." Can you think of a joke or anecdote that epitomizes the voice of your home region?
3. Is there a regional voice common to the writers in the area you are from? Can you characterize that voice? Compare it with the New England voice described by Thomas Williams. (New Englanders: Does your own idea of a New England voice match Williams's?)
4. Analyze your own writing voice for traces of a regional voice. What particular turns of phrases and habits of inflection inform your writing?

TO DO

1. Make a list of writers from your region. Use the library to supplement what you already know. Then spend a day or two browsing among the works of those writers. Pay close attention to the sounds and sensibilities of their voices.
2. Then write an essay about the voice of your region. (You may define region as broadly or narrowly as you like: the voice of the great Southwest, the Minnesota voice, the Brooklyn voice.) Write the essay *in the voice of the region*. (If you are unsure about how to begin,

you might start by imitating the voice of your favorite writer from your region.)

TIP

Keep in mind that there is plenty of room for variety within any given regional voice. It is a good idea to think of a regional voice the same way you think of your own voice: It is actually many voices, each one distinctly different from the others. Your own voices are bound together by the values and sensibilities of their owner, you; so too are the many voices of a region bound together by the characteristics distinguishing that region from all others.

55

Fresh Crayolas: A Busy First Day in Kindergarten

Michael Winerip

*It is an assignment many newspaper reporters dread: Write a
story about the first day of school. After all, what's to write? School
is school.*

Michael Winerip of The New York Times *knows better. And
so in early September 1988, he spent the first day of school with
Rhoda Zimmerman's kindergarten class in Westbury, New York.
And then, using only about 800 words, he captured the substance
and spirit of the classroom in a way that anyone who has ever gone
to kindergarten can appreciate. His ingredients: a generous helping
of anecdotes, just enough (but not too much) background information, and the knowing voice of a kindergartner.*

1   "My name is Mrs. Zimmerman," said the full-grown person standing in front of the Park Avenue School. "You probably don't know who I
am, since this is the very first day. I want it to be a very special day.
Don't you?"

2   "YES!"

3   "Good," Mrs. Zimmerman said. It was time to sing "God Bless
America." Piece of cake. They learned it last year in pre-K. No one's
voice was louder than Anika Davis's as she sang, "From the mountains,
to the fairy."

4   "Lovely," Mrs. Zimmerman said, "such lovely singing." And they
all followed Mrs. Zimmerman into the building, walking along the line
in the middle of the corridor, so they wouldn't get crooked.

5   When Rhoda Zimmerman started teaching 24 years ago, the first
day of kindergarten was the Battle of San Juan Hill Part II. "I used to wear
old clothes," she said. "There were kids tearing at my dress, crying, it
was a mess." Now with working mothers, day care, nursery school, Head

Start, preschool, early childhood development centers, by the time the average suburban child reaches kindergarten, he has 27 years of educational experience. In her two new kindergarten classes, Mrs. Zimmerman had just one first-day cryer.

. . .

6   More typical was 4-year-old Kristen Wilson. Her mother, Lisa, came to school opening day, and Kristen looked about ready to die from public humiliation. "She wants me to go," said the mother. Mrs. Wilson gave her a kiss and reminded her to take the yellow bus home. "I'm talking to you," Mrs. Wilson said.

7   "I know what to do," Kristen said.

8   On the first day, the principal, Delores Hunter, was everywhere. "Look at these second graders," she said. "They've grown up so." They looked enormous.

9   In kindergarten, the first order of business was making sure everyone knew their names. "What do we call you?" Mrs. Zimmerman said.

10   "Salvatore Jerome LoCascio," said a boy.

11   "But what can we call you?" said Mrs. Zimmerman.

12   "Salvatore Jerome LoCascio."

13   They sang the good-morning song, then Mrs. Zimmerman had them close their eyes and think of a nice summer memory. "You don't have to crunch your eyes," she said. She was afraid they were concentrating so much on closing their eyes, they might not be able to think.

14   Brenda O'Rilley went to Memphis on a plane by herself. Jason Labriola saw Niagara Falls.

15   "Did you love it?" Mrs. Zimmerman said.

16   "Yes!"

17   Rocky Buffolino flew to Disney World. Christina Lynch went to Flushing, Queens.

18   Twenty minutes after school opened, Gregory Gary had to go to the bathroom. This was not a record. Then Christina had to go, and Matt, and Tamieka. When Salvatore Jerome LoCascio returned from the bathroom, he announced in a loud voice so everybody could hear, "I'm back, Mrs. Zimmerman."

19   She showed them all the corners of the room, the science table, workbench, play kitchen, the Leggos and where the computer and typewriter would go next week.

20   "This," she said, "is the special table where Mrs. Slezak"—the teacher's aid—"prepares the snack." That sounded awfully good.

21   During play time, they practiced walking like ducks, elephants and frogs. The new boxes of thick-size Crayolas had a fresh smell.

22   "Boys and girls," said Mrs. Zimmerman. "Every day when it's time to stop playing, I'll say: 'I look at the clock and what does it say? Time to put the toys away.' Can you say that?"

23   They could!

24   "One, two, three, four," said Mrs. Slezak. "Everybody on the floor."

25   They sang the ABC song, and Mrs. Zimmerman said: "You know what we're going to have for snack? My favorite, peanut butter and jelly." So they sang the peanut butter and jelly song.

26   By 10:15, Mrs. Zimmerman knew everyone's name.

. . .

27   During snack, Andrew Ciccone showed them his Bugs Bunny digital watch. "It's 10:21," said Andrew.

28   "I love that watch," said Mrs. Zimmerman.

29   At 10:30, John Ingram said, "Is it time to leave?"

30   Mrs. Zimmerman had a basket of farm goods. "How does a lemon taste," she said, "Sweet?"

31   "Yes!"

32   "A lemon tastes sweet?" Mrs. Zimmerman said.

33   "Sour!"

34   Mrs. Zimmerman had a bus safety workbook for everyone. "I know in pre-K the teachers used to pin things on you but now that you're in kindergarten," she said, "I don't have to pin it on you, do I?"

35   "No way!"

36   Everyone got on the bus beautifully, but James forgot to get off and wound up back at school.

37   After class, Mrs. Zimmerman said to the principal, "A lot went on today, Delores, a lot of teaching." The class of 2000 was on its way.

TO THINK ABOUT

1. Winerip writes: "And they all followed Mrs. Zimmerman into the building, walking along the line in the middle of the corridor, so they wouldn't get crooked." Here, and elsewhere, he uses the vocabulary and cadence of a kindergartner. What is the effect of this voice on you, the reader?

2. What can you infer about the personalities of Mrs. Zimmerman and two of her pupils—Kristen Wilson and Salvatore Jerome LoCascio? How are you able to reach these judgments?

3. The narrative voices in "Fresh Crayolas" and Henry Allen's "The Corps" (Chapter 1) are very different. But the writers use similar techniques. How are these pieces alike?

TO DO

1. Make a list of your own early memories of school: specific incidents that deepened your understanding of yourself or the world around you. Pick one that appeals to you. Write an essay about it. Do your best to capture the essence of the classroom—the smells, the sounds, the atmosphere.
2. Visit a world where you are a stranger—an elementary school classroom, a theater company in rehearsal, a shelter for the homeless. Observe. Interview. Take notes. Then write an essay in which you capture the essence of that world. If the inhabitants of your chosen world speak with a distinctive voice, try imitating it.

TIP

Show, don't tell. In a piece about a world (no matter how small) it is necessary to *show* your reader the world: the sights, the sounds, the smell, the feel of it. Show through description, anecdote, dialogue, and through the sound of your own voice. The more you show, the more you allow your reader to experience your world viscerally as well as intellectually. The more you show, the less you have to explain. The less you have to explain, the more your readers will learn on their own. The more they learn on their own, the longer they will remember your essay.

(But how much *should* I explain, I hear you asking. The answer is: just enough to give your reader a comprehensible context. And not a word more.)

Thematic Contents

Life and Death

Moral Questions, and Answers

Subcultures

Social Commentary

Writers are always full of ideas about what's wrong with the world and how to make it a better place.

Rhetorical Contents

* Denotes informal, indirect, or implied argument.

Cause and Effect

Classification

Definition

Description

Humor, Irony, and Satire

Illustration

Narration

Acknowledgments

Henry Allen. "The Corps," *The Washington Post*, March 5, 1972. Copyright © 1972, The Washington Post. Reprinted with permission.

Jennifer Allen. Untitled, *The New York Times* ("Hers" column), May 1982. Copyright by the author. We have made dilligent efforts to contact the copyright holder to obtain permission to reprint this selection.

Barbara Lazear Ascher. Untitled, *The New York Times* ("Hers" column), February 1983. Copyright by the author. We have made dilligent efforts to contact the copyright holder to obtain permission to reprint this selection.

Dave Barry. "UnNintended Benefits," from *Dave Barry Talks Back*. Copyright © 1991 by Dave Barry. Reprinted by permission of Crown Publishers, Inc.; "Commencement," *Miami Herald*. Reprinted with permission of the Miami Herald.

Andrei Codrescu. "Stalin," from *A Craving for Swan* by Andrei Codrescu. A Sandstone Book, Ohio State University Press, 1986. Reprinted with permission of Ohio State University Press.

Richard Cohen. "A Newspaper We Can Do Without," syndicated column printed in *The Boston Globe*, March 25, 1985. Copyright © 1993, The Washington Post Writers Group. Reprinted with permission.

Sara Davidson. "Rolling into the Eighties," *Esquire*, February 1980. Reprinted by permission of International Creative Management, Inc. Copyright © 1980 by Sara Davidson.

Annie Dillard. Excerpt from *The Writing Life* by Annie Dillard. Reprinted by permission of Russell & Volkening as agents for the author. Copyright © 1989 by Annie Dillard.

Elissa Ely. "So long 4 ever," *The Boston Globe*, July 1, 1990. Copyright by the author. Reprinted by permission of the author.

Nora Ephron. "A Few Words About Breasts: Shaping Up Absurd," from *Crazy Salad*. Reprinted by permission of International Creative Management, Inc. Copyright © 1972 by Nora Ephron.

Judy Foreman. "Handicapped" by Judy Foreman, *The Boston Globe*, August 19, 1979. Reprinted courtesy of The Boston Globe.

Eduardo Galeano. "Bureaucracy 2 & Bureaucracy 3." Reprinted from *The Book of Embraces* by Eduardo Galeano, translated by Cedric Balfrage and Mark Schafer, with the permission of W. W. Norton & Company, Inc. Copyright © 1991 by Eduardo Galeano.

Martin Gansberg. "38 Who Saw Murder Didn't Call the Police," *The New York Times*, March 27, 1964. Copyright © 1964 by The New York Times Company. Reprinted by permission.

Henry Louis Gates, Jr. "Canon Confidential: A Sam Slade Caper," *The New York Times,* March 25, 1990. Reprinted by permission of Brandt & Brandt Literary Agents, Inc.

Natalie Goldberg. "Obsessions," from *Writing Down the Bones* by Natalie Goldberg. Copyright © 1986 by Natalie Goldberg. Reprinted by arrangement with Shambhala Publications, Inc., 300 Massachusetts Ave., Boston, MA 02115.

Ellen Goodman. "Dick & Jane Play Tennis," "Rating the Kids," from *Making Sense* by Ellen Goodman; "Real Foes, False Foes," *The Boston Globe,* May 23, 1991. Copyright © 1993, The Boston Globe. Reprinted with permission.

Lois Gould. "On Pornography and the First Amendment," *The New York Times* ("Hers" column), March 1977. Copyright © 1988 by The New York Times Company. Reprinted by permission.

Stephen J. Gould. "The Streak of Streaks," reprinted from *Bully for Brontosaurus: Reflections in Natural History* by Stephen Jay Gould, with the permission of W. W. Norton & Company, Inc. Copyright © 1991 by Stephen Jay Gould.

Paul Harasim. "Hello, CIA?" by Paul Harasim. Copyright © 1983, *The Cincinnati Post.* Used with permission.

Jamaica Kincaid. "Girl," from *At the Bottom of the River* by Jamaica Kincaid. Copyright © 1978, 1983 by Jamaica Kincaid. Reprinted by permission of Farrar, Straus & Giroux, Inc.

Martin Luther King, Jr. "I Have A Dream." Reprinted by arrangement with The Heirs to the Estate of Martin Luther King, Jr., c/o Joan Daves Agency as agent for the proprietor.

Maxine Hong Kingston. "Reunion," *The New York Times* ("Hers" column), 1978. Reprinted by permission of the author.

Susan Landgraf. "After Deadline," *Journal American.* Reprinted by permission of Journal American.

Lewis H. Lapham. "Achievement Test," *Harper's* Magazine, July 1991. Copyright © 1991 by Harper's Magazine. All rights reserved. Reprinted from the July issue by special permission.

Fran Lebowitz. "Sound of Music: Enough Already," from *Metropolitan Life* by Fran Lebowitz. Copyright © 1974/75/76/77/78 by Fran Lebowitz. Reprinted by permission of Dutton, an imprint of New American Library, a division of Penguin Books USA, Inc.

Richard Lederer. "The Case for Short Words." Copyright © 1991 by Richard Lederer. Reprinted by permission of Pocket Books, a division of Simon & Schuster, Inc.

Alan Lupo. "A House and Its Memories," by Allan Lupo, *The Boston Globe,* March 1, 1991. Reprinted courtesy of The Boston Globe.

Nancy Mairs. "On Being a Cripple" and "On Not Liking Sex," from *Plaintext: Deciphering a Woman's Life,* by Nancy Mairs. Copyright © 1986, University of Arizona Press. Reprinted by permission from the University of Arizona Press.

Andrew Merton. "It Hurts to Be in Love" and "What a Freshman Needs to Know," *The Boston Globe,* February 1976 and September 3, 1989, respectively. Reprinted by permission of the author.

Gail Y. Miyasaki. "Obachan," reprinted in *New Worlds of Literature.* W. W. Norton & Company. We have made dilligent efforts to contact the copyright holder to obtain permission to reprint this selection.

A. G. Mojtabai. "On Wearing the Chador," *The New York Times* ("Hers" column), June 19, 1980. Copyright © 1982 by The New York Times Company. Reprinted by permission.

Judith Ortiz-Cofer. "Silent Dancing," from *Silent Dancing* by Judith Ortiz-Cofer. Copyright 1990. Reprinted by permission of Arte Publico Press.

Grace Paley. "Three Days and a Question." We have made dilligent efforts to contact the copyright holder to obtain permission to reprint this selection.

Anna Quindlen. "Life in the 30's," *The New York Times*, April 7, 1988. Copyright © 1988 by The New York Times Company. Reprinted with permission.

Caryl Rivers. "High Heels," *The Boston Globe*. Reprinted by permission of the author.

Richard Selzer. *Specimen Collectors.* Copyright © 1979 by Richard Selzer. Reprinted by permission of John Hawkins & Associates, Inc.

Randy Shilts. "Talking AIDS to Death," *Esquire*, March 1989. Reprinted by permission of the author.

Charles Simic. "Reading Philosophy at Night," from *Wonderful Words, Silent Truths* by Charles Simic. Published by the University of Michigan Press, copyright © 1990 by the University of Michigan. First published in *Antaeus*, Fall 1987. Reprinted by permission of the University of Michigan Press.

Harry Stein. "The Big A," "On Becoming Mr. Ethics," "Uncommon Decency," from *Ethics (and Other Liabilities)* by Harry Stein. Copyright © 1982 by Harry Stein. Reprinted by permission of St. Martins Press, Inc., New York.

Cynthia Vann. "A Death in the Family," *The News and Observer*, March 15, 1987. We have made dilligent efforts to contact the copyright holder to obtain permission to reprint this selection.

Gore Vidal. "Drugs," from *Homage to Daniel Shays: Collected Essays 1952–1972* by Gore Vidal. Copyright © 1970 by Gore Vidal. Reprinted by permission of Random House, Inc.

Patricia Volk. "Choices," *The New York Times* ("Hers" column), September 24, 1987. Copyright © 1987 by The New York Times Company. Reprinted by permission.

Kurt Vonnegut. "Palm Sunday: Introduction," "First Amendment," from *Palm Sunday* by Kurt Vonnegut. Copyright © 1981 by Kurt Vonnegut. Reprinted by permission of Delacorte Press/Seymour Lawrence, a Division of Bantam Doubleday Dell Publishing Group, Inc.

Alice Walker. "Right to Life: What Can the White Man Say to the Black Woman?" from *Her Blue Body, Everything We Know, Earthling Poems, 1965–1990.* Copyright © 1991 by Alice Walker. Reprinted by permission of Hartcourt Brace & Co.

Joy Williams. "Save the Whales, Screw the Shrimp," *Esquire*, 1989. Reprinted by permission of International Creative Management, Inc. Copyright © 1989 by Joy Williams.

Thomas Williams. "New England Voices," *The New York Times*, January 19, 1986. Copyright © 1986 by The New York Times Company. Reprinted by permission.

Michael Winerip. "Fresh Crayolas: A Busy First Day in Kindergarten," *The New York Times*, September 11, 1987. Copyright © 1987 by The New York Times Company. Reprinted by permission.

Index of Authors and Titles